THE
CHARITIES
ACTS
HANDBOOK

Published by
Jordan Publishing Ltd
21 St Thomas Street
Bristol BS1 6JS

© Jordan Publishing Ltd 1996

British Library Cataloguing-in-Publication Data
A catalogue record for this book is available from the British Library.

ISBN 0 85308 292 8

Typeset by Mendip Communications Limited, Frome, Somerset
Printed by Hobbs the Printers of Southampton

CONTENTS

TABLE OF CASES

TABLE OF STATUTES

References in the right-hand column are to paragraph numbers.

TABLE OF STATUTORY INSTRUMENTS

References in the right-hand column are to paragraph numbers.

CHAPTER 1

THE CHARITY COMMISSIONERS AND OFFICIAL CUSTODIAN FOR CHARITIES

Introduction – The Commissioners – General Functions – Advice-giving – Investigating and Checking Abuse – No Power to Manage Charities – Official Custodian for Charities

1.1 Introduction

The reforms introduced by the Charities Act 1992 are now consolidated with the Charities Act 1960 in the Charities Act 1993, which came into force on 1 August 1993. The Charity Commissioners have been given a more positive role in monitoring charities, fed by the flow of information which charity trustees must supply to the Commissioners on an annual basis. The Commission now derives its authority from the 1993 Act but its fundamental constitution and the general functions of the Commissioners are unchanged.

1.2 The Commissioners

Section 1 of and Sch 1 to the 1993 Act provide for a body of up to five Charity Commissioners – a Chief Commissioner, and between two and four other Commissioners of whom two must be legally qualified. At present, there are five Charity Commissioners comprising the Chief Commissioner, two legally qualified Commissioners and two lay Commissioners. They are appointed by the Home Secretary.

In practice, many of the functions of the Commissioners under the 1993 Act, for example conducting inquiries, giving directions and making orders are carried out by assistant Commissioners who are appointed by the Commissioners and authorised under Sch 1 to act on their behalf and in their name.

1.3 General Functions

Section 1(3) of the 1993 Act gives the Commissioners three general functions:

(a) to promote the effective use of charitable resources by encouraging the development of better methods of administration;

(b) giving charity trustees information or advice on any matter affecting the charity; and

(c) investigating and checking abuses.

According to s 1(4), the general object of the Commissioners, in respect of any particular charity, is to act:

'as best to promote and make effective the work of the charity in meeting the needs designated by its trusts.'

Unless there are statutory grounds for altering the trusts of the charity (see Chapter 9), the Commissioners are as much bound by the existing trusts of a charity as are the trustees.

1.4 Advice-giving

Much of the information and advice-giving is provided in a general way through the publications of the Commissioners, including the Commissioners' annual reports, or informally to individual charities. However, s 29 of the 1993 Act confers a specific power on the Commissioners to advise charity trustees on any matter affecting the performance of their duties. Provided the application for advice is made in writing – and it is advisable to refer expressly to s 29 when making the application – trustees who act on the Commissioners' advice will be deemed to have acted in accordance with the trusts of the charity unless they knew or had reason to suspect that the Commissioners were ignorant of material facts or a court decision on the matter has been given or is pending.

Where trustees are in doubt as to how to act, advice under s 29 is a valuable protection. However, s 29 is permissive. The Commissioners are not obliged to give advice and may well decline to do so if, for example, the matter is contentious.

1.5 Investigating and Checking Abuse

The general function of investigating and checking abuse is reflected in a raft of detailed statutory provisions consolidating powers in the 1960 Act with the increased powers to inquire into charities and to act to protect charity property introduced by the 1992 Act (see Chapter 5).

1.6 No Power to Manage Charities

The Commissioners are prohibited by s 1(4) of the 1993 Act from acting in the administration of a charity. Although they have extensive powers to inquire into charities and to take steps to protect charity property, they cannot intervene in the legitimate decision-making process of the charity trustees nor directly take over the management of a charity.

1.7 Official Custodian for Charities

Section 2 of the 1993 Act requires the Commissioners to appoint one of their officers to be the official custodian for charities, a corporation sole, whose function was formerly to hold property, whether land or investments, for charities. As the holder of investments, the official custodian provided a useful service to charity trustees free of charge.

In May 1989, when the White Paper, 'Charities: A Framework for the Future' ('The White Paper') was published, the official custodian's holdings amounted to approximately £1.25 billion, involving almost 40,000 charities. The White Paper recommended that the official custodian should cease to hold investments on behalf of the charities except in special circumstances. This recommendation was implemented by the 1992 Act, now consolidated in the 1993 Act (see Chapter 7). The official custodian continues to hold land as a custodian trustee for charities (see Chapter 6), but the investment-holding function is now restricted to circumstances where it is necessary to protect charity property (see Chapter 5).

CHAPTER 2

REGISTRATION AND DECLARATION OF REGISTERED CHARITY STATUS

Introduction – The Register: Contents and Access – The Need to Register – Exempt Charities – Small Charities – The Meaning of 'Income' – The Registration Process – Removal from the Register – Declaration of Registered Charity Status – Penalties for Non-compliance – Summary of Requirements

2.1 Introduction

A public register of charities has been maintained by the Charity Commissioners since 1960. By the mid-1980s, however, this was regarded as defective in many ways. Reforms were introduced by the 1992 Act, both in respect of the charities required to register and in the system for updating information on the register on a regular basis. These have been consolidated with the provisions of the 1960 Act in the 1993 Act.

2.2 The Register: Contents and Access

The register

2.2.1 Section 3(3) of the 1993 Act requires the Commissioners to keep a register of charities in such a manner as they think fit. The register is computerised.

Contents

2.2.2 Section 3(3) of the 1993 Act requires the register to contain the name of every registered charity. This is relevant to the provisions governing charity names (see Chapter 3). Section 3(3) also requires the register to contain, in respect of every registered charity, such other particulars of and such other information as the Commissioners think fit. The Commissioners record such details as the governing instrument, any popular or alternative working name of a charity, its acronym, objects, financial year end and the name and address of the correspondent for the charity. Section 3(3) is sufficiently wide to enable the Commissioners to enter on the register more general information about a charity, such as whether or not the statutory duties of the charity trustees to file accounts, reports and returns have been discharged.

Access

2.2.3 The register is a public register. Section 3(8) of the 1993 Act gives the public the right to inspect the register and to obtain particulars of entries on the register. Section 3(9) provides that, where information contained on the register is not in documentary form, which is quite possible in the case of a computerised register, it should be available for public inspection in legible form. Reading the information from a visual display unit would suffice. Section 3(10) enables the Commissioners, at their discretion, to exclude certain information from public access.

It is now possible to obtain information about a particular charity by visiting one of the Commission's offices or by telephone. It is also possible to obtain more general information, for example lists of charities with an income in excess of a particular figure or of charities with the same or similar objects. The Charity Commission publishes a leaflet, 'Central Register of Charities: Services Available' (cc 45), describing the services which the Central Register is able to provide.

At one time, the services of the Central Register were provided without charge. However, s 51 of the 1992 Act now consolidated in s 85 of the 1993 Act empowers the Secretary of State to make regulations setting out the fees to be charged by the Commission in respect of its functions. The Charity Commissioners' Fees (Copies and Extracts) Regulations 1992, SI 1992/2986 specifies fees for the supply of extracts from the register. The Regulations empower the Commissioners to waive fees and it is their practice to do so where the trustees of a charity request a copy of the charity's constitution.

2.3 The Need to Register

Section 3(2) of the 1993 Act requires all charities to be registered unless they fall into one of the categories listed in s 3(5). Section 3(7)(a) requires the trustees of any charity which should be registered, but which is not, to apply to the Commissioners to register the charity.

The charities listed in s 3(5), which are not required to register, are as follows:

(a) exempt charities listed in Sch 2 to the Act: for example, universities, industrial and provident societies, national institutions such as the British Museum and grant maintained schools;
(b) charities excepted from the need to register by order or regulations: for example charities associated with the armed forces and scout and guide associations;
(c) small charities without permanent endowment (capital which may not be expended – see s 96(3)) or the use or occupation of land and whose income from all sources in aggregate does not exceed £1,000 per year;
(d) a place of worship registered under s 9 of the Places of Worship Act 1855.

Section 3(2) permits charities falling into these categories, other than exempt charities, to apply to the Commissioners for registration on a voluntary basis.

2.4 Exempt Charities

Under the 1960 Act, exempt charities were permitted to register on a voluntary basis. However, the Commissioners developed a policy of declining to register exempt charities, since they had no means of compelling an exempt charity to submit to their jurisdiction, for example to submit accounts.

The Charities Act 1992 effected two changes. It cancelled the existing voluntary registrations of exempt charities and it prohibited any future voluntary registration of an exempt charity. That prohibition is consolidated in s 3(2) of the 1993 Act.

As a result, an exempt charity formerly registered on a voluntary basis may no longer claim that it is a registered charity or refer to a registered charity number. As evidence of its charitable status, it may state that it is an exempt charity under Sch 2 to the 1993 Act, recognised as charitable by the Inland Revenue, and quote its Inland Revenue reference number. If an exempt charity wishes to become a registered charity, it would need to change its legal status, for example by converting an industrial and provident society to a charitable company limited by guarantee.

2.5 Small Charities

Under s 3(2) of the 1993 Act, a small charity will require registration if:

(a) it has a permanent endowment; or
(b) it has the use or occupation of land; or
(c) its income from all sources in aggregate amounts to at least £1,000 per year.

Many charities with an income below £1,000 per year will have registered under the 1960 Act, where the equivalent provision was an income from investments in excess of £15 per year. The threshold of £15 was increased to £1,000 by the 1992 Act (now consolidated in s 3(5) of the 1993 Act), but the source of the income is irrelevant. It may be investment income, but equally it may be income from donations. (For the meaning of 'income' see **2.6**). A small charity which was subject to compulsory registration, but no longer requires to be registered as a result of the change in the income qualifications, may continue its registration on a voluntary basis relying on s 3(2). Alternatively, it may apply to the Commissioners to be removed from the register. The Commissioners are bound to comply with that request.

There is flexibility in the £1,000 threshold. Section 3(12) enables the Secretary of State to alter the figure of £1,000 by order, either to keep pace with inflation or to exclude more charities from compulsory registration (and so prevent the Commissioners from becoming overburdened).

2.6 The Meaning of 'Income'

2.6.1 Elsewhere in the 1993 Act, the terms 'gross income' and 'annual income' are used. For the meaning of 'annual income' see **4.2**. 'Gross income' is defined by s 97 to mean the gross recorded income of a charity from all sources, including special trusts. Section 3 refers simply to 'income' in the phrase 'whose income from all sources does not in aggregate amount to £1,000', but the phrase is further defined by s 96(3) to mean the gross revenues of the charity or the Commissioners' estimate of the likely gross revenues. Furthermore, under s 96(4) the Commissioners are to determine whether any institution established for the special purposes of a charity should be treated as part of the charity – so that the revenues will be taken together – or a distinct charity. Under s 96(6), added by the Charities (Amendment) Act 1995, the Commissioners may direct that two or more charities having the same trustees shall be treated as a single charity and so the income of the charities would be aggregated.

2.6.2 As a result, the term 'income' in s 3 of the 1993 Act is similar to the term 'gross income' used elsewhere in the Act, but it is not identical. The key differences are as follows.

(a) Income, in s 3, is assessed according to the 'gross revenues' of a charity as distinct from the 'gross recorded income'. It is not clear if there is any substantial difference between these terms, for example whether a legacy would fall within one but not the other.

(b) The meaning of 'income' in s 3 is not as certain as the definition of gross income, which automatically includes income of special trusts. A charity may be uncertain whether it is subject to compulsory registration until the Commissioners have given a direction under s 96(4) or (6) as to whether the income from the special trusts or another charity with the same trustees should be aggregated with the income from the main charity. However, if a main charity is already registered with subsidiary charities under the same charity registration number, it would seem appropriate to aggregate the income.

2.7 The Registration Process

2.7.1 To be eligible for registration, an organisation must be a charity within the meaning of s 96(1) and s 97(1) of the 1993 Act. It must be an institution, corporate or not, which is established for purposes which are exclusively charitable according to the law of England and Wales and which is subject to the control of the High Court in the exercise of the court's jurisdiction with respect to charities. The Commissioners interpret the requirement of 'control' to mean that the institution must be established in England and Wales (whether as a trust, company or association) and there must be some means of exerting control, so that either the institution should have property in England and Wales or the majority of the trustees should be resident in England and Wales.

2.7.2 Where the trustees apply to the Commissioners for registration on a compulsory or voluntary basis, s 3(6) requires them to provide to the Commissioners copies of the trusts of the charity or, if they are not in documentary form, evidence of the trusts and such other documents or information as the Commissioners may require or as the Secretary of State may prescribe by regulation. In most cases, the trustees will be able to provide a copy of the governing instrument of the charity (or a draft in the case of an informal application by a proposed charity). Very rarely, evidence of the trusts may be in some other form, for example a statutory declaration where the original deeds are lost. In addition, the Commissioners require applicants to complete a questionnaire providing information about the activities of the charity, the charity trustees and other relevant information. The Commissioners may call for supporting material, for example copies of past accounts, publications, newspaper cuttings or minutes of meetings.

2.7.3 The Commissioners are not the sole arbiters of charitable status. Section 4(2) permits any person who is or may be affected by the registration of a charity to object to registration or, if the charity has been registered, to apply for its removal. (The Inland Revenue is the most often quoted example of a body with a right of objection under s 4(2).) Section 4(3) provides that an appeal may be made to the High Court against a decision of the Commissioners to register or not to register a charity by the purported charity, by a person whose objection or application under s 4(2) has been disallowed or by the Attorney-General.

2.7.4 Section 4(1) of the 1993 Act provides that an institution which is registered is conclusively presumed to be a charity when on the register for all purposes other than rectification. A charity may, for example, rely on registration in order to claim the mandatory rate relief available to charities under s 43(6) of the Local Government Finance Act 1988. However, the presumption is not absolute. The register may be rectified by the removal of an organisation. This may be the result of a successful application under s 4(2) (see **2.7.3**) or removal by the Commissioners under s 3(4) (see **2.8**).

2.7.5 The registration particulars need to be updated. Section 3(7) of the 1993 Act requires trustees to inform the Commissioners of any change in the particulars of the charity entered in the register, for example an amendment of the governing instrument. This is in addition to the obligation to provide annual reports and returns (see Chapter 4) which provide an additional source of information for updating the register.

2.7.6 At present, no charge is made for registering a charity or amending the registered particulars. However, this is another area where the Government has indicated that it proposes to introduce charges under s 85(1) of the 1993 Act and it is current Government policy that charges should cover the cost of the service provided. In the 'Proposals for Reform of the Charities and Voluntary Organisations Task Force' ('the Deregulation Task Force'), published in July 1994, concern was expressed that the payment of considerable fees will impose a burden or act as a barrier for many charities which have few or no assets at the time of registration. The Charity Commission and the Treasury are committed to reviewing the registration process to ensure that it is as efficient as possible, but the Treasury rejected the proposal that any charge for registering a charity should be nominal only.

2.8 Removal from the Register

Section 3(4) of the 1993 Act requires the Commissioners to remove from the register any organisation which no longer appears to the Commissioners to be a charity because of a change in its purposes or trusts, or where a charity has ceased to exist or does not operate.

Seemingly, the Commissioners cannot cancel a registration if they take the view that the initial registration was a mistake on their part. Section 4(1) allows rectification of the register (see **2.7.4**), but s 3(4) restricts the Commissioners' powers of removal to cases where there has been a change in the purposes or trusts or where the charity has ceased to exist or does not operate. If the Commissioners wish to cancel a mistaken registration, they may only do so in response to an application under s 4(1), perhaps from the organisation itself or from the Inland Revenue (see **2.7.4**).

Section 3(7)(b) requires the trustees of a charity to notify the Commissioners if it ceases to exist.

Cancelled entries are in fact retained on the register in accordance with s 3(8), but they are clearly marked as such so that the register fulfils its purpose of being an up-to-date source of information about currently active charities.

2.9 Declaration of Registered Charity Status

2.9.1 Under s 5 of the 1993 Act, a registered charity with a gross income[1] in the previous financial year in excess of £10,000,[2] must state that it is a registered charity on certain documents specified in s 5(2). The Government's declared purpose in introducing this provision is to alert people dealing with a charity to the fact that it is subject to the supervisory regime of the Commissioners and to the legal constraints which bind charities.

The documents to which the provision relates are set out in s 5(2) and are:

(a) notices, advertisements and other documents issued by or on behalf of the charity and soliciting money or other property for the benefit of the charity;
(b) bills of exchange, promissory notes, endorsements, cheques and orders for money or goods purporting to be signed on behalf of the charity; and
(c) bills, invoices, receipts and letters of credit.

With the exception of Welsh charities, the statement of registered charity status must be in English in legible characters, even if the literature of the charity is normally published in another language. In that case, the charity may wish to make the statement in both English and in the language which it would normally use. Welsh charities are permitted by s 3(2) of the Welsh Language Act 1993 to use the words 'elusen cofrestredig' on documents in Welsh.

2.9.2 Section 5 is similar, but not identical, to s 68 of the 1993 Act, which requires a charitable company, which does not include the word 'charity' or 'charitable' in its name, to state that it is a charity on certain documents (similar to those listed in s 5), but incuding business letters, which are not listed in s 5. However, s 68 is concerned with charitable status rather than registered charity status. It applies to all charitable companies, whether registered or not and regardless of income. Charitable companies will need to ensure that they comply with both sections. For example, the word 'charity' on a cheque issued by a charitable company which is a registered charity is not sufficient. The words 'registered charity' are necessary to comply with both statutory provisions.

The point made at (a) (above) applies whether the solicitation is expressed or implied, and whether or not the money or other property is given for consideration. Therefore, it applies not only to direct fund-raising material, but also to newsletters providing information about projects which have the indirect purpose of raising funds. It would apply to documents seeking outright donations, but also to documents inviting contributions in exchange for some benefit, for example admission to some fundraising event. Since the provision relates to solicitations issued on behalf of a charity, it is also relevant to solicitations issued on behalf of a charity by professional fundraisers and commercial participators (see Chapters 12 and 13).

---

1 'Gross income' is defined by s 97 to mean gross recorded income from all sources, including special trusts (see **4.3.2**).
2 Section 5 specified a threshold of £5,000. This figure was raised to £10,000 with effect from 1 December 1995 by the Charities Act 1993 (Substitution of Sums Order) 1995 made under s 5(6) in response to proposals of the Deregulation Task Force.

2.10 Penalties for Non-compliance

2.10.1 The most controversial aspect of s 5 of the 1993 Act is the imposition of criminal penalties for failing to comply with its provisions. Under s 5(4), any person who issues or authorises the issue of any document which does not carry the necessary statement is guilty of an offence and liable on summary conviction to a fine. Section 5(5) imposes a similar penalty on any person who signs a document falling within s 5(2)(b) – a cheque being the most obvious example – without the necessary statement of registered charity status. Liability rests on the individual who issues, authorises or signs the document, whether a trustee or an employee of the charity, or even, in the case of an advertisement soliciting funds, a professional fundraiser or a commercial participator.

2.10.2 These offences are ones of strict liability. The individual is guilty, whether or not the default was committed knowingly. Section 94 of the 1993 Act does, however, provide that no proceedings may be instituted except by or with the consent of the Director of Public Prosecutions. Proceedings would be instituted by the Crown Prosecution Service. During the passage of the Charities Bill (leading to the Charities Act 1992) through the House of Lords, it was suggested that proceedings would not be instituted except in the most extreme cases. No indication was given of what might constitute a 'most extreme case'. The Deregulation Task Force proposed that the requirement of mens rea should be introduced, so that the offender must be aware of his or her fault. However, the proposal has not been implemented.

2.11 Summary of Requirements

Table 1

This table indicates, according to charity type, the need for a charity to register under s 3 of the 1993 Act, as amended, to declare its status as a registered charity under s 5 of the 1993 Act, if its income in the last financial year exceeded £10,000 and to declare its status as a charity under s 68 of the 1993 Act, if the name 'charity' or 'charitable' does not appear in the name of the charity.

KEY TO CHARITY TYPES

1 Exempt charity, including industrial and provident society.
2 Charity excepted from registration by order or regulation.
3 Charity with permanent endowment, not falling into categories 1 or 2.
4 Charity having use or occupation of land, not falling into categories 1 or 2.
5 Charity with gross income in excess of £1,000 per year, not falling into categories 1 or 2.
6 Charity with gross income not exceeding £1,000 per year, or falling into categories 1 or 4.

Charity type	Registration	Declaration of registered status ★	Declaration of charitable status ★★
1	None possible	Not applicable	If a company
2	Voluntary	Compulsory	If a company
3	Compulsory	Compulsory	If a company
4	Compulsory	Compulsory	If a company
5	Compulsory	Compulsory	If a company
6	Voluntary	Not compulsory	If a company

★ If income in the last financial year exceeded £10,000.
★★ If the word 'charity' or 'charitable' does not appear in the name.

CHAPTER 3

CHARITY NAMES

Introduction – Which Charities? – Reasons for Change – Time-limits – The Direction – The Resolution – Checklist

3.1 Introduction

Before the 1992 Act there was a lacuna in the Commissioners' powers. They could not refuse to register a charity with a name similar to that of another charity or with a name which was misleading in some way. For example, the name of a local charity might suggest that it was associated with some national charity, when in fact there was no connection. Sections 4 and 5 of the 1992 Act gave the Commissioners power to require charity trustees to change the name of their charity. These provisions are consolidated as ss 6 and 7 of the 1993 Act.

3.2 Which Charities?

The powers of the Commissioners to require a change of name apply to all charities, whether registered or not, save for exempt charities which are excluded by s 6(9). However, the power in s 6(2)(a) (see below) is concerned specifically with changing the registered name of a registered charity.

3.3 Reasons for Change

3.3.1 There are five sets of circumstances when the Commissioners may require a change of name.

(a) If the registered name is the same or too like the name of another charity at the time the name is entered in the register. The key points of this power are as follows:
   (i) the registered name is the name entered in the charities register, not an acronym or popular name used as an alternative (see **2.2.2**);
   (ii) the other charity, whose name is protected by the Commissioners' action, need not be a registered charity;
   (iii) the similarity must exist when the name is entered in the charities register. This power cannot be used to protect the former name of an existing charity which has been changed or the name of a charity which has ceased to exist;
   (iv) the Commissioners may disregard minor differences in the names of the two charities in reaching a conclusion that the names are the same or too alike (s 6(7)).
   In the *British Diabetic Association v The Diabetic Society* [1995] 4 All ER 812, Robert Walker J made an order requiring the society to change its name and restraining it from using the name or mark 'The Diabetic Society', 'The British Diabetic

Society', 'Diabetic Society', 'The Diabetes Society' and/or 'Diabetes Society' on the grounds that 'association' and 'society' were very similar in derivation and meaning and were not dissimilar in form.

The Commissioners may be expected to follow this precedent when acting under s 6.

(b) If a charity's name is likely to mislead the public as to the true nature of the purposes or activities of the charity.

(c) If a charity's name includes a word or expression specified in the Charities (Misleading Names) Regulations 1992 and the Commissioners are of the opinion that this is likely to mislead the public as to the status of the charity. Example words which denote national or international status or royal patronage.

(d) If a charity's name is likely to give a misleading impression that it is connected in some way with HM Government, a local authority or some other body or individual.

(e) If a charity's name is offensive. There is no statutory indication of what may be regarded as offensive.

3.4 Time-limits

The Commissioners must give the direction to require a charity to change its registered name under s 6(2)(a) within 12 months of the date when the name was entered in the register. However, the powers to require change under s 6(2)(b), (c), (d) and (e) are not subject to any time-limit. These powers could be used by the Commissioners to require a charity to change a name which has been in use for some time.

3.5 The Direction

The Commissioners exercise their power to require a charity to change its name by giving a formal direction to the charity trustees under s 6(1). Under this direction the charity trustees are required to change the name of the charity. The new name is to be determined by the trustees, with the approval of the Commissioners. The direction will also specify the period within which the change must be effected.

Section 90 of the 1993 Act deals with directions of the Commissioners generally. The principal features of a direction are:

(a) a direction must be in writing but does not require any other formality – a letter will suffice;

(b) there is no right of appeal against a direction, but the Commissioners can vary or revoke a direction by a further direction; and

(c) a direction can be enforced by contempt proceedings in the High Court under s 88 of the 1993 Act.

3.6 The Resolution

3.6.1 The charity trustees must pass a resolution to change the name of the charity, regardless of any provisions in the trusts of the charity. They cannot refuse to comply on the grounds that they have no power to amend the trusts or that the power to amend rests with others or is subject to the consent of some other individual. In particular, ss 6(8) and 7 of the 1993 Act make it clear that in the case of a charitable company, the name is to be changed by resolution of the directors rather than by special resolution of the members, which would be the normal procedure under company law. A resolution to change the name of a charitable company must, however, be filed with the Registrar of Companies in the usual way and will not be completed until a certificate of incorporation on change of name has been issued. The Registrar of Companies retains the power to object to new name and it is, therefore, essential that the Charity Commission and the Registrar of Companies adopt a co-ordinated approach.

3.6.2 Under s 6(5), the trustees must notify the Commissioners of the charity's new name and of the date on which the change occurred. If the charity is a registered charity, the Commissioners will then enter that new name in the register.

3.7 Checklist

Charity trustees should take the following steps if they receive a direction from the Commissioners to change the name of their charity.

(a) Consider whether there is evidence to justify the name and, if so, submit this to the Commissioners with a request that they revoke the direction.

(b) If the direction is to be complied with, select a new name and submit this to the Commissioners for approval.

(c) If the charity is a company, check that the new name is not the same or too like that of a registered company.

(d) Pass a resolution to change the name, following the trustees' normal rules of procedure.

(e) If the charity is a company, transmit a certified copy of the resolution to the Registrar of Companies with the statutory fee on change of name (currently £20) and await the certificate of incorporation on change of name.

(f) Transmit a certified copy of the resolution to the Commissioners (with a certified copy of the certificate of incorporation on change of name, if a company). If the charity is a registered charity, ask for confirmation that the charity register has been amended.

(g) If it is not possible to complete the change of name within the time-limit specified by the Commissioners in the direction, ask the Commissioners to vary the directions to permit more time.

CHAPTER 4

CHARITY ACCOUNTS: ACCOUNTING AND REPORTING PROCEDURES

Introduction – Graduated System – Financial Year – Accounting Records – Annual Statements of Accounts – Audit or Independent Examination – Commissioners' Power to Order Audit – Annual Reports – Annual Returns – Public Access to Accounts – Penalties for Non-compliance – Summary of Requirements

4.1 Introduction

4.1.1 The 1992 Act introduced radical changes to the accounting and reporting procedures of charities to improve the quality of charity accounts and to establish systems for supplying information to the Commissioners on a regular basis – essential if the Commissioners are to monitor charities effectively. These changes have been consolidated in the 1993 Act and are implemented by the Charities (Accounts and Reports) Regulations 1995 (SI 1995/2724). The new accounting and reporting regime came into effect on 1 March 1996 and applies to a charity in respect of its financial year beginning on or after that date.

The principal changes under the new regime are:

(a) for the first time, many charities will be required not only to maintain accounting records, but also to send annual accounts, an annual report and an annual return to the Commissioners;

(b) for the first time, there is a general requirement that the accounts of many charities be subject to external scrutiny by an independent examiner or, in certain circumstances, a registered auditor;

(c) charities should model their accounts on 'Accounting by Charities: The Statement of Recommended Practice' (SORP), issued by the Charity Commissioners in October 1995 and approved by the Accounting Standards Committee. This brings a measure of uniformity to the preparation of charity accounts;

(d) charity trustees are required to make copies of their charity's accounts available to the public upon request.

4.1.2 The statutory regime is contained in the 1993 Act and the Charities (Accounts and Reports) Regulations 1995. The Regulations provide the basic framework for:

(a) the form of accounts;
(b) auditor's report;
(c) independent examiner's report;
(d) financial year.

The statutory regime is supplemented by the SORP, which is the principal source of accounting methods and principles for all charities, regardless of size.

4.2 Graduated System

4.2.1 There has always been a concern that the new accounting and reporting regime should not become an unnecessary burden on smaller charities. What is appopriate for a charity with an annual income of £250,000 will not be appropriate for a charity with an annual income of only £10,000. The requirements of the new regime are therefore graduated according to the size of the charity, determined by its gross income or total expenditure. The term 'gross income' is defined by s 97 to mean the gross recorded income of a charity from all sources, including special trusts. Total expenditure is not defined. Confusingly, there are different thresholds to determine the form of accounts and annual report on the one hand, and auditing requirements on the other. The thresholds themselves were increased even before the new regime came into force.

4.2.2 Sections 28, 29 and 30 of the Deregulation and Contracting Out Act 1994 amended the 1993 Act to introduce a 'light touch regime' for charities whose gross income or total expenditure does not exceed £10,000 (in the relevant year). The light touch regime is as follows:

(a) accounts may be prepared on a simplified receipts and payments basis;
(b) the accounts do not have to be independently examined or audited (unless this is a specific requirement of the governing document of the charity);
(c) a simplified annual report is required, prepared in accordance with Charity Commission guide-lines;
(d) the accounts and report need only be filed with the Charity Commission if requested; and
(e) a simplified annual return is required.

4.2.3 For charities which fall outside the light touch regime, the form of accounts is governed by the gross income of the charity in the year for which the accounts are being prepared. Charities with an income not exceeding £100,000 may prepare accounts on a receipts and payments basis which may be accompanied by a Statement of Assets and Liabilities at the year end and simplified annual report. Charities with a gross income of £100,000 and above must prepare accounts on an accruals basis and comply with a full statutory regime. The original sum of £25,000 was raised to £100,000 by the Charities Act 1993 (Substitution of Sums) Order 1995 (SI 1995/2696).

4.2.4 Auditing requirements are governed by the gross income or total expenditure in the year for which accounts are being prepared or either of the two previous years. Section 43, as amended by the Charities Act 1993 (Substitution of Sums) Order 1995, requires the accounts of a charity whose gross income or total expenditure exceeds the threshold of £250,000 to be subject to audit by an auditor qualified to audit company accounts. If the gross income or total expenditure falls below £250,000, the trustees may choose to have the accounts examined by an independent examiner rather than audited by a registered auditor, unless the governing instrument of the charity requires a full audit.

Section 43 does not apply to companies (s 43(9)). The auditing requirements for charitable companies are governed by the Companies Act 1985 (Audit Exemption) Regulations 1994 (SI 1994/1935). A charitable company can claim exemption from audit if its gross income for the year for which the accounts have been prepared does not exceed £90,000 and its balance sheet total for that year is not more than £1.4 million. If its gross income exceeds £90,000 but does not exceed £250,000 and the balance sheet total for the year is not more than £1.4 million, the trustees may produce unaudited accounts accompanied by a report of a reporting accountant as defined by s 249D of the Companies Act 1985.

4.3 Financial Year

Under the Charities Act 1960, charities were required to prepare statements of account for consecutive periods not exceeding 15 months. However, the concept of the financial year is central to the new regime. The annual statement of accounts (s 42), the annual report (s 45) and annual return (s 48) are all to be prepared in respect of a charity's financial year and the form of accounts and auditing requirements are determined according to the gross income or total expenditure in respect of a financial year.

Paragraph 5 of the Charities (Accounts and Reports) Regulations 1995 introduces provisions for determining a charity's financial year, which are similar to rules governing companies. A charity's financial year will normally be a 12-month period ending on the charity's accounting reference date. Trustees have some flexibility in selecting the accounting reference date in the first year under the new regime, so that the first financial year may be somewhere between six months and 18 months. Trustees also have power to change the accounting reference date. However, these powers may be exercised only in exceptional circumstances and the power to change the accounting reference date may not be exercised in consecutive years.

4.4 Accounting Records

4.4.1 Section 41 of the 1993 Act requires charity trustees to ensure that accounting records are kept which record the financial transactions of the charity on a day-to-day basis.

The accounting records must be sufficient:

(a) to show and explain all the charity's transactions;
(b) to disclose at any time and with reasonable accuracy the financial position of the charity at that time;
(c) to show entries on a day-to-day basis for all sums received and expended, identifying the matter in respect of which the transaction took place and to include a record of assets and liabilities; and
(d) to enable the trustees to ensure that any statements of accounts required by the 1993 Act comply with the statutory requirements (see **4.5**).

The requirement that the records should disclose a charity's financial position at any time with reasonable accuracy does not mean the charity must update its accounting records daily. The records should be sufficiently detailed, showing transactions on a daily basis, to enable the accounts to be drawn up to reveal the financial position of the charity on any particular date in the past.

Section 41 does not apply to charitable companies. They are excluded by s 41(5), but they must maintain identical accounting records by virtue of s 221 of the Companies Act 1985, the wording of which is mirrored in s 41. Similarly, s 41 does not apply to exempt charities. They are excluded by s 46(1), but are required to keep proper books of account.

4.4.2 By s 41, accounting records must be preserved for at least six years from the end of the financial year to which they relate. The Commissioners may, however, agree to the destruction or disposal of records in some other way if a charity ceases to exist. A similar rule is imposed on exempt charities by s 46(2). Section 222 of the Companies Act 1985 deals with the preservation of company accounting records. A public company must preserve records for six years, but a private company need only preserve records for three years. Since charitable companies are established as private companies, it would appear that they need only preserve records for three years. This would seem to be an oversight and charitable companies would be well-advised to observe the six-year requirement.

4.5 Annual Statements of Accounts

4.5.1 Section 42 requires charity trustees to prepare annual statements of accounts. Two categories of charity are excluded from these requirements, although they may be subject to other obligations to prepare annual accounts. The excluded categories are as follows:

(a) charitable companies are excluded by s 42(7). The format of the accounts should comply with Companies Act 1985 requirements and they should be prepared in accordance with the SORP, which does apply to charitable companies;

(b) exempt charities are excluded by s 46(1). However, they are required to prepare consecutive statements of account consisting of an income and expenditure account and a balance sheet for periods not exceeding 15 months. They should comply with SORP and may also be subject to special requirements imposed on them by some other statutory regime.

4.5.2 Section 42(3) permits trustees of a charity with a gross income in the relevant year not exceeding £100,000 (see **4.2**) to elect to prepare the simplified accounts in the form of a receipts and payments account and a statement of assets and liabilities. Trustees of a charity whose gross income for the year in question exceeds £100,000 are required to prepare annual statements of accounts whose form and contents comply with the Charities (Accounts and Reports) Regulations 1995. The form and contents are set out in para 3 of and Sch 1 to the Regulations. The principal requirements are:

(a) a statement of financial activities (SOFA) showing total incoming resources, the application of the resources and the movement in total resources;

(b) incoming resources divided between resources from donors, from investment, from trading activities and 'other' incoming resources. Income from trading activities should be divided between activities in furtherance of the objects of the charity and activities for commercial or fundraising purposes;

(c) expenditure should be divided between expenditure directly relating to the objects of the charity, expenditure on fundraising and publicity and expenditure on the cost of managing and administering the charity;

(d) the SOFA should distinguish between unrestricted and restricted income funds and capital funds. These divisions should also be made in the balance sheet;

(e) the SOFA and a balance sheet are required to give a true and fair view of the charity. If, in special circumstances, a true and fair view would not be given by complying with the statutory requirements, trustees may depart from the Regulations, but this must be explained in the notes to the accounts;

(f) Part IV of the Schedule deals with notes to the accounts and highlights significant points which will be of interest to the Commissioners, for example whether remuneration or other benefits have been paid to the charity trustees or persons connected with the trustees, the cost of trustee indemnity insurance or any other form of indemnity for the trustees and details of any transactions between the charity and a charity trustee or a person connected with a trustee.

The requirements of para 3 of and Sch 1 to the Regulations are supplemented by the SORP.

The Regulations make special provision for the form of accounts of common investment and common deposit funds established under ss 24 and 25 (see **7.8**), registered housing associations and higher educational institutions.

4.5.3 There is an obligation to preserve any statement of accounts for six years from the end of the financial year to which it relates. This is similar to the obligation to preserve accounting records (see **4.4.2**).

4.6 Audit or Independent Examination

4.6.1 Section 43 of the 1993 Act requires the annual accounts of a charity to be audited or examined by an independent examiner. The following categories of charity are excluded from this requirement:

(a) charitable companies (s 43(9)), which must, however, comply with the audit requirements of the Companies Act 1985 (see **4.2**);

(b) exempt charities (s 46(1));

(c) charities which have neither any permanent endowment nor the use or occupation of land, nor an income in the relevant year exceeding £1,000 and which are not registered on a voluntary basis (s 46(2)); and

(d) charities whose gross income in the year to which the accounts relate does not exceed £10,000 (see **4.2**).

4.6.2 If the gross income or total expenditure of a charity exceeds £250,000 in the year for which the accounts are being prepared or either of the two immediately preceding years, the accounts must be audited by a person who is eligible to act as a company auditor under s 25 of the Companies Act 1985 (ie a registered auditor).

If the gross income or total expenditure of a charity exceeds £10,000 but not £250,000, s 43(3) permits the trustees to have the accounts examined by an independent examiner as an alternative to an audit. An independent examiner is defined, in s 43(3) as an independent person who is reasonably believed by the trustees to have the requisite ability and practical experience to carry out a competent examination of the accounts. This does not necessarily mean a professional accountant, but could include a bank or building society manager, a retired accountant or a local authority treasurer. Under s 43(7), the Commissioners may give guidance to trustees – either generally or to trustees of a particular charity – about the selection of an independent examiner and may give directions relating to the carrying out of an examination. The Commissioners are expected to issue guidance well before March 1997 when it will be necessary to implement the new regime in respect of financial years beginning on or after 1 March 1996. Section 43(3) has been amended by s 28 of the Deregulation and Contracting Out Act 1994 so that a charity whose gross income in the year for which the accounts are prepared does not exceed £10,000 need not submit accounts for audit or independent examination, unless that is a requirement of its constitution.

4.6.3 The duties of an auditor carrying out an audit of charity accounts and the duties of an independent examiner carrying out an examination of accounts under s 43 are specified in paras 6 and 7 of the Charities (Accounts and Reports) Regulations 1995, made under s 44. Some of the information which auditors or independent examiners are required to include in their report is surprisingly routine: for example the name and address of the auditor (or independent examiner), the name of the charity, the financial year to which the report relates and a statement that the report is prepared under s 43. Auditors and independent examiners are also required to sign their reports.

An auditor is required to state that in his opinion the statement of accounts complies with the Regulations and gives a true and fair view of the state of affairs of the charity. In the case of simplified accounts (for a charity whose gross income does not exceed £100,000), an auditor or independent examiner must confirm that the accounts and statement of assets and liabilities properly represent the receipts and payments during the year and assets and liabilities at the end of the year and that they distinguish any material special trust or other restricted fund.

If an auditor has formed the opinion that:

(a) proper accounting records have not been kept; or
(b) the accounts do not accord with the records; or
(c) the statement of accounts is inconsistent with the trustees' report; or
(d) information or explanations to which the auditor is entitled under the regulations have not been made available;

then the report must include a statement to that effect.

4.6.4 Paragraph 6(5) of the Regulations requires an auditor to communicate with the Commissioners in writing any matter of which he becomes aware in his capacity as an auditor which relates to the charity or a connected body and which the auditor has reasonable cause to believe is, or is likely to be, of material significance for the exercise of the Commissioners' functions in relation to the charity under ss 8 or 18 (instituting inquiries and acting for the protection of charities) (see **5.3** and **5.4**). This introduces a statutory 'whistle blowing' obligation on auditors. It is not sufficient for the auditor to draw the attention of the trustees to the irregularity.

Paragraph 6(6) of the Regulations introduces a 'signing off' obligation for auditors. On ceasing to hold office, an auditor must give trustees a statement of any circumstances connected with the termination of his office which he considers should be brought to the attention of the trustees or, if there is none, a statement to that effect. Unless the statement is a negative statement, the auditor must also send a copy to the Commissioners.

4.6.5 There are subtle differences in the obligations placed on an independent examiner compared with an auditor. For example, an auditor must include in his report a statement that accounting records have not been kept or the statement of accounts does not accord with those records if he has come to this opinion. On the other hand, an independent examiner must state in his report 'whether or not any matter has come to his attention in connection with the examination which gives him reasonable cause to believe that in any material respect accounting records have not been kept or the accounts do not accord with the records'. The independent examiner is required to give a negative assurance that these matters have not come to light.

An independent examiner must also state whether or not any matter has come to his attention in connection with the examination to which, in his opinion, attention should be drawn in the report in order to enable a proper understanding of the accounts to be reached. Again, a negative assurance is required.

No statutory whistle blowing obligation or signing off obligation is imposed on an independent examiner, but if it becomes apparent to the examiner that there has been material expenditure or action which appears not to be in accordance with the trusts of the charity, the report must state this opinion.

4.7 Commissioners' Power to Order Audit

4.7.1 Section 43 places the obligation to submit accounts for audit or independent examination on the trustees. In those circumstances, the costs of the audit or independent examination will be an administrative expense, to be met from the charity's funds. Section 43(4), (5) and (6) does, however, confer power on the Commissioners to make an order requiring the audit of accounts. In certain circumstances, the costs of such an audit fall automatically on the trustees personally.

Section 43(4) confers on the Commissioners a power to order the audit (or examination of accounts, if appropriate) if the statutory requirement for accounts to be audited or examined has not been complied with within 10 months of the end of the relevant financial year.

In these circumstances, the appointment of the auditor or examiner is a matter for the Commissioners but the costs are the responsibility of the trustees. Section 43(6) provides that expenses, including the auditor's remuneration, are to be met, in the first place, by the trustees, who are personally liable jointly and severally. The Commissioners, therefore, may seek to recover the expenses from one of several trustees. The expenses can only be met from the funds of the charity if the Commissioners are of the view that it is not practical to recover the expenses from the trustees. There is no discretion in the matter.

Section 43(4) also confers on the Commissioners a power to order the audit of accounts, which have already been subject to independent examination, if the Commissioners are of the view that an audit is desirable. In these circumstances, the auditor may be appointed by the trustees and, provided the trustees comply with the Commissioners' order, the costs of the audit will be met from the funds of the charity.

The Commissioners' powers to order an independent examination or audit of accounts under s 43 do not apply to those categories of charity excluded from the scope of s 43 (see **4.6.1**). However, the Commissioners may require the accounts of a charitable company (other than an exempt charity) to be audited at their expense under s 69.

4.8 Annual Reports

4.8.1 Under s 45, the trustees must prepare an annual report in respect of the financial year of a charity. The annual report of a charity whose gross income in that year exceeded £10,000 must be sent to the Commissioners within 10 months of the end of that financial year with the accounts and with the report of the auditor or independent examiner if appropriate. The Commissioners may extend the 10-month period if it has not been possible for good reason to produce the accounts and report within that time. Section 45(3) was amended by the Deregulation and Contracting Out Act 1994 so that the report of a charity with a gross income below £10,000 need only be sent to the Commissioners if so requested.

4.8.2 Section 45 requires the annual report of the charity to comply with the Charities (Accounts and Reports) Regulations 1995. The requirements are specified in para 10 of the Regulations.

For small charities, with a gross income not exceeding £100,000, a brief summary of the main activities and achievements of the charity during the year in relation to its objects is required. For charities with a gross income exceeding the £100,000 threshold, the report is required to include:

(a) a review of all activities, including material transactions, significant developments and achievements of the charity during the year in relation to its objects;
(b) any significant changes in those activities during the year;
(c) any important events affecting those activities which have occurred since the end of the year; and
(d) any likely future developments in those activities.

The report is also required to include routine information such as the name of the charity, charity registration number, principal address, summary of the trusts, name of the charity trustees (or the first 50 if there are more than 50), a description of the organisational structure of the charity and a description of any assets held by the charity for another charity. The Commissioners have power to dispense with the requirement to disclose the names of trustees or the principal address of the charity where to do so would lead individuals into personal danger. An example where this might be appropriate would be in the case of a women's refuge.

Special provisions are made for the report of a common investment fund or common deposit fund established under ss 24 or 25 (see **7.8**).

4.8.3 Two categories of charity are excluded from the provisions of s 45 by s 46(2). These are exempt charities and charities which have neither any permanent endowment, nor the use or occupation of land nor an income in the relevant year exceeding £1,000 which are not registered on a voluntary basis.

Charitable companies are required to prepare an annual report to send to the Commissioners with accounts prepared under Part VII of the Companies Act 1985 and auditor's report attached.

Charities which are both excepted from the need to register by an order of the Commissioners made under s 3(5) and are not registered on a voluntary basis, are partially exempt from the requirements of s 45. Under s 46, these charities need only prepare and send an annual report when they are required to do so by the Commissioners. In such cases, the annual report should have attached to it the accounts and report of the auditor or independent examiner.

4.8.4 Section 47 provides for the annual report of a charity, including the accounts and report prepared by the auditor or independent examiner kept by the Commissioners, to be open to public inspection and for the Commissioners to supply copies of such documents on request. Fees for the supply of copies of or extracts from documents are prescribed by the Charity Commissioners' Fees (Copies and Extracts) Regulations 1992 (SI 1992/2986).

4.9 Annual Returns

Section 48 requires every registered charity whose gross income or total expenditure for the year exceeds £10,000 to prepare an annual return to be sent to the Commissioners within 10 months of the end of the financial year to which the return relates.

Under s 48(3), the Commissioners may waive the need to prepare an annual return in the case of a particular charity or particular class of charities or, in the case of a particular financial year, of a charity or class of charities.

4.10 Public Access to Accounts

Section 47(2) and (3) effects a radical change in the public accountability of charities. Sections 41 to 46 are concerned with the obligations of charity trustees to maintain accounts and, broadly speaking, in the case of registered charities, to prepare annual accounts, reports and returns to be sent to the Commissioners. The right of members of the public to inspect documents sent to the Charity Commission (see **4.8.4**) ensures that the public have access to information about registered charities.

Section 47(2) and (3) goes further. Section 47(2) confers the right on any member of the public to submit a written request to charity trustees, whether the charity is registered or not, to supply a copy of the charity's recent accounts. Provided he or she pays whatever reasonable fee the trustees require to cover the cost of supplying the accounts, the trustees must comply with the request within two months of the receipt of the request. (Section 47(3) identifies which accounts are 'the most recent accounts' of a charity.)

Therefore, any member of the public may obtain the accounts of any charity, even exempt charities which would, in the past, have been difficult to obtain.

4.11 Penalties for Non-compliance

A controversial aspect of the new accounting and reporting requirements has been the introduction of criminal sanctions for failure to fulfil the statutory obligations.

Section 49 provides that a person is guilty of an offence if, without reasonable excuse, he is persistently in default:

(a) in submitting the annual report with accounts attached or the annual return; or
(b) in supplying copies of the most recent accounts of the charity to a member of the public under s 47(2).

Such a person will be liable on summary conviction to a fine.

Since s 49 is subject to s 94, proceedings may not be instituted without the consent of the Director of Public Prosecutions.

The individuals likely to be prosecuted under s 49 are the charity trustees, because the statutory obligations are placed on the trustees rather than on the officers of the charity. It is the trustees' responsibility to ensure that the statutory obligations have been complied with. Where a prosecution is authorised by the Director of Public Prosecutions, it is possible that all the trustees would be prosecuted unless they could establish that they acted reasonably in delegating the obligation to send the accounts, report and return to one of their number or to an officer of the charity. This is because the charity trustees are jointly responsible for the proper conduct of the affairs of the charity. It would be less easy to establish a reasonable excuse if no steps had been taken to prepare the documents in the first place.

4.12 Summary of Requirements

Tables 2 and 3 summarise the accounting and reporting requirements for registered charities and non-registered charities, respectively. Registered charities include charities registered on a voluntary basis. A charity may also be subject to another accounting and reporting regime not shown in the table, for example a registered housing association will need to comply with the requirements of the Housing Corporation.

Table 2 Registered Charities

This table shows the accounting and reporting requirements of registered charities according to the charity type. A charity may also be subject to other accounting and reporting regimes not shown in the table.

KEY TO REGISTERED CHARITIES

1 With gross income or total expenditure exceeding £250,000.
2 With gross income between £100,000 and £250,000.
3 With gross income between £10,000 and £100,000.
4 With gross income below £10,000.
5 Charitable company, regardless of income.
6 Excepted charity, registered on voluntary basis.

Charity type	Accounting records (s 41)	Annual accounts (s 42)	Audit/independent examination (s 43)	Annual report (s 45)	Annual return (s 48)	Accounts to public (s 47)
1	Yes	Full accounts	Full audit	Yes	Yes	Yes
2	Yes	Full accounts	Independent examination	Yes	Yes	Yes
3	Yes	Simplified accounts	Independent examination	Yes	Yes	Yes
4	Yes	Simplified accounts*	No	Yes*	No	Yes
5	No, but must comply with Companies Act 1985	No, but must comply with Companies Act 1985	No, but must comply with Companies Act 1985	Yes, in addition to Companies Act 1985	Yes, in addition to Companies Act 1985	Yes
6	Yes	Yes. Full accounts if income in excess of £100,000	Yes. Full audit if gross income exceeds £250,000, otherwise independent examination	Yes	Yes	Yes

*Need only be filed with the Charity Commissioners on request.

Table 3 Unregistered Charities

This table shows the accounting and reporting requirements of unregistered charities according to charity type. A charity may also be subject to other statutory regimes not shown in the table.

KEY TO UNREGISTERED CHARITY TYPES
1 Exempt charity.
2 Unregistered charitable company, regardless of income.
3 Charity (other than company) with income below £1,000.
4 Excepted charity with income exceeding £1,000 but not registered on voluntary basis.

Charity type	Accounting records (s 41)	Annual accounts (s 42)	Audit/independent examination (s 43)	Annual report (s 45)	Annual return (s 48)	Accounts to public (s 47)
1	Yes (s 46(1))	No, but must comply with s 46(1)	None	None	None	Yes
2	No, but must comply with Companies Act 1985	No, but must comply with Companies Act 1985	No, but must comply with Companies Act 1985	No, but must comply with Companies Act 1985	No, but must comply with Companies Act 1985	Yes
3	Yes	None	None	None	None	Yes
4	Yes	Yes. Full accounts if gross income in excess of £100,000	Yes. Full audit if gross income exceeds £250,000	On request	None	Yes

CHAPTER 5

POWERS TO DEAL WITH ABUSE: PREVENTION, INVESTIGATION AND PROTECTION

Introduction – Disqualification – Commissioners' Information Powers – Intervention – Appointment of Receiver and Manager – Supervision of Scottish Charities – Court Proceedings

5.1 Introduction

The 1960 Act conferred on the Commissioners power to investigate charities and to take protective action where, as a result of an inquiry, they were satisfied that there had been misconduct or mismanagement or they were satisfied that protective action was desirable.

The 1992 Act introduced reforms to give greater force to the role of the Commissioners to prevent, investigate and initiate action against abuse. These reforms are now consolidated in the 1993 Act.

5.2 Disqualification

5.2.1 The disqualification of individuals with convictions for fraud or dishonesty from acting as a trustee of a charity is one of the preventive measures introduced by the 1992 Act. Other preventive measures were the requirement for all registered charities to declare their status and certain documents (see **2.9**) and the power conferred on the Commissioners to require a charity to change its name if too similar to that of another charity or otherwise likely to mislead (see Chapter 3).

A person is disqualified from acting as a trustee of a charity by s 72(1) of the 1993 Act if:

(a) he has been convicted of an offence involving dishonesty or deception (including theft, fraud or forgery) provided that the conviction is not a spent conviction under the Rehabilitation of Offenders Act 1975;

(b) he has been adjudged bankrupt or sequestration of his estate has been awarded and he has not been discharged in either case;

(c) he has made a composition or arrangement with, or granted a trust deed for, his creditors and has not been discharged in respect of it;

(d) he has been removed as trustee of a charity by order of the Commissioners or the High Court on the grounds of misconduct or mismanagement in the administration of a charity for which he was responsible or to which he was privy, or which, by his conduct, he contributed to or facilitated;

(e) he has been removed under s 7 of the Law Reform (Miscellaneous Provisions) (Scotland) Act 1990 (powers of the Court of Session to deal with management of charities) from being concerned in the management or control of any charity; or

(f) he is subject to a disqualification order by the Company Directors Disqualification
     Act 1986 or to an order made under s 429(2)(b) of the Insolvency Act (failure to pay
     under county court administration order) and has not obtained leave under the
     provisions of the appropriate Act to act as director (trustee) of the charity.

The disqualification from acting as a trustee applies to all charities, including exempt
charities and other unregistered charities. It applies both to the office of managing
trustee and to the office of holding trustee and is effective even if the grounds for
disqualification arose before s 72 of the 1993 Act (or its predecessor s 45 of the 1992
Act) was implemented.

5.2.2 Disqualification is automatic unless the Commissioners exercise their power of
waiver, under s 72(4) of the 1993 Act. The waiver may authorise the individual to act as
trustee of a particular charity or of a particular class of charities. The Commissioners may
not waive the disqualification of an individual who is disqualified under the Company
Directors Disqualification Act 1986 and who has not obtained leave under that Act to
act as director of a company.

5.2.3 Section 73 imposes penalties for acting as a trustee while disqualified.

(a) Under s 73(1) it is an offence, punishable by a term of imprisonment or a fine or
     both, to act as a trustee while disqualified. This does not apply to a trustee who is
     disqualified under grounds (b) or (f) above (see **5.2.1**) in which case the offence is
     dealt with under company law. The proceedings may only be instituted with the
     consent of the Director of Public Prosecutions.
(b) Under s 73(4), the Commissioners may order an individual who has acted as a
     trustee while disqualified, to repay to the charity the whole or part of any such sums
     received by way of remuneration or expenses or the value of any benefit received in
     kind. In normal circumstances, a trustee would not receive any remuneration or
     benefit in kind from the charity. However, out-of-pocket expenses may have been
     paid to the trustee.

5.2.4 Section 72(6) requires the Commissioners to keep a register, open to the public,
of all individuals who have been removed from office by the Commissioners at
whatever date, or by the High Court if removed after s 45(1) of the Charities Act 1992
came into force.

5.2.5 In *Decisions of the Charity Commissioners* (Vol 1) published in August 1993, the
Commissioners explained their policy when considering applications for waiver made
under s 72(4).
    The Commissioners analysed the cases involving the removal of a trustee in
circumstances of bankruptcy (but not dishonesty) and identified the following
underlying principles:

(a) the general rule is that the court will remove a trustee in cases of bankruptcy on the
     basis either of impecuniosity, or that a person who has shown lack of prudence in
     managing his own affairs is not likely to be successful in managing the affairs of
     others;
(b) no separate misconduct either in the affairs of the charity or, generally, need be
     shown; and

(c) the fact that a trustee is not in a position under the trust where he is likely to be in receipt or custody of property, and that he is a person of means will weigh in favour of not removing him.

The Commissioners went on to identify the following issues as relevant, recommending that they be addressed in any application submitted under s 72(4):

(a) the specific nature of the offence in respect of which the disqualification arises;
(b) the gravity of the offence and the sentence passed by the court;
(c) the seriousness of the bankruptcy of composition or the circumstances of any removal by the court or the Commissioners as the case may be;
(d) the nature of the trust property, for instance whether it only consists of land used in the performance of the charity's objects or whether there are investments and money which would or might pass through the trustee's own hands;
(e) the degree of risk of misappropriation of the funds or property of any charity concerned if the trustee remains in office;
(f) whether in the case of a relevant offence or bankruptcy or composition with creditors, the nature and extent of any misconduct relating to the administration of any charity may itself warrant removal from office as a trustee;
(g) whether and, if so, how seriously, the reputation of charity in general or of a particular charity will be impugned by the grant of a waiver;
(h) where relevant, the interests of the charity or class of charity in the rehabilitation of offenders through charitable works;
(i) whether the applicant is prohibited from acting as a director of the company under the Company Directors Disqualification Act 1986 and, if so, whether leave has been given under the Act for him to act as a director of any other company;
(j) if a disqualification order has not been made in circumstances where the applicant has been convicted of a criminal offence involving dishonesty or deception in the course of a company's administration, the reason why no such order was made;
(k) whether the trusts of the charity otherwise contain provisions disqualifying or determining trusteeship in any of the circumstances covered by the statutory disqualification. Waiver would extend only to the statutory provision. It would not override the trust provisions;
(l) the views of the other trustees of the charity or charities concerned.

5.3 Commissioners' Information Powers

5.3.1 Sections 8 and 9 of the 1993 Act empower the Commissioners to institute inquiries into charities and to call for documents and to search records. These powers do not extend over exempt charities.

Where the Commissioners institute an inquiry under s 8, they may conduct the inquiry themselves or appoint a person to conduct it and to report to them. The Commissioners (or a person appointed by them to conduct the inquiry) may direct an individual:

(a) to provide accounts or written statements on any matter under investigation on which he has or can reasonably obtain information;
(b) to provide copies of documents under his custody or control; and

(c) to attend in person to give evidence or produce documents.

Evidence may be taken on oath and statutory declarations may be required to verify accounts, documents or other information provided.

The power under s 8 to obtain information is initiated by a direction of the Commissioners (or person appointed by them to conduct the inquiry). Section 90 of the Act deals with the giving and enforcement of directions (see **3.5**).

Section 9 confers on the Commissioners an additional power, which may be exercised independently of an inquiry, to make an order to require an individual to provide information in his possession or documents in his custody or under his control which relate to any charity and which are relevant to the functions of the Commissioners or the official custodian. Sections 87 to 91 of the Act deal with the making and enforcement of orders of the Commissioners. The fundamental difference between an order and a direction is in the formality of the documentation. All that is required for a direction is that it is in writing, whereas an order will be made under seal.

5.3.2 Section 10 of the 1993 Act enables the Commissioners to exchange information with the organisations listed in s 10(6) for the purpose of enabling or assisting the Commissioners or the other organisation to fulfil its functions. The organisations listed are:

(a) any government department (including a Northern Ireland department);
(b) any local authority;
(c) any constable;
(d) any other body or person discharging functions of a public nature (including a body or person discharging regulatory functions in relation to any description of activities).

Section 10(2) excludes from this list the Commissioners of Customs and Excise (who deal with VAT) and the Commissioners of Inland Revenue. However, those bodies are expressly authorised to disclose to the Commissioners information relating to:

(a) the name and address of any institution which has been treated as established for charitable purposes (so helping the Commissioners to track down unregistered charities);
(b) information about the purpose of the institution and its trusts in order to provide assistance in determining whether the institution ought to be treated as a charity (so helping the Commissioners to reach a decision on the charitable status of the organisation);
(c) information about an organisation which has been treated as a charity but which appears to be carrying on activities which are not charitable or to have applied its funds for purposes which are not charitable (so helping the Commissioners to monitor charities and check abuse).

5.3.3 Section 11 of the 1993 Act creates an offence of knowingly or recklessly providing the Commissioners (including an individual appointed to conduct an inquiry under s 8) with information which is false or misleading in a material particular. The offence exists if the information is provided supposedly in compliance with a statutory requirement (for example the requirement to provide information under s 9) or the individual providing the information intends, or could reasonably be expected to know, that the information would be used by the Commissioners for the purpose of discharging their statutory functions.

No proceedings may be brought under s 11 without the consent of the Director of Public Prosecutions (s 94).

5.4 Intervention

5.4.1 Section 18 of the 1993 Act confers on the Commissioners a number of powers to act for the protection of charities. A distinction is drawn between temporary protective powers designed to enable the Commissioners to intervene swiftly to protect assets which they believe to be at risk, and remedial powers which are designed to provide a permanent solution for a charity where the Commissioners have discovered misconduct or mismanagement.

5.4.2 The temporary protective powers are set out in s 18(1). These are:

(a) to suspend a trustee (whether a holding trustee or a managing trustee), or an officer, agent or employee of the charity, for a period of up to 12 months pending consideration being given to the removal of that individual;
(b) to appoint additional charity trustees if the Commissioners consider this to be necessary for the proper administration of the charity;
(c) to invest property of the charity in the official custodian of charities (whether the property consists of land or investments);
(d) to prevent a person holding property on behalf of the charity or on behalf of any trustee of the charity from parting with the property without the approval of the Commissioners;
(e) to prevent a debtor of the charity making any payment to the charity without the approval of the Commissioners;
(f) to restrict transactions which the charity may enter into without the approval of the Commissioners (for example transactions which exceed a specified value); and
(g) to appoint a receiver and manager in respect of the property and affairs of the charity.

The power of the Commissioners to appoint a receiver and manage is dealt with in greater detail in s 19 (see **5.5**).

5.4.3 The temporary protective powers under s 18(1) may be exercised by the Commissioners if they are satisfied that either:

(a) there is or has been any misconduct or mismanagement in the administration of the charity; or
(b) it is necessary or desirable to act to protect the property of the charity.

It is not necessary to have instituted an inquiry under s 8 before exercising these powers, nor is it necessary to serve charity trustees with notice of the intention to exercise the powers.

5.4.4 The permanent remedial powers of the Commissioners under the amended s 18 are:

(a) to remove a trustee (whether a charity trustee or holding trustee), officer, agent or employee of the charity who is in the view of the Commissioners responsible for or privy to misconduct or mismanagement or has by his conduct contributed to or facilitated the misconduct or mismanagement; and

(b) to make a scheme for the administration of the charity without the need for an application from the trustees or, indeed, any other person empowered to apply for a scheme under s 16 of the Act (see **9.3.1**).

These permanent remedial powers are exercisable only if:

(a) a s 8 inquiry has been instituted, although the inquiry need not have been concluded; and

(b) the Commissioners are satisfied both that there is or has been misconduct or mismanagement in the administration of the charity and that the course proposed is necessary to protect the property of the charity; and

(c) before exercising these powers, the Commissioners have served notice on each charity trustee in the UK.

5.4.5 The powers of the Commissioners under s 18 are exercised by order of the Commissioners. There is a right of appeal to the High Court against such orders under s 16, although under s 16(3) it is a preliminary requirement for instituting an appeal that the Commissioners have issued a certificate stating that it is a proper case for an appeal, or leave of a judge attached to the Chancery Division has been obtained. This preliminary requirement does not apply to Commissioners' order appointing a receiver and manager or to Commissioners' order suspending or removing an officer or employee of a charity (s 18(9)).

5.4.6 Section 18(14) imposes penalties for contravening an order of the Commissioners made under s 18(1)(i), (iv), (v) or (vi) (see **5.4.2**(d)(e) and (f)). Any person who contravenes such an order will be guilty of an offence and liable on conviction to a fine. Conviction under s 18(14) does not preclude the institution of proceedings for breach of trust (s 18(15)).

5.5 Appointment of Receiver and Manager

5.5.1 Section 19 of the 1993 Act supplements the provisions of s 18(1) which enables the Commissioners to appoint a receiver and manager for a charity.

The order appointing the receiver and manager should specify the functions to be discharged by him. These may include all or any of the powers of the charity trustees. Furthermore, the order may provide that the receiver and manager will act in conjunction with the charity trustees or, alternatively, to the exclusion of the charity trustees.

The receiver and manager is subject to the supervision of the Commissioners to whom he may turn for advice and the Commissioners may, in turn, seek directions from the court. The costs of any such proceedings must be met by the charity.

5.5.2 The Charities (Receiver and Manager) Regulations 1992 (SI 1992/2355) were made under s 9(6) of the 1992 Act, which has now been consolidated in s 19(6) of the 1993 Act. The Regulations deal with the following:

(a) authorising the Commissioners to require security from a receiver and manager for the proper discharge of his functions;

(b) authorising the Commissioners to determine the amount of remuneration of a receiver and manager to be paid out of the income of the charity;

(c) requiring a receiver and manager to submit an initial report to the Commissioners within three months of the date of his appointment, annual interim reports where office is held for a period of more than 12 months and a final report within three months of ceasing to hold office;

(d) specifying the procedure to be followed by the Commissioners in order to remove a receiver and manager from office where he has failed to give the specified security or to discharge any function satisfactorily, including power for the Commissioners to disallow remuneration.

5.6 Supervision of Scottish Charities

In order to prevent abuse of the system, s 80 of the Act gives the Commissioners certain powers over charities which are either established in Scotland but managed and controlled wholly or mainly in England or Wales, or which are established and managed in Scotland but which have property in England.

The Commissioners may exercise their powers of inquiry or to obtain information under ss 8 and 9. They may also exercise their powers to act for the protection of charity property under ss 18 and 19 in respect of a charity established in Scotland but managed or controlled wholly or mainly in England or Wales. The Commissioners may not, however, use their power to appoint additional trustees.

The Commissioners may order an individual who holds property of a Scottish charity not to part with the property without their approval if:

(a) the charity is established in Scotland and managed or controlled wholly or mainly in Scotland; and

(b) the property is held on behalf of the charity in England or Wales; and

(c) the Commissioners are satisfied that there has been misconduct or mismanagement in the administration of the charity and that it is necessary or desirable to act to protect the property of the charity.

Finally, s 80(4) gives the Commissioners powers in respect of persons in England or Wales who hold property for a Scottish charity, regardless of whether the charity is managed and controlled mainly in Scotland or mainly in England and Wales. In such circumstances, if the Commissioners are satisfied that there has been misconduct or mismanagement in the administration of the charity and that it is necessary or desirable to protect the property, they may order that the property held in England or Wales be transferred to another charity with purposes as similar in character as possible to those of the original Scottish charity. The transferee charity may be a Scottish charity or an English charity.

5.7 Court Proceedings

5.7.1 Under the 1960 Act, the Commissioners had no power to institute proceedings against trustees. If the Commissioners were of the view that legal proceedings were desirable, they were required to refer the matter to the Attorney-General. The decision whether or not to institute proceedings on the basis of the information provided by the Commissioners, and the conduct of those proceedings, were entirely a matter for the Attorney-General.

In order to strengthen the role of the Commissioners in dealing directly with abuse, the 1992 Act conferred powers to initiate proceedings which are now consolidated in s 32 of the 1993 Act. The Commissioners are given concurrent jurisdiction with the Attorney-General to initiate legal proceedings relating to charities or the property or affairs of charities or, alternatively, to compromise claims with a view to avoiding such proceedings. For example, if the Commissioners are of the view that a charity has suffered loss as a result of the negligence of the charity trustees, they can reach agreement with the trustees concerning what recompense the trustees should make to the charity without instituting proceedings.

However, the Commissioners still need the Attorney-General's consent to institute proceedings and to compromise claims.

5.7.2 Section 34 is also relevant. It provides that a copy of the report of an inquiry under s 8, if certified by the Commissioners to be a true copy, will be admissible in proceedings instituted by the Commissioners under s 34 or by the Attorney-General. The report is evidence of any fact stated in the report and evidence of the opinion of the person appointed by the Commissioners to conduct the inquiry.

A s 8 inquiry may, therefore, be the first step towards legal proceedings instituted by the Commissioners against any one or more of the charity trustees or others involved in the administration of the charity who are criticised in the report.

Hence, it will be important for individuals, who are the subject matter of a report, to challenge anything with which they disagree as soon as practicable after publication of the report.

CHAPTER 6

LAND TRANSACTIONS

Introduction – Summary of Rules on Disposals of Freehold Land and Leases (Other than Mortgages) – Disposals of Freehold Land and Leases by Charities (Other than Mortgages) – The Usual Procedure for Disposing of Land under s 36(3) of the 1993 Act – The Charities (Qualified Surveyors' Reports) Regulations 1992 – Exemptions from the General Rule in s 36(3) – Section 37 Statements – Controls on Mortgages by Charities – Miscellaneous – Section 82 Authority

6.1 Introduction

6.1.1 Under s 29 of the 1960 Act the trustees of registered charities required the Commissioners' consent:

(a) to mortgage or otherwise charge any part of the charity's permanent endowment; or

(b) to grant leases of more than 22 years or otherwise dispose of land which formed part of the permanent endowment or which had, at any time, been occupied for the charity's purposes.

This did not apply to exempt charities and certain excepted charities.

The wide drafting of the section and, in particular, the phrase 'or otherwise dispose of land which has at any time been occupied for the charity's purposes', meant that a large number of land transactions were subject to the Commissioners' scrutiny. For example, a simple grant of a right of way or easement required consent, as did the assignment or surrender of a lease of property which had been occupied for charitable purposes.

6.1.2 The Woodfield Report recommended that trustees should be given a general power to sell land without the Commissioners' consent, provided that they complied with certain statutory requirements. The White Paper accepted this recommendation. It stated, at p 39:

'In considering what might take the place of section 29 (the Government) have been concerned to provide continuing protection for charity property against mismanagement and abuse, and to focus the Commissioners' efforts on the sorts of financial transaction for which closer supervision and control remain necessary. They have also been concerned to do as much as possible to assist purchasers in obtaining good title to charity land.'

6.2 Summary of Rules on Disposals of Freehold Land and Leases (Other than Mortgages)

1 Disposal to connected person – Commissioners' consent required.

2 Disposal of freehold, grant of lease of more than seven years, or other disposal – qualified surveyor's report required; advertise (if necessary).

3 Grant of lease of less than seven years – report by person with requisite ability required; no advertisement required.

4   Disposal of functional land (in cases under 1, 2 and 3 (above)) – give public notice
     and take into account representations, unless:
     (a) a Charity Commission exemption order has been acquired; or
     (b) a lease is granted for less than two years.
5   Leases to beneficiaries – no need for Commissioners' consent or to comply with 2,
     3 or 4 (above).

6.3 Disposals of Freehold Land and Leases by Charities (Other than Mortgages)

6.3.1 Section 36(1) of the 1993 Act provides that land held by or in trust for a charity
may be sold, leased or otherwise disposed of only with an order of the court or the
Commissioners. Again, this applies to registered charities and charities excepted from
registration only and not to exempt charities. Under the old s 29(4) of the 1960 Act,
charities could be excepted from the provisions of s 29 by an order of the court or the
Commissioners. A number of categories of charities were excepted, for example certain
non-conformist religious charities.

Section 36 of the 1993 Act does not apply to mortgages of charity land. They are dealt
with in ss 38 and 39.

6.3.2 The general rule in s 36(1) (ie no disposal of land without an order of the court or
the Commissioners) is subject to various exemptions set out in the rest of s 36. The
exemptions do not apply if land is disposed by a charity to a connected person or a
trustee of a connected person. In that case, the consent of the Commissioners must be
obtained.

6.3.3 Schedule 5 to the 1993 Act defines a connected person as:

(a) a trustee of the charity;
(b) a person who is the donor of any land to the charity;
(c) a child (including stepchild and an illegitimate child), parent, grandchild,
    grandparent, brother or sister of any trustee or donor;
(d) an officer, agent or employee of the charity;
(e) the spouse of any person falling within any of the above;
(f) an institution which is 'controlled' (as defined in para 3 of the Schedule) by any of
    the above defined persons or any two or more such persons together; or
(g) a body corporate in which any connected person has a 'substantial interest' (as
    defined in para 4 of the Schedule) or two or more such persons have a substantial
    interest.

6.4 The Usual Procedure for Disposing of Land under s 36(3) of the 1993 Act

Under s 36(3) the usual procedure which charity trustees must follow before entering
into an agreement for the sale or lease or other disposition of land (other than a
mortgage) will be as follows.

(a) They must obtain and consider a written report on the proposed disposition from a qualified surveyor instructed by the trustees and acting exclusively for the charity.

For these purposes, qualified surveyor means a Fellow or Professional Associate of the Royal Institution of Chartered Surveyors or the Incorporated Society of Valuers and Auctioneers, who is reasonably believed by the charity trustees to have ability in and experience of the valuation of land of the particular kind and in the particular area in question.

The report issued by the qualified surveyor will have to contain such information and deal with such matters as may be prescribed by regulations made by the Secretary of State. The current regulations are contained within the Charities (Qualified Surveyors' Reports) Regulations 1992 (SI 1992/2980) (see **6.5**).

It is clear that the qualified surveyor can act only for the charity and not, for example, for any other party to the transaction.

(b) The trustees must advertise the proposed disposal for such period and in such manner as the qualified surveyor advises. However, this requirement will not apply if the surveyor has advised that it would not be in the best interests of the charity to advertise the proposed disposal.

(c) The trustees must consider the surveyor's report and satisfy themselves that the proposed terms of disposal are the best that can be reasonably obtained.

The rules cover all dispositions, for example granting of easements, surrenders or assignments of leases of whatever length.

The trustees do not have to meet in person to consider the disposal. It is possible for the trustees to delegate the decision whether or not to dispose of land to a sub-committee of the trustees. Moreover, that sub-committee does not need to meet; it will be sufficient if its members duly consider the surveyor's report and decide in the light of the report that they are satisfied that the terms offered are the best that can be reasonably obtained.

Earl Ferrers commented for the Government during the introduction of the legislation:

'I have no doubt that it is right that trustees must have the final responsibility for approving the terms of any sale and in seeing that the new statutory requirements have been complied with. But this need not be at a meeting of the trustees. The governing instrument of the charity may contain powers to delegate certain functions of the trustees to a committee of their number. We see no reason why the trustees should not set the policy for disposals and then delegate decisions in this area to a committee of their numbers who would report back to the trustee body at regular intervals.' (HL Deb, Vol 535, col 416 (6 February 1992).)

6.5 The Charities (Qualified Surveyors' Reports) Regulations 1992

The Regulations prescribing the information which the qualified surveyor is to supply came into force on 1 January 1993. The requirements are sometimes cumbersome and inappropriate for certain dispositions, in particular with regard to surrenders or assignments of short-term leases which unlike leases granted for seven years are not exempt (see **6.6**). The Regulations set out in detail the information the surveyor must advise on and it is recommended that the surveyor sets out his report following closely the format of the Schedule to the Regulations answering in turn each section, subsection or paragraph.[1] In brief, the report must contain the following information:

(a) a physical description of the property including a plan and even room measurements;
(b) basic details of any lease including advice on liability for repairs and dilapidations and any other provisions in the lease which may affect the value of the land.
(c) details of easements, restrictive covenants and any periodic charges other than rent affecting the land;
(d) the state of repair of buildings and whether it would be in the best interests of the charity to carry out any works prior to disposal;
(e) whether in the surveyor's opinion it would be in the best interests of the charity to carry out any alterations prior to disposal;
(f) whether it is in the interests of the charity to subdivide the property for the purpose of disposition; whether or not the property should be advertised; whether or not there should be a delay in the disposition;
(g) advise on VAT where the surveyor feels competent to give such advice or a statement to the effect that the surveyor does not feel able to give such advice;
(h) advice on the value of the property and whether it is in the best interests of the charity to proceed with a disposition;
(i) where the surveyor does not recommend a disposition as the best use of the land, his opinion and reasons for the type of disposition which would be the best use of the land.

---

1 This is only a summary. The exact wording should be referred to in each instance.

6.6 Exemptions from the General Rule in s 36(3)

Leases under seven years

6.6.1 Charities were concerned that the requirements of s 32(3) of the 1992 Act, as originally drafted, were excessively onerous in the case of granting short-term leases. The Government agreed. Section 36(5) now provides that where a charity proposes to grant a lease of not more than seven years, the charity trustees must:

(a) obtain and consider the advice on the proposed disposition of a person (not necessarily a qualified surveyor) who is reasonably believed by the trustees to have the requisite ability and practical experience to provide them with competent advice on the proposed lease; and
(b) decide that they are satisfied, having considered that person's advice, that the proposed terms are the best that can be reasonably obtained.

Earl Ferrers commented, when introducing the amendment during the passing of the legislation that led to this subsection:

'In Committee there was some anxiety that the regime that was imposed by Clause 32 [now s 36 of the 1993 Act] on trustees for disposals of charity land should be more flexible in the case of short leases. I accepted then that the arguments in favour of relaxing the regime to short leases were strong. I have no wish either to be inflexible or to saddle trustees with undue and burdensome requirements which are simply not justified by transactions at hand. These amendments therefore introduce a less strict regime for those kinds of leases.

On the other hand, we need to ensure that trustees act responsibly in the administration of their trust. Therefore, their duty to get the best rent available on the grant of a lease is properly reflected in these new provisions which will replace Section 29 of the Charities Act 1960. For leases of 7 years or less these amendments will allow trustees to take advice more appropriate to the transaction concerned from someone who need not be a qualified surveyor but who they reasonably consider has the appropriate expertise to give them advice before deciding whether the terms are the best available. Such advice need not be in the form of a written report.' (HL Deb, Vol 535, cols 415–416 (6 February 1992).)

Disposals of functional land

6.6.2 Additional requirements apply by virtue of s 36(6) to land which is held by a charity to be used for the purposes or any particular purposes of the charity. This is called functional land. For example, land may have been given to a school on condition that it is used as a sports field.

Functional land cannot be sold, leased or otherwise disposed of unless the charity trustees in addition to complying with s 36(3) or (5) have previously:

(a) given *public notice* of the proposed disposal, inviting representations to be made to them within a time specified in the public notice, being not less than one month from the date of the notice; and

(b) taken into consideration any representations made to them within that time about the proposed disposition.

There is no need for a public notice if the charity intends either to replace the land disposed of with other property which is to be held on the same trusts or if the disposal is the granting of a lease of under two years. However, again, assignments and surrenders are caught by the main rule.

Questions may arise about the distinction between an advertisement of the proposed disposal under s 36(3) and the public notice of the proposed disposition of functional land under s 36(6). Clearly, a public notice is a form of advertisement, although it goes further in inviting representations to be made (s 36(6)(b)(i)). The form of the public notice is not prescribed by the 1993 Act nor will it be in any future regulations. Therefore, the trustees must decide on an appropriate form of public notice. No doubt the notice could incorporate the advertisement (if necessary).

Functional land – leases of less than two years

6.6.3 No public notice has to be given in the case of a lease of functional land of less than two years (s 36(7) of the 1993 Act). This was introduced by the Government after much pressure, particularly from the churches. A report under s 36(5) will still be required.

Functional land – exemption orders

6.6.4 Under s 36(8), the Commissioners may direct that the charities may be exempted from the obligation to advertise disposals of functional land. The

Commissioners will make the order if they are satisfied that this would be in the interests of the charity. The charity must apply in writing to the Commissioners for such a direction.[1]

This was a late amendment to the 1992 Act and followed representations by Lord Chorley as Chairman of the National Trust, who commented, at the report stage of the Bill:

'The problems so far as concerns the National Trust can be put quite simply. The statutory objects of the Trust are to own and manage property for conservation. The great bulk of that property is held inalienably; that is to say, it may never be sold. In this respect the National Trust and the National Trust for Scotland are unique in this Bill. The Trust is now a very large landowner and I feel that I should give some figures to demonstrate the problem. We own, for example, more than 6,000 inalienable cottages; we have more than 12,000 farm tenancies and there are wayleaves, easements and so forth. Altogether we estimate that we have about 10,000 separate let properties that will be affected by sub-section (6). Properties are let for relatively short terms – the cottages, typically for eight years. What all this means is that we are dealing with up to 1,000 dispositions, to use the phrase, a year. In other words we will be required to issue about 1,000 public notices every year. That would involve heavy expenditure in advertising, in staff time, which is expensive and in management delay. And one is bound to ask; to what end? These are matters – I emphasise this – of routine property management in almost all cases of modest size; for example, cottage lease renewals. I find it hard to believe that advertising would serve in this respect any useful purpose.' (HL Deb, Vol 535, cols 418–419 (6 February 1992).)

It must be emphasised that s 36(8) only exempts charities from the requirements of s 36(6) (ie disposals of functional land). It does not exempt them from the requirements to comply with s 36(3) or 36(5).

---

1 The Charity Commission does not grant formal orders as such but directions by way of letter. The Commission estimates that in the region of 50 directions have been made to date for specific transactions. The Commission gave the following examples of where such a direction might be justified, but it is up to the charity trustees to prove the case:

   – where an urgent transaction which is not significant to the trusts of the charity, for example the grant of an easement or lease which does not materially affect the charity's trusts and urgency means that time for the notice cannot be found;
   – where there has been public discussion of proposed disposal, for example coverage by the media;
   – where there is a voluntary conveyance of land under threat of a compulsory purchase order.

Exemption in respect of disposals to charities

6.6.5 A charity does not need to comply with s 36 in the case of the disposal of land to another charity at a price which is not the best price that can be reasonably obtained. This exemption only applies if the disposal is in fulfilment of the trusts of the charity making the disposal.

Exemption in respect of the grant of leases to beneficiaries of a charity

6.6.6 Section 36(9)(c) makes it clear that s 36 does not apply in the case of the grant by a charity of a lease to a beneficiary of that charity where the lease:

(a) is granted otherwise than for the best rent that can be reasonably obtained; and
(b) is intended to enable the premises to be occupied for the purposes of the charity.

This was introduced after concern had been expressed particularly in relation to the grant of leases by alms houses charities to beneficiaries. Earl Ferrers commented:

'A number of charities have trusts which provide for leases to be granted to beneficiaries who occupy charity property in furtherance of its objects. Such charities may provide charitable relief for housing for the poor or other disadvantaged in society. Very often such leases are for less than a market rent.

It would be entirely inappropriate for the provisions of Section 32 [now s 36 of the 1993 Act] to apply to those cases. The Section is designed to ensure that the trustees obtain the best price when disposing of charity property. Where the lease is to a beneficiary of the charity, that criteria clearly should not apply.' (HL Deb, Vol 535, cols 420–421 (6 February 1992).)

6.7 Section 37 Statements

6.7.1 Under s 37 of the 1993 Act, any contract for the sale or lease or other disposition of land which is held by a charity and any conveyance, transfer, lease or other instrument, for example a deed, effecting a disposal of such land must state:

(a) that the land is held by or in trust for a charity;
(b) whether the charity is an exempt charity and whether the disposition is one falling within s 37(9); and
(c) if it is not an exempt charity and the disposition does not fall within s 36(9), that the land to be disposed of is land to which the restrictions on disposition contained in s 36 apply.

The wording currently to be used is set out in the Land Registration (Charities) Rules 1993 (SI 1993/1704) ('the Rules') and also in HM Land Registry Practice Advice Leaflet No 1 (second edition) 'Charity Land Transactions'.

Under new 128 of the Rules the wording for registered land should be as follows:

'The land transferred [*or as the case may be*] is held by or in trust for a charity by the proprietor and the charity is an exempt charity

or

the charity is not an exempt charity and the transfer [*or as the case may be*] is one falling within paragraph [*(a), (b) or (c) as the case may be*] of subsection (9) of section 36 of the Charities Act 1993

or

the charity is not an exempt charity and the restrictions on disposition imposed by section 36 of the Charities Act 1993 apply to the land (subject to subsection (9) of that section).'

New r 62 deals with the statement on first registration at HM Land Registry. The wording may be adapted for unregistered dispositions.

6.7.2 By s 37(2), the charity trustees have to certify, in the instrument by which the disposition is effected, either:

(a) that the disposition has been sanctioned by an order of the court or of the Commissioners (as the case may be); or

(b) in the case of a transaction under s 37(2), that the charity trustees have power under the trusts of the charity to effect the disposition and that they have complied with the provisions of that section so far as applicable to it.

6.7.3 Does the certificate in the contract conveyance, transfer, lease or deed disposing of the land have to be signed by all the trustees? Section 37(2) requires that the 'charity trustees shall certify in the instrument etc'. This is different from the requirement under the stamp duty legislation, where the instrument must contain a statement concerning the value of the transaction.

Do the charity trustees have to sign the certificate themselves or is it sufficient for the instrument to contain a certificate which could read as follows?

'It is certified that the charity trustees of the vendor have power under the trusts of the vendor to effect the provisions of this deed and that they have complied with the provisions of s 36 of the Charities Act 1993 so far as applicable to this deed.'

Under s 82 of the Charities Act 1993, trustees of an unincorporated trust may sanction two or more trustees to execute documents in the names and on behalf of the trustees. Hence, trustees so empowered should be able to sign the s 36(2) certificate. However, at Section F2 of HM Land Registry Practice Leaflet No 1 (second edition), HM Land Registry state that all charity trustees must join in and execute the disposition in order to give the required certificate even if they are not the registered proprietors of the land. There is no prescribed form for the certificate although the Practice Leaflet makes some suggestions. In the case of an incorporated charity, two trustees can usually witness the execution of documents. The implication of this must be that the certificate can be in the deed and requires no additional signatures from the trustees.

6.7.4 However, in the case of any incorporated charity, if HM Land Registry Practice Leaflet is correct, the charity trustees' certificate would appear to lift the veil of incorporation and render the charity trustees personally liable to any person acquiring the land. Neither the 1993 Act nor HM Land Registry Practice Advice Leaflet No 1 makes any reference to this aspect. Furthermore, it would be inaccurate for charity trustees to state that they have the power to effect the provisions of the deed as it is the incorporated charity as a separate legal entity which has the power. This certificate could read as follows:

It is certified by the charity trustees of the vendor/transferor that the vendor/transferor has power in its Memorandum and Articles of Association to effect the provisions of this Deed and that the vendor/transferor has complied with the provisions of Section 36 of the Charities Act 1993 so far as applicable to this Deed.

Thus whilst a delegated power to two or more trustees is an effective means of executing the transfer, it may (or may not) be an effective means of giving the certificate.

6.7.5 If s 33(2) has been satisfied, any person who later acquires an interest in the land for money or money's worth may presume that the facts were as stated in the certificate.

6.7.6 If land is disposed of which is subject to s 36(1) or s 36(2), but s 37(2) has not been complied with, ie the charity trustees have not given a certificate, the disposal of the land is still valid in favour of a person who, in good faith, acquires an interest in the land for money or money's worth. This is so notwithstanding that the requisite court order or Commissioners' order has not been obtained or that the charity trustees have failed to comply with s 37(2).

6.7.7 If, on a disposal of land, the land will be *acquired* by a charity or held in trust for a charity, both the contract for the sale or lease or other disposition and any conveyance, transfer, lease or other instrument has to state:

(a) that the land will, as a result of the disposition, be held by or in trust for a charity;
(b) whether the charity is an exempt charity; and
(c) if it is not an exempt charity, that the restrictions on disposition imposed by s 36 will apply to the land.

Hence, if a vendor is disposing of land to a charity, the conveyance or other documents of transfer, as well as the contract, will have to follow the prescribed wording of new r 122 of the Rules for registered land (which may be adapted for unregistered acquisitions):

'The land transferred [*or as the case may be*] will, as a result of this transfer [*or as the case may be*], be held by or in trust for the [*named*] charity and *either* the charity is an exempt charity *or* the charity is not an exempt charity and the restrictions on disposition imposed by section 36 of the Charities Act 1993 will apply to the land (subject to subsection (9) of that section).'

6.7.8 Where the land is registered at HM Land Registry, the Registrar shall enter a restriction in the prescribed form. The most common entry will be Form 12 applying to charities which are not exempt charities to read as follows:

'Except under an Order of the Registrar no disposition or dealing by the proprietor of the land is to be registered unless the instrument giving effect to it contains a certificate complying with Section 37(2) or in the case of a charge with Section 39(2) of the Charities Act 1993.'

There are variations on this form of restriction for exempt charities, for titles with rent charges and also a restriction Form 12D which warns the intending purchaser of a Charity Commission intervention to protect the assets of the charity.

6.7.9 Where charities are unincorporated under Section H2 of HM Land Registry Practice Advice Leaflet No 1, HM Land Registry states that the Registrar will not require any evidence of a delegation to two or more trustees of the right to execute documents on behalf of the trustees if the transfer, charge or other disposition states that it has been executed in pursuance of s 82 of the Charities Act 1993. The recommended wording from HM Land Registry (although there is no prescribed form by way of statutory instrument) reads as follows:

'This transfer [*or as the case may be*] is executed by [A and B] being two of the registered proprietors of the land in this title as charity trustees and on behalf of all the charity trustees under a general authority given pursuant to Section 82 of the Charities Act 1993.'

Even if the disposition is for money or money's worth and there is no reason to doubt the good faith of the person in whose favour it is made, HM Land Registry will require strict proof that the authority has been properly conferred and is still subsisting without such a statement.

However, given HM Land Registry's view on s 37(2) (see **6.7.3**), there would appear to be little point in such delegation.

6.8 Controls on Mortgages by Charities

6.8.1 The Woodfield Report made no recommendation for mortgages and charges by trustees. Section 29 of the 1960 Act applied equally to mortgages as to other disposals of land.

In the White Paper, the Government proposed to give trustees a general power to borrow money on the security of a mortgage without the Commissioners' consent. Before creating any mortgage or charge, however, the Government wished trustees to be obliged to obtain and consider 'proper advice' on:

(a) whether the terms of the proposed borrowing are reasonable having regard to the charity's circumstances;
(b) the charity's ability to repay the sum borrowed on the terms proposed; and
(c) whether the borrowing is properly needed for the purposes of the charity.

6.8.2 As in s 36, with disposals of land under s 38(1) the general rule is that there can be no mortgage of land held by a charity without an order of the court or of the Commissioners. This rule does not apply to exempt charities.

6.8.3 Equally, the rule in s 38(1) does not apply if s 38(3) (see below) has been complied with. This derogation applies only to a mortgage of land by way of security for the repayment of a loan. It would not apply to the grant of a mortgage to secure any other obligation, for example a guarantee. If s 38(3) has been complied with, the charity trustees do not need the Commissioners' consent. However, before executing the mortgage they must obtain and consider proper written advice.

Under s 38(3) that advice must cover:

(a) whether the proposed loan is necessary;
(b) whether the terms are reasonable; and
(c) the ability of the charity to repay, on those terms, the sum proposed to be borrowed.

6.8.4 Who can give the proper advice? It need not be a qualified surveyor (as defined in s 36(4)). Instead, the adviser must:

(a) be reasonably believed by the charity trustees to be qualified by his ability in and practical experience of financial matters; and
(b) have no financial interest in the making of the loan in question. The person who gives the advice can be an employee, a trustee or an officer of the charity.

6.8.5 Surprisingly, the restrictions on disposals of land to connected persons do not apply in the case of mortgages to secure moneys borrowed from a connected person. Accordingly, such a transaction does not require the consent of the Commissioners if s 38(3) is complied with.

6.8.6 Section 38 does not apply to any mortgage which has been authorised under s 36(9)(a); that is, a mortgage authorised by any statutory provision contained in or having effect under an Act of Parliament or by any scheme (s 38(5)). Hence, if a category of mortgages for charities is exempted either by an Act of Parliament or by statutory instrument in the future or by a scheme, the requirements of s 38 will not apply to those types of mortgages.

Section 39 statements

6.8.7 Under s 39, any mortgage of land held by or in trust for a charity must state:

(a) that the land is held by or in trust for a charity;
(b) whether the charity is an exempt charity and whether the mortgage falls within s 38(5) (see **6.8.6**); and
(c) if it is not an exempt charity and the mortgage is not within s 38(5) that the mortgage is one to which the restrictions imposed by s 38 apply.

6.8.8 The Land Registry form of statement in the case of registered land is set out in new r 128 of the Rules and may be adapted for unregistered land. The wording states:

'The land charged is held by or in trust for a charity by the proprietor and the charity is an exempt charity

or

the charity is not an exempt charity and the charge is one falling within subsection (5) of section 38 of the Charities Act 1993

or

the charity is not an exempt charity and the charge is one to which the restrictions imposed by section 38 of the Charities Act 1993 apply.'

6.8.9 By s 39(2), if the provisions in either s 38(1) or (2) apply, then the charity trustees have to certify in the mortgage either:

(a) that the mortgage has been sanctioned by an order of the court or the Commissioners; or
(b) that the charity trustees have power under the trusts of the charity to grant the mortgage and that they have obtained and considered such advice as is mentioned in s 38(2).

The certificate as suggested by HM Land Registry, although there is no prescribed form, reads as follows:

'The [chargors] certify that as charity trustees they have power under the trusts of the charity to effect this charge and that they have obtained and considered such advice as is mentioned in sub-section (2) of Section 38 of the Charities Act 1993.'

The same grey area affects incorporated charities and the trustees' certificate required in the case of disposals by charities (see **6.7.3**).

Section 39(3) and (4) provides for good title to be given to anyone who acquires an interest in charity land where s 38(2) has been complied with. If it has not been complied with, but a person acquires the charity land in good faith and for money's worth, the mortgage shall be deemed valid notwithstanding a breach of s 38.

6.9 Miscellaneous

1   The usual rule that only four legal owners may be registered at HM Land Registry does not apply to charitable trustees.

2   Some charities have other restrictions on powers, for example Housing Associations requiring Housing Corporation consent in addition to complying with the Charities Act 1993.

3   Not every transfer document will require a Charities Act 1993 statement, for example registration of a new trustee.

4   HM Land Registry prescribes the statements for unregistered land on first registration in HM Land Registry Practice Advice Leaflet No 1 and which are virtually identical to those for registered land.

5   The onus is upon trustees to ensure that the appropriate restriction is entered at HM Land Registry when any changes occur, for example:
    – if a body obtains charitable status;
    – where a charity becomes an exempt charity;
    – where a registered proprietor holds on trust for a charity (new r 124 of Land Registry Rules).

6.10 Section 82 Authority

By s 82, the trustees of a charity may, subject to whatever is stated in the constitution of the charity, confer on any number of trustees (but not less than two) a general authority, or an authority limited in such manner as the trustees think fit, to execute in the names and on behalf of the trustees assurances or other deeds or instruments for giving effect to transactions to which the trustees are a party. Any deed or instrument executed under the authority conferred in s 82(1) shall have the same effect as if executed by all the trustees. This is an extremely useful provision for an unincorporated trust which has not taken advantage of the capacity to incorporate (see Chapter 8) or for unincorporated associations.

This does not, however, avoid the need where an unincorporated trust or unincorporated association takes an interest in land for all the names of the trustees or committee members to be recited as the persons interested in the land as trustees of the charity, but merely means that the execution of the documents is facilitated. If a charity finds that its conveyancing or investment transactions are complicated by the number of trustees, then the charity should consider either incorporation (see Chapter 8) or, at the very least, appointing custodian trustees to hold the charity's lands and investments on behalf of the charity. It will be necessary to amend the charity's constitution to allow for the appointment of custodian trustees if the constitution does not so provide. None of these comments apply to an incorporated charity since, in the case of limited liability companies, any two directors (who are the equivalent of trustees) or one director and the company secretary can usually execute documents on behalf of the company unless the Articles of Association specify differently. Equally, in the case of industrial and provident societies, organisations incorporated by Royal Charter or companies created by statute, it is normal to provide that any two of the members of the executive body (trustees, directors, etc) may execute documents on the companies' behalf.

CHAPTER 7

CHARITY INVESTMENTS AND THE OFFICIAL CUSTODIAN FOR CHARITIES

Introduction – Trustee Investments Act 1961 – Apportionment of Funds – Permitted Investments – Application to Scotland – Further Reform – Divestment from the Official Custodian – Common Investment and Common Deposit Funds

7.1 Introduction

The 1992 Act made important changes to the investment powers of charities and to the legal administrative arrangements for holding charity investments. An attempt was also made to introduce into the Act a general power for charity trustees to delegate the exercise of their investment powers. However, the attempt failed. Trustees still lack a power of delegation unless it is provided for in the governing instrument of their charity.

7.2 Trustee Investments Act 1961

7.2.1 The Trustee Investments Act 1961 ('the 1961 Act') extended the scope of authorised investments for trusts, with statutory powers of investment, whether private trusts or charitable trusts. Under that Act, it was possible for trustees to invest in equities, provided that they first divided the trust fund into two equal parts, the 'narrower range' part and the 'wider range' part. The trustees could invest the wider range part in equities, but such investments were restricted to securities issued in the UK, in a company incorporated in the UK with a total issued and paid-up share capital of at least £1 million. The company must also have paid a dividend on all shares issued by it, in each of the five years immediately preceding the calendar year in which the investment was made.

7.2.2 The operation of the 1961 Act was the subject of increasing criticism over the years. Comparative studies of the performance of equities and gilts indicated that the value of fixed interest assets had been undermined by high levels of inflation, whereas equities had, by and large, kept pace with inflation. A charity required by the statutory powers of investment to divide capital into two equal parts before investing in equities was bound to see its capital devalued. The provisions of the 1961 Act had also failed to take account of the developments in investment practice which had taken place since 1961. This was recognised by Sir Robert Megarry in *Trustees of the British Museum v Att-Gen* [1984] 1 All ER 337. There was mounting pressure to amend the provisions of the Act, particularly in their application to charities which were more likely than private trusts to be restricted to the statutory powers of investment.

7.2.3 The Government conceded to pressure to include provisions in the 1992 Act which would enable the 1961 Act to be modified by subordinate legislation insofar as they applied to charities. These provisions appear as ss 70 and 71 in the 1993 Act.

7.3 Apportionment of Funds

7.3.1 Section 70 of the 1993 Act empowers the Secretary of State (in this case the Secretary of State for the Home Department – the Home Secretary) by order to vary the apportionment required by s 2(1) of the 1961 Act in so far as it applies to charities. The Charities (Trustee Investments Act 1961) Order 1961 has been made under s 70 so that the wider range is no longer required to be equal to the narrower range, but may be up to three times its value. Apportionment need no longer be according to the ratio of 50:50 but 25:75. (Any such order will not alter the investment powers of any private trust caught by the restrictive investment powers of the 1961 Act.)

Section 70(2) provides that the revised apportionment will apply to future and existing charitable funds restricted to the statutory power of investment. Newly acquired capital, for example a legacy, may be divided according to the new ratio. Equally, funds which have already been divided 50:50 between narrower and wider range may be re-divided according to the new ratio.

Example

Trustees may have divided the property of the charity into two equal parts, in accordance with the 1961 Act, in order to invest one half in wider-range investments. As a result of the better performance of equities, the wider-range part may have grown to represent 60 per cent of the trust fund, so that the actual apportionment between narrower and wider range is 40:60. (There is no obligation under the 1961 Act to maintain equality between the two halves). If the trustees wish to take advantage of their increased power to invest in equities conferred by the Home Secretary's order they may re-divide their fund according to the new ratio of 25:75 between narrower and wider range, so freeing a further 15 per cent of the fund for investment in equities.

7.4 Permitted Investments

7.4.1 As mentioned in **7.2.2**, the range of investment permitted by the 1961 Act failed to take account of developments in investment practice since 1961 or the new range of investment opportunities open to charity trustees with wider powers of investment, for example direct investment in land, investment in shares of newly privatised State undertakings and investment overseas, particularly in the other States of the European Union.

Section 71 of the 1993 Act empowers the Secretary of State, by regulations (with the consent of the Treasury), to extend the range of investments authorised for charity investment beyond the range permitted for trustee investment in the 1961 Act. The regulations may specify what proportion of a charity's property may be invested in the new range or in any particular investment within the new range and may impose requirements for obtaining and considering advice before investment. For example, direct investment in land, as distinct from investment in mortgages, is not within the scope of narrower- or wider-range investment. Regulations might permit direct investment in land but:

(a) restrict the proportion of a charity's funds which may be invested in this way;
(b) restrict the percentage of funds which may be invested in any one State; and
(c) require the trustees to obtain specialist advice on investing in land.

The underlying purpose would be to ensure that the funds were diversified and that the trustees received proper advice when making and reviewing their investments.

7.4.2 Under s 71(4), the new forms of investment envisaged would be open to any charity unless its trusts specifically exclude such investment or unless it is prohibited from making such investment by a contrary intention in an Act of Parliament or in a statutory instrument under an Act. For example, the trusts of a charity may specifically exclude any form of investment other than investment in ethical unit trusts. This charity could not take advantage of any new forms of investment permitted by the regulations. The regulations themselves, introducing the new forms of investment, may also exclude certain categories of charity from exercising the new powers. For example, if regulations permitted investment overseas, charities below a certain size might be excluded.

7.4.3 The power to make regulations under s 71 relates to the powers of investment of charities generally, rather than to any particular charity. If the charity trustees of a charity wish to extend the range of investment open to them and have no power to amend the administrative provisions of their trust, they should seek an order from the Commissioners under s 26 of the 1993 Act.

7.4.4 No regulations have been made under s 71. However, regulations have been made by the Treasury under s 12 of the 1961 Act to make technical changes and changes imposed by European law to the range of permitted investments in the Trustee Investments (Additional Powers) Order 1994 and the Trustee Investments (Additional Powers) (No 2) Order 1994.

7.5 Application to Scotland

The Trustees Investments Act 1961 applies to trusts throughout the UK, whereas the Charities Act 1993 is, for the most part, concerned with charities in England and Wales. Sections 70 and 71 of the 1993 Act are two of the few exceptions. Any order or regulations made under those sections will apply to charities in Scotland (a charity being defined as a recognised body within the meaning of s 1(7) of the Law Reform (Miscellaneous Provisions) (Scotland) Act 1990).

7.6 Further Reform

Sections 70 and 71 of the 1993 Act owe their existence to pressure from the charity sector exerted in 1991 when the Charities Bill was passing through the House of Lords.

Since that time, further pressure has been exerted not least by the Deregulation Task Force which pressed the Treasury on the issue.

In May 1996, the Treasury published a consultation document 'Investment Powers of Trustees', inviting comment on proposals to remove the restrictions on trustee investment imposed by the 1961 Act under the Deregulation and Contracting Out Act 1994, but without prejudice to the trustees' duty of care: for example to take proper advice and have regard to the need for diversification. If the proposals are implemented they will supersede ss 70 and 71 of the 1993 Act.

7.7 Divestment from the Official Custodian

7.7.1 As the holder of investments, the official custodian provided useful services to charity trustees. These included avoiding the need to transfer title to newly appointed trustees, receiving and paying to trustees dividends and interest without deduction of tax (so that there was then no need for the trustees to reclaim tax), informing trustees when investments were due for redemption and being a source of general advice on investment matters. However, the 1989 White Paper recommended that this service should be terminated and investments returned to charity trustees or their nominees.

7.7.2 Despite opposition to these proposals, ss 29 and 30 of the 1992 Act introduced provisions to divest the official custodian of investments held on behalf of charities. These provisions have not been consolidated in the 1993 Act but remain in force as unrepealed provisions of the 1992 Act.

(a) Section 29(1) authorises the official custodian to divest himself of all property except land or property vested in him by an order made under s 20 of the 1960 Act (now s 18 of the 1993 Act) for the protection of a charity.

(b) The investments may be returned to the charity trustees or to a person nominated by the charity trustees to receive and hold the property.

　　A nominee must be either an individual resident in England and Wales or a body corporate which has a place of business in England and Wales.

　　It is inadvisable to transfer investments to one single individual. The trustees should request that investments be transferred instead to two or more of their number, to a holding company or to a body corporate entitled to act as a custodian trustee under the Public Trustee Act 1906. A body corporate entitled to act as custodian trustee will be entitled, by s 4(3) of the 1906 Act, to charge fees not exceeding those chargeable by the Public Trustee. In all other cases, unless the trusts of the charity authorise the remuneration of a trustee, no payment may be made, except repayment of out of pocket expenses. This follows the rule established since *Robinson v Peet* (1734) 3 P Wms 249, that a trustee should act gratuitously.

　　The introduction of rolling settlement for UK share transactions means that, for equities, a nominee company is a more practicable proposition than vesting shares in the trustees. Rolling settlement requires completion of a deal by the tenth working day after the day of the transaction, shortening eventually to five working days or possibly less. However, charity trustees must not delegate the exercise of their investment powers to the nominee unless authorised to do so by the trusts of the charity or by an order of the Commissioners.

(c) Section 29(4) empowers the Commissioners to make directions for the process of divestment to be effected in stages and to make directions for dealing with different types of holding in different ways. Some types of holding can be transferred in kind to the charity trustees or their nominees and others can be realised and the proceeds of sale returned to the charity trustees or their nominees.

In August 1992 the official custodian published a booklet *Divestment Guide 1* describing how the programme of divestments is to be achieved. It started in January 1993 and will be carried out in phases timetabled to end in June 1997.

Besides issuing the booklet to all charities with investments held in the name of the official custodian, two help-lines have been set up to deal with queries (051 227 3191 ext 2469 and 071 210 4646).

7.7.3 The White Paper anticipated that one of the problems of divestment would be the discovery of a number of dormant charities where it would not be possible to trace the charity trustees in order to seek instructions or transfer holdings. Section 29(7)–(11) makes provision for dealing with the assets of dormant charities (see **9.5**).

7.7.4 When the Commissioners are satisfied that the official custodian has completed the programme of divestment, any remaining funds (excluding, of course, land and any property transferred for protection to the official custodian under s 18 of the 1993 Act) are to be paid by the official custodian into the Consolidated Fund.

7.7.5 The trusts of many charities provide for the property of the charity to be vested in the official custodian. Similarly, the Commissioners may have made schemes or orders requiring trustees to recoup permanent endowment, which has been expended for the purposes of the charity, by making payments into an accumulation account maintained by the official custodian. Section 30 of the 1992 Act overrides those provisions so that nothing in the trusts of a charity or in an order or scheme of the Commissioners will prevent the process of divestment in s 29. Furthermore, a requirement in the trusts of a charity that the investments be held in the name of the official custodian ceased to have effect when ss 29 and 30 came into force on 1 September 1992. The trustees will be able to transfer the investments of the charity (but not the interests in land) to a nominee or into the names of the trustees, without waiting for the official custodian's programme of divestment to run its course.

7.8 Common Investment and Common Deposit Funds

7.8.1 The Commissioners made a number of schemes, under s 22(1) of the 1960 Act, to set up common investment funds. These are essentially pooling arrangements, enabling charities to transfer property into a common investment fund which is invested under the control of the trustees of the fund. A common investment fund operates in much the same way as a unit trust fund. Surprisingly, s 22 did not permit the Commissioners to set up free-standing, common deposit funds, by which charities could pool money to be placed on deposit at a more advantageous rate of interest.

7.8.2 The omission was rectified in the 1992 Act, which introduced a provision to permit the court or the Commissioners, on the application of two or more charities, to make schemes to establish common deposit funds. The provisions relating to common investment funds and to common deposit funds are now consolidated in ss 24 and 25 of the 1993 Act. As a result, every charity is empowered to invest in common deposit funds, unless their trusts specifically exclude such investment.

CHAPTER 8

INCORPORATION: TRUSTEES AND CHARITABLE COMPANIES

Introduction – Incorporation and Trustee Liability – Incorporation Under the 1993 Act – Trust Companies – Status of Charitable Companies

8.1 Introduction

Incorporation may be relevant to a charity in one of two different ways: the trustee body may be incorporated or the charity may be incorporated. Before the 1992 Act, trustees might be incorporated under the Charitable Trustees Incorporation Act 1872 ('the 1872 Act') but without the benefit of limited liability, or, if the trusts of the charity permitted a sole corporate trustee. The 1992 Act updated the 1872 Act, but without introducing limited liability. The relevant provisions are now set out in ss 50 to 62 of the 1993 Act.

Alternatively, and more usually, the charity itself may be incorporated as a company, industrial and provident society or a body incorporated by Royal Charter. The 1992 Act developed the special body of law relating to charitable companies, setting them apart from commercial companies which operate for the benefit of shareholders.

8.2 Incorporation and Trustee Liability

8.2.1 An incorporated body has a legal identity of its own. It may acquire property, enter into contracts and incur liabilities in its own name, even though its affairs are managed by individuals. However, the issue of legal identity is distinct from the question of legal liability. Limited liability is not an automatic consequence of incorporation.

For charities, the issue of trustee liability is of increasing concern. This is partly because of a greater awareness among charity trustees of their responsibilities, but also because of the increased responsibilities being placed on trustees as charities extend their activities to fulfil functions formerly undertaken by local authorities and other statutory bodies.

Where a body of charity trustees – as distinct from the charity – is incorporated as a company, the individuals will have the same protection from personal liability as they would if the charity itself were incorporated. If, however, the trustee body is incorporated under the Charitable Trustees Incorporation Act 1872, and now the 1993 Act, the trustees continue to be liable as if there were no incorporation (see **8.3.1**(e)).

8.2.2 The 1989 White Paper addressed the issue of incorporation. However, its primary purpose was not to minimise the risk of personal liability for trustees but to ensure that charitable companies would be subject to regulation and supervision by the Attorney-General and Charity Commission. It considered two possibilities:

(a) the creation of a new charity structure, fully under the Commissioners' jurisdiction but involving some form of incorporation coupled with limited liability;
(b) provisions for the trustee body to be incorporated, with limited liability, but with the charity itself remaining as a charitable trust.

In fact, the 1992 Act adopted neither course. The Act amended the Charitable Trustees Incorporation Act 1872, to facilitate the incorporation of charity trustees, but without the benefits of limited liability. This met a need created by the withdrawal of the investment-holding function of the official custodian for charities but did not answer questions about the potential liability of trustees.

However, during the passage of the Bill through the House of Lords, Earl Ferrers indicated that the Government was committed to exploring the problem of liability and possible solutions to it.

8.3 Incorporation Under the 1993 Act

8.3.1 Sections 50 to 62 of the 1993 Act have now replaced the 1872 Act providing a procedure for trustees of an unincorporated charity, whether a trust or an association, to apply to the Commissioners for a certificate of incorporation of the trustees.

Key features of the procedures are as follows.

(a) Section 52 requires the application to be in writing, signed by the trustees and accompanied by such docments or information as the Charity Commissioners may require. In practice, the Commissioners require the completion of an application form.
(b) The Commissioners' decision will normally be favourable if they are satisfied that the charity has sufficient investments to benefit from incorporation. However, the Commissioners would not normally consider incorporation where the charity's only investments are of a nature that may be held in the name of the charity (eg shares in common investment funds, building society or bank accounts and government stocks held on the National Savings Stock Register) or in the name of office holders of the charity such as secretary and treasurer (eg government stocks on the Bank of England Register) or shares in a common investment fund established under s 24 (see **7.8**) or land which can be vested in the official custodian for charities (see **1.7**).
(c) The certificate issued by the Commissioners may contain conditions or directions relating to the trustee body, for example the number of trustees, the method of appointment and their term of office. In the absence of such conditions or directions, the constitution and method of appointing trustees will continue to be governed by the trusts of the charity. For example, if the trusts provide for nine trustees to be appointed on a three-year rotating basis, that will continue to be the case after the granting of a certificate of incorporation in the absence of any provisions in the certificate to the contrary.

(d) Section 51 provides that on the granting of the certificate all real and personal property held in trust for the charity is vested in the incorporated trustees. Formal steps may be required to effect a transfer, for example where registered land is held in the name of individual trustees or a nominee for the charity, it will be necessary to apply to the Land Registry to transfer the title into the name of the incorporated trustees. Section 51 specifically requires any person or persons (other than the official custodian) in whose name any stocks, funds or securities are standing in trust for the charity to transfer them into the name of the incorporated trustees. In the case of equities, the formal transfer may not be desirable or practicable given the introduction of rolling settlements for share transactions (see **7.7.2**). Whilst the nominee might comply with s 51 and the incorporated trustees then transfer the shares back to the nominee, it is preferable for the shares to remain with the nominee who would record that they were held for the incorporated trustees. The exemption for the official custodian ensures that property vested in the official custodian as a protective measure will remain with the official custodian, as well as minimising any interference in the divestment programme.

(e) Section 54 makes clear that incorporation will not diminish the liability of trustees, stating:

> 'after a certificate of incorporation has been granted under this Part of this Act all trustees of the charity, notwithstanding their incorporation, shall be chargeable for such property as shall come into their hands, and shall be answerable and accountable for their own acts, receipts, neglects, and defaults, and for the due administration of the charity and its property, in the same manner and to the same extent as if no such incorporation had been effected.'

(f) Section 56 empowers the Commissioners to amend the certificate of incorporation. They may initiate the amendment, provided that they inform the trustees of the proposed change and allow one month for the trustees to make representations. However, in the normal course of events, change would be initiated at the request of the trustees, for example seeking some change in the constitution of the incorporated trustees, such as the number of trustees or length of term of office. A new certificate of incorporation will be issued following the amendment.

(g) Section 61 gives the Commissioners power to dissolve an incorporated trustee body on the application of the trustees, if they are satisfied that this course is in the interests of the charity. Alternatively, the Commissioners may dissolve a trustee body on their own initiative if the incorporated trustee body has no assets or has ceased to operate or to exist. Section 61 provides that any assets held by the trustee body immediately before dissolution will be transferred either to the individuals who constituted the incorporated trustee body as trustees for the charity or to a person nominated by the trustees to receive the property.

(h) The Commissioners' powers apply to all charities, including exempt charities. However, s 50(2) prohibits the grant of a certificate to the trustees of a charity which is required to be a registered charity but which is not registered and s 53(1) prohibits the grant of a certificate to trustees who are not properly appointed to the satisfaction of the Commissioners. If the appointment of the trustees is defective and cannot be corrected by the trustees, the Commissioners would need to make an order under s 16 to formalise the appointment and then consider an application from those trustees.

8.3.2 Arrangements for the execution of documents on behalf of incorporated trustees are set out in s 60. There are three possible methods.

(a) If there is a seal, by affixing the seal.
(b) Whether or not there is a seal, a deed may be expressed to be executed by the incorporated trustees and signed by at least a majority of the trustees.
(c) Whether or not there is a seal, s 60(4) enables the trustees to confer on any two or more of their number, power to execute a document on behalf of the incorporated trustees. This authority may be general, relating to any transaction approved by the incorporated trustees or it may be restricted to a particular transaction. The authority may be restricted to named trustees or it may require the signature of any two of the trustees.

A document which is executed by individual trustees under s 60 should make clear the basis on which they act, since a document which purports to be signed by a majority of the trustees or by two of the trustees acting under the authority of a resolution of the incorporated trustees is deemed to be properly executed in favour of any purchaser in good faith for valuable consideration. Appropriate clauses would be:

> This deed has been approved and ordered to be executed by resolution passed at a duly constituted meeting of the Incorporated Trustees of [. . .] and is intended to be executed by a majority of them.

> This deed has been approved and ordered to be executed by resolution passed at a duly constituted meeting of the Incorporated Trustees of [. . .] and is intended to be executed by two of the trustees on whom acting under s 60 of the Charities Act 1993 the Incorporated Trustees of [. . .] have duly conferred a general authority to execute in the name of that body and on its behalf documents for giving effect to transactions to which it is a party.

8.4 Trust Companies

8.4.1 Although it is rare for charity trustees to be incorporated, it is more common for a charity to have a company to act as nominee, to hold land and investments.

The trust company holds the assets of the charity to deal with in accordance with the instructions of the charity trustees. However, an ordinary trust company incorporated with power to act as trustee and to hold land, does not come within the statutory definition of a trust corporation. If charity land held by a trust company is sold, the payment of the proceeds of sale to the trust company does not, in itself, satisfy the rule of trust law that either two trustees or a trust corporation are required to give a good receipt for capital moneys.

This problem does not arise when property is held by the Official Custodian (which is still a possibility where land is involved), nor by a corporate body authorised to act as custodian trustee under the Public Trustee Rules 1912, SR&O 1912/348. Paragraph 30 of those Rules included any corporation incorporated under the Charitable Trustees Incorporation Act 1872, and now under s 50 of the 1993 Act, and any corporation authorised by the Lord Chancellor to act in relation to any charitable trusts as a trust corporation. However, few trust companies set up by individual charities to act as nominees will satisfy these conditions.

8.4.2 Section 35 of the 1993 Act provides a solution to these difficulties. It provides that a corporation appointed to act as trustee by an order of the Commissioners will be included in the definition of trust corporations.

If charity trustees have appointed a trust company to act as nominee to hold property on behalf of the charity, it is advisable for the trustees to seek an order from the Commissioners under s 16 of the 1993 Act to ensure that the nominee company is a trust corporation able to give a valid receipt for capital money arising on the sale of land. Alternatively, an additional person will need to be appointed to act with the nominee in any sale to give a receipt for the proceeds of sale. The nominee and the additional person will then hold the proceeds of sale on trust for the charity to deal with them as directed by the charity trustees.

These steps would also be necessary in those cases where a corporate body, which is not a trust corporation, is to act as charity trustee, but an order is not required if the charity itself is a company. In those circumstances, the company is not acting as trustee but as the owner of the property.

8.5 Status of Charitable Companies

8.5.1 The 1989 White Paper expressed concern at the ability of the Attorney-General and the Charity Commission to exercise their full supervisory role over charitable companies.

The 1960 Act had acknowledged the special status of charitable companies to some extent. This was developed further by s 111 of the Companies Act 1989 and by the 1992 Act, both of which amended the 1960 Act. The provisions are now consolidated in ss 63 to 68 of the 1993 Act.

8.5.2 Section 63 confers on the Attorney-General the power to apply to the court to wind up a charitable company under the Insolvency Act 1986. The Commissioners may also do so if they have instituted an inquiry into the charity concerned under s 8 (see **5.3.1**) and are satisfied that there has been mismanagement or misconduct or that action should be taken to protect the charity or to ensure that its property is applied for the purposes of the charity. The Commissioners may also apply to the court to have a winding-up set aside or to the Registrar of Companies for the reinstatement of a charitable company which has been struck off the Companies' Register as a defunct company. The powers of the Commissioners under s 63 are exercisable only with the agreement of the Attorney-General.

8.5.3 Section 64(1) ensures that a charitable company may not exercise its statutory power to amend its Memorandum and Articles of Association in order to divert property dedicated for the charitable purposes of the company to some other purpose.

Section 64(2) makes it necessary to obtain prior written approval to amend the objects of a charitable company or any provision in the Memorandum or Articles of Association which direct or restrict the manner in which the property of the charitable company may be used or applied. There is some ambiguity in the phrase 'the manner in which the property may be used or applied'. This is thought to refer to the purpose for which the property may be used for, rather than how the decision is reached. For example, an amendment of the objects of a charitable company would fall within the scope of s 64(2), an amendment to permit the trustees to delegate the exercise of their powers to a sub-committee would not.

It is necessary to obtain the written consent of the Charity Commissioners before the special resolution to effect the amendment is put to the general meeting. A copy of the special resolution should be sent to the Commissioners seeking their approval. They will return the copy bearing their official stamp of approval which should, in turn, be sent to the Registrar of Companies when filing a copy of the special resolution.

8.5.4 Section 65 effectively excludes charities from the relaxation of the ultra vires rule, which enables other companies in certain circumstances to undertake activities otherwise unauthorised by their Memorandum and Articles of Association. There is, however, protection for a person who acquires an interest from a charity for full consideration and without knowing that the transaction was beyond the powers of the charitable company or did not know that the company was a charity.

8.5.5 Section 66 requires a charitable company to obtain prior written consent from the Commissioners before approving certain arrangements for the benefit of directors or persons connected with a director, which are authorised by the Companies Act 1985 but which would be inconsistent with the normal rule of charity law that trustees should not benefit from their charity (*Re French Protestant Hospital* [1951] Ch 567).

8.5.6 Section 67 rectifies an anomaly by amending the Companies Act 1985 so that charitable companies are required to comply with s 349(1) of that Act to publish the company's name on business letters and other documents.

8.5.7 Section 68 requires a charitable company whose name does not include the word 'charity' or 'charitable' to declare its status as a charity on business letters and other documents. This requirement applies to all charitable companies whether registered or not (see **2.9.2**).

CHAPTER 9

SCHEMES

Introduction – Concurrent Jurisdiction with the High Court – Scheme Applications – Publicity – Failed Charity Appeals

9.1 Introduction

The impetus for the 1992 Act came from an acknowledgement that the role of charities had changed substantially since 1960. To minimise the possibility of abuse, the accounting and reporting procedures needed urgent improvement and a modern central database was required to facilitate the monitoring of charities. At the same time, the opportunity was taken to modernise a number of procedures affecting charities including some aspects of the Commissioners' statutory powers to establish schemes. The 1960 Act powers and the amendments made by the 1992 Act are now brought together in the 1993 Act.

9.2 Concurrent Jurisdiction with the High Court

9.2.1 Section 16 of the 1993 Act confers on the Commissioners concurrent jurisdiction with the High Court for the following purposes:

(a) establishing a scheme for the administration of a charity;
(b) appointing, discharging or removing a charity trustee or trustee of the charity, or removing an officer or employee; and
(c) vesting or transferring property, or requiring or entitling any person to call for or make any transfer of property or any payment.

9.2.2 A substantial proportion of schemes established by the Commissioners are cy-près schemes made under s 13 to alter the original purposes of a charity. One or more of the conditions specified in s 13(1) must be present: for example the original purposes must have been fulfilled or cannot be carried out according to the directions given and to the spirit of the gift. A substantial proportion of schemes are also established to amend administrative provisions specified in the trusts of a charity. For example, a charity with an income well below £250,000 but with a requirement in its constitution that accounts be audited, might, in the absence of a power of amendment in the constitution, apply for a scheme to substitute a requirement for independent examination (see **4.2.4**).

In *Decisions of the Charity Commissioners* (Vol 3) published in January 1995, the Commissioners indicated that they would be willing to exercise their power under s 16 to establish a scheme for a charity without a power of amendment which would confer such a power, making further schemes for purely administrative changes unnecessary.

9.2.3 Section 16(3) prohibits the Commissioners from exercising their concurrent jurisdiction with the High Court to determine the title to property or any question as to the existence or extent of any charge or trusts. Section 16(10) further prohibits the Commissioners from exercising their jurisdiction in any case which by reason of its contentious character or because it involves special questions of law or of fact would, in the opinion of the Commissioners, be more fit to be adjudicated by the court.

Special provisions are made for charities governed by a Royal Charter (s 15) and charities governed by Act of Parliament (s 17). To a large degree, the Charity Commission has been relieved of the need to make schemes for small charities by ss 74 and 75 which empower trustees to amalgamate their charity with another or to amend the trust provisions without the need for a scheme and even to spend permanent endowment and so bring the charity to an end (see **10.2** and **10.3**).

9.3 Scheme Applications

9.3.1 Except in exceptional circumstances (s 16(6)), the Commissioners cannot make a scheme on their own initiative, but only in pursuance of an order of the court or on an application made under s 16. Most applications are made by the trustees under s 16(4). This may not be possible if, for example, the trustees disagree among themselves or with the Commissioners over the need for a scheme, or if there are insufficient trustees to make a valid decision.

The 1992 Act introduced changes in the application procedure to facilitate the scheme-making process, which are now incorporated into s 16 of the 1993 Act.

A scheme or order may now be established by the Commissioners in the following circumstances.

(a) On the application of the charity trustees (s 16(4)(a)).
(b) In pursuance of an order of the court (s 16(2) and (4)(b)).
(c) On the application of the Attorney-General, provided that the charity is not an exempt charity (s 16(4)(c)).
(d) If the total income of the charity from all sources does not exceed £500 per year, on the application of:
    (i) any one or more of the charity trustees;
    (ii) any person interested in the charity, for example a potential beneficiary;
    (iii) any two or more of the inhabitants of the area of benefit of the charity if the charity is a local charity.
    The sum of £500 may be varied by order of the Secretary of State either to take account of inflation or to bring more charities within the scope of this provision. (As to the meaning of 'income from all sources', see **2.6**.)
(e) A scheme for the administration of the charity (as distinct from an order appointing or removing trustees or removing an officer of the charity or an order dealing with property) may be established under s 16 in the following circumstances:
    (i) if charity trustees are willing to apply for a scheme, but are prevented from doing so because of a vacancy in their number, or the absence or incapacity of any of them, the Commissioners may establish a scheme on an application of

however many of the charity trustees as the Commissioners think appropriate. This avoids the need for the Commissioners to make a preliminary order to appoint trustees to comply with the requirements of the trusts of the charity, and then to invite those trustees to apply for a scheme to alter the trusts of the charity. The appointment of trustees and the alteration of the trusts can be dealt with in one document;

(ii) if the Commissioners are satisfied that the charity trustees ought, in the interests of the charity, to apply for a scheme, but have unreasonably refused or neglected to do so and if the Commissioners have given the trustees an opportunity to make representations to them, the Commissioners may proceed to establish a scheme on their own initiative without an application being made to them (s 16(6)).

Section 16(6) does not apply to exempt charities.

9.3.2 If the charity trustees dispute the need for a scheme, they may either:

(a) institute proceedings in the High Court to seek directions as to whether they should apply for a scheme or not (these proceedings would be charity proceedings under s 33 and would need to be authorised by an order of the Commissioners, although the trustees could appeal to the High Court against a refusal of the Commissioners to make an order); or

(b) the trustees may wait until the Commissioners have made a scheme under s 16(6) and then exercise the statutory right to appeal to the High Court within three months of the making of the scheme under s 6(12). (The appeal requires a certificate from the Commissioners that the case is a proper one for an appeal (unlikely to be forthcoming in the circumstances) or the leave of one of the judges of the High Court attached to the Chancery Division.)

9.4 Publicity

In addition to a formal application, publicity is the other essential element in the procedure of establishing a scheme. Section 16(9) requires the Commissioners to give notice of their intention to establish a scheme for a charity to every trustee of the charity unless he or she is a party or privy to the application or cannot be found or has no known address in the UK.

Section 20(1) requires public notice of an intention to establish a scheme to be given at least one month before the scheme is to be established, inviting representations to be made within a specified time and which will then be considered by the Commissioners under s 20(4). In the case of a local charity, s 20(1) requires a copy of the draft scheme to be sent to the local parish or community council or, if there is no council, to the chairman of the parish meeting.

Once a scheme has been established, s 20(6) requires a copy of the scheme to be made available for public inspection for at least one month at the Charity Commission and within the area if it is a local charity. This requirement is normally fulfilled by the publication of a further notice confirming that the scheme has been established and stating where a copy may be inspected.

9.5 Failed Charity Appeals

9.5.1 From time to time, a public charitable appeal fails to raise sufficient funds to carry out the intended purpose. Often the trustees omit to include a provision enabling the funds which have been raised to be used for another charitable purpose.

Section 14 of the 1993 Act enables the Commissioners to establish a scheme to apply the proceeds of a failed appeal for charitable purposes similar to those of the appeal.

9.5.2 A scheme may be made if:

(a) the funds fall within s 14(3), so that the donor is presumed to be unidentifiable (eg funds raised by street collections or through lotteries or competitions); or

(b) the donor falls within s 14(1)(a) in that he or she cannot be identified or found after the trustees have published advertisements and made inquiries in the form and for the period prescribed in the Charities (Cy-près Advertisements, Inquiries and Disclaimers) Regulations 1993 made by the Commissioners under s 14(8); or

(c) the donor falls within s 14(1)(b) in that he or she has executed a written disclaimer. That, too, will be in a form prescribed by the regulations made by the Commissioners under s 14(8).

Under s 14(4), the court may direct that property be treated as though it belonged to unidentifiable donors if attempts to trace donors would be unreasonable in view of the amounts likely to be returned to donors or in view of the nature, circumstances and amounts of the gifts and the lapse of time since the gifts were made. This power could be invaluable if, for example, small sums have been donated through sponsored activities but where each donor might be traced through sponsorship forms. The difficulty is that an application has to be made to the court. A more practical arrangement would have been to give the Commissioners power to waive the requirements in appropriate cases.

9.5.3 Donors who are deemed to be unidentifiable under s 14(3) and (4) have a right to reclaim their donations (less expenses incurred by the trustees in respect of the claims) within six months of the date of a scheme (s 14(5)). Section 14(5) enables the Commissioners to direct charity trustees to set aside a specific amount to meet such claims. If the amount set aside is insufficient to meet the claims, the Commissioners may authorise the trustees to reduce proportionately the amount paid to each claimant and to deduct expenses properly incurred by the trustees in dealing with claims. This ensures that neither the expenses nor any shortfall become the personal liability of the trustees, but are deducted from the donors' funds.

CHAPTER 10

SMALL CHARITIES AND DORMANT CHARITIES

Introduction – Amalgamation, Division and Amendment – Power to Spend Permanent Endowment – Dormant Bank Accounts – Dormant Investment Accounts

10.1 Introduction

10.1.1 There has been concern for many years about the effectiveness of small charities which have a small endowment fund, producing what is, in real terms, an ever-decreasing income. The Charities Act 1985 was intended to facilitate the modernising and amalgamation of small charities and, in some cases, the winding up of charities. However, the Act was of limited use. It was replaced by ss 43 and 44 of the 1992 Act (now ss 74 and 75 of the 1993 Act).

10.1.2 There has also been concern about the existence of dormant charities which have ceased to function. The updating of the register, the increased reporting requirements and the process of divesting the official custodian are all likely to reveal numbers of dormant charities. Arrangements for disposing of the assets of dormant charities introduced by the 1992 Act are now set out in s 28 of the 1993 Act. In addition, s 29 of the 1992 Act, which provides for the divestment of investments from the official custodian, and which remains in force, includes arrangements for the investments of dormant charities.

10.2 Amalgamation, Division and Amendment

10.2.1 Section 74 of the 1993 Act confers on charity trustees the power to transfer property of a charity to one or more other charities, to amend the objects and administrative powers of a charity. Section 74 does not enable the trustees to spend the permanent endowment of their charity. This is dealt with in s 75 (see **10.3**).

10.2.2 Section 74 applies to a charity if the following three conditions are all satisfied.

(a) The gross income of the charity in its last financial year does not exceed £5,000. Gross income, as defined by s 97 of the Act, includes gross income from all sources, including special trusts (see **4.3.2**). (Section 74(2) confers on the Secretary of State power by order to amend the £5,000 threshold.) The Home Office has agreed in response to a proposal from the Deregulation Task Force to raise the threshold to £10,000, but this proposal has yet to be implemented.

(b) The charity does not hold any land subject to trusts which stipulate that the land must be used for the purposes of the charity (eg an almshouse charity or a village hall charity would be excluded, whereas a charity which holds land as an investment, producing income for the charity, would satisfy the condition).

(c) The charity is not an exempt charity or a charitable company.

Section 74(12) defines a charitable company to include a charity incorporated by Royal Charter. Industrial and provident societies are exempt charities. These charities do not need to rely on s 74, since they have mechanisms for amendment and dissolution in their governing instruments.

10.2.3 Section 74(2)(a) and (b) empower charity trustees to resolve to transfer their charity's property to another charity or to divide the property among two or more charities if two conditions specified in s 74(4) are satisfied. These are:

(a) the purposes of their charity have ceased to be conducive to a suitable and effective application of the charity's resources; and

(b) the purposes of any transferee charity are as similar in character to the purposes of their charity as is reasonably practicable.

In response to proposals from the Deregulation Task Force it has been accepted 'in principle' by the Home Office and the Commissioners that it is virtually impossible for charity trustees to establish that the first condition is satisfied and therefore the condition should be removed.

A transferee charity must be a registered charity or an unregistered charity which does not require registration. A charity which should be registered, but is in breach of that statutory requirement, cannot benefit.

Section 74(2)(c) empowers charity trustees to resolve to modify all or any of the purposes of their charity or to change the purposes to other charitable purposes if they are satisfied both that:

(a) the existing purposes of the charity have ceased to be conducive to a suitable and effective application of the charity's resources; and

(b) the purposes specified in the resolution are as similar in character to those existing purposes as is practical in the circumstances.

Section 74(2)(d) empowers charity trustees to resolve to modify their administrative powers and procedures.

A resolution passed by the charity trustees under s 74(2) must be approved by a majority of not less than two-thirds of those trustees voting on the resolution.

10.2.4 When a resolution has been passed in accordance with s 74, the charity trustees are required by s 74(7):

'(a) to give public notice of the resolution in such manner as they think reasonable in the circumstances; and

(b) to send a copy of the resolution to the Commissioners, together with a statement of their reasons for passing it.'

There is no prescribed form for resolutions passed under s 74 or for the notice but the Commissioners have published a booklet, *Small Charities: Alteration of Trusts, Transfer of Property, Expenditure of Capital*, giving guidance on s 74 and s 75 procedures. It is strongly recommended that charity trustees of a small charity who are contemplating using s 74 should obtain a copy of the booklet and follow that guidance to avoid any unnecessary difficulties.

The Commissioners must indicate, within three months of receiving the resolution, that either they concur with the resolution or they do not. If they concur with the resolution to modify or replace the purposes of the charity or to amend the administrative powers or procedures of the trustees, the Commissioners should also specify the date when the resolution is to take effect. In reaching their conclusion, the Commissioners are entitled to call for further information or explanation from the trustees. They must also take into consideration any representations made to them by any person who appears to them to be interested in the charity (eg a trustee or potential beneficiary) and which are made within six weeks of the Commissioners receiving the resolution.

10.2.5 Where a resolution to transfer the property of the charity to one or more other charities has been passed, the trustees must make arrangements to effect the transfer. The Commissioners may assist in this process, at the request of the transferor charity, by making orders under s 74(10) to vest the property in the new trustees or in their nominees. The new trustees will hold the property on the trusts of their charity, but subject to any restrictions on expenditure which applied when the property was held by the transferor charity. So, if the property was permanent endowment of the transferor charity, it will remain permanent endowment in the hands of the transferee charity, even though the transferee charity has no other permanent endowment.

10.3 Power to Spend Permanent Endowment

10.3.1 Section 75 of the 1993 Act empowers trustees of certain small charities with a permanent endowment to spend the permanent endowment and so bring the charity to an end. To come within the scope of s 75, a charity must satisfy the following three conditions.

(a) The permanent endowment of the charity must not consist of any land. It makes no difference whether the land is used for the charitable purposes of the charity or is only a source of income.

(b) The gross income in the last financial year of the charity must not have exceeded £1,000. Gross income is defined in s 97 of the 1993 Act to mean gross recorded income from all sources, including special trusts. Section 75(9) confers on the Secretary of State power, by order, to amend the threshold figure of £1,000 and it has been agreed in response to the Proposals for Reform of the Deregulation Task Force, that the threshold should be raised to £10,000. The proposal has yet to be implemented.

(c) The charity must not be an exempt charity or a charitable company. As in s 74, a charitable company is defined to include a charity which is incorporated by Royal Charter (see **10.2.2**(c)).

10.3.2 Section 75 empowers charity trustees to resolve that their charity shall be free from restrictions against spending permanent endowment:

(a) if they are satisfied that the property of the charity is too small, in relation to its purposes, for any useful purpose to be achieved by the expenditure of its income alone; and

(b) if they have considered whether there is any reasonable possibility of transferring the property to one or more other charities under s 74.

For this purpose, the charity trustees must disregard the issue of whether the transfer to other charities under s 74 would impose on the charity an unacceptable burden of costs. In fact, any costs of transfer should be minimal if the transfer is made by order of the Commissioners under s 74(10) (see **10.2.5**).

A resolution passed by charity trustees must be approved by a majority of not less than two-thirds of those trustees voting on the resolution.

10.3.3 Having passed the resolution, the trustees and the Commissioners must then follow a procedure similar to that set out in s 74 for giving public notice of the resolution and for obtaining confirmation that the Commissioners concur with the resolution (see **10.2.5**). The trustees' resolution is effective on the date specified by the Commissioners in their notification to the trustees that they concur with the resolution. The trustees may then apply both capital and income for the purpose of the charity and bring the charity to an end. If the charity is a registered charity, the Commissioners would remove the charity from the register, having received from the trustees their final report and accounts confirming that all capital has been expended.

10.4 Dormant Bank Accounts

10.4.1 A number of financial institutions, including banks and building societies, hold accounts in the name of a charity, but no transactions have been initiated in the account by the charity trustees for a number of years and the financial institution is unable to trace any of the trustees. The funds lie dormant, without achieving the purpose for which they are held. Section 18 of the 1992 Act introduced a mechanism for these funds to be released for use by an active charity. This is now set out in s 28 of the 1993 Act. For s 28 to apply, the following conditions must be satisfied.

(a) The charity must not be an exempt charity.
(b) The account must have been dormant for five years immediately preceding the date on which the financial institution informs the Commissioners of the existence of the account. The account will be treated as dormant if no transaction has taken place in the account other than a payment into the account or a transaction initiated by the financial institution itself. For example, an account might exist which receives income on a regular basis which is accumulated in the account. If no transaction takes place apart from the receipt of income and possibly the deduction of charges made by the financial institution holding the account, it is a dormant account.
(c) The financial institution must be unable, after making reasonable inquiries, to locate the charity or any of its trustees.

10.4.2 If these conditions are satisfied, the financial institution should inform the Commissioners of the existence of the account and of its inability to trace the trustees or the charity. (Section 28(7) removes the normal obligation of confidentiality which would bind the financial institution and which might otherwise be an impediment to the operation of s 28.)

The Commissioners may direct the financial institution to transfer the funds to one or more charities specified by the Commissioners. In identifying transferee charities, the

Commissioners are required to have regard to the purposes of the original charity if those purposes are known to them and to obtain written confirmation from the trustees of a transferee charity that they are willing to accept the property.

A transferee charity will hold the funds received from a dormant account for its purposes, but subject to any restrictions on expenditure (eg as permanent endowment) which applied to the original charity. This assumes that the Commissioners will have sufficient knowledge about the transferor charity to know whether the funds were permanent endowment or not. Section 28 does not indicate whether there should be a presumption for or against permanent endowment when the status of the funds is unknown.

The receipt of the funds by the trustees of the transferee charity is complete discharge to the financial institution.

10.4.3 There may be occasions when the procedure under s 28 is implemented, but the circumstances change subsequently, so that a transaction takes place in the dormant account, or the financial institution now has the means to trace the transferor charity or its trustees. Section 28(5) provides that if the Commissioners have made a direction under s 28, but it has not been implemented, the financial institution has a duty to inform the Commissioners, in writing, of the changed circumstances.

If it appears to the Commissioners that the account is no longer dormant, they are required to revoke the direction, so that no funds are transferred to the intended transferee charity. However, s 28 does not make any provision for the recovery of funds by the transferor charity if the financial institution has already implemented the Commissioners' direction. In those circumstances, the funds have become the property of the transferee charity and cannot be recovered.

10.5 Dormant Investment Accounts

The White Paper recognised that in the process of transferring investments from the official custodian to trustees, the official custodian would be unable to contact trustees of a number of charities. In order to complete the process of divesting investments, arrangements for dealing with the investments of dormant charities would be needed. The White Paper concluded that the most appropriate solution would be for the Commissioners to transfer the assets to some other charity with similar purposes, in accordance with the cy-près doctrine. The Commissioners' powers are contained in s 29(7)–(10) of the 1992 Act. Section 29 has not been consolidated into the 1993 Act because it is a transient provision which will be defunct once the divestment process has been completed. The powers in s 29(7)–(10) are similar in many respects to the arrangements dealing with dormant bank accounts (see **10.4**). They provide as follows.

(a) If the official custodian holds property in trust for a charity, but after making reasonable inquiries is unable to locate the charity or any of its trustees, he is required to sell the property, unless it is already money, and to hold the proceeds of sale or money pending instructions from the Commissioners.

(b) The Commissioners may direct the official custodian to transfer the money or proceeds of sale to one or more charities whose purposes are as similar in character as those of the dormant charity as is reasonably practicable. Before making their direction, the Commissioners must obtain written confirmation from the trustees of the transferee charity that they are willing to receive the amount proposed.

(c) The trustees of the transferee charity hold the funds for the purposes of the transferee charity, but subject to any restrictions on expenditure (eg a permanent endowment), which applied to the funds in the hands of the transferor charity.

Section 29 does not make provision for the dormant charity, should it come to life, to recover property which has been transferred to another charity under the provisions of s 29(7)–(10).

CHAPTER 11

MISCELLANEOUS REFORMS

Introduction – Ex Gratia Payments – Almshouse Contributions – Reverter of Sites Act 1987 – Redundant Churches

11.1 Introduction

The 1992 Act was used as a vehicle for introducing a number of miscellaneous reforms which required statutory authority. Those concerning ex gratia payments and the Reverter of Sites Act 1987 have been consolidated in the 1993 Act. The provisions of the 1992 Act concerning almshouse contributions and redundant churches remain in force and have not been consolidated.

11.2 Ex Gratia Payments

11.2.1 The Commissioners have power, now in s 26 of the 1993 Act, to make an order authorising trustees to enter into a particular transaction or compromise or follow a course of action where the Commissioners are satisfied that the action proposed is expedient in the interests of the charity, although it may not be within the powers of the trustees. Such an order will protect the trustees from a charge of breach of trust.

There are occasions when charity trustees believe they are under a moral obligation to make a payment to an individual, although the payment is neither consistent with the purposes of the charity nor can it be said to be expedient in the interests of the charity. These are known as ex gratia payments. In *Re Snowden and Re Henderson* [1969] 3 WLR 273, Cross J established that such payments could be authorised by the Attorney-General or the court, and laid down an appropriate procedure to be followed to obtain authority.

11.2.2 The 1992 Act conferred power on the Commissioners to authorise ex gratia payments. That power is now set out in s 27 of the 1993 Act. It is, however, subordinate to the Attorney-General's power in three ways.

(a) The exercise of the power is subject to the supervision of the Attorney-General, and must be exercised in accordance with any directions he may give. For example, he may direct the Commissioners not to exercise the power in particular cases (perhaps according to the value of the payment) or require them to consult him before they exercise their power.

(b) The Commissioners may, of their own accord, decide that a case should be referred to the Attorney-General for decision.

(c) There is a right of appeal to the Attorney-General against a decision by the Commissioners to refuse authorisation.

Any charity trustees wishing to make an ex gratia payment should, in the first place, seek the consent of the Commissioners.

11.3 Almshouse Contributions

11.3.1 Almshouse charities are occupied by their residents under licence. The residents do not pay a rent, but make a weekly payment to the charity as a contribution to the cost of maintaining the almshouses and meeting the cost of essential services. In many cases, the authority for the trustees to charge weekly maintenance contributions was conferred by a scheme established by the Commissioners, which also required any changes in the weekly amount to be approved by the Commissioners.

The 1989 White Paper recommended an end to this practice. It took the view that the work of the Commissioners in approving increases in weekly maintenance contributions had become a matter of routine and was inappropriate, since it involved the Commissioners in management decisions which were a matter for the trustees. Section 1(4) which re-enacts s 1(4) of the 1960 Act prohibits the Commissioners from acting in the administration of a charity.

11.3.2 Section 50 of the 1992 Act implemented the recommendation of the White Paper. Section 50 continues in force and has not been consolidated in the 1993 Act. It provides that any condition in the trusts of an almshouse charity requiring the Commissioners to specify, approve or authorise the amount (or the maximum amount) of weekly maintenance contributions should cease to have effect. The basic power to make such charges therefore continues, free of the condition. However, s 50 does not confer power to make charges where no power exists at present. Any almshouse charity in that position would need a scheme from the Commissioners to give the charity trustees power to charge (see **9.2**).

11.3.3 Section 50(2) defines an 'almshouse charity' as a charity which is authorised, under its trusts, to maintain almshouses. 'Almshouses' is defined as any premises maintained as an almshouse, whether they are called an almshouse or not. These definitions are not particularly helpful. An almshouse charity is traditionally a charity providing housing for the poor, particularly the elderly poor.

If any charity trustees are in doubt about the status of their charity and whether they may rely on s 50, they may formally seek the advice of the Commissioners under s 29 of the 1993 Act (see **1.4**).

11.4 Reverter of Sites Act 1987

11.4.1 The School Sites Act 1841, the Literary and Scientific Institutions Act 1854 and the Places of Worship Act 1873 encouraged landowners to give land for charitable purposes by granting a statutory right of reverter.

If, at any time in the future, the land ceased to be used for the purpose for which it had been given, the land would revert to the original owner or to his successors. In practice, the right gave rise to significant difficulties. When land ceased to be used for the charitable purposes for which it was given, the trustees of the charity became trustees for the successors of the original landowner, who often could not be identified or traced. The trustees were without power to sell the property or the means to repair it. The Reverter of Sites Act 1987 ('the 1987 Act') overcame this difficulty in part, by replacing the statutory right of reverter with a statutory trust for sale for the benefit of the successors of the original landowner, including powers to manage, repair and sell the land.

11.4.2 There was, however, a problem in relation to the statutory right of reverter and the statutory trust for sale under the 1987 Act. If the legal title to the land had been transferred to the official custodian, the official custodian became a trustee of land held subject to private non-charitable trusts as soon as the land ceased to be used for the charitable purposes for which it had been given. That was inconsistent with the function of the official custodian to act as trustee of charity property. Section 23 (formerly s 31 of the 1992 Act) empowers the Commissioners, on their own initiative, to make an order to discharge the official custodian. The power may be exercised where either:

(a) a trust for sale has arisen under the 1987 Act; or
(b) in the opinion of the Commissioners, a trust for sale under the 1987 Act is likely to arise at a particular time or in particular circumstances (ie a trust for sale is foreseeable).

The Commissioners' order will:

(a) discharge the official custodian; and
(b) transfer the title of the property into the names of the charity trustees or, if the trust for sale has already arisen, into the names of the individuals who were the charity trustees immediately before the trust for sale arose.

The Commissioners may, at the request of the charity trustees, transfer the title into the names of other persons.

11.4.3 If a trust for sale has arisen under the 1987 Act, but the official custodian has not yet been discharged by an order of the Commissioners, s 23(5) makes clear that the powers of management and the liabilities under the trust for sale fall on the trustees of the charity rather than on the official custodian. The trustees may exercise all powers of management in the name of the official custodian. However, s 23(6) also makes clear that the trustees cannot sell the land while it remains vested in the name of the official custodian. No sale can take place until the Commissioners have made an order under s 23(2) to transfer the property into the names of individual trustees, who will then receive the proceeds of sale.

11.5 Redundant Churches

11.5.1 As a general rule, trustees of a charity have a duty to dispose of land or buildings which have been used by the charity, but which have ceased to be suitable for its purposes, and to obtain the best price reasonably obtainable. At one time, this rule presented a particular difficulty for buildings which were classified as ancient monuments or buildings of historic or architectural interest and which were used as places of public worship by religious charities. If the building fell into disuse or was otherwise unsuitable for the purposes of the charity, the trustees were required to sell to the highest bidder, even though this might not be in the best interests of the continued preservation of the building and public access to the building.

11.5.2 Sections 4 and 5 of the Redundant Churches and Other Religious Buildings Act 1969 (amended by the National Heritage Act 1983) overcame this problem, empowering the court or the Commissioners to establish a scheme to permit charity trustees to give or sell at an undervalue a redundant church or place of public worship to the Secretary of State (acting under his power to preserve buildings of historical or architectural interest and ancient monuments) or to the Historic Buildings and Monuments Commission for England.

There are a number of ancillary provisions enabling:

(a) adjacent land, for example a churchyard, to be disposed of in the same way;
(b) rights of way to be granted by the trustees to give necessary access, including public access;
(c) the Commissioners to establish schemes to permit public worship to continue in the building, even if it is not by the original charity or according to its tenets of faith; and
(d) ancillary charities, whose purposes were to maintain and repair a redundant church, to continue to be used for the repair and maintenance of the building.

11.5.3 Section 49 of and Sch 5 to the 1992 Act, which remain in force, amend ss 4 and 5 of the 1969 Act. The power to give or sell premises at an undervalue to the Secretary of State or to the Historic Buildings and Monuments Commission for England is extended to such charities as may be prescribed by the Secretary of State. It is now open to the Secretary of State to transfer to certain charities the function of preserving redundant churches which are listed buildings of historical or architectural interest or ancient monuments.

Redundant churches and chapels of the Church of England situated in England are not governed by the 1969 Act, but by the Pastoral Measure 1983.

CHAPTER 12

CONTROL OF FUND-RAISING: PROFESSIONAL FUND-RAISERS

Introduction – Proposals for Reform – Control of Professional Fund-raisers – Charitable Institutions – Summary of Exemptions from the Definition of Professional Fund-raiser – What is a Professional Fund-raiser? – Examples of Professional Fund-raisers – Section 59 Agreements – Section 60 Statements – Regulations

12.1 Introduction

12.1.1 Part II of the Charities Act 1992 was not consolidated in the Charities Act 1993, and came into force on 15 March 1995. Before then, the 1939 House to House Collections Act regulated (as one might expect) house to house collections. Different rules applied, however, to street collections under the Police, Factories, etc (Miscellaneous Provisions) Act 1916. In the background lurked the criminal law, in particular the Theft Act 1968. Under that Act any person guilty of abusing fund-raising can be prosecuted for:

(a) theft (defined as dishonestly appropriating property belonging to another); and
(b) fraud (defined as obtaining a financial advantage by deception).

12.1.2 In 1991, Parliament had not addressed itself specifically to the problems of charity fund-raising since 1939. Since then, a huge number of new charities had been established. In 1965, when the compulsory registration of charities under the 1960 Act was underway, the number of registered charities was 57,500, in December 1994, the figure was 178,609.

12.1.3 Many of these charities are unendowed and are dependent on a wide range of sources of income, fund-raising being one. This is true of many of the great household names in the voluntary sector (not just charities), for example Oxfam, World Wide Fund for Nature, Greenpeace and Friends of the Earth, which have all been started since 1939.

12.1.4 Fund-raising practices have developed and become more sophisticated in response to this rising tide of demand. Examples are the telethon, TV and radio appeals, sponsored activities etc, direct mail and telephone campaigns and mass charity concerts like Band Aid.

12.2 Proposals for Reform

12.2.1 Public concern about malpractice in fund-raising by charities has prompted a number of independent reviews of fund-raising practice. A working party of the National Council for Voluntary Organisations (NCVO) in 1985 reviewed the means currently available for protecting charities from dubious fund-raising practices and made recommendations. Its report was quoted, with approval, by the Woodfield Report of 1988. The working party identified the following abuses in particular:

(a) excessive sums retained by some fund-raising practitioners;
(b) claims that part of the proceeds from the sale of goods or services will go to charity when, in fact, the share given to charity is much smaller than donors might suppose; and
(c) dubious fund-raising practices, carried on in a charity's name but without its knowledge or approval.

The Woodfield Report and the White Paper

12.2.2 These particular abuses were considered by the Woodfield Report, which made the following recommendations.

(a) That it should be a criminal offence for fund-raising practitioners to deduct their remuneration (however calculated) from donations received before paying them to the charity, unless they could prove that their intention to do so was made clear to every donor. The White Paper rejected this but recommended that 'all those who receive funds raised for or on behalf of a charity should remit the full amount to the charity without deducting fees or expenses' (at p 56).
(b) That whenever goods or services were offered for sale with the indication that some part of the proceeds was to be devoted to charity, there should be specified:
   (i) the charity or charities that were to benefit (and, if more than one, in what proportion);
   (ii) the *manner* in which the sums they were to receive would be calculated.

   In the White Paper, the Government expressed its concern about the practicability of these proposals, and commented (at p 56):

   'Basic details of the agreement reached between charity and the "co-venturer", should be provided, however, with some latitude being allowed as to the form of expression chosen. Under the kind of provision envisaged charity catalogues, for example, would be required to incorporate a simple, single, statement to the effect that X per cent of net profits, gross profits or receipts would go to the named charity or charities. Some formulae may be more complex. Even so, it should be possible to give some indication of their effect, by reference, for example, to the minimum proportion going to charity.'

(c) That a charity should be able, in certain circumstances, to obtain an injunction against the use of its name by a named person or organisation.

There was concern that this recommendation did not go far enough because the onus of detecting the abuse of its name and the initial liability for legal costs would fall on the charity. The charity might be able to recover some of its legal costs but this would be by no means certain, as it would depend, in each case, on the financial strength of the defendant. An alternative might have been a blanket ban on all fund-raising in a charity's name without its written consent. This alternative was rejected. If implemented, it would doubtless have destroyed local grassroots fund-raising initiatives – many people are moved, especially in cases of emergencies, to 'do their bit', raise money and send it off to the relevant charity. If such heartfelt responses had to be first processed through a bureaucratic mill they would no doubt be frequently stifled by the time the requisite written consent came through.

12.3 Control of Professional Fund-raisers

The recommendations of the Woodfield Report are important, for they are the basis of Part II of the 1992 Act. Part II is concerned to control, to a certain extent:

(a) the activities of professional fund-raisers;
(b) certain types of fund-raising practice (TV, radio and telephone appeals);
(c) the activities of people who sell goods or services and represent that a proportion is to go to charity; and
(d) the use of a charity's name by unauthorised fund-raisers.

It must also be emphasised that the 1992 Act only applies (save in certain very limited cases) to England and Wales. It does not apply to Scotland or Northern Ireland.

12.4 Charitable Institutions

12.4.1 It is vital to understand that Part II of the 1992 Act does not apply simply to charities but to *charitable institutions* as defined by the 1992 Act.

Section 58(1) defines a 'charitable institution' as:

'a charity or an institution (other than a charity) which is established for charitable, benevolent or philanthropic purposes.'

This wording follows the House to House Collections Act 1939. The definition includes registered charities and those charities which are *exempt* from registration under the Charities Act 1993 (such as Universities) and those charities which are *excepted* by statutory instrument from registration as charities (such as the Boy Scouts). Section 97 of the 1993 Act defines 'charitable purposes' as 'purposes which are exclusively charitable according to the laws of England and Wales'. An organisation established under the laws of another country, for example France, could qualify as an institution established for charitable purposes *provided* its objects were exclusively charitable under English law.

Hence, it must be emphasised that there is a very important and clear distinction between the two phrases, 'charitable purposes' and 'charitable institution'. When coupled with 'purposes', 'charitable' means exclusively charitable according to the laws of England. But when 'charitable' is joined with 'institution' it does *not* mean that. It means something much wider. It encompasses 'benevolent and philanthropic purposes' as well.

Benevolent

12.4.2 There is a dearth of reported cases on the meaning of 'benevolent and philanthropic' under the 1939 Act. The word 'benevolent' has been held to include purposes which are not exclusively charitable. It is defined in the Shorter Oxford Dictionary as 'of a kindly disposition, charitable, generous'. In 1891, Lord Branwen distinguished 'benevolent' and 'charitable' in *Income Tax Commissioners v Pemsel* (1891) AC 531.

'I think there is some fund for providing oysters at one of the Inns of Court for the Benchers. This, however benevolent, would hardly be called charitable.'

In Australia, a public benevolent institution has been construed to mean institutions which promote the relief of poverty, sickness, destitution or helplessness (see *Perpetual Trustee Co Ltd v FCT* (1931) 45 CLR 224).

Philanthropic

12.4.3 In *Re Macduff* (1896) 2 Ch 481, a name whose Shakespearian connections hardly evoke philanthropy, Stirling J said (at p 481):

> '"Philanthropic" is no doubt a word of narrower meaning than "benevolent". An act may be benevolent if it indicates goodwill to a particular individual only; whereas an act cannot be said to be philanthropic unless it indicates goodwill to mankind at large. Still, it seems to me that "philanthropic" is wide enough to comprise purposes not technically charitable.'

Philanthropic is defined in the Shorter Oxford Dictionary to mean 'benevolent, humane'. The same phrase is used in the National Lottery etc Act 1993 in relation to the National Lottery Charities Board. It is considered that the phrase covers organisations which are not strictly charitable in law but which have a charitable character. The essential attributes of charity were considered in the Irish case of *Re Cranston* [1898] 1 IR 446 at p 452. This statement, which was quoted with approval in the English Court of Appeal by Kennedy LJ in *In re Wedgewood* [1915] 1 Ch 113 at p 119, is that charity:

> 'should be unselfish – that is for the benefit of other persons than the donor – that it shall be public, that is that those to be benefited shall form a class worthy in numbers or in importance of consideration as a public object of generosity, and that it shall be philanthropic or benevolent, that is dictated by a desire to do good.'

But is the phrase wide enough to include organisations such as Greenpeace or Friends of the Earth, which are primarily dedicated to preserving the environment (rather than 'mankind') as benevolent or philanthropic organisations? The phrase should be wide enough to cover the non-charitable work of Amnesty International or charitable-type organisations established in other jurisdictions concerned with mankind, for example Médecins sans Frontières, which, if not charitable under English law (see **12.4.1**), should fall within the definition of 'philanthropic'.

If, for example, Friends of the Earth is not a philanthropic organisation, then Parts II and III of the 1992 Act will not apply to it. However, in the discussions in the House of Lords on Part III of the 1992 Act, it was clear that their Lordships thought that Greenpeace was a philanthropic institution.

12.5 Summary of Exemptions from the Definition of Professional Fund-raiser

Fund-raising by any of the following is exempt from the controls of Part II of the 1992 Act.

(a) Charitable institutions (see **12.5.1**).
(b) Companies connected with charitable institutions (see **12.5.2**).
(c) Low-paid workers (see **12.5.3**).

(d) Collectors (see **12.5.4**).

(e) Celebrities (see **12.5.5**).

Exemption for charitable institutions

12.5.1 It is important to note that the controls introduced by Part II of the 1992 Act do not apply to direct fund-raising undertaken by a charitable institution. Equally, fund-raising by one charitable institution on behalf of other charitable institutions, for example the BBC's 'Children in Need Appeal' (itself a registered charity), is outside the 1992 Act. The definition of professional fund-raiser (s 58(1)) expressly excludes 'a charitable institution'.

Exemption for connected companies

12.5.2 This exemption of charitable institutions is further extended by s 58(2)(a) of the 1992 Act to *any company connected with a charitable institution* provided that company is not carrying on a fund-raising business (see **12.6.1**). If a company is connected with a charitable institution but carries on a fund-raising business as defined in the first part of the definition of professional fund-raiser, that company can be a professional fund-raiser and subject to the controls set out in the Act even though it is connected with a charitable institution. This distinction seems at first sight to present considerable difficulties of interpretation. When is a company set up by a charitable institution to put on fund-raising events *not* carrying out a fund-raising business within the definition? But the answer becomes clear if the definition is applied. Whilst such a company will be 'wholly ... engaged in soliciting or otherwise procuring money or other property for charitable, benevolent or philanthropic purposes' it will not, it is submitted, be carrying on that business 'for gain', since that expression signifies the notion of personal profit or profit for shareholders, whilst a trading company owned by a charity will normally donate any profits to the charity. Hence, such a company will fall within the second definition of a 'professional fund-raiser' in s 58(1), and is therefore exempt from the controls on professional fund-raisers.

A company is defined in s 97 of the 1993 Act (as amended by the Companies Act 1989), as being 'a company formed and registered under the Companies Act 1985, or to which the provisions of that Act apply as they apply to such a company'.

A company is 'connected with' a charitable institution if the institution or the institutions and one or more other charitable institutions taken together, is or are entitled (whether directly or through one or more nominees) to exercise, or control the exercise of, the whole of the voting power at any general meeting of the company (s 58(5)).

Hence, provided they fall within the second definition of 'professional fund-raiser' in s 58(1), trading subsidiaries or trading companies owned by a number of charitable institutions, for example to co-ordinate the sale of Christmas cards, are outside the scope of Part II of the 1992 Act. As originally defined, the Bill would have made charities' trading subsidiaries comply with the disclosure requirements in what is now s 60. As Lord Allen of Abbeydale pointed out in the Public Committee, National Trust Enterprises Limited sold over 11 million individual items and 1,600 lines of products in 1990. If the proposals in the Bill had been enacted this would have imposed a very considerable bureaucratic burden on the National Trust in particular and the charity sector in general.

Exemption for low-paid workers

12.5.3 When the Bill was first published there was considerable concern that the definition of 'professional fund-raiser' was so wide that it would include people who collected money for charity and were paid expenses and a nominal fee. The Government addressed this concern in s 58(3), which provides that a person is not a professional fund-raiser if he does not receive more than £5 per day or £500 per year by way of remuneration in connection with soliciting money or other property. The person paid £5 per day or less for 'rattling his tin' in the street is not, therefore, a professional fund-raiser. If someone is paid less than £5 per day or £500 per year *plus* expenses, he or she will still be within the exemption.

Section 58(3)(b) excludes from the definition anyone paid a small fee (£500 or less) for organising or otherwise undertaking other kinds of fund-raising events or activities for a charitable institution. So, for example, if a person is paid £400 for organising a garden fete at which he solicits money or other property for the benefit of a charitable institution, he is not a professional fund-raiser.

However, some difficult questions could arise.

Example

Mrs Jones organises a garden fete for XYZ charity. She is paid £600 for doing so. At the garden fete, solicitations for money are made by the stallholders who are not themselves professional fund-raisers. The fete is run by the charity and not by Mrs Jones. Mrs Jones is not responsible for the money. She has, therefore, not solicited money herself and s 58(3) of the 1992 Act requires her to solicit money, for that section to apply and for her to be treated as a 'professional fund-raiser'. Hence, even though Mrs Jones has been paid more than £500 per year she is not a professional fund-raiser. If, on the other hand, she was responsible for receiving the money under an arrangement with XYZ charity, she would be deemed to have solicited (see s 58(7)(b)), and (by virtue of being paid more than £500), would be treated as a professional fund-raiser.

Exemption for collectors

12.5.4 If a professional fund-raiser uses paid collectors or agents to solicit funds for a charitable institution, those collectors or agents are not themselves professional fund-raisers. They are, in effect, sheltered by the professional fund-raiser who contracts their services (s 58(2)(c)).

Exemption for appeals by celebrities

12.5.5 The first draft of the Bill caused concern that celebrities employed by professional fund-raisers or charitable institutions to make appeals on radio and television would be caught in the net of the professional fund-raiser definition. The Bill was amended.

Section 58(2)(d) excludes from its definition of professional fund-raiser for the purposes of s 58(1):

'any person who in the course of a relevant programme, that is to say a radio or television programme in the course of which a fund-raising venture is undertaken by:

(i)   a charitable institution; or
(ii) a company connected with such an institution,

makes any solicitation at the instance of that institution or company.'

Hence, even if a celebrity is paid to make an appeal on behalf of a charity, he will not be a professional fund-raiser.

12.6 What is a Professional Fund-raiser?

12.6.1 A professional fund-raiser is defined in s 58(1) as:

'(a) any person (apart from a charitable institution) who carries on a fund-raising business, or
(b) any other person (apart from a person excluded by virtue of subsection (2) or (3)) who for reward solicits money or other property for the benefit of a charitable institution, if he does so otherwise than in the course of a fund-raising venture undertaken by a person falling within paragraph (a) above.'

A fund-raising business is defined in s 58(1) as 'any business carried on for gain and wholly or primarily engaged in soliciting or otherwise procuring money or other property for charitable, benevolent or philanthropic purposes'.

Hence, the definition of professional fund-raiser includes people who for *gain* specialise 'wholly or primarily' in soliciting money, etc, for charitable institutions or who for *reward* solicit money otherwise than in the course of a 'fund-raising venture' undertaken by someone who runs a fund-raising business.

For the purposes of determining whether a business is a fund-raising business, 'wholly or primarily' engaged in soliciting, etc, money for charitable etc, purposes, presumably one must consider the overall activities of that business in the course of its financial year.

On the other hand, the person who is paid £501 for soliciting money or other property for a charitable institution will be a professional fund-raiser even if he does not carry on a 'fund-raising business', because he will be soliciting for reward. Equally, the business which carries on fund-raising activities for charitable institutions for reward but which does not do this 'wholly or primarily', will be caught under this second test.

'Otherwise procuring'

12.6.2 The phrase 'otherwise procuring' in the definition of fund-raising business requires consideration. Concern was expressed by Lord Swinfen at the report stage of the Bill that the definition could include outside agencies in support of charitable fund-raising. For example, is a direct mail house, which specialises in carrying out work for charitable institutions, 'otherwise procuring' money for the charitable institutions and, hence, a professional fund-raiser? Alternatively, is a company which specialises in writing advertising copy for charitable institutions a professional fund-raiser because it 'otherwise procures' money for charitable institutions through the power of its design of advertisements?

Earl Ferrers had earlier stated in the committee stage of the Bill on 11 December 1991:

'We do not want to catch as a professional fund-raiser the marketing consultant, for example, who gives advice to a charity on how it should prepare its fund-raising pamphlet, or indeed a direct mailing firm which might simply send out appeal letters on behalf of a charity, or another firm which might put the appeal notices in the envelopes. This type of indirect involvement does not fall within Clauses 57 to 60 [now ss 58 to 61 of the 1992 Act] as they are currently drafted. These people, such as the ones who print the document, put it in the envelope and mail it are acting as contractors. They are providing a service to the charity in the same way as a catering contractor might provide food for the charity. It is not intended that those people should be caught. Only when a person falling within the definition of professional fund-raiser makes the solicitation himself will he be regulated by the Bill and rightly so.' (Public Bill Committee, Fifth Sitting, col 220 (11 December 1991).)

This statement begs a number of questions. The fact that a particular supplier is acting as a contractor is irrelevant. Professional fund-raisers are contractors. The crucial issue is: where does the boundary lie between a professional fund-raiser and someone who helps raise money for a charitable institution but who does not solicit money or other property? In other words, what does 'otherwise procure' mean? Lord Swinfen sought to have the words removed. He commented:

'In Committee my noble friend Lord Ferrers clarified the Government's intention with respect to that aspect of the Bill. He indicated that outside agencies contracting services to charities and other voluntary organisations in the course of their fund-raising activities would not be regulated under the Bill ... In order to ensure that that intention is properly clarified on the face of the Bill and so as to allay the considerable anxiety which still exists within the charity sector in that respect, [this] amendment seeks to remove the words "or otherwise procuring" from the definition of the type of activity undertaken by fund-raising businesses.' (HL Deb, Vol 535, col 1201 (18 February 1992).)

Viscount Astor replied:

'The words are intended to deal with a situation where, although an appeal or a campaign is undertaken solely by a professional fund-raiser, the appeal literature appears to come from the charity itself with the name and address of the fund-raiser appearing, sometimes inconspicuously, as the recipient of donations and so forth. The key factor is that the fund-raiser is the agent who makes the appeal and gathers in the funds. In such a case the reference to soliciting alone would probably be inadequate because the solicitation would appear to come from the charity even if, in reality, it was from the fund-raiser. The expression "procuring" is used in preference to "obtaining" in order to make clear that the fund-raiser in question must actively achieve the obtaining of funds for charitable purposes and not simply be a passive recipient by accident.' (HL Deb, Vol 535, col 1202–1203 (18 February 1992).)

One can sympathise with the Government's desire to ensure that professional fund-raisers do not try to avoid the Act's requirements by following the common practice of putting out fund-raising literature in the charity's name. On the other hand, there can be no doubt that the phrase 'otherwise procuring' could sweep up into the definition of professional fund-raiser certain types of activity which were not intended to be included, for example the writing of advertising copy if it is undertaken by a business which is 'wholly or primarily' engaged with the charitable sector. We must wait and see how the courts will interpret this phrase.

12.7 Examples of Professional Fund-raisers

A covenant renewal agency

12.7.1 Some charities employ the services of outside firms to organise their covenant renewals. These firms telephone covenantors to explain that their covenants have lapsed and ask them to renew. The donors send no money to the agency. It could be argued that the agency was merely performing a service on behalf of the charity, ie like a contractor. Clearly it is. But one needs to go further and ask 'what is the nature of that agency?'. Is the agency soliciting money for charitable purposes? The answer must be 'yes'. In soliciting the renewal of covenants it is soliciting money, and hence the agency is a professional fund-raiser and its relationship with the charity and the donors must comply with the 1992 Act.

Telephone appeals

12.7.2 A telephone appeal for charitable donations carried out by a telemarketing organisation will amount to fund-raising. The telemarketing organisation will be caught under the definition of 'fund-raising business' if it is 'wholly or primarily' engaged in soliciting money '. . . for charitable, benevolent or philanthropic purposes' (s 58(1)). What is the position if it is not 'wholly or primarily' engaged in soliciting money for charitable, etc, purposes, for example if it mainly does telemarketing on behalf of non-charitable institutions? The telemarketing organisation will still be subject to the 1992 Act, because the second limb of the definition of professional fund-raiser includes any other person who is not running a fund-raising business (see **12.6.1**) but 'who for reward solicits money or other property for the benefit of a charitable institution' (s 58(1)).

This is the case even if (as is usual) the telemarketing organisation requests that all payments be made to the charity or, alternatively, if a donor responds positively to the telephone appeal, that the agency sends the donor appeal literature and asks the donor to send the donation direct to the charity. It could be argued that the agency is like the contractor who prints a document, addresses it and posts it, and whom Earl Ferrers did not consider to be a professional fund-raiser (see **12.6.2**). As Earl Ferrers said in the same speech:

> '. . . only when a person falling within the definition of professional fund-raiser makes the solicitation himself will he be regulated by the Bill.' (Public Bill Committee, Fifth Sitting, col 220 (11 December 1991).)

'Solicitation' is extremely widely drafted in s 58(6) (see **12.9.3**) and must cover the telemarketing agency which will, therefore, be a professional fund-raiser for the purposes of the Act.

Secondees

12.7.3 Some organisations, for example banks, second their staff to work for charities. The bank continues to employ (and pay) the secondee. If the secondee solicits funds on behalf of the charity with whom he is working, is he a professional fund-raiser? He will be soliciting money and be being paid (by his employer). Therefore, will he be soliciting money *for reward* (see **12.6.1**)? It could be that the secondee, in these circumstances, will be classified as a professional fund-raiser.

Consultants

12.7.4 The activity of a consultant who is paid to advise a charitable institution about how to go about fund-raising would not in itself make the consultant a professional fund-raiser controlled by the Act. Unless he *solicits* funds or property for the charitable institution, he will *not* be a professional fund-raiser.

Agency agreements

12.7.5 Some charities pay an agency a fee to obtain contributions to the charity through, for example, a payroll-giving scheme. The agency then pays a success fee to independent agents if they manage to sign up donors to the charity. The agency prepares standardised materials to facilitate the agents in mounting the appeal and advises the agents where to visit in order to solicit support. The agents are self-employed and pay their own tax and National Insurance contributions. The relationship raises the question: *who is the professional fund-raiser?*. Although the agency is not itself actively concerned to solicit money on behalf of the charities, it is probably engaged in a fund-raising business. The agents are not within the definition 'professional fund-raiser' in s 58(1) because of the exclusion contained in the second definition of a professional fund-raiser as someone who is engaged in fund-raising in the course of a fund-raising venture undertaken by a person carrying on fund-raising business. Such an analysis would be in line with the statement of Earl Ferrers in the House of Lords at p 1198 of Hansard (18 February 1992) on the Charities Bill:

> 'The provisions of Part II are intended to regulate the affairs of professional fundraisers – the men who run fundraising businesses – in relation to the appeals and campaigns they organise for charitable institutions.'

Hence, in these circumstances, it is the agency which organises the fund-raisers rather than the individual agent who makes the solicitation who should be treated as the professional fund-raiser and subject to the controls set out in the Act.

12.8 Section 59 Agreements

12.8.1 Broadly speaking, the 1992 Act introduces controls on professional fund-raisers which follow the recommendations of the White Paper (see **12.2**).

By s 59(1), 'it shall be unlawful for a professional fund-raiser to solicit money or other property for the benefit of a charitable institution unless he does so in accordance with an agreement with the institution satisfying the prescribed requirements'.

The prescribed requirements are laid down in the Charitable Institutions (Fund-Raising) Regulations 1994 (SI 1994/3024). Regulation 2 provides that the agreement between the charitable institution and a professional fund-raiser shall be in writing and shall be signed by or on behalf of the charitable institution and the professional fund-raiser.

The agreement has to specify:

(a) the name and address of each of the parties to the agreement;

(b) the date on which the agreement was signed by or on behalf of those parties;
(c) the period for which the agreement is to subsist;
(d) any terms relating to termination of the agreement prior to the date on which the period expires;
(e) any terms relating to the variation of the agreement during that period.

The agreement also has to contain:

(a) a statement of its principal objectives and the methods to be used in pursuit of those objectives;
(b) if there is more than one charitable institution party to the agreement, provision as to the manner in which the proportion in which the institutions which are so party are respectively to benefit under the agreement is to be determined;
(c) provision as to the amount by way of remuneration or expenses which the professional fund-raiser is to be entitled to receive in respect of things done by him in pursuance of the agreement and the manner in which that amount is to be determined.

Section 59(1) uses the word 'unlawful'. Something may be unlawful in two senses:

(a) unenforceable by law; and
(b) punishable by law.

It is clear from the rest of s 59(3) and (4) that 'unlawful' is used here to denote unenforceability.

Breach of s 59

12.8.2 By s 59(3), the court may grant an injunction on the application of a charitable institution if it is satisfied:

(a) that any person has breached s 59(1) (ie a professional fund-raiser is soliciting money for the benefit of a charitable institution without having entered into a s 59(1) agreement); and
(b) that unless restrained, such a contravention is likely to continue or be repeated.

The court in question is either the High Court or a county court. In injunction cases, either court could be used.

12.8.3 Note that an agreement is not enforceable if a charitable institution enters into a s 59(1) agreement with a professional fund-raiser and the agreement does not comply with the prescribed requirements set out in the regulations. In that case, the agreement can only be enforced by the professional fund-raiser to such an extent (if any) as may be provided by an order of the court. Hence, it is imperative for professional fund-raisers that all agreements with charitable institutions conform to the requirements of the regulations.

12.8.4 This is equally vital for charity trustees. For example, if a charity enters into an agreement with a professional fund-raiser which breached s 59(1), that agreement would not be enforceable against the charitable institution without the order of the court (see s 58(4)), but the charity, none the less, might make payments under it. Could the trustees be held personally liable to reimburse the charity for payments made in breach of s 59(1) on the basis that the charity has suffered as a result of their negligence? The argument would be that, but for their negligence (in permitting payments under a non-enforceable agreement), the charity could have resisted paying out under the agreement, unless payment had been sanctioned by the court.

Enforceability

12.8.5 Section 59(5) makes it clear that any provision under an agreement between a charitable institution and a professional fund-raiser is only enforceable by the professional fund-raiser if:

(a) the agreement satisfies the prescribed requirements (ie it conforms to the regulations under s 59(1)); or
(b) a court orders that the provision of the agreement can be enforced.

In addition to the standard requirements laid down in reg 2 of the Charitable Institutions (Fund-Raising) Regulations 1994, reg 5 provides that a professional fund-raiser who is party to an agreement under s 59:

> 'Shall, on request and at all reasonable times, make available to any charitable institution which is a party to that agreement any books, documents or other records (however kept) which relate to that institution and are kept for the purposes of the agreement.'

By reg 5(2), the records have to be kept in legible form. By reg 6, the professional fund-raiser has, unless he has a reasonable excuse, to pay over any money or any negotiable instrument received by him to the account of the charitable institution as soon as is reasonably practicable after receipt, and in any event not later than the expiration of 28 days after that receipt unless another period has been agreed with the institution. Payment has to be made to the charitable institution itself or into an account in the name of the institution.

If the professional fund-raiser receives property other than money then it has to be dealt with in accordance with any instructions given for that purpose by the charitable institution. Pending the handing over of any property it has to be kept securely by the professional fund-raiser.

Breach of reg 5(1) or reg 6(2) is a criminal offence which can give rise to a maximum fine of £500 (second level on the standard scale).

The requirements laid down by the Charitable Institutions (Fund-Raising) Regulations 1994 are the legal minimum. Charitable institutions may well want to build on the requirements set out in the Regulations to protect themselves on other issues. For example, a charitable organisation may wish to impose a penal rate of interest on the professional fund-raiser should it delay making payments due to the charitable institution under the fund-raising agreement. A charitable institution may require the professional fund-raiser to hold regular meetings to monitor the fund-raising appeal. The agreement should also consider such items as copyright, for example who owns copyright in artwork or any copy produced by the professional fund-raiser? What is the position of the ownership of data, for example lists of names created by the professional fund-raiser? Is the professional fund-raiser under a duty of confidentiality? Should the professional fund-raiser be restrained from undertaking any work of a similar nature for any organisation which operates within the same or a similar field of activity as the charitable institution for the duration of the agreement? What is the governing law of the contract?

The charitable institution should ensure that a s 59 agreement is signed by a trustee.

12.9 Section 60 Statements

12.9.1 Section 60(1) of the 1992 Act requires that where a professional fund-raiser solicits money or other property for the benefit of one or more particular charitable institutions, the solicitation shall be accompanied by a statement clearly indicating:

'(a) the name or names of the institutions concerned [eg 'XYZ charity'];
(b) if there is more than one institution concerned, the proportions in which the institutions are respectively to benefit [eg 'XYZ charity 50 per cent, ABC charity 50 per cent']; and
(c) (in general terms) the method by which the fund-raiser's remuneration in connection with the appeal is to be determined [eg 'the organisers of this appeal will be paid X per cent of the proceeds of the appeal'].'

12.9.2 Section 60(2) deals with the situation where a professional fund-raiser is soliciting money or other property for charitable, benevolent or philanthropic purposes of any description, rather than for the benefit of one or more particular charitable institutions. Thus, it covers, for example, an appeal for 'Victims of Famine' or 'The Handicapped' rather than an appeal for Oxfam or Mencap (which falls within s 60(1)).

In this case, the professional fund-raiser has to accompany his solicitation with a statement clearly indicating:

'(a) the fact that he is soliciting money or other property for those purposes [eg 'Famine'] and not for any particular charitable institution or institutions;
(b) the method by which it is to be determined how the proceeds of the appeal are to be distributed between different charitable institutions; and
(c) (in general terms) the method by which his remuneration in connection with the appeal is to be determined.'

12.9.3 Subsections (1) and (2) of s 60 raise similar issues and can be dealt with together. It is worth emphasising the meaning of 'solicit'. Under s 58(6), soliciting can occur:

(a) by speaking directly to the person being solicited (whether in his presence or not) [hence, a solicitation can be made face to face, or by telephone]; or
(b) by means of a statement published in any newspaper, film, radio or television programme;
(c) 'or otherwise'.

Therefore, solicitations can be made in many different ways. Whenever a solicitation is made, a s 60(1) or (2) statement has to accompany it. If, for example, a professional fund-raiser organises a street collection, the collector will have to display the statement. If a professional fund-raiser arranges a charity ball, the tickets will have to bear the statement. If a professional fund-raiser arranges a telephone appeal, the statement will have to be given on each call. It will not be enough to send the statement with the appeal documentation to the potential donor.

12.9.4 How detailed does the s 60 statement have to be?

Earl Ferrers clarified the position:

'As regards the statement it will have to be true and correct. That is the first point. It need not go into the detail and precision that a test of accuracy would impose.

  I accept that such a test would be too rigid given the variety of fund-raising methods used. That is why I introduced the element of flexibility which is contained in these amendments. I appreciate that Clause 60 places new duties on professional fund-raisers and commercial participators. They will be at the bottom of what one might call a fairly daunting learning curve. It is only right that the Government should help fund-raisers along that new curve. I am happy to undertake that we shall, in consultation with practitioners, give appropriate help and guidance to them so that they do not fall into any unfortunate traps.' (HL Deb, Vol 535, cols 1206–1207 (18 February 1992).)

It should be noted that the 1992 Act is drafted in such a way that the form of statement will not be prescribed in regulations. However, by s 64(1) the Secretary of State may make such regulations as appear to him to be necessary or desirable for any purposes connected with Part II of the 1992 Act. In years to come, the government might issue regulations laying down guide-lines on the contents of s 60 statements. At the report stage of the Bill, Lord Swinfen moved an amendment requiring the government to issue guide-lines on the content of s 60 statements. Earl Ferrers rejected this. He did not consider statutory guidance would be helpful because it would have to deal with every contingency. Instead, he reiterated that the government would consult with practitioners on this issue. In the interim, it is for the professional fund-raiser to draw up the statement.

Example of s 60(1) statement

12.9.5 A possible format for a statement under s 60(1) might be as follows.

Charity Appeal

For XYZ charity, a registered charity★ and ABC Charity, a registered charity. XYZ and ABC will each receive 50 per cent of the net proceeds of this appeal. Scrouge and Co, the organisers of this appeal, will be paid a flat fee by XYZ and ABC.

[or]

Scrouge and Co, the organisers of this appeal, will receive 10p for every £ raised by the appeal.

If you make a donation of more than £50 by credit or debit card, you have the right to cancel your donation within seven days of this broadcast.★★

NOTES

★Under s 5 of the 1993 Act, if a registered charity had an income of more than £10,000 in its last financial year, it must state the fact that it is a registered charity in legible characters on all notices, advertisements, etc, issued by or on behalf of the charity and soliciting money or other property. As already explained (see **2.8**) breach of s 5 can give rise to criminal liabilities – and this could include liability on a professional fund-raiser.

★★If the appeal is made in the course of a radio or television programme and in association with an announcement that payment may be made by credit or debit card, the statement must include details of the donor's right to cancel his donation and demand a refund so long as the demand for a refund is made within seven days of the broadcast.

Is it necessary to state that XYZ and ABC will each receive 50 per cent 'of the net proceeds of this appeal'? The 1992 Act merely requires a statement 'of the proportions in which the institutions are respectively to benefit'. That begs the question: from what shall the institutions benefit? Will they benefit from the total proceeds of the appeal? If that is the case, how does the fund-raiser get his reward? But if one uses the phrase 'net proceeds', that raises the question, 'net of what'? Should the fund-raiser, in the example above, in order to make the statement a clear indication, state '50 per cent of the net proceeds after deduction of Scrouge and Co's remuneration'?

If the public becomes aware that professional fund-raisers are receiving large proportions of moneys ostensibly raised for charitable institutions, the effect on public generosity could be dramatic. The degree of disclosure needed about the fund-raiser's remuneration could be crucial. The 1992 Act only calls for a statement in general terms about the *method* by which the fund-raiser's remuneration is to be determined. Is it sufficient to state that Scrouge and Co is being paid a flat fee (of an unspecified amount)? It seems that that would comply with the Act. It shows the *method* by which the fund-raiser is to be paid. Equally, in the case of a telephone appeal, a fund-raiser might be paid £1 per call. Does the fund-raiser have to state that he is being paid £1 per call (which might be a considerable turn-off for potential donors) or is it sufficient to state that he is being paid a flat rate per call? It would appear that the latter would suffice. But what happens if the potential donor then asks 'how much per call?'? Does the fund-raiser have to reply? It seems not. His obligation under the 1992 Act is to give a statement clearly indicating the method by which his remuneration is to be determined and it would seem that the statement 'We are being paid a flat rate per call' would comply with that requirement.

Telephone fund-raising raises a number of problems. The Home Office publication *Charitable Fund-raising: Professional and Commercial Involvement* (February 1995) states at p 10:

'Incoming telephone services; if a company *answers* telephone calls, simply to record credit card details for people who have decided to make a donation, eg in response to an appeal by direct mail or newspaper or television advertisement, *and* the donations are credited direct to the institutions' (not the company's) bank account, the company may not be a professional fundraiser. However, the distinction is a narrow one and care is needed; if, for example, the operator repeats or explains details about the appeal, even in response to a request for clarification from the caller, this may well amount to professional fundraising, and operators must therefore be able to recognise this distinction and respond appropriately in each case.

Where incoming telephone services are provided by automated (eg computer based) answering equipment owned by a service provider and rented to an institution, then even when a solicitation is made by a person whose voice is recorded provided that person is from the charitable institution, the service provider may not be regarded as a professional fundraiser.'

It must be emphasised that these conclusions are tentative. As Earl Ferrers recognised, there is much learning to be done. The precise meaning and requirements of the statement will have to await judicial scrutiny or possible regulations.

The Home Office Voluntary Services Unit commented at p 5 of its publication *Charitable Fund-raising: Professional and Commercial Involvement* (February 1995):

'We recognise that each situation may be different and that it is difficult to lay down precise rules, but recommend that in general as clear information as possible is given in statements – in many cases going further than the minimum required by law. Where Part II applies the formulation "in general terms, the method by which . . ." does, *at least* require a distinction to be drawn between calculations based on a proportion of sales of income, and those based on a fixed charge or for work undertaken. Codes of practice . . . such as the Advertising Standards Authority's Code of Advertising and Sales Promotion . . . may impose further non-statutory requirements, which may go further than the law and regulations. . . . We also encourage the public to *ask* for more detail if they are unclear or uncertain about what they are told.'

The requirements in Part II are, however, the minimum legal requirements.

Example of s 60(2) statement

12.9.6 A possible format for a statement under s 60(2) might be as follows.

Save the Whale Appeal

This is an appeal on behalf of whales and not for the benefit of any particular charitable institution.

Ninety per cent of the proceeds of this appeal shall go to such charitable institutions as are chosen by the management committee of this appeal.

Scrouge and Co, as organisers of this appeal, will receive 10p for every £1 raised by the appeal.

If you make a donation of more than £50 by credit or debit card you have the right to cancel your donation within seven days of this broadcast.

The same notes concerning the statement under s 60(1) which are mentioned above apply to this statement.

The Home Office Voluntary Services Unit in the same pamphlet as mentioned at **12.9.5** states:

'It is recommended that charitable fundraising is undertaken for specific charitable institutions rather than general charitable purposes. The public are warned to be more cautious in responding to appeals for general charitable purposes' (p 4).

The right to cancel – ss 60 and 61

12.9.7 Reference has already been made (see **12.9.5**) to the obligation of a professional fund-raiser, under s 60(4), to notify potential donors who may give more than £50 in response to a radio or TV appeal, of their right to demand a refund if the donation is made by credit or debit card. By s 60(5), if a solicitation is made by a professional fund-raiser *by telephone*, the fund-raiser must notify, within seven days, the donor of:

(a) the full details of the s 60 statement (see **12.9.1**); and
(b) his right to cancel the donation within seven days and demand a refund if he pays more than £50 to the professional fund-raiser.

This does not apply if the payment is made to a charitable institution (s 60(5)) even if the solicitation has been made by a professional fund-raiser. It must be noted that in the case of a telephone appeal, the donor has the right to cancel irrespective of how he has paid the £50 or more. In the case of a TV or radio appeal, the right to cancel only applies if payment is made by a debit or credit card.

12.9.8 The professional fund-raiser must give the donor who has paid more than £50 in response to a telephone appeal details of the donor's right to cancel within seven days. This seven-day period is determined as follows (s 60(6)):

(a) if the donor pays in person – the seven days run from the time of payment;
(b) if the donor pays by post – the seven days run from the time of posting the donation;
(c) if the donor pays via telephone or fax or other telecommunication apparatus and orders an account to be debited – the seven days run from the time when such authority is given.

The donor then has seven days from the date he is *given* the written statement (s 61(2)(b)) to exercise, if he so wishes, his right to cancel the donation.

Does that mean that the donor has literally to be given the notice, ie must it be physically *handed* to him, or is the statement given when it is posted through his letter box or when it is put into the post (if posted)?

12.9.9 Section 7 of the Interpretation Act 1978 provides that where an Act authorises or requires any document to be served by post (whether the expression 'serve' or the expression 'give' is used) then, unless the contrary intention appears, the service is deemed to be effected by properly addressing, prepaying and posting a letter containing the document and, unless the contrary is proved, to have been effected at the time when the letter would be delivered in the ordinary course of post. The implication is that 'to give' is synonymous with 'to serve'. This is confirmed by a case under the Law of Property Act 1925, s 36(2), which uses the phrase 'give . . . notice in writing' in which it was held that 'give' meant the same as 'serve' (*Re 88 Berkeley Road, Rickwood v Turnesk* [1971] Ch 648).

Section 76 of the 1992 Act states that any notice or other document to be given or served under Part II may be served on or given to a person by:

(a) delivering it to that person;
(b) leaving it at his last known address in the UK; or
(c) sending it by post to him at that address.

In the case of a body corporate (eg a limited company, or a body incorporated by Royal Charter) notice is effected by delivering it or sending it by post:

(a) to the registered or principal office of the body in the UK; or
(b) if it has no such office in the UK, to any place in the UK where it carries on business or conducts its affairs.

The right to cancel notice is deemed to be effected under the Interpretation Act 1978 'at the time at which the letter would be delivered in the ordinary course of post' (s 7). This means that delivery will be presumed to have taken place on the next working day or the next but one, depending on whether first- or second-class post is used. The court will normally assume that second-class post is used.

Example

Gullible responds to a telephone appeal run by Scrouge and Co on behalf of the XYZ charity and sends £100 by post on 1 May to Scrouge. Scrouge receives the donation on 3 May. Scrouge has to give to Gullible the right to cancel notice within seven days (s 60(5)) of the postmark on Gullible's letter – (s 60(6) states that payment shall be regarded as made at the time when it is posted) ie by 7 May.

Scrouge posts the right to cancel notice on 7 May. Gullible will be deemed to have received the notice two workings days after 7 May unless the 'contrary is proved' (Interpretation Act 1978, s 7). If he receives the notice, Gullible must exercise his right to cancel within seven days of being given the right to cancel notice. If he receives the notice on 9 May, he will have to post his notice exercising his right to cancel by 16 May (letter posted on 7 May and served on 9 May).

There is no approved format for the notice exercising the right to cancel. It merely has to indicate the donor's intention to cancel.

How much refund?

12.9.10 The Bill allowed no right for the professional fund-raiser to deduct any administrative costs before refunding any donation over £50 where the donor had exercised the right to cancel. This was criticised. As a result, s 61(4) allows the fund-raiser to deduct 'administrative expenses reasonably incurred' in connection with making the refund. Viscount Astor explained:

> 'administrative expenses' is intended to cover the direct costs of refunding the payment, for costs such as staff time, postage, bank charges and so forth. It will also cover the costs of dealing with any notice of cancellation of an agreement to make payment.' (HL Deb, Vol 535, col 1215 (18 February 1992).)

Breach of s 60

12.9.11 Section 60(7) imposes a strict criminal liability on a professional fund-raiser who is in breach of s 60, ie a professional fund-raiser who fails to give the statements required under s 60(1), (2), (4) or (5). The maximum fine is currently £5,000.

It will be a defence for a person charged with any offence under s 60 'to prove that he took all reasonable precautions and exercised all due diligence to avoid the commission of the offence' (s 60(8)). This is similar to a phrase used in the Trade Descriptions Act 1968, s 24. It shifts the burden of proof from the prosecution, who would, under normal rules of criminal law, have to prove that the defendant had mens rea and committed the offence, onto the defendant, who has to show that he took all reasonable precautions, etc. That is a heavy burden. In one case under the Trade Descriptions Act 1968, *Tesco Supermarkets v Nattrass* [1971] 2 All ER 127, the House of Lords ruled that the defendants had exercised all due diligence by devising a proper system for the operation of their supermarket and by securing its implementation as far as was reasonably practicable.

Thus, professional fund-raisers will need to ensure that they have proper procedures, adequately monitored, to ensure that their staff comply with the requirements of s 60. If they do not, they will be unable to establish that they have taken all reasonable precautions and exercised all due diligence. Viscount Astor commented on behalf of the Government:

'In order to avail himself of this defence the person charged must establish, on the balance of probabilities, that he was not negligent in failing to avoid the commission of the offence.' (HL Deb, Vol 535, col 1210 (18 February 1992).)

The Act is notably silent about who is responsible for its enforcement. There is no section empowering trading standards officers to do so. In the absence of such a section, it is the police who are responsible for enforcement. However, in the war against crime, breaches of Part II will come fairly low down any list of priorities. Hence, the Charity Commission is endeavouring to monitor the position and liaise with the relevant local police force.

12.9.12 Section 60(9) contains a sting. It provides that where there is a breach of s 60 which is due to the act or default of some other person, that other person shall be guilty of the offence. The same defence of having taken all reasonable precautions, etc, can be pleaded. The subsection is principally designed to allow charges to be brought against employees who break the requirements of the Act, in breach, for example, of their employer's rule book. But the subsection could have wider implications. The original clause 4 of the Bill (now s 5 of the 1993 Act) contained a similar subclause (4(5)). The Law Society was most concerned about its effect because it feared that solicitors who failed to advise their clients of the requirements of what is now s 5, could have been guilty of a criminal offence. The solicitor who failed to advise might have been guilty of a 'default' under the section. The Government was persuaded to drop clause 4(5) but s 60(9) remained.

Viscount Astor commented:

'The provision [s 60(9)] is designed to ensure that, where a professional fund-raiser's employees or agents go off on a frolic of their own and neglect to make the necessary disclosures, they are guilty of an offence whether or not the fund-raiser is prosecuted. Of course if the employer has taken steps to institute a proper system to ensure the making of the statement he will be able to rely on subsection (8).

It has been suggested that the wording of subsection (9) could catch solicitors or accountants who advise professional fund-raisers or commercial participators. We have looked at this matter again and I have to say we do not see how that could be so. The duty placed on the professional fund-raiser is to disclose certain information when soliciting funds. The act or default relates to the failure to disclose that information when soliciting funds.

Subsection (9) of Clause 60 cannot render solicitors liable to prosecution under this clause if they advise their client incorrectly about when the provisions of Clause 60 apply. They are under no duty to make any disclosure. The offence relates to the failure to make the required statements of disclosure.' (HL Deb, Vol 535, col 1210 (18 February 1992).)

12.10 Regulations

12.10.1 It is worth reiterating that Part II of the 1992 Act in relation to fund-raising does not apply to charitable institutions or companies controlled by them provided they fall within the second definition of professional fund-raiser (see **12.5.2**). However, the Government did consider applying the right to cancel in the case of donations over £50 to appeals made directly by charitable institutions. In the end the Government decided not to. In part, this was because the Home Office has given financial support towards the development of a voluntary code of practice for broadcast appeals. The charities involved in broadcast appeals had indicated their willingness to include in that voluntary code a requirement that donors of money over a certain sum should be informed in writing or by telephone of the right to cancel the donation.

However, the Government has reserved the right to introduce regulations to extend the statutory right to cancel to radio or television appeals made by charitable institutions or their connected companies (as defined in s 58). Indeed, s 64(2)(e) is much wider. It states:

'Any such regulations may ... make other provisions regulating the raising of funds for charitable, benevolent or philanthropic purposes (whether by professional fund-raisers or commercial participators or otherwise).'

These are wide powers and could cover far more than the imposition of the right to cancel upon appeals made by charitable institutions or their connected companies, as indeed has already happened (see **13.7**).

CHAPTER 13

CONTROL OF FUND-RAISING: COMMERCIAL PARTICIPATORS AND OTHER MATTERS

Introduction – What is a Commercial Participator? – Application of the Definition – Section 59 Agreements – Section 60 Statements – Criminal Sanctions – Quasi Commercial Participators – Right of Charitable Institutions to Prevent Unauthorised Fund-raising – Section 63 – Section 75

13.1 Introduction

13.1.1 As noted (see **12.2.2**), one of the recommendations of the Woodfield Report was that whenever goods or services were advertised or offered for sale, with an indication that some part of the proceeds was to be devoted to charity, there should be specified:

(a) the charity or charities that were to benefit; and
(b) the manner in which the sums they were to receive would be calculated.

13.1.2 The White Paper endorsed this. There had been some doubts about the practicability of the Woodfield proposal but the authors of the White Paper were sure that 'the public, when being encouraged to make a purchase on the grounds that it will benefit charity, have a right to certain basic information, which should not be difficult to provide' (at para 10.20).
   The Government followed that when drafting the Act.

13.2 What is a Commercial Participator?

13.2.1 The 1992 Act introduces a new phrase to the dictionary of the voluntary sector: 'the commercial participator'. In essence, a commercial participator is someone who encourages purchases of goods or services on the ground that some of the proceeds will go to a charitable institution or that a donation will be made to a charitable institution.

13.2.2 Section 58(1) defines a commercial participator as:

'in relation to any charitable institution . . . any person who –

(a) carries on for gain a business other than a fund-raising business, but
(b) in the course of that business, engages in any promotional venture in the course of which it is represented that charitable contributions are to be given to or applied for the benefit of the institution.'

A number of the expressions used in this definition are also defined in the Act. The definition of 'a charitable institution' and the definition of 'a fund-raising business' have been considered (see **12.4** and **12.6**, respectively). 'Promotional venture' is defined by s 58(1) of the Act as 'any advertising or sales campaign or any other venture undertaken for promotional purposes'. 'Venture' has not, apparently, been defined in any statute or, remarkably, considered in any judgment. The Oxford English Dictionary defines a venture as: 'that which is ventured or risked in a commercial enterprise or speculation'.

'Represent' is defined by s 58(6) as meaning to represent:

'in any manner whatever, whether done by speaking directly ... or by means of a statement published in any newspaper, film or radio or television programme or otherwise...;'

'Charitable contributions' is defined by s 58(1) as meaning:

'in relation to any representation made by any commercial participator or other person ...

(a) the whole or part of –
    (i) the consideration given for goods or services sold or supplied by him, or
    (ii) any proceeds (other than such consideration) of a promotional venture undertaken by him, or
(b) sums given by him by way of donation in connection with the sale or supply of any such goods or services (whether the amount of such sums is determined by reference to the value of any such goods or services or otherwise)'.

'Services' is defined by s 58(9) as including:

'facilities, and in particular –
(a) access to any premises or event;
(b) membership of any organisation;
(c) the provision of advertising space; and
(d) the provision of any financial facilities;
and references to the supply of services shall be construed accordingly.'

13.2.3 In debate at the committee stage of the Bill, Viscount Astor, referring to the definition of commercial participator, stated:

'It is a wide definition drafted to ensure that a broad range of types of facility or service that may be offered by a person acting as a commercial participator are encompassed within the Bill.' (Public Bill Committee, Fifth Sitting, col 221 (11 December 1992).)

13.3 Application of the Definition

The following questions arise on the definition of commercial participator.

Companies controlled by charitable institutions

13.3.1 Under the Charities Act 1992 as originally drafted, companies controlled by charitable institutions, although outside the controls of professional fund-raisers, fell within the controls on commercial participators. This was unexpected as it had generally been thought that charities' trading companies would be outside the controls given the potential implications set out at **12.5.2**. In order to rectify this, an amendment was included in the Deregulation and Contracting Out Act 1994 which excludes from the definition of a commercial participator 'a company connected with the institution'. This is a reference to a particular charitable institution in relation to which the representation is made. Hence, if a trading company is owned by charity A, all statements concerning charitable contributions made by that trading company to charity A are excluded from the Act. But if the trading company is owned by charity A but carries on activities for the benefits of charities B, C and D and makes representations concerning payments to B, C and D, then that trading company is a commercial participator in respect of its dealings with charities B, C and D because it is not a company 'connected' (as defined in s 58(5)) with B, C or D.

However, the Voluntary Services Unit of the Home Office has stated in *Charities Fund-raising: Professional and Commercial Involvement* (February 1995) at p 3:

> '... the need for good practice in fund-raising by charities, other charitable institutions and connected companies is just as strong as it is for those subject to Part II, including the need to have full regard to professional codes and other recommended practice. Although some regard has to be made for the different circumstances where a charitable institution or its connected company undertakes direct fund-raising, as far as is applicable, the Home Offcice (and in relation to charities) the Charity Commission *strongly recommends, as a matter of good practice* [my emphasis] that these bodies follow the same requirements (eg for agreements and statements ...) as for others who are subject to the requirements of Part II.'

The same publication also comments:

> 'Compliance with such arrangements may be straightforward in many cases; for example in a charity shop it may be possible to make the appropriate statement by notice displayed prominently by the tills saying that all profits are covenanted to the charity' (p 10).

Broadcast appeals

13.3.2 Much concern was expressed in the House of Lords about broadcast appeals, where all the contributions go to the charitable institution on whose behalf the broadcast appeal is made. The appeals use building societies and credit card companies which provide facilities for the receipt of donations and charge for their services. Are they commercial participators? Viscount Astor confirmed:

> 'the definition [   ] of commercial participator [is] not intended to include commercial organisations providing services for broadcast appeals as part of their normal business.' (Public Bill Committee, Fifth Sitting, col 222 (11 December 1992).)

This clearly accords with the definition of commercial participator which requires the participator to be engaged in a 'promotional venture' in the course of which it is represented that charitable contributions will be given. If a bank charges a charity for running pledge lines during a broadcast appeal, it is not engaging in a 'promotional venture' (as defined in s 58(1)).

What if a bank gave its facilities free of charge and this was mentioned in the appeal? This would not alter the position. The bank would not be a commercial participator – it would not be representing that 'charitable contributions' (as defined) would be made. In advertising that it was donating free services to the charity, it could be argued that the use of the charity's name was consideration given for the free service. But s 58(1) requires that the representation must be in relation to 'the whole or part of the consideration given ... for services sold'. In this case, although the charity is giving consideration for the free service (ie use of its name) no part of *that* consideration is being given to the charity.

Affinity cards

13.3.3 Under this system, banks issue credit cards dedicated to a particular charity and donate a percentage of the customer's monthly payments to a charity. Clearly, in this situation, the bank is:

(a) engaging in a business (banking) which is not a fund-raising business; but
(b) in the course of that, is engaging in a promotional venture in which it is representing that a percentage of the consideration paid for the services provided by the bank will go to a charitable institution.

Hence, the bank is a commercial participator.

This is made clear by s 58(9)(d) of the 1992 Act where the definition of 'services' includes 'the provision of any financial facilities'.

Given this, the affinity card should, it is submitted, bear the statement required under s 60(3) (see **13.5.2**).

Christmas cards

13.3.4 Many commercial organisations sell charity Christmas cards, ie cards which state 'sold in aid of XYZ charity'. Is a high street retailer who sells such cards a commercial participator? The retailer carried on, for gain, a business other than fund-raising. In the course of his business, is he engaging in a promotional venture of any sort? Since a promotional venture includes a sales campaign (s 58(1)), displaying the cards for sale constitutes a promotional venture. But it is also necessary to establish that in the course of that promotional venture it is represented that charitable contributions (as defined) will be made. Like a solicitation (see **12.9.3**), a representation can be made in any manner whatever, expressly or impliedly. Hence, the sale of a Christmas card stating 'sold in aid of XYZ charity' is an implied representation that part of the price paid for the card will go to XYZ charity. Therefore, on this analysis, the retailer is a commercial participator with the consequences analysed below (see **13.4** and **13.5**).

Is the position different if the Christmas card merely states 'XYZ charity'? This is more difficult, but it may be an implied representation that part of the price paid will go to the charity.

Other examples of commercial participators

13.3.5 Other examples of commercial participators include the following.

(a) The maker of a product who prints a charity's logo on the product and states:

  '1p will go to XYZ charity for each packet sold'.

(b) The events organiser (eg the Glastonbury Festival) who states that the net proceeds of the event will go to a charitable institution.

  Glastonbury raises an interesting issue. The net proceeds used to go to the Campaign for Nuclear Disarmament. Is that a benevolent or philanthropic institution? Probably not, as it is established for political purposes. The net proceeds now go to Greenpeace. Is that a benevolent or philanthropic institution? (For a discussion, see **12.4.2**.)

(c) The travel company which offers to pay one per cent of the price of a holiday to a named charitable institution.

13.4 Section 59 Agreements

13.4.1 Just as the professional fund-raiser has to have an agreement with a charitable institution before it can solicit money for its benefit, so too must the commercial participator. Section 59(2) states that it is unlawful for a commercial participator to represent that charitable contributions are to be given to a charitable institution 'unless he does so in accordance with an agreement with the institution satisfying the prescribed requirements'.

Under the Charitable Institutions (Fund-Raising) Regulations 1994 (SI 1994/3024) (the Regulations), the agreement between charitable institution and commercial participator required by s 59(2) of the 1992 Act has to be in writing and signed by or on behalf of the charitable institution and the commercial participator.

The agreement has to specify:

(a) the name and address of each of the parties to the agreement;
(b) the date on which the agreement was signed by or on behalf of each of those parties;
(c) the period for which the agreement is to subsist;
(d) any terms relating to the termination of the agreement prior to the date on which that period expires;
(e) any terms relating to the variation of the agreement during that period.

The agreement also has to contain:

(a) a statement of its principal objectives and the methods to be used in pursuit of those objectives;
(b) provision as to the manner in which are to be determined:
    (i) if there is more than one charitable institution party to the agreement, the proportion in which the institutions which are so party are respectively to benefit under the agreement; and
    (ii) the proportion of the consideration given for goods or services sold or supplied by the commercial participator or of any other proceeds of a promotional venture undertaken by him, which is to be given to or applied for the benefit of the charitable institution; or
    (iii) the sums by way of donations by the commercial participator in connection with the sale or supply of any goods or services sold or supplied by him which are to be so given or applied;
    as the case may require;
(c) provision as to any amount by way of remuneration or expenses which the commercial participator is to be entitled to receive in respect of things done by him in pursuance of the agreement in the manner in which any such amount is to be determined.

As with the agreement for professional fund-raisers, this list is the minimum.

If a commercial participator seeks to represent that charitable contributions are to be given to a charitable institution without the benefit of a s 59 agreement complying with the prescribed requirements, or there is an agreement but it does not satisfy those requirements, then any such agreement is unenforceable without the approval of the High Court or county court. In addition, under s 59(5) the commercial participator will not be entitled to receive any remuneration under a defective agreement until the agreement satisfies the prescribed requirements or a court orders that the commercial participator may be paid. It is unlikely, however, that this provision will be of much use to charitable institutions. This is because money will normally pass from the commercial participator to the charitable institution (eg '5p per bottle of water sold goes to XYZ Charity'). In this case, sales have been made by the commercial participator with a proportion of sales income being forwarded to the charity. It is only where moneys are going from the charitable institution to the commercial participator that the charitable institution could refuse to pay until the court has ordered it to do so or the agreement had been rectified so as to ensure that it complied with the prescribed requirements. It is difficult to envisage commercial circumstances where this provision could be of much use to charitable institutions.

Under reg 5, a commercial participator has to on request and at all reasonable times make available to any charitable institution which is a party to an agreement with the commercial participator any books, documents or other records however kept which relates to the institution and kept for the purposes of the agreement. These records have to be kept in legible form.

Under reg 6, any money due to the charitable institution from a commercial participator has to be paid over as soon as is reasonably practicable after its receipt and 'in any event not later than the expiration of 28 days after that receipt or such other period as may be agreed with the institution'.

Payment has to be made to the charitable institution or into a bank account controlled by it.

Breach of regs 5 and 6 are criminal offences which give rise to a maximum fine of £500 per offence (level 2 on the scale).

Although the protection afforded by the Regulations for charitable institutions contracting with commercial participators are considerable, none the less charitable institutions should also consider whether or not there are other clauses that should be inserted in such a contract to cover their positions. In particular, charities should consider the fact that licensing their name through a commercial organisation can give rise to a number of problems. The Charity Commissioners considered this in their 1991 report as follows:

'106. We also had an occasion to consider the use of charity names by commercial concerns. In our view, charities trustees should be wary of entering into arrangements whereby the charity's name is to be used by a commercial company in return for money. This might involve the endorsement of a commercial product by a charity or the use of the charity's name in relation to a commercial product. There are cases where a charity can properly associate with a commercial organisation to their mutual benefit, but care must be taken to protect the interests of the charity and to ensure that the relationship is, and remains, appropriate.

107. The charity's name is a valuable asset. It is the means by which it is identified in the central register of charities and to the public. Before allowing the use of a charity's name on a commercial basis, charity trustees must first consider the needs of a charity, and whether funds could be raised by other methods. The name of a charity must not be exploited for non-charitable purposes. If a charity's name is used commercially it must be shown that the arrangement is expedient, in the interests of the charity and on terms which are advantageous to the charity. Any such arrangement must be precisely defined by the charity trustees in every detail and kept under review. They must ensure that there is no misuse of the charity name nor any improper exploitation of its association

with a commercial organisation and that the arrangements made allow them to prevent any such misuse.'

A careful analysis reveals that this statement is less than helpful – at one point it states 'the name of the charity must not *be exploited for non-charitable purposes*' [my emphasis] but then states that a charity can use its name 'commercially' (which is surely a non-charitable use)! The regime introduced by the 1992 Act concerning commercial participators implies that a charity can lawfully licence its name and logo provided the safeguards laid down by the 1992 Act are complied with. Hence, it is submitted that the Charity Commissioners do not consider that a charity cannot exploit its name or logo commercially.

However well drafted the agreement may be, each charity which enters into arrangements whereby its name is to be associated with the goods and/or services provided by a third party needs to appreciate that there is a risk that the charity's name could be brought into disrepute through the activities of some members of the licensees' group of companies. Modern transnational companies have tentacles spread throughout many countries. The company with which a charity has a licensing arrangement in the UK may be involved in many different industries in many different countries of the world, and it is impossible for the charity to check adequately on the performance of all those companies prior to entering into any arrangement whereby the charity licences its name. Hence, the charity may take warranties from the licensee that, for example, in all companies controlled by it the licensee will ensure that all employees are employed on conditions which comply with the standards laid down by the International Labour Organisation. But such a clause will not give any solace to the cancer relief charity which suddenly discovers that its licensees' subsidiary in India is selling cigarettes!

Alternatively, there could be a sudden scandal about the company upon whose products the charity's logo appears, for example an environmental charity might have licensed its logo to Shell only to be overtaken by the publicity surrounding Ken Sarowiwa.

Nothing can be 100 per cent watertight in these circumstances and charities need to proceed with considerable caution. It is therefore suggested that where a charity is licensing its name, in addition to the requirements laid down by the Regulations, a charity could seek clauses such as:

(a) a warranty by the licensee that neither it nor any of its associated companies (ie subsidiaries or joint ventures) will at any time during the duration of the agreement do anything which could bring the reputation of the charity into disrepute;

(b) a termination clause allowing the charity to terminate the licence immediately should, in its opinion, its name be brought into disrepute or if the licensee is in a material breach of any of the terms of the agreement;

(c) a term relating to what happens to stock bearing the charity's logo in the event of early termination of the agreement due to its breach by the licensee;

(d) strict controls on the use of the charity's name and logo and recognition of its copyright.

A charity might also wish to seek other clauses such as:

(a) an agreement that the commercial participator will not enter into a similar arrangement with any other organisation operating in the same field as the charity for the duration of the agreement;

(b) an indemnity in respect of any losses or damage suffered by the charity as a result of any action by the commercial participator;

(c) an obligation on the commercial participator to segregate moneys due to the charitable institution in a separate bank account preferably marked with the name of the charity so that, should the commercial participator go into liquidation, the moneys in the account will be deemed to be trust moneys and not part of the general assets of the commercial participator available for distribution to the general body of its creditors.

Possible problems with s 59 agreements

13.4.2 Under s 59(2), the commercial participator has to have the charitable institution's consent before he can engage in a promotional venture in the course of which it is represented that charitable contributions will be given. An interesting question arises in terms of the tax treatment of any payment made by the commercial participator to a charity. This point does not apply to any payments made by a commercial participator to a benevolent or philanthropic institution because such organisations are not charities and do not enjoy the tax benefits available to charities. Will the payment received by the charity from a commercial participator be treated as an implied licence fee paid by the commercial participator to the charity for the use and exploitation of the charity's name?

One could take the example of a pen manufacturer, which encourages the public to buy its pens by saying that five per cent of the purchase price will be donated to a named charity. The charity's name and logo is used in connection with the marketing of the pen. Is the charity, therefore, engaged in a business of exploiting its name and logo commercially? If it is, then the receipts from that exploitation could be treated by the Inland Revenue as profits of a business which has not been carried on in fulfilment of the charity's main objects. If that is the case, the Inland Revenue will be entitled to levy corporation or income tax (depending on how the charity is constituted) upon those profits, under s 505 of the Income and Corporation Taxes Act 1988.

Similar problems have already arisen in connection with affinity cards. In these cases, the Inland Revenue has approved treating such income as Schedule D, Case III royalty income in the hands of charities. This is on the basis that the royalties will be paid under a legal obligation, will be annually recurring and will be pure income profit (as opposed to a licence fee).

However, if the agreement with the affinity card company covers more than use of the charity's name and logo, for example use of a mailing list, any payments will not be susceptible to being treated as pure income profit.

One method which has been adopted by charities to get round this problem is to appoint its trading subsidiary as its licensee to exploit the other commercial activities, for example mailing lists. The trading subsidiary negotiates with commercial partners for use of the mailing list, and payments are then made to the trading subsidiary in respect of those activities.

In addition, in relation to affinity cards, Customs & Excise were prepared to grant a concession whereby it treated four-fifths of the payment made to the charity by the affinity card company as a donation and only one-fifth of the payment as being a payment for services rendered by the charity and which thereby attracted VAT.

In the case of other forms of commercial relations with commercial participators, Customs & Excise have not been prepared to be so generous. In other words, the impact of VAT has to be considered on all arrangements whereby charities license their names to commercial participators. If the charitable institution's turnover exceeds £46,000 (1995 figure), it will be obligated to register for VAT and charge VAT on the licence fee and any other services that it renders to the commercial participator.

So far as direct taxation is concerned, the affinity cards precedent is useful but not conclusive. The nature of an affinity card contract is that it is long term – traditionally at least five years. Hence, the payments made by the affinity card company to the charity can be constructed as an annual payment, ie one that has the capacity of lasting at least one year. Annual payments are exempt from taxation in the hands of a charity under s 505 of the Income and Corporation Taxes Act 1988. However, many commercial promotions last for less than one year and therefore payments in this case are not capable of being constructed as annual payments. In addition, under many arrangements with commercial participators, charities are asked to do more than merely license their name. They are frequently asked to join in promotional and marketing activities or to make available to the commercial participator their database of supporters. If the charity undertakes any promotional activities or anything other than merely licensing its name, then any payment to it cannot qualify as an annual payment.

Hence, in those circumstances where the agreement with the commercial participator lasts less than one year or if joint promotional services are being rendered or the charity's database is being licensed, those services have to be undertaken by the charity's trading company. The charity's trading company will then license the charity's name and logo and database to the commercial participator and undertake the joint promotional activities. In that case, payments will then be made (plus VAT if appropriate) to the charity's trading company by the commercial participator, and the charity's trading company will in turn covenant its taxable profits or pay them up by way of gift aid to the charity hence avoiding direct taxation on its profits.

Fitting the need to comply with these requirements of taxation into the framework imposed by the Charities Act 1992 is not always easy.

Where the payment can qualify as an annual payment, then the agreement can be between the charity and the commercial participator as required by s 59(2) of the 1992 Act. The separate services (if required) of licensing the database or undertaking joint promotional activities should, even in this case, be undertaken by the trading company and a separate payment made to it for those services. Where the agreement with the commercial participator is not capable of being constructed as an annual payment, for example because it is only a one-off short-term promotion, then the agreement has to be constructed as a tri-partite agreement between the charity, its trading company and the commercial participator. In that case, the charity joins into the agreement so as to comply with the obligations of s 59 but with the agreement making it clear that all payments are made to the trading company.

It is also necessary to ensure that the trading company has the benefit of the provisions of reg 5 of the Regulations (the charity's right to inspect the books and records of the commercial participator) by having such a clause expressly included in the agreement.

There is also a possible problem under reg 6 of the Regulations (see above), as under that regulation a commercial participator has to 'unless he has a reasonable excuse' pay moneys due to the charitable institution to that institution 'as soon as is reasonably practicable after its receipt and in any event not later than the expiration of 28 days after that receipt or such other period as may be agreed with the Institution'.

In the case where payments are made to a charity's trading company, those moneys will usually be held until virtually the year end before any profits (if any) are paid out by Deed of Covenant or gift aid to the charity. In order to protect the commercial participator, it is suggested that the agreement between the trading company and the commercial participator should make it clear that the charity accepts that payments will be made by the commercial participator to the trading company and that the profits of the trading company are only paid up at certain specified intervals.

13.4.3 The rest of s 59 (which is discussed at **12.8**) applies to commercial participators just as it does to professional fund-raisers. Therefore, in summary, the position is as follows.

(a) A commercial participator who represents that charitable contributions will be made, without having entered into a s 59(2) agreement, can be restrained by injunction.

(b) If a charitable institution makes an agreement with a commercial participator but the agreement does not satisfy the prescribed requirements, the agreement is unenforceable unless a court orders that it is enforceable.

13.5 Section 60 Statements

13.5.1 Section 60(3) makes similar provisions, in terms of statements to be made by commercial participators, as s 60(1) and (2) makes for professional fund-raisers.

13.5.2 Section 60(3) provides that where any representation is made by a commercial participator to the effect that charitable contributions are to be given to or applied for the benefit of one or more particular charitable institutions the representation shall be accompanied by a statement clearly indicating:

'(a) the name or names of the institution or institutions concerned;
(b) if there is more than one institution concerned, the proportions in which the institutions are respectively to benefit; and
(c) (in general terms), the method by which it is to be determined –
    (i) what proportion of the consideration given for goods or services sold or supplied by him, or of any other proceeds of a promotional venture undertaken by him, is to be given to or applied for the benefit of the institution or institutions concerned; or
    (ii) what sums by way of donations by him in connection with the sale or supply of any such goods or services are to be so given or applied,
as the case may require.'

13.5.3 Section 60(3) requires that any representation made by a commercial participator has to be accompanied by a statement. A representation, as we have already seen, can be made expressly or impliedly and can be made by speaking directly or by means of a statement published in a newspaper, film, radio or television programme or otherwise. Whenever the representation is made, the statement has to accompany it. In the case of an oral representation, the statement has to be made at the same time or be visible; in the case of a newspaper advertisement, the advertisement must contain the statement. In shops, it will be sufficient that the statement is made by a clear and legible sign, provided it is readily visible when the representation is made.

13.5.4 As can be seen, there are two different ways in which the statement can be made 'as the case may require'. Unfortunately, s 60(3) is not satisfactorily worded.

The first possibility as the statement indicates:

'(in general terms) the method by which it is to be determined (i) what proportion of the consideration given etc.'

On close analysis this could be ludicrously easy to comply with.

Example

A high street retailer XYZ with its own brand of products decides to give 10p for each can of baked beans sold to ABC charity. The statement required under s 60(3)(c)(i) could be as general as:

The directors of XYZ shall meet each year in the Ritz Hotel to decide what proportion of the price paid for this can of beans will be given to ABC charity, a registered charity.

Such a statement does indicate in (*general terms*) the *method* by which it is to be determined what proportion of the price of the can of beans will be given to ABC charity! Obviously, this is ridiculous. But it illustrates one of the problems with the drafting of this subsection of the Act. Charitable institutions negotiating arrangements with commercial participators should be advised to ignore completely the statement 'in general terms the method by which it is to be determined' if possible, and seek to ensure that the statement clearly indicates what proportion the consideration given for the goods or services sold will be given to the charitable institution concerned.

This view is substantiated by the Home Office in their publication *Charitable Fund-raising: Professional and Commercial Involvement* (February 1995) at p 5 where it is stated:

'We strongly recommend that in the case of commercial participation . . . or similar activities by charitable institutions or their connected companies not subject to Part II, that the exact amount going to charitable institutions is given in the statement, expressed *net* (ie after deduction of all expenses, costs etc); for example, "*X% of the purchase price goes to charity Y*" or "*£X per item sold goes . . . etc*". Where this cannot be stated exactly then a reasonable alternative is recommended, such as "*a minimum X% . . . etc*", or "*it is estimated that X% . . . etc*" provided this is a reasonable statement to make and meets the requirements of the law in the particular circumstances of the case.

We recommend that only where no such statement can meaningfully be made should a percentage be expressed as a gross figure. In such a case it is most important that attention is drawn in the statement to the significance of that fact, ie that further expenses will have to be paid, reducing the benefit that the charitable institution will receive from the donation.'

The Home Office recommendations seek to deal with the problem thrown up by the phrase '(in general terms) the method by which it is to be determined etc'. The Home Office recommendations go beyond the express letter of the law in requiring rather more precise statements. However, it should also be borne in mind that at times it is very difficult for commercial participators to make precise statements as to what proportion of the price paid will go to the charity because of the complexities of particular commercial arrangements.

The second method of making the required statement under s 60(3)(c) is to state '(in general terms) the method by which it is to be determined … what sums by way of donation' by the commercial participator in connection with the sale or supply of such goods are to be given. The best and most easy example of this is a trading company owned by a charity. In this case, the statement could be '100% of the taxable profits of XYZ Trading Limited are given each year by Deed of Covenant to XYZ Charity a registered charity'.

Such a statement is not strictly necessary in any event because of the exemptions from the controls for companies controlled by a charitable institution (see **13.3.1**). However, as already noted (see **13.3.1**) the Home Office recommends that charities do make such a statement. Another example would be where a commercial participator states 'ABC Corporation has agreed to give £50,000 to XYZ Charity, a registered charity. Each purchase you make helps ABC reach that target'.

Such a statement clearly gives the information of what sum (by way of donation) by the commercial participator is to be made in connection with the sale or supply of the goods in question.

13.5.5 Who is the commercial participator? Problems can arise as to who precisely is the commercial participator. Not all arrangements are as simple as where a retailer itself enters directly into an agreement with a charitable institution that a product will be sold with a representation that part of the proceeds will go to the institution. Suppose the manufacturer or producer of goods initiates the principal agreement with the charitable institution and then supplies the products to many different retailers. The items in question will bear the charitable institution's logo; does this make the retailer an implied commercial participator given the breadth of the definition 'to represent' contained in s 58(5)? In such cases, it is helpful to ensure that any statement included on the product clearly identifies the producer as opposed to the retailer as being the commercial participator. None the less, as the Home Office comments in *Charitable Fund-raising: Professional and Commercial Involvement* at p 11:

> 'However statements declaring retailers not to be commercial participator should be approached with caution; the producer is unable to prevent the retailer making himself a commercial participator by making a relevant representation, and such a declaration may give unjustified reassurance.'

However, it is unlikely that the retailer will make any representation that part of the proceeds of sale received by him will be paid to the charitable institution, and, if he does, then that will make him a commercial participator and, unless he has an agreement under s 59(2), he will be acting unlawfully.

The sale of Christmas cards

13.5.6 Section 58(6) defines 'to represent' in such a wide way that the high street retailer which sells Christmas cards which bear the emblem 'sold in aid of XYZ Charity' will almost certainly be construed as being a commercial participator. The retailer is carrying on a commercial business selling cards in the course of which it is impliedly representing that part of the proceeds will go to XYZ Charity. The average consumer who buys such a Christmas card will assume that part of the proceeds of sale will go to XYZ Charity as a result of the statement printed on the card. Hence, in theory, the retailer will need to have a s 59 agreement and make the statement under s 60(3). So far so easy. In reality, the position is far more complicated. The high street retailer will not in many cases pay a penny to XYZ Charity despite the statement on the card!

In fact, XYZ Charity will probably set up a trading company, XYZ Trading Limited to carry out the sale of Christmas cards. XYZ Charity will have licensed XYZ Trading Limited to use the charity's name on the card. XYZ Trading Limited will then have sold the cards to a wholesaler. XYZ Trading Limited will, hopefully, have made a profit on that transaction. After deductions of all expenses etc, XYZ Trading Limited will covenant its profits to XYZ Charity or give them by gift aid. In that very limited sense, the cards are sold in aid of XYZ Charity. The wholesaler will then sell the cards either outright or on a sale or return basis to a retailer which will then seek to sell them to the public. Hence, whilst a high street retailer would appear to be a commercial participator, in fact, it is not because it is not paying any part of the proceeds of sale of the Christmas card to a charitable institution, although it is impliedly representing that it is!

The high street retailer will need to make it very clear that it is not a commercial participator. It will not, however, want to put up a statement to the effect that:

> Not a single penny from the sale of these charity Christmas cards is paid by this company to any of the named charities!

That would be commercially disastrous. Instead, it will want a more bland statement probably to appear on the Christmas card itself (or packet if the cards are sold in packets) such as:

> These cards were sold by XYZ Trading Limited which covenants all its taxable profits to XYZ Charity a registered charity. XYZ Trading Limited took its profits on the sale of this card at that point. All subsequent sellers of this card are not commercial participators for the purposes of Part II of the Charities Act 1992.

Inevitably, there will be old but as yet unsold stock in circulation printed prior to the legislation coming into effect. Consequently, a statement may have to be put up in shops so as to ensure that the representation made by the sale of a Christmas card which states 'sold in aid of XYZ Charity' is accompanied by the statement required by s 60(3), which in this case would be a statement to the effect that the subsection does not apply.

13.5.7 As stated above at **13.4.2**, it may well be necessary for charities' trading companies to be involved in relationships with commercial participators. In this case, the statement that will have to be made to comply with s 60(3) will be, for example:

> Xp per item is paid to XYZ Trading Limited which covenants all its taxable profits to XYZ a registered charity.

This statement is the best that can be made in order to comply with the spirit of the 1992 Act and to ensure that the charity's affairs are structured in the most tax-efficient manner. There must be an argument as to whether or not a payment made to a trading company is, to quote s 60(3)(c)(i) 'given to or applied for the benefit of the institution or institutions concerned'. The best argument is that the payment being made to the trading company is 'applied for the benefit of the institution' since the trading company covenants its profits to the charity.

13.5.8 All of the problems noted in this section concerning direct taxation only apply to charities. In the case of a charitable institution which is not a charity, ie a benevolent or philanthropic institution, it does not enjoy the benefits of exemption from tax accorded to charities. Income that it receives from licensing its name will be taxable and there is no point in using a trading company. Consequently, in the case of benevolent or philanthropic organisations, there can be straightforward arrangements between the organisation itself and the commercial participator to comply with the 1992 Act.

Examples of a s 60(3) statement

(a) *In a shop*

> Five per cent of the retail price of this bottle will be given to XYZ charity.

> [*or*]

> In respect of each bottle sold, five pence will be paid to XYZ charity.

(b) *A statement made on radio or TV – sale of goods, for example a lawnmower*

> Five per cent of the price you pay for your lawnmower will be given to XYZ charity. If you pay for goods which cost more than £50 by credit or debit card you have the right to cancel your purchase within seven days of this broadcast.★

NOTE
★ By s 60(4), if a representation under s 60(3) is made in the course of a radio or television programme and payment can be made by credit or debit card, the broadcast has to include details of the right to cancel under s 61(1). In the case of goods purchased by virtue of s 61(4)(b), any right to cancel and have a refund paid is conditional upon restitution being made by the purchaser of the goods in question.

Telephone sales

If a representation under s 60(3) is made by telephone, the commercial participator is obliged, within seven days of any payment of £50 or more to the commercial participator, to give any person making a payment in response to the telephone appeal the s 60(3) statement and details of the right to cancel under s 61(2) (see **12.9.7**).

13.6 Criminal Sanctions

Just as the professional fund-raiser who breaches s 60(1) to (5) is guilty of a criminal offence, so also is the commercial participator with a maximum fine of £5,000 per offence. The same points concerning the criminal sanctions for breaching s 60 which applied to professional fund-raisers, also apply to commercial participators (see **12.9.11**).

13.7 Quasi Commercial Participators

One of the anomalies in Part II of the 1992 Act is that the controls on commercial participators only apply if the commercial participator claims that part of the proceeds of sale of goods or services will go to a named charitable institution. There are no controls in the Act itself on a commercial party which seeks to sell goods or services coupled with the inducement that part of the proceeds will go to a general charitable cause, for example 'to relieve poverty in the Third World'. This was different from the position in relation to professional fund-raisers (see **12.9.2**).

Despite this oversight in primary legislation, the Charitable Institutions (Control of Fund-raising) Regulations 1994 seek to control such activities. Regulation 7 applies to 'any person who carries on for gain a business other than a fundraising business' and who 'engages in any promotional venture in the course of which it is represented that charitable contributions are to be applied for charitable, benevolent or philanthropic purposes of any description (rather than for the benefit of one or more particular charitable institutions)'. For the purposes of this book, such persons are called quasi commercial participators.

For example, the owner of a pizza restaurant states '£1 per pizza will be sent to the victims of the Japanese earthquake'. In these circumstances, by reg 7(2) the quasi commercial participator has to ensure that the representation is accompanied by a statement clearly indicating:

(a) the fact that charitable contributions are to be applied for those purposes and not for the benefit of any particular charitable institution; and
(b) (in general terms), a statement identical to that required under s 60(3) (see **13.5**), although in this case the statement is in relation to the charitable purposes rather than a charitable institution and the method by which it is to be determined, and how the charitable contributions are to be distributed between different charitable institutions.

Example of a statement under reg 7(2):

> £1 per pizza sold will be applied for the benefit of children in Bosnia and not for the benefit of a particular charitable institution. The proprietor of the restaurant will decide which charitable institutions will be supported.

Breach of reg 7(2) is a criminal offence but as this is laid down by statutory instrument and not by primary legislation the maximum fine is £500.

13.8 Right of Charitable Institutions to Prevent Unauthorised Fund-raising

As mentioned at **12.2.2**, the Woodfield Report and the White Paper both considered that there should be some mechanism for charities to prevent unauthorised fund-raising being carried on in their name. This is reflected in s 62 of the 1992 Act, which applies not only to charities but to charitable institutions.

By s 62(1), where the court (ie the High Court or county court) is satisfied that any person has, or is, either soliciting money or other property for the benefit of a charitable institution or representing that charitable contributions are to be given, and that unless restrained he is likely to do further acts of that nature, if the court is satisfied as to one or more of the matters set out in s 62(2) it may grant an injunction restraining the unauthorised fund-raising.

The charitable institution has to establish, to the court's satisfaction, one or more of the following under s 62(2):

(a) that the person in question is using methods of fund-raising to which the institution objects;
(b) that that person is not a fit and proper person to raise funds for the institution; and
(c) in the case where it is represented that charitable contributions (as defined in s 58(1)) are to be given, that the institution does not wish to be associated with the particular promotional or other fund-raising venture in which that person is engaged.

Before the charitable institution can obtain an injunction it must have given not less than 28 days' notice in writing to the person in question. The notice must request him to cease forthwith and state that if he does not comply with the notice the institution will make an application for an injunction. The form of the notice may be prescribed by regulations to be issued under s 64(2).

To help charitable institutions which may be plagued by unauthorised fund-raisers, where a charitable institution has given the 28-day notice under s 62(3), but the person, having initially complied with the notice, subsequently begins to carry on the same activities, the charitable institution can immediately apply for an injunction without having to serve a further notice. This only applies if the application for the injunction is made not more than 12 months after the date of service of the relevant notice upon the fund-raiser. Service can be effected by complying with s 76 of the 1992 Act. (For further details, see **12.9.9.**)

13.9 Section 63

Criminal offences

Section 63 makes it a criminal offence for a person who is representing that an institution is a registered charity to solicit money or other property for the benefit of that institution when it is not a registered charity.

Therefore, for example, it would be a criminal offence under s 63 for a person to solicit money on behalf of Eton coupled with the representation that Eton is a registered charity. Eton is not a registered charity, although it is a charity which is exempt from registration. Equally, it would be a criminal offence for a person to solicit money on behalf of the Girl Guides together with a representation that the Girl Guides are a registered charity. The Girl Guides are an excepted charity, ie excepted from registration and are, therefore, not registered. These fine distinctions may be lost on fund-raisers, particularly in the case of such charities as the Girl Guides, Boy Scouts and other excepted charities.

The maximum fine that can be imposed under this section is currently £5,000.

13.10 Section 75

This applies to Part II and Part III of the Charities Act 1992, ie those matters dealt with in Chapters 12, 13 and 14 of this book. Under this section, where any offence under the Charities Act 1992 is committed by a body corporate and is proved to have been committed with the consent or connivance of, or to be attributable to any neglect on the part of, any director, manager, secretary or other similar officer of the body corporate, or any person who was purporting to act in any such capacity, he as well as the body corporate shall be guilty of that offence and shall be liable to be proceeded against and be punished accordingly.

Such section appears in a number of Acts of Parliament (including, for example, the House to House Collections Act 1939) but there have been very few cases to elucidate the meaning of such a section. For example, does a director of a corporation have to have actual knowledge in order to have consented or is implied knowledge sufficient? The existence of this section in relation to Part II means that potentially if, for example, a company which was a commercial participator acted in breach of Part II then possibly the directors of that company could also be made personally liable under s 75.

CHAPTER 14

PUBLIC CHARITABLE COLLECTIONS: CURRENT CONTROLS AND PART III OF THE 1992 ACT

Background – Static Collecting Boxes – The Existing Law: House to House Collections – Street Collections – The 1992 Reforms – Definition of Public Place – Exceptions to the Public Place Definition – Charitable Appeals – Controls on Public Charitable Collections – Obtaining a Local Authority Permit – Section 68 Permits: Conditions – Appeal Against Conditions Contained in a Permit – Refusal of a Local Authority Permit – Appeal Against Refusal to Grant a Permit – Withdrawal of a Local Authority Permit – Criminal Offences – Section 72 Orders – Conclusion

14.1 Background

Charitable fund-raising by street and house to house collections prior to implementation of the relevant parts of the Charities Act 1992 and its Regulations will continue to be controlled by s 5 of the Police, Factories, etc (Miscellaneous Provisions) Act 1916 and the House to House Collections Act 1939 (both amended by the Local Government Act 1972). Both Acts involve the issue of licences or permits by district councils, the Metropolitan Police or the Common Council of the City of London. Both Acts contain detailed regulations covering the conduct of collections with submission of accounts and so forth.

Oddly, there are significant differences between the two pieces of legislation and the associated regulations. The Woodfield Report saw no reason why the two types of collections should be regulated differently. The White Paper endorsed this and proposed combing the provisions in a single piece of legislation, under the umbrella of 'public charitable collections' to be accompanied by standard regulations applicable throughout England and Wales. Part III of the 1992 Act will do this when implemented.

Schedule 7 to the 1992 Act will repeal most of the old legislation. Section 5 of the 1916 Act and all of the 1939 Act will be repealed, although the 1916 Act will still apply in Northern Ireland as will the House to House Collections Act (Northern Ireland) 1953.

The 1992 legislation has been subject to a number of criticisms with the result that it has not yet been implemented. Consequently, the pre-1992 law is still in operation and this chapter therefore considers both the current law and the 1992 reforms. The Home Office is aiming to bring Part III of the Act finally into force in June 1998 following further public consultation.

14.2 Static Collecting Boxes

The 1992 Act does not extend the controls on public charitable collections to static collecting boxes found in shops, public houses or elsewhere – which is made clear by s 65(2)(c). This caused some concern in the debate at the committee stage. The Government responded that the amount of money collected by static collection boxes was usually relatively small and such collections did not have the potential to cause inconvenience to the public. The Government clearly hopes that a code of practice on static collecting boxes covering the kinds of container to be used, the appointment of an individual as responsible for each container and the identification to be carried by a static box, will be sufficient to deal with such problems as they arise. The Institute of Charity Fundraising Managers has produced a guidance note on the management of static collecting boxes.

In addition, the Charity Commissioners do have the power to transfer abandoned funds to the official custodian for safekeeping while an inquiry is underway. This function of the official custodian will continue.

14.3　The Existing Law: House to House Collections

14.3.1　The House to House Collections Act 1939 provides for a system of licensing and regulation for door-to-door fund-raising activities. With very few exceptions, the Act requires that any one who promotes a house to house collection for any charitable purpose must hold a licence.

Definitions

14.3.2　Under s 11 of the 1939 Act 'a promoter' is a person who causes other persons to act, whether for remuneration or otherwise as collectors for the purpose of the collection. 'Collection' means an appeal to the public made by means of visits from house to house, to give, whether for consideration or not, money or other property. The sale of goods or the solicitation of jumble falls within this definition. 'House' includes a place of business such as a public house. 'Charitable purpose' means any charitable, benevolent or philanthropic purpose whether or not charitable within the meaning of any rule of law (see **12.4**). A 'collector' is a person who makes the appeal in the course of such visits.

Obtaining a licence

14.3.3　The promoter (but not the collector) of a house to house collection is required to obtain a licence from the relevant authority. An application has to be made to the appropriate authority and must specify the purpose of the collection and the locality (whether the whole of an area or part of it) within which the collection is to be made. The licensing authority is the Common Council of the City of London; in the Metropolitan Police District, the Commissioner of Police for the Metropolis; and elsewhere, the local district council. Application must be made in the prescribed manner and in the form specified in the House to House Collections Regulations 1947.

Notably, there is no legal duty for anyone to inform the charity or receive its permission to collect. Sir Philip Woodfield's report recommended that any house to house collection should have the prior permission of the charity concerned. This is dealt with to some degree in s 62 of the 1992 Act (see **13.8**).

Collections which take place in one 'house' only are outside the 1939 Act.

The licence can be granted for such period as the licensing authority authorises, up to a maximum of 12 months. If it appears expedient to the licensing authority, it may grant a licence for up to 18 months.

Refusal or revocation of a licence

14.3.4 A licensing authority may refuse to grant a licence or revoke an existing one, if it appears to them that:

(a) the total amount likely to be applied for charitable purposes as a result of the collection, including any amount already so applied, is inadequate in proportion to the value of the proceeds likely to be or already received;

(b) remuneration is excessive in relation to the total amount which is likely to be or has been retained out of the proceeds of the collection by any person;

(c) the grant of a licence would facilitate an offence of begging or that such an offence has been committed in connection with the collection;

(d) the applicant or licensee is not a fit and proper person to hold a licence by reason of conviction for certain offences;

(e) the applicant or licensee has failed in promoting a licensed collection to exercise due diligence to secure that persons authorised by him to act as collectors were fit and proper persons, to secure the compliance of persons so authorised with the regulations under the House to House Collections Act 1939, or to prevent prescribed badges or certificates being obtained by unauthorised persons;

(f) the applicant or licensee has refused or neglected to furnish the authority with such information as it has reasonably required.

14.3.5 When refusing or revoking a licence, the licensing authority must give written notice to the applicant or licensee, stating the grounds for refusal or revocation and informing him of his right to an appeal. Appeals may be made to the Secretary of State within 14 days of the notice. The Secretary of State's decision is final. If an appeal is allowed, the authority must forthwith issue or restore the licence (s 2(6) of the 1939 Act).

Exemptions from the licence requirements

14.3.6 There are two possible exemptions from the requirement to obtain a licence.

First, under s 1(4) of the 1939 Act, a local exemption certificate may be granted by the chief officer of police for the proposed collection area where he is satisfied that the purpose of the collection is local in character and will be completed in a short time. The exemption is given to the person who appears to be principally concerned in the promotion of the collection. This means that a licence is not required but other requirements still apply, such as those referring to misuse of badges by collectors. The use of these exemption permits vary from area to area but possibly as many as 5,000 such approvals are given each year in London, mainly for Christmas carol collections. Secondly, under s 3, if the Home Secretary is satisfied that a promoter is pursuing a charitable purpose throughout the whole or a substantial part of England and Wales he may make an order granting an exemption from the need to obtain a licence for collections in specific localities described in the order. It is normally considered appropriate for the head of fund-raising of the organisation to make the application.

Such an order allows national charitable, benevolent or philanthropic organisations who have obtained an order to carry out house to house collections across the country without individual licences for each collection. However, this section has been construed very narrowly and exemption orders have been rare and strictly controlled. In July 1994 there were 46 such orders. There have been some complaints by local authorities and local charities of excessive collecting, out of local control, by exemption order holders.

Applications for an exemption certificate are made to the Voluntary Service Unit, Home Office, Room 1382, 50 Queen Anne's Gate, London SW1H 9AT. A promoter who promotes a collection without proper authority under the licensing system commits a criminal offence under s 1(2) of the 1939 Act and is liable on summary conviction to a maximum penalty of six months' imprisonment or a maximum fine of £5,000.

14.3.7 Any person who contravenes or fails to comply with the provisions of the House to House Collections Regulations 1947 and the House to House Collections Regulations 1963 is guilty of an offence under s 4(3) of the 1939 Act and liable on summary conviction to a fine not exceeding £200.

An offence is committed by any person who displays or uses:

(a) a prescribed badge or certificate of authority which is not held for the purposes of the appeal pursuant to regulations made under the 1939 Act; or
(b) any badge or device or certificate or other document which is almost a copy of a prescribed badge or certificate of authority as to be calculated to deceive.

The expression 'calculated to deceive' has been held to mean 'likely to deceive', see *R v Davidson* (1972) 3 All ER 1121. Any person guilty of an offence under this section is liable on summary conviction to imprisonment for a term not exceeding six months or a fine not exceeding £1,000 or both (s 8(4)).

A police constable may require any person whom he believes to be acting as a collector for the purposes of a collection for a charitable purpose to declare to him immediately his name and address and to sign his name, and if any person fails to comply with that requirement he shall be guilty of an offence for which on summary conviction has a fine not exceeding £200.

Knowingly or recklessly making a false statement when furnishing any information for the purposes of the 1939 Act is an offence and any person guilty of this is liable on summary conviction to imprisonment for a term not exceeding six months or to a fine not exceeding £1,000 or both (s 8(6)).

Under s 8(7), where an offence under the 1939 Act is committed by a corporation and is proved to have been committed with the consent or connivance of, or to be attributable to any culpable neglect of duty on the part of any director, manager, secretary or other officer of the corporation, he as well as the corporation shall be deemed to be guilty of that offence and shall be liable to be proceeded against and punished accordingly. It seems that trustees of an organisation are 'officers' and therefore trustees of charitable, benevolent or philanthropic organisations which are established as corporations (whether limited liability companies, established by Royal Charter, industrial and provident societies or statutory corporations) and could be proceeded against personally under this section.

Conduct of house to house collections

14.3.8 A promoter must provide collectors with a certificate of authority and badges. A sealed collecting box or receipt book is required if money is collected. The promoter has a general duty of due diligence and this includes ensuring that all collectors are fit and proper persons and that all certificates of authority and badges are destroyed when no longer required.

In *Tesco Supermarkets v Nattrass* [1971] 2 All ER 127, Lord Diplock said, 'to exercise due diligence to prevent something from being done is to take all reasonable steps to prevent it' (see **12.9.11**).

A collector must be at least 16 years of age. He or she must sign the certificate of authority and badge, wear the badge during collections and produce the certificate on demand returning both to the promoter on completion of the collection.

The sealed collection boxes and receipt books along with the moneys collected must be passed to the promoter on completion. Collection boxes must be opened in the presence of the promoter and one other responsible person or by a bank official.

No collector is allowed to importune any person to the annoyance of such person or remain at the door of any house if requested to leave by any occupant (reg 9). The word 'annoyance' is construed more widely than negligence and includes anything which disturbs the sensible ordinary English inhabitant's reasonable peace of mind!

It is considered that many promoters are somewhat lax in exercising their duty of due diligence to ensure that all collectors are fit and proper persons in accordance with the regulations. The Charity Commissioners have criticised the recruitment of collectors by unsolicited telephone calls made at random and without any checks to see if the individual is a fit and proper person to conduct a collection, not least because the level of managerial and financial control is often inadequate (see the report of the Charity Commissioners for 1992 at para 97).

Accounts

14.3.9 The Regulations set out the forms of account required for collections. Accounts in prescribed form must be sent to the licensing authority within one month of the expiration date of the licence and must be audited. Where an exemption order has been made, accounts must be made on a yearly basis to the Secretary of State.

14.4 Street Collections

Street collections are often confused with house to house collections but from the legal point of view they are quite distinct, although there may well be an overlap, for example in relation to accounts.

14.4.1 The activities of collecting money or selling goods for the benefit of charitable or other purposes in any street or public place are still governed by s 5 of the Police, Factories, etc (Miscellaneous Provisions) Act 1916 as amended by s 251 of the Local Government Act 1972. This Act allows regulations for street collections to be made by the Common Council of the City of London, the Commissioner for the Metropolitan Police District and district councils. A model for local regulations is contained in the Charitable Collections (Transitional Provisions) Order 1974, although it is not obligatory on local authorities to introduce such a system of licensing in each area. Regulations do not come into operation until they have been confirmed by the Secretary of State and published for such time and in such manner as the Secretary of State may direct. They do not apply to the selling of articles in any street or public place when they are sold in the ordinary course of trade and for the purposes of earning a livelihood, and no representation is made by or on behalf of the seller that any part of the proceeds will be devoted to any charitable purpose. Note that if regulations based upon the model contained in the Charitable Collections (Transitional Provisions) Order 1974 are adopted, they do not require confirmation by the Secretary of State.

14.4.2 Street collections are any collections made in any street or public place. 'Street' according to s 5(4) of the 1916 Act includes 'any highway and any public bridge, road, lane, footway, square, court, alley or passage whether a thoroughfare or not'. 'Public place' is not defined although according to case-law it has been held that a public place is a place where members of the public go even when they may have no legal right to do so or when they are invited to go, for example a private field which members of the public were invited to use to watch point-to-point races; *R v Collinson* (1931) 75 SJ 491.

14.4.3 There is no equivalent to the national exemption order for house to house collections available for street collections.

Street collections in London are regulated by the Street Collections (Metropolitan Police District) Regulations 1979. Any person in contravention is liable to a fine. According to reg 2, no collection may be made in any street or public place unless the persons responsible have obtained a permit.

14.4.4 Regulation 5(1) stipulates that the application for a permit must be written in the prescribed form and made no later than the first day of the month preceding the month proposed for the collection. The application must be made by a body consisting of not less than three members jointly responsible for the collection (reg 5(2)).

14.4.5 The permit must specify the hours and date of the collection. All taking part in the collection must have written authority from the chief promoter which must be produced on the request of any constable.

14.4.6 Other regulations state that the collector must remain stationary, that a collector or two collectors together shall not be nearer to another collector than 25 metres and that no collection shall be made in a manner likely to inconvenience or annoy any person. Collectors must be over 16 years of age, must not receive any payment and may not be accompanied by an animal. Under reg 13, the Commissioner in some cases may authorise persons as young as 14 years of age to act as collectors if accompanied at all times by a responsible adult.

14.4.7 Collectors must have numbered and securely sealed collecting boxes bearing the name of the charity or fund for which a collection is being made and these must be delivered unopened to the promoter following the collection. Collecting boxes must be opened in the presence of the promoter and one other responsible person such as a bank official.

14.4.8 Within three months after the collection date, the promoter must forward to the authority a statement of receipt and expenditure certified by two persons responsible for the collection and a qualified accountant.

14.5 The 1992 Reforms

What is a public charitable collection?

14.5.1 When the Bill was first published there was an outcry from the voluntary sector because the definition of a public charitable collection was so wide that it would have encompassed coffee mornings and jumble sales.

14.5.2 As Earl Ferrers said at the committee stage of the Bill:

'During the debate on Second Reading a number of members of the Committee expressed anxiety that the scope of the definition of public place cast the net of regulation too wide. It was argued that the Bill would require charity shops to have a permit in order to be able to trade and that permits might also be necessary for coffee mornings in private houses. I undertook to consider the drafting of the Bill in order to ensure that inappropriate regulations such as this were not imposed by the Bill … The amendments will ensure that the Bill will regulate collections that are taken in places which, although technically private, are for many purposes, including access by members of the public, no different to purely public places. I have in mind the forecourts of railway stations and privately owned shopping centres. Such places can be lucrative sites for public collections.' (Public Bill Committee, Sixth Sitting, col 243 (11 December 1992).)

14.5.3 A public charitable collection means a charitable appeal which is made (s 65(1)(a)):

'(i) in any public place, or
(ii) by means of visits from house to house.'

14.6 Definition of Public Place

A public place is defined (s 65(8)) as:

'(a) any highway; and
(b) … any other place to which at any time when the appeal is made, members of the public have or are permitted to have access and which is either –
      (i) not within a building; or
      (ii) if within a building, is a public area within any station, airport or shopping precinct or any other similar public area.'

As Earl Ferrers stated (see **14.5.2**), s 65(8)(b) is designed to cover railway stations and shopping precincts, etc. Lord Swinfen was most concerned about the phrase 'or any other similar public area' and introduced a probing amendment on the report stage of the Bill to ascertain what the phrase meant.

Viscount Astor responded:

'In general terms the answer to my noble friend's first question is that the words in sub-section (7) of Section 65 [now s 65(8)] are designed to ensure that collections in places which are buildings but to which the public has already access are regulated by Part III of the Bill. These places include railway stations, airports or ports for ferries to which the public has access without the need for a ticket, covered and uncovered shopping precincts and so on. Places such as the interiors of shops or theatres would certainly be excluded.

As to the question of who will know whether an area is similar or not I think that the specific examples in sub-section (7) [now (8)] of the public areas within a station, airport or shopping precinct sufficiently indicate the types of areas which fall within sub-section (7)(b)(ii) [now subsection (8)(b)(ii)]. The characteristics of these areas are that, even though they are within buildings and not privately owned, the public has unrestricted access for much of the day.

It will of course be for the local authority to judge in the first instance whether the proposed site for a public collection falls within the scope of the sub-section.' (HL Deb, Vol 535, col 1231 (18 February 1992).)

The prospect of licensing collections on private land has raised the question of what steps will be necessary to co-ordinate effectively between local authorities, applicants for permits and the owners/occupiers of the premises involved.

14.7 Exceptions to the Public Place Definition

14.7.1 The definition of public place excludes, by implication, any building, except for public areas such as stations, etc. Hence, collections in hospitals, schools or offices are not public charitable collections. An interesting question arises with public houses. Presumably, a collection within one public house is not a public charitable collection but moving from one pub to another would be.

14.7.2 By s 65(9), the definition of public place does not apply to:

'(a) any place to which members of the public are permitted to have access only if any payment or ticket required as a condition of access has been made or purchased [eg a jumble sale]; or

(b) to any place to which members of the public are permitted to have access only by virtue of permission given for the purposes of the appeal in question [eg a coffee morning].'

14.7.3 Collections in a churchyard or in the course of a public meeting are excluded (s 65(2)).

In January 1996, the Home Office Voluntary Services Unit and the Charity Commission issued *Public Charitable Collections: Response to the Consultation*, and this noted that 60 per cent of those questioned favoured extension of licences to private places 'that are in effect public'. Some local authorities said they would demand evidence of the landowner's approval before granting a public collection licence.

14.8 Charitable Appeals

14.8.1 A charitable appeal is defined (s 65(1)(b)) as an appeal to members of the public to give money or other property (whether for consideration or otherwise) which is made in association with a representation that the whole or any part of its proceeds is to be applied for charitable, benevolent or philanthropic purposes (see **12.4**).

14.8.2 The definition covers not only the donation of money but also property. This means that collections of jumble, books, newspapers, stamps, old clothes or milk bottle tops will be charitable appeals if it is stated that the whole or any part of the proceeds is to be applied for charitable, etc, purposes. This is not a change from the current law so far as house to house collections are concerned, as the 1939 Act applies to collections for money 'or other property'.

14.8.3 A charitable appeal can also take place if goods or services are offered for sale or to be supplied in any public place or by means of visits from house to house and is coupled with a representation that the whole or any part of the proceeds of sale is to be applied for charitable, benevolent or philanthropic purposes (s 65(7)). Hence, the itinerant salespersons going from door to door, selling goods made by handicapped people for the purposes of selling those goods to benefit a charity for the handicapped, will be conducting a public charitable collection. Again, this is not different from the position under the 1939 Act which covered the sale of goods conducted from house to house in order to raise money for charities or benevolent or philanthropic organisations.

14.9 Controls on Public Charitable Collections

14.9.1 Under s 66(1) no public charitable collection shall be conducted in the area of any local authority except in accordance with:

(a) a permit issued by the authority under s 68; or
(b) an order made by the Charity Commissioners under s 72.

For these purposes, a local authority means a District Council or a London borough, the Common Council of the City of London or the Council of the Isles of Scilly. The promoter of any public charitable collection which is conducted in breach of s 66(1) shall be guilty of a criminal offence and liable on conviction to a fine not exceeding £2,500.

This is a major change so far as London is concerned. Hitherto, the Metropolitan Police has been the licensing authority, which role will be taken over by the 37 London Boroughs if Part III of the 1992 Act is brought into force. This is one of the key criticisms of the 1992 reforms. Many charities have expressed concerns about increased numbers of applications that would be needed for London-wide collections, and local authorities have also expressed concerns about making the necessary amendments locally and whether some form of central administration could be continued.

An Opposition amendment was debated but withdrawn during the Lords committee stage of the Deregulation and Contracting Out Act on 29 June 1994, proposing that Part III be amended to place responsibility for the licensing of collections in London (back) with the Metropolitan Police. The consultation response (see **14.7.2**) found a clear wish for a single point of application in London. The second major change is that all major charitable collections will require a licence, in contrast to the current position whereby, under s 1(4) of the House to House Collections Act 1939, the police may approve a temporary, local, house to house collection outside normal licensing controls (see **14.3.6**). In addition, a minority of local authorities do not apply a licensing regime for street collections at present, whereas if the 1992 Act is implemented, all local authorities will be required to implement the licensing system. The consultation response (see **14.7.3**) revealed a balance in favour of ending the police power to grant exemptions from control for small local house to house collections. If the exemption *is* removed, further thought needs to be given to small-scale collections such as for example carol singing door to door and 'bob-a-job' week.

14.9.2 Section 66(1) states that no public charitable collection can take place without either a local authority permit or a Charity Commissioner's order. In view of the wide definition of public charitable appeal, Lord Allen of Abbeydale made strenuous attempts for local authorities to be given the power to waive these requirements in certain cases. As he commented at the report stage of the Bill:

> 'People undertaking all kinds of collections, whether for funds or goods, are required under the Bill to obtain licences. It seems that that could include people who call around to collect for a jumble sale for charity, groups singing carols for children's charities or scouts for washing parked cars to raise funds. They could face the threat of criminal sanctions if no licence is obtained. It may be worth noting that the DPP's consent would not be required ... The wording of the amendment may be susceptible to improvement but there is a case for giving some discretion over the need for permits for fund-raising activities. The Secretary of State should have the ability, perhaps after a more detailed consultation than has so far been possible with local authorities and voluntary organisations to prescribe circumstances under which some of the requirements for permits might be waived.' (HL Deb, Vol 535, col 1232 (18 February 1992).)

For the Government, Earl Ferrers commented:

> '... there is a balance to be struck here between public accountability and private inconvenience. I do not think that the need to obtain a permit is an onerous one for small local groups. They are collecting from local people, and I see no reason why they should not be accountable locally for the moneys which they raise.
>
> The noble Lord, Lord Allen of Abbeydale, referred to jumble sales. He said people are always conducting house to house jumble collections. That is perfectly true and bags are left outside people's houses and people are invited to put all kinds of things in the bags which have to be sold for the benefit of the charity involved. A rag-and-bone merchant may then sell the items collected on behalf of a charity. However, a rag-and-bone merchant or whoever it may be may retain 95% of the proceeds and send the charity concerned only a small percentage of the proceeds. That is precisely the kind of thing that we wish to stop. The noble Lord ... referred to carol singers. If I wished to collect for a charity in the street, I would need a permit. I would feel fairly miffed if all someone else did was to go down the street and sing a carol outside someone's door and that obviated the need for a permit. It is important that the same regulations apply in every case. The responsibility we are discussing is not an onerous one.' (HL Deb, Vol 535, col 1234 (18 February 1992).)

On the Third Reading the question came up again. Lord Allen returned to the attack. But Earl Ferrers resisted any amendment, principally because he considered that drafting the kind of regulations would be very difficult to accomplish, without either creating absurdities or loopholes for the less scrupulous.

> 'It would be easy enough to specify carol singing as an exempt activity. But if one did so the group which sings "The Holly and the Ivy" would be able to take advantage of the concession

but the group which sang "White Christmas" would not because that is not a carol. It will be difficult to think of a more absurd situation than one in which the application of the criminal law depends on the classification of the item sung.

Likewise it ought to be possible to cover what is known as Bob-a-Job Week. But a detailed provision of this kind would create its own anomalies since similar activities by groups other than scouts would not be covered ... Exception seems at odds with what Part III is trying to do. It serves two purposes. First it ensures that those who raise money or collect property locally are also accountable locally for what they collect. That is why it requires local authorities to give permission for public charitable collections and why the regulations to be made under the Bill will require promoters to keep proper accounts.

Secondly, Part III serves to ensure that public charitable collections do not cause a nuisance to the public as a result of their sheer number or the places in which they are conducted. Both of those purposes might be undermined by the system of waivers which are suggested by the amendment.' (HL Deb, Vol 535, col 217 (25 February 1992).)

A system of supervision along the lines set out in the 1992 Act has been operating in Scotland by virtue of the Civic Government (Scotland) Act 1982. There is no exemption or waiver system in the Scottish legislation.

14.10 Obtaining a Local Authority Permit

14.10.1 The promoter of a collection has to apply for a permit to the relevant local authority (see **14.9.1**). Hence, a different permit has to be obtained from each separate local authority area in which a public charitable collection is to be conducted, unless a Charity Commission order is obtained under s 72 (see **14.17**).

14.10.2 The promoter is defined, in s 65(3), as the person who organises or controls the conduct of the charitable appeal in question. Hence, this could be (but is probably not) a charity trustee.

14.10.3 The application for the permit will have to comply with regulations to be issued under s 73 of the 1992 Act. The application has to specify the period for which it is desired that the permit will last, up to a maximum of 12 months.

14.10.4 The application normally has to be made at least one month before the day on which the collection is to be conducted or, if it is to be collected on more than one day, on the first of those days. However, in cases of emergency, the local authority can allow an application to be made less than a month before the day of the collection. No application can be made more than six months before the first day of the collection. It will be a criminal offence knowingly or recklessly to furnish false information in an application (s 74(3)) (maximum fine £2,500).

14.10.5 The local authority is obliged to consult the chief officer of police for the police area which comprises or includes the local authority area.

Having enquired of the chief officer of police, the local authority then, by s 68, has either to:

(a) issue a permit; or
(b) refuse the application in accordance with s 69.

If a local authority fails to determine an application for the issue of a permit then the applicant would have the right to seek an order of judicial review from the High Court in respect of the local authority's failure to determine the application.

14.11 Section 68 Permits: Conditions

14.11.1 A local authority may attach such conditions as it thinks fit to any permit (s 68(2)). However, all such conditions have to be consistent with the requirements of any regulations issued by the Secretary of State under s 73(2). Those regulations may make provision:

(a) about the keeping and publication of accounts;
(b) for the prevention of any annoyance to members of the public;
(c) to provide for the use by collectors of badges and certificates of authority including in particular a provision:
    (i) prescribing the form of badges and certificates; and
    (ii) requiring a collector, on request, to permit his badge or certificate to be inspected by a constable or a duly authorised officer of a local authority or by an occupier of any premises visited by him in the course of the collection;
(d) prohibiting persons under a prescribed age from acting as collectors.

14.11.2 By s 68(3), a local authority may, in particular, attach conditions on a permit:

(a) specifying the day of the week, date, time or frequency of the collection;
(b) specifying the locality or localities within their area in which the collection may be conducted; and
(c) regulating the manner in which the collection is to be conducted.

Where a local authority attaches any condition to a permit, it must serve notice in writing on the applicant of their decision and of the reasons for their decision. The notice also has to state the right of appeal, set out in s 71(2).

14.12 Appeal Against Conditions Contained in a Permit

A person to whom a permit has been issued under s 68 may appeal to a magistrates' court against the decision of the local authority to attach a condition to the permit (s 71(2)). The appeal has to be lodged within 14 days of the date of service on the person of a notice under s 68. An appeal can be made from the decision of the magistrates' court to the Crown Court.

14.13 Refusal of a Local Authority Permit

Under s 68(1)(b), the local authority can refuse to issue a permit provided it is on the basis of one or more of the grounds specified in s 69. Written notice of the refusal has to be given to the applicant, together with the reasons for the decision. The notice also has to state the right of appeal conferred by s 71(2). The grounds for refusal by a local authority to grant a permit are set out in s 69 of the 1992 Act.

They are as follows:

(a) If it appears to the local authority that the collection would cause undue inconvenience to members of the public by reason of:
  (i) the day of the week or date on which;
  (ii) the time at which;
  (iii) the frequency with which; or
  (iv) the locality or localities in which;
  it is proposed to be conducted.
(b) If the collection falls on the same day or within one day of another public charitable collection already authorised. This is qualified by s 69(2) whereby the local authority cannot refuse to issue a permit if it appears to them that the collection will only be conducted in one location, which is on land on which members of the public will have access only by virtue of the permission of the occupier of the land.
(c) If the amount likely to be applied for charitable, benevolent or philanthropic purposes would be inadequate, having regard to the likely amount of the collection proceeds. The local authority's judgment on this was questioned in the committee stage of the Bill, but Viscount Astor pointed out that a similar test had been applied for 50 years under the 1939 Act (s 2(3)(a)) and it had not given rise to any problems.
(d) If the applicant or any other person is likely to receive an excessive amount by way of remuneration in connection with the collection. This ground also appeared in the 1939 Act.
(e) If the applicant has been convicted:
  (i) of an offence under s 5 of the Police, Factories, etc (Miscellaneous Provisions) Act 1916, under the House to House Collections Act 1939, under s 119 of the Civic Government (Scotland) Act 1982 or regulations made under it, or under Part III of the 1992 Act or regulations made under s 73 of the 1992 Act; or
  (ii) of any offence which involves dishonesty or an offence which would, in the opinion of the local authority, be likely to be facilitated by the issuing to him of a permit.
(f) If the applicant is a person other than a charitable, benevolent or philanthropic institution for whose benefit the collection is proposed to be conducted, but the local authority are not satisfied that the applicant is authorised by the relevant institution.
(g) If the local authority consider that the applicant, when promoting any collection authorised under Part III of the 1992 Act or under s 119 of the Civic Government (Scotland) Act 1982, did not exercise due diligence:
  (i) to ensure that persons authorised by him to act as collectors were fit; and
  (ii) to ensure that those persons complied with the provisions of regulations under s 73 of the 1992 Act or s 119 of the Civic Government (Scotland) Act 1982; or
  (iii) to prevent badges or certificates of authority being obtained by persons other than those he had so authorised.

14.14 Appeal Against Refusal to Grant a Permit

If the local authority refuses to issue a permit, the applicant may appeal to the magistrates' court against the decision of the authority within 14 days of the date of the service of the notice under s 68(4). An appeal against the decision of the magistrates' court can be brought to the Crown Court.

14.15 Withdrawal of a Local Authority Permit

14.15.1 Under s 70 of the 1992 Act, a local authority has power to withdraw the permit, to attach any condition to the permit or to vary any existing condition of the permit.

The local authority can do this only if it satisfies s 70(1), ie that it has reason to believe:

(a) that there has been a change in the circumstances which prevailed at the time when it issued the permit and is of the opinion that if the application for the permit had been made in the new circumstances of the case the permit would not have been issued by them; or

(b) that any information furnished to it by the promoter for the purposes of the application for the permit was false in a material particular.

14.15.2 If the local authority decides to impose conditions on an existing permit, they must comply with s 68(2) – ie be in accordance with regulations to be issued under s 73. It does not appear that the local authority can, at this stage, impose any of the conditions set out in s 68(3) and in particular s 68(3)(c), regulating the manner in which the collection is to be conducted. Any notice imposing new conditions has to be advised to the promoter in writing. The notice has to state the right of appeal conferred by s 71(2) and the 14-day period within which such appeal must be brought.

14.15.3 The local authority can also, by s 70(3), withdraw a permit if it has reason to believe that there has been or is likely to be a breach of any condition of the permit. The permit holder has the right to appeal to the magistrates' court within 14 days of the date of service of written notice withdrawing the permit (s 71(2)(b)).

The permit continues to have effect as if it had not been withdrawn or, in the case of an additional condition, if the condition had not been attached until either:

(a) the time for bringing an appeal under s 71(2) has expired; or

(b) until the determination or abandonment of the appeal, if such an appeal is brought.

14.16 Criminal Offences

14.16.1 Under s 73(3), the regulations that will be issued under s 73 may provide that any failure to comply with any part of the regulations will be an offence punishable by a fine on summary conviction, not exceeding £500. This will cover, inter alia, the keeping and publication of accounts, the use of badges and certificates and the banning of persons under a prescribed age from acting as collectors.

14.16.2 It will be an offence, under s 74, to use any badge or certificate or authority which is not being used in accordance with an appeal or to use any false badge or certificate or article to deceive a member of the public. Breach of this section can give rise to a fine not exceeding £2,500 on conviction.

14.16.3 Any person who makes an application under s 67 for a local authority licence and knowingly or recklessly furnishes any information which is false in a material particular, shall be guilty of a criminal offence and on conviction will be liable to a fine not exceeding £2,500.

14.17 Section 72 Orders

Introduction

14.17.1 The obligation to obtain a local authority permit to conduct a public charitable collection is reduced to an extent by s 72 which states:

'(1) Where the Charity Commissioners are satisfied, on the application of any charity, that that
      charity proposes –
      (a) to promote public charitable collections –
           (i) throughout England and Wales, or
           (ii) throughout a substantial part of England and Wales,
      in connection with any charitable purposes pursued by the charity, or
      (b) to authorise other persons to promote public charitable collections as mentioned in
           paragraph (a),
      the Commissioners may make an order under this subsection in respect of the charity.'

14.17.2 It must be noted that the capacity to give a national order only applies to charities, ie registered, exempt or excepted charities. In contrast to the position under the House to House Collections Act 1939, it does *not* apply to institutions established for benevolent or philanthropic purposes. This gave rise to great debate in the House of Lords where certain of their Lordships pressed the Government to allow such national organisations as Amnesty International or Greenpeace to be able to benefit from some similar national exemption. The Government refused on the grounds that such benevolent or philanthropic organisations were not susceptible to supervision by the Charity Commissioners and the Government was not prepared to set up a special regime for those organisations.

14.17.3 What is meant by 'throughout England and Wales or throughout a substantial part of England and Wales'? Unless the public charitable collections are to be conducted throughout England and Wales or throughout a substantial part of England and Wales, no exemption order will be issued. The phrase is used in s 3 of the 1939 Act but there have been no reported cases on it.

In the House of Lords debate on the report stage of the Bill, Earl Ferrers commented:

'My Lords, there is an inherent flexibility in the phrase: "a substantial part of England and Wales".

In the first instance it will be for the Charity Commissioners and ultimately for the courts to decide whether a proposed public charitable collection covers a substantial part of England and Wales. That is an alternative to a collection throughout England and Wales. I suggest that the collection will need to take place in a majority of the districts in England and Wales. For example, collections in association with a long distance sponsored walk will be unlikely to cover a substantial part of England and Wales. To do so the walk would have to pass through at least the majority of districts of England and Wales. A walk around the coastline of England and Wales will probably just about satisfy the requirements; a walk across the Pennines would not.

My noble friend Lord Swinfen was worried about Exemption Orders for disaster appeals. The amendment will allow disaster appeals which are established for charitable purposes to apply for an exemption order under this Clause. They will be eligible for such an Order whether they were concerned with the disaster in this country or abroad. The amendment would not allow disaster appeals established for benevolent or philanthropic purposes to obtain an Exemption Order.' (HL Deb, Vol 535, cols 1241–1242 (19 February 1992).)

Hence, it appears that it will be extremely difficult to obtain an exemption order if the applicant charity has to show that collections will take place in a majority of the districts in England and Wales. In response to the consultation document (see **14.7.2**), a majority of those questioned opposed national exemption orders. It should be borne in mind that under the 1992 Act they will apply to *all* collections, ie street and house to house.

14.17.4 What will be the position with a charity with a number of branches? The position will vary according to how the charity is established. If the branches are part of one national charity so that the branches and the national organisation comprise one legal entity, it could be that the charity will be able to seek an exemption order if it can comply with the terms of s 72(1). On the other hand, a charity whose branches are each independent, separate, legal entities will almost certainly not be able to comply with the Act because it will rely upon the local branches to carry out collections in their localities and, therefore, each local branch will have to obtain the necessary permit from the relevant local authority.

It may be possible, in this case, for the national charity to authorise the independent local branches to collect on the national charity's behalf. In this case, the collection would be carried out by persons authorised by the national charity and might then fall within s 72. The moneys would all have to be paid to the national charity, but it could then (depending on the terms of the appeal) make grants to the local branches.

14.17.5 The exemption order can apply to a collection not only made directly by the charity but by other persons authorised by the charity to promote a public charitable collection. This will cover a collection organised by a professional fund-raiser.

14.17.6 The area covered by the exemption order will be decided by the Charity Commissioners. Section 72(2) gives the Commissioners the power to order that the collections be conducted 'in such an area or areas as may be specified in the order'.

In addition, by s 72(3) an order under s 72(1) may:

(a) include such conditions as the Commissioners think fit, for example to notify the relevant local authorities;
(b) be expressed to have effect without limit of time or for a specified period only; or
(c) be revoked or varied by a further order of the Commissioners.

14.17.7 If the Commissioners decide to revoke or vary an order they have to serve written notice of their reasons for making a further order on the charity. However, this is qualified by the words 'unless it appears to them (ie the Commissioners) that the interests of the charity would not be prejudiced by the further order'. Whether or not the Commissioners' judgment on any such question is fair or not will be an interesting question. What will be the position if the Commissioners revoke an order but decide that the interests of the charity would not be prejudiced by the revocation of the order and, therefore, do not give reasons? There is no right of appeal against a decision of the Commissioners in this regard. An aggrieved charity could apply to the High Court for an order of judicial review against the Commissioners in these circumstances.

14.17.8 Any collections conducted in accordance with an order from the Charity Commissioners under s 72 will have to comply with regulations to be issued by the Secretary of State under s 72(1). An obligation to inform and consult local authorities may be included.

14.18 Conclusion

The provisions of Part III of the 1992 Act cover a very large range of fund-raising activities, undertaken directly by or on behalf of charitable, benevolent or philanthropic institutions. It must be emphasised that, unlike Part II, Part III not only applies to professional fund-raisers and commercial participators, it regulates fund-raising directly, by charitable institutions (as defined). Although the definition of public place was considerably narrowed after debate in the House of Lords, many fund-raising activities by or on behalf of charitable institutions are covered by the Act. Accordingly, the following activities will require either a local authority permit or, in the case of charities, a Charity Commission exemption order under s 72.

(a) All forms of collection on highways and in 'public' places, including railway forecourts, shopping precincts, airport lounges, etc.
(b) House to house collections.
(c) Jumble collections.
(d) All sales of goods on behalf of charities on highways and in a public place.

When Part III will come into force is still unclear as some of the proposed changes would appear to require primary legislation, and whether Parliamentary time will be forthcoming is perhaps uncertain.

APPENDIX 1

STATUTES

CHARITIES ACT 1992

(1992 c 41)

ARRANGEMENT OF SECTIONS

PART I

CHARITIES

PART II

CONTROL OF FUND-RAISING FOR CHARITABLE INSTITUTIONS

Preliminary

Control of fund-raising

Supplementary

PART III

PUBLIC CHARITABLE COLLECTIONS

Preliminary

Prohibition on conducting unauthorised collections

Permits

PART I

CHARITIES

Charity property

29. Divestment of charity property held by official custodian for charities

(1) The official custodian shall, in accordance with this section, divest himself of all property to which this subsection applies.

(2) Subsection (1) applies to any property held by the official custodian in his capacity as such, with the exception of –

(a) any land; and

(b) any property (other than land) which is vested in him by virtue of an order of the Commissioners under section 20 of the 1960 Act (power to act for protection of charities).

(3) Where property to which subsection (1) applies is held by the official custodian in trust for particular charities, he shall (subject to subsection (7)) divest himself of that property in such manner as the Commissioners may direct.

(4) Without prejudice to the generality of subsection (3), directions given by the Commissioners under that subsection may make different provision in relation to different property held by the official custodian or in relation to different classes or descriptions of property held by him, including (in particular) –

(a) provision designed to secure that the divestment required by subsection (1) is effected in stages or by means of transfers or other disposals taking place at different times;

(b) provision requiring the official custodian to transfer any specified investments, or any specified class or description of investments, held by him in trust for a charity –

   (i) to the charity trustees or any trustee for the charity, or

   (ii) to a person nominated by the charity trustees to hold any such investments in trust for the charity;

(c) provision requiring the official custodian to sell or call in any specified investments, or any specified class or description of investments, so held by him and to pay any proceeds of sale or other money accruing therefrom –

   (i) to the charity trustees or any trustee for the charity, or

   (ii) into any bank account kept in its name.

(5) The charity trustees of a charity may, in the case of any property falling to be transferred by the o fficial custodian in accordance with a direction under subsection (3), nominate a person to hold any such property in trust for the charity; but a person shall not be so nominated unless –

    (a) if an individual, he resides in England and Wales; or

    (b) if a body corporate, it has a place of business there.

(6) Directions under subsection (3) shall, in the case of any property vested in the official custodian by virtue of section 22(6) of the 1960 Act (common investment funds), provide for any such property to be transferred –

    (a) to the trustees appointed to manage the common investment fund concerned; or

    (b) to any person nominated by those trustees who is authorised by or under the common investment scheme concerned to hold that fund or any part of it.

(7) Where the official custodian –

    (a) holds any relevant property in trust for a charity, but

    (b) after making reasonable injuries is unable to locate the charity or any of its trustees,

he shall –

      (i) unless the relevant property is money, sell the property and hold the proceeds of sale pending the giving by the Commissioners of a direction under subsection (8);

      (ii) if the relevant property is money, hold it pending the giving of any such direction;

and for this purpose 'relevant property' means any property to which subsection (1) applies or any proceeds of sale or other money accruing to the official custodian in consequence of a direction under subsection (3).

(8) Where subsection (7) applies in relation to a charity ('the dormant charity'), the Commissioners may direct the official custodian –

    (a) to pay such amount as is held by him in accordance with that subsection to such other charity as is specified in the direction in accordance with subsection (9), or

    (b) to pay to each of two or more other charities so specified in the direction such part of that amount as is there specified in relation to that charity.

(9) The Commissioners may specify in a direction under subsection (8) such charity or charities as they consider appropriate, being in each case a charity whose purposes are, in the opinion of the Commissioners, as similar in character to those of the dormant charity as is reasonably practicable; but the Commissioners shall not so specify any charity unless they have received from the charity trustees written confirmation that they are willing to accept the amount proposed to be paid to the charity.

(10) Any amount received by a charity by virtue of subsection (8) shall be received by the charity on terms that –

    (a) it shall be held and applied by the charity for the purposes of the charity, but

    (b) it shall, as property of the charity, nevertheless be subject to any restrictions on expenditure to which it, or (as the case may be) the property which it represents, was subject as property of the dormant charity.

(11) At such time as the Commissioners are satisfied that the official custodian has divested himself of all property held by him in trust for particular charities, all remaining funds held by him as official custodian shall be paid by him into the Consolidated Fund.

(12) Nothing in subsection (11) applies in relation to any property held by the official custodian which falls within subsection (2)(a) or (b).

(13) In this section 'land' does not include any interest in land by way of mortgage or other security.

30. Provisions supplementary to section 29

(1) Any directions of the Commissioners under section 29 above shall have effect notwithstanding anything –
  (a) in the trusts of a charity, or
  (b) in section 17(1) of the 1960 Act (supplementary provisions as to property vested in official custodian).

(2) Subject to subsection (3), any provision –
  (a) of the trusts of a charity, or
  (b) of any directions given by an order of the Commissioners made in connection with a transaction requiring the sanction of an order under section 29(1) of the 1960 Act (restrictions on dealing with charity property),
shall cease to have effect if and to the extent that it requires or authorises personal property of the charity to be transferred to or held by the official custodian; and for this purpose 'personal property' extends to any mortgage or other real security, but does not include any interest in land other than such an interest by way of mortgage or other security.

(3) Subsection (2) does not apply to –
  (a) any provision of an order made under section 20 of the 1960 Act (power to act for protection of charities); or
  (b) any provision of any other order, or of any scheme, of the Commissioners if the provision requires trustees of a charity to make payments into an account maintained by the official custodian with a view to the accumulation of a sum as capital of the charity (whether or not by way of recoupment of a sum expended out of the charity's permanent endowment);
but any such provision as is mentioned in paragraph (b) shall have effect as if, instead of requiring the trustees to make such payments into an account maintained by the official custodian, it required the trustees to make such payments into an account maintained by them or by any other person (apart from the official custodian) who is either a trustee for the charity or a person nominated by them to hold such payments in trust for the charity.

(4) The disposal of any property by the official custodian in accordance with section 29 above shall operate to discharge him from his trusteeship of that property.

(5) Where any instrument issued by the official custodian in connection with any such disposal contains a printed reproduction of his official seal, that instrument shall have the same effect as if it were duly sealed with his official seal.

36. Removal of requirements under statutory provisions for consent to dealings with charity land

(1) Any provision –
  (a) establishing or regulating a particular charity and contained in, or having effect under, any Act of Parliament, or
  (b) contained in the trusts of a charity,
shall cease to have effect if and to the extent that it provides for dispositions of, or other dealings with, land held by or in trust for the charity to require the consent of the Commissioners (whether signified by order or otherwise).

(2) Any provision of an order or scheme under the Education Act 1944 or the Education Act 1973 relating to a charity shall cease to have effect if and to the extent that it requires, in relation to any sale, lease or other disposition of land held by or in trust for the charity, approval by the Commissioners or the Secretary of State of the amount for which the land is to be sold, leased or otherwise disposed of.

(3) In this section 'land' means land in England or Wales.

49. Amendment of Redundant Churches and Other Religious Buildings Act 1969

The Redundant Churches and Other Religious Buildings Act 1969 shall have effect subject to the amendments specified in Schedule 5 to this Act.

50. Contributions towards maintenance etc of almshouses

(1) Any provision in the trusts of an almshouse charity which relates to the payment by persons resident in the charity's almshouses of contributions towards the cost of maintaining those almshouses and essential services in them shall cease to have effect if and to the extent that it provides for the amount, or the maximum amount, of such contributions to be a sum specified, approved or authorised by the Commissioners.

(2) In subsection (1) −
'almshouse' means any premises maintained as an almshouse, whether they are called an almshouse or not; and
'almshouse charity' means a charity which is authorised under its trusts to maintain almshouses.

PART II

CONTROL OF FUND-RAISING FOR CHARITABLE INSTITUTIONS

Preliminary

58. Interpretation of Part II

(1) In this Part −
'charitable contributions', in relation to any representation made by any commercial participator or other person, means −
  (a) the whole or part of −
    (i) the consideration given for goods or services sold or supplied by him, or
    (ii) any proceeds (other than such consideration) of a promotional venture undertaken by him, or
  (b) sums given by him by way of donation in connection with the sale or supply of any such goods or services (whether the amount of such sums is determined by reference to the value of any such goods or services or otherwise);
'charitable institution' means a charity or an institution (other than a charity) which is established for charitable, benevolent or philanthropic purposes;
'charity' means a charity within the meaning of the Charities Act 1960;
'commercial participator', in relation to any charitable institution, means any person (apart from a company connected with such an institution) who −
  (a) carries on for gain a business other than a fund-raising business, but
  (b) in the course of that business, engages in any promotional venture in the course of which it is represented that charitable contributions are to be given to or applied for the benefit of the institution;
'company' has the meaning given by section 46 of the Charities Act 1960 (as amended by the Companies Act 1989);

'the court' means the High Court or a county court;

'credit card' means a card which is a credit-token within the meaning of the Consumer Credit Act 1974;

'debit card' means a card the use of which by its holder to make a payment results in a current account of his at a bank, or at any other institution providing banking services, being debited with the payment;

'fund-raising business' means any business carried on for gain and wholly or primarily engaged in soliciting or otherwise procuring money or other property for charitable, benevolent or philanthropic purposes;

'institution' includes any trust or undertaking;

'professional fund-raiser' means –

(a) any person (apart from a charitable instutiton or company connected with such an institution) who carries on a fund-raising business, or

(b) any other person (apart from a person excluded by virtue of subsection (2) or (3)) who for reward solicits money or other property for the benefit of a charitable institution, if he does so otherwise than in the course of any fund-raising venture undertaken by a person falling within paragraph (a) above;

'promotional venture' means any advertising or sales campaign or any other venture undertaken for promotional purposes;

'radio or television programme' includes any item included in a programme service within the meaning of the Broadcasting Act 1990.

(2) In subsection (1), paragraph (b) of the definition of 'professional fund-raiser' does not apply to any of the following, namely –

(a) any charitable institution or any company connected with any such institution;

(b) any officer or employee of any such institution or company, or any trustee of any such institution, acting (in each case) in his capacity as such;

(c) any person acting as a collector in respect of a public charitable collection (apart from a person who is to be treated as a promoter of such a collection by virtue of section 65(3));

(d) any person who in the course of a relevant programme, that is to say a radio or television programme in the course of which a fund-raising venture is undertaken by –

(i) a charitable institution, or

(ii) a company connected with such an institution,

makes any solicitation at the instance of that institution or company; or

(e) any commercial participator;

and for this purpose 'collector' and 'public charitable collection' have the same meaning as in Part III of this Act.

(3) In addition, paragraph (b) of the definition of 'professional fund-raiser' does not apply to a person if he does not receive –

(a) more than –

(i) £5 per day, or

(ii) £500 per year,

by way of remuneration in connection with soliciting money or other property for the benefit of the charitable institution referred to in that paragraph; or

(b) more than £500 by way of remuneration in connection with any fund-raising venture in the course of which he solicits money or other property for the benefit of that institution.

(4) In this Part any reference to charitable purposes, where occurring in the context of a reference to charitable, benevolent or philanthropic purposes, is a reference to charitable purposes whether or not the purposes are charitable within the meaning of any rule of law.

(5) For the purposes of this Part a company is connected with a charitable institution if –

(a) the institution, or

(b) the institution and one or more other charitable institutions, taken together, is or are entitled (whether directly or through one or more nominees) to exercise, or control the exercise of, the whole of the voting power at any general meeting of the company.

(6) In this Part –

(a) 'represent' and 'solicit' mean respectively represent and solicit in any manner whatever, whether expressly or impliedly and whether done –

  (i) by speaking directly to the person or persons to whom the representation or solicitation is addressed (whether when in his or their presence or not), or

  (ii) by means of a statement published in any newspaper, film or radio or television programme,

or otherwise, and references to a representation or solicitation shall be construed accordingly; and

(b) any reference to soliciting or otherwise procuring money or other property is a reference to soliciting or otherwise procuring money or other property whether any consideration is, or is to be, given in return for the money or other property or not.

(7) Where –

(a) any solicitation of money or other property for the benefit of a charitable institution is made in accordance with arrangements between any person and that institution, and

(b) under those arrangements that person will be responsible for receiving on behalf of the institution money or other property given in response to the solicitation.

then (if he would not be so regarded apart from this subsection) that person shall be regarded for the purposes of this Part as soliciting money or other property for the benefit of the institution.

(8) Where any fund-raising venture is undertaken by a professional fund-raiser in the course of a radio or television programme, any solicitation which is made by a person in the course of the programme at the instance of the fund-raiser shall be regarded for the purposes of this Part as made by the fund-raiser and not by that person (and shall be so regarded whether or not the solicitation is made by that person for any reward).

(9) In this Part 'services' includes facilities, and in particular –

(a) access to any premises or event;

(b) membership of any organisation;

(c) the provision of advertising space; and

(d) the provision of any financial facilities;

and references to the supply of services shall be construed accordingly.

(10) The Secretary of State may by order amend subsection (3) by substituting a different sum for any sum for the time being specified there.

NOTE

Section shown as amended by the Deregulation and Contracting Out Act 1994.

Control of fund-raising

59. Prohibition on professional fund-raiser etc raising funds for charitable institution without an agreement in prescribed form

(1) It shall be unlawful for a professional fund-raiser to solicit money or other property for the benefit of a charitable institution unless he does so in accordance with an agreement with the institution satisfying the prescribed requirements.

(2) It shall be unlawful for a commercial participator to represent that charitable contributions are to be given to or applied for the benefit of a charitable institution unless he does so in accordance with an agreement with the institution satisfying the prescribed requirements.

(3) Where on the application of a charitable institution the court is satisfied –
  (a) that any person has contravened or is contravening subsection (1) or (2) in relation to the institution, and
  (b) that, unless restrained, any such contravention is likely to continue or be repeated,
the court may grant an injunction restraining the contravention; and compliance with subsection (1) or (2) shall not be enforceable otherwise than in accordance with this subsection.

(4) Where –
  (a) a charitable institution makes any agreement with a professional fund-raiser or a commercial participator by virtue of which –
    (i) the professional fund-raiser is authorised to solicit money or other property for the benefit of the institution, or
    (ii) the commercial participator is authorised to represent that charitable contributions are to be given to or applied for the benefit of the institution,
    as the case may be, but
  (b) the agreement does not satisfy the prescribed requirements in any respect,
the agreement shall not be enforceable against the institution except to such extent (if any) as may be provided by an order of the court.

(5) A professional fund-raiser or commercial participator who is a party to such an agreement as is mentioned in subsection (4)(a) shall not be entitled to receive any amount by way of remuneration or expenses in respect of anything done by him in pursuance of the agreement unless –
  (a) he is so entitled under any provision of the agreement, and
  (b) either –
    (i) the agreement satisfies the prescribed requirements, or
    (ii) any such provision has effect by virtue of an order of the court under subsection (4).

(6) In this section 'the prescribed requirements' means such requirements as are prescribed by regulations made by virtue of section 64(2)(a).

60. Professional fund-raisers etc required to indicate institutions benefiting and arrangements for remuneration

(1) Where a professional fund-raiser solicits money or other property for the benefit of one or more particular charitable institutions, the solicitation shall be accompanied by a statement clearly indicating –
  (a) the name or names of the institution or institutions concerned;
  (b) if there is more than one institution concerned, the proportions in which the institutions are respectively to benefit; and
  (c) (in general terms) the method by which the fund-raiser's remuneration in connection with the appeal is to be determined.

(2) Where a professional fund-raiser solicits money or other property for charitable, benevolent or philanthropic purposes of any description (rather than for the benefit of one or more particular charitable institutions), the solicitation shall be accompanied by a statement clearly indicating –
  (a) the fact that he is soliciting money or other property for those purposes and not for the benefit of any particular charitable institution or institutions;
  (b) the method by which it is to be determined how the proceeds of the appeal are to be distributed between different charitable institutions; and

(c) (in general terms) the method by which his remuneration in connection with the appeal is to be determined.

(3) Where any representation is made by a commercial participator to the effect that charitable contributions are to be given to or applied for the benefit of one or more particular charitable institutions, the representation shall be accompanied by a statement clearly indicating –
   (a) the name or names of the institution or institutions concerned;
   (b) if there is more than one institution concerned, the proportions in which the institutions are respectively to benefit; and
   (c) (in general terms) the method by which it is to be determined –
      (i) what proportion of the consideration given for goods or services sold or supplied by him, or of any other proceeds of a promotional venture undertaken by him, is to be given to or applied for the benefit of the institution or institutions concerned, or
      (ii) what sums by way of donations by him in connection with the sale or supply of any such goods or services are to be so given or applied,
   as the case may require.

(4) If any such solicitation or representation as is mentioned in any of subsections (1) to (3) is made –
   (a) in the course of a radio or television programme, and
   (b) in association with an announcement to the effect that payment may be made, in response to the solicitation or representation, by means of a credit or debit card,
the statement required by virtue of subsection (1), (2) or (3) (as the case may be) shall include full details of the right to have refunded under section 61(1) any payment of £50 or more which is so made.

(5) If any such solicitation or representation as is mentioned in any of subsections (1) to (3) is made orally but is not made –
   (a) by speaking directly to the particular person or persons to whom it is addressed and in his or their presence, or
   (b) in the course of any radio or television programme,
the professional fund-raiser or commercial participator concerned shall, within seven days of any payment of £50 or more being made to him in response to the solicitation or representation, give to the person making the payment a written statement –
      (i) of the matters specified in paragraphs (a) to (c) of that subsection; and
      (ii) including full details of the right to cancel under section 61(2) an agreement made in response to the solicitation or representation, and the right to have refunded under section 61(2) or (3) any payment of £50 or more made in response thereto.

(6) In subsection (5) above the reference to the making of a payment is a reference to the making of a payment of whatever nature and by whatever means, including a payment made by means of a credit card or a debit card; and for the purposes of that subsection –
   (a) where the person making any such payment makes it in person, it shall be regarded as made at the time when it is so made;
   (b) where the person making any such payment sends it by post, it shall be regarded as made at the time when it is posted; and
   (c) where the person making any such payment makes it by giving, by telephone or by means of any other telecommunication apparatus, authority for an account to be debited with the payment, it shall be regarded as made at the time when any such authority is given.

(7) Where any requirement of subsections (1) to (5) is not complied with in relation to any solicitation or representation, the professional fund-raiser or commercial participator concerned shall be guilty of an offence and liable on summary conviction to a fine not exceeding the fifth level on the standard scale.

(8) It shall be a defence for a person charged with any such offence to prove that he took all reasonable precautions and exercised all due diligence to avoid the commission of the offence.

(9) Where the commission by any person of an offence under subsection (7) is due to the act or default of some other person, that other person shall be guilty of the offence; and a person may be charged with and convicted of the offence by virtue of this subsection whether or not proceedings are taken against the first-mentioned person.

(10) In this section –
'the appeal', in relation to any solicitation by a professional fund-raiser, means the campaign or
    other fund-raising venture in the course of which the solicitation is made;
'telecommunication apparatus' has the same meaning as in the Telecommunications Act 1984.

61. Cancellation of payments and agreements made in response to appeals

(1) Where –
    (a) a person ('the donor'), in response to any such solicitation or representation as is
        mentioned in any of subsections (1) to (3) of section 60 which is made in the course of a
        radio or television programme, makes any payment of £50 or more to the relevant
        fund-raiser by means of a credit card or a debit card, but
    (b) before the end of the period of seven days beginning with the date of the solicitation or
        representation, the donor serves on the relevant fund-raiser a notice in writing which,
        however expressed, indicates the donor's intention to cancel the payment,
the donor shall (subject to subsection (4) below) be entitled to have the payment refunded to him
forthwith by the relevant fund-raiser.

(2) Where –
    (a) a person ('the donor'), in response to any solicitation or representation falling within
        subsection (5) of section 60, enters into an agreement with the relevant fund-raiser under
        which the donor is, or may be, liable to make any payment or payments to the relevant
        fund-raiser, and the amount or aggregate amount which the donor is, or may be, liable to
        pay to him under the agreement is £50 or more, but
    (b) before the end of the period of seven days beginning with the date when he is given any
        such written statement as is referred to in that subsection, the donor serves on the relevant
        fund-raiser a notice in writing which, however expressed, indicates the donor's intention
        to cancel the agreement,
the notice shall operate, as from the time when it is so served, to cancel the agreement and any
liability of any person other than the donor in connection with the making of any such payment
or payments, and the donor shall (subject to subsection (4) below) be entitled to have any
payment of £50 or more made by him under the agreement refunded to him forthwith by the
relevant fund-raiser.

(3) Where, in response to any solicitation or representation falling within subsection (5) of section
60, a person ('the donor') –
    (a) makes any payment of £50 or more to the relevant fund-raiser, but
    (b) does not enter into any such agreement as is mentioned in subsection (2) above,
then, if before the end of the period of seven days beginning with the date when the donor is
given any such written statement as is referred to in subsection (5) of that section, the donor serves
on the relevant fund-raiser a notice in writing which, however expressed, indicates the donor's
intention to cancel the payment, the donor shall (subject to subsection (4) below) be entitled to
have the payment refunded to him forthwith by the relevant fund-raiser.

(4) The right of any person to have a payment refunded to him under any of subsections (1) to (3)
above –

   (a) is a right to have refunded to him the amount of the payment less any administrative expenses reasonably incurred by the relevant fund-raiser in connection with –
      (i) the making of the refund, or
      (ii) (in the case of a refund under subsection (2)) dealing with the notice of cancellation served by that person; and
   (b) shall, in the case of a payment for goods already received, be conditional upon restitution being made by him of the goods in question.

(5) Nothing in subsections (1) to (3) above has effect in relation to any payment made or to be made in respect of services which have been supplied at the time when the relevant notice is served.

(6) In this section any reference to the making of a payment is a reference to the making of a payment of whatever nature and (in the case of subsection (2) or (3)) a payment made by whatever means, including a payment made by means of a credit card or a debit card; and subsection (6) of section 60 shall have effect for determining when a payment is made for the purposes of this section as it has effect for determining when a payment is made for the purposes of subsection (5) of that section.

(7) In this section 'the relevant fund-raiser', in relation to any solicitation or representation, means the professional fund-raiser or commercial participator by whom it is made.

(8) The Secretary of State may by order –
   (a) amend any provision of this section by substituting a different sum for the sum for the time being specified there; and
   (b) make such consequential amendments in section 60 as he considers appropriate.

62. Right of charitable institution to prevent unauthorised fund-raising

(1) Where on the application of any charitable institution –
   (a) the court is satisfied that any person has done or is doing either of the following, namely –
      (i) soliciting money or other property for the benefit of the institution, or
      (ii) representing that charitable contributions are to be given to or applied for the benefit of the institution,
   and that, unless restrained, he is likely to do further acts of that nature, and
   (b) the court is also satisfied as to one or more of the matters specified in subsection (2),
then (subject to subsection (3)) the court may grant an injunction restraining the doing of any such acts.

(2) The matters referred to in subsection (1)(b) are –
   (a) that the person in question is using methods of fund-raising to which the institution objects;
   (b) that that person is not a fit and proper person to raise funds for the institution; and
   (c) where the conduct complained of is the making of such representations as are mentioned in subsection (1)(a)(ii), that the institution does not wish to be associated with the particular promotional or other fund-raising venture in which the person is engaged.

(3) The power to grant an injunction under subsection (1) shall not be exercisable on the application of a charitable institution unless the institution has, not less than 28 days before making the application, served on the person in question a notice in writing –
   (a) requesting him to cease forthwith –
      (i) soliciting money or other property for the benefit of the institution, or
      (ii) representing that charitable contributions are to be given to or applied for the benefit of the institution,
   as the case may be; and

(b) stating that, if he does not comply with the notice, the institution will make an application under this section for an injunction.

(4) Where –
   (a) a charitable institution has served on any person a notice under subsection (3) ('the relevant notice') and that person has complied with the notice, but
   (b) that person has subsequently begun to carry on activities which are the same, or substantially the same, as those in respect of which the relevant notice was served,
the institution shall not, in connection with an application made by it under this section in respect of the activities carried on by that person, be required by virtue of that subsection to serve a further notice on him, if the application is made not more than 12 months after the date of service of the relevant notice.

(5) This section shall not have the effect of authorising a charitable institution to make an application under this section in respect of anything done by a professional fund-raiser or commercial participator in relation to the institution.

63. False statements relating to institutions which are not registered charities

(1) Where –
   (a) a person solicits money or other property for the benefit of an institution in association with a representation that the institution is a registered charity, and
   (b) the institution is not such a charity,
he shall be guilty of an offence and liable on summary conviction to a fine not exceeding the fifth level on the standard scale.

(1A) In any proceedings for an offence under subsection (1), it shall be a defence for the accused to prove that he believed on reasonable grounds that the institution was a registered charity.

(2) In this section 'registered charity' means a charity which is for the time being registered in the register of charities kept under section 4 of the Charities Act 1960.

NOTE
Section shown as amended by the Deregulation and Contracting Out Act 1994.

Supplementary

64. Regulations about fund-raising

(1) The Secretary of State may make such regulations as appear to him to be necessary or desirable for any purposes connected with any of the preceding provisions of this Part.

(2) Without prejudice to the generality of subsection (1), any such regulation may –
   (a) prescribe the form and content of –
       (i) agreements made for the purposes of section 59, and
       (ii) notices served under section 62(3);
   (b) require professional fund-raisers or commercial participators who are parties to such agreements with charitable institutions to make available to the institutions books, documents or other records (however kept) which relate to the institutions;
   (c) specify the manner in which money or other property acquired by professional fund-raisers or commercial participators for the benefit of, or otherwise falling to be given to or applied by such persons for the benefit of, charitable institutions is to be transmitted to such institutions;

(d) provide for any provisions of section 60 or 61 having effect in relation to solicitations or representations made in the course of radio or television programmes to have effect, subject to any modifications specified in the regulations, in relation to solicitations or representations made in the course of such programmes –
   (i) by charitable institutions, or
   (ii) by companies connected with such institutions,
and, in that connection, provide for any other provisions of this Part to have effect for the purposes of the regulations subject to any modifications so specified;

(e) make other provision regulating the raising of funds for charitable, benevolent or philanthropic purposes (whether by professional fund-raisers or commercial participators or otherwise).

(3) In subsection (2)(c) the reference to such money or other property as is there mentioned includes a reference to money or other property which, in the case of a professional fund-raiser or commercial participator –

(a) has been acquired by him otherwise than in accordance with an agreement with a charitable institution, but

(b) by reason of any solicitation or representation in consequence of which it has been acquired, is held by him on trust for such an institution.

(4) Regulations under this section may provide that any failure to comply with a specified provision of the regulations shall be an offence punishable on summary conviction by a fine not exceeding the second level on the standard scale.

PART III

PUBLIC CHARITABLE COLLECTIONS

Preliminary

65. Interpretation of Part III

(1) In this Part –
(a) 'public charitable collection' means (subject to subsection (2)) a charitable appeal which is made –
   (i) in any public place, or
   (ii) by means of visits from house to house; and

(b) 'charitable appeal' means an appeal to members of the public to give money or other property (whether for consideration or otherwise) which is made in association with a representation that the whole or any part of its proceeds is to be applied for charitable, benevolent or philanthropic purposes.

(2) Subsection (1)(a) does not apply to a charitable appeal which –
(a) is made in the course of a public meeting; or
(b) is made –
   (i) on land within a churchyard or burial ground contiguous or adjacent to a place of public worship, or
   (ii) on other land occupied for the purposes of a place of public worship and contiguous or adjacent to it,
being (in each case) land which is enclosed or substantially enclosed (whether by any wall or building or otherwise); or

(c) is an appeal to members of the public to give money or other property by placing it in an unattended receptacle;

and for the purposes of paragraph (c) above a receptacle is unattended if it is not in the possession or custody of a person acting as a collector.

(3) In this Part, in relation to a public charitable collection –

(a) 'promoter' means a person who (whether alone or with others and whether for remuneration or otherwise) organises or controls the conduct of the charitable appeal in question, and associated expressions shall be construed accordingly; and

(b) 'collector' means any person by whom that appeal is made (whether made by him alone or with others and whether made by him for remuneration or otherwise);

but where no person acts in the manner mentioned in paragraph (a) above in respect of a public charitable collection, any person who acts as a collector in respect of it shall for the purposes of this Part be treated as a promoter of it as well.

(4) In this Part –

'local authority' means the council of a district or of a London borough, the Common Council of the City of London, or the Council of the Isles of Scilly; and

'proceeds', in relation to a public charitable collection, means all money or other property given (whether for consideration or otherwise) in response to the charitable appeal in question.

(5) In this Part any reference to charitable purposes, where occurring in the context of a reference to charitable, benevolent or philanthropic purposes, is a reference to charitable purposes whether or not the purposes are charitable within the meaning of any rule of law.

(6) The functions exercisable under this Part by a local authority shall be exercisable –

(a) as respects the Inner Temple, by its Sub-Treasurer, and

(b) as respects the Middle Temple, by its Under Treasurer;

and references in this Part to a local authority or to the area of a local authority shall be construed accordingly.

(7) It is thereby declared that an appeal to members of the public (other than one falling within subsection (2)) is a public charitable collection for the purposes of this Part if –

(a) it consists in or includes the making of an offer to sell goods or to supply services, or the exposing of goods for sale, to members of the public, and

(b) it is made as mentioned in sub-paragraph (i) or (ii) of subsection (1)(a) and in association with a representation that the whole or any part of its proceeds is to be applied for charitable, benevolent or philanthropic purposes.

This subsection shall not be taken as prejudicing the generality of subsection (1)(b).

(8) In this section –

'house' includes any part of a building constituting a separate dwelling;

'public place', in relation to a charitable appeal, means –

(a) any highway, and

(b) (subject to subsection (9)) any other place to which, at any time when the appeal is made, members of the public have or are permitted to have access and which either –

(i) is not within a building, or

(ii) if within a building, is a public area within any station, airport or shopping precinct or any other similar public area.

(9) In subsection (8), paragraph (b) of the definition of 'public place' does not apply to –

(a) any place to which members of the public are permitted to have access only if any payment or ticket required as a condition of access has been made or purchased; or

(b) any place to which members of the public are permitted to have access only by virtue of permission given for the purposes of the appeal in question.

Prohibition on conducting unauthorised collections

66. Prohibition on conducting public charitable collections without authorisation

(1) No public charitable collection shall be conducted in the area of any local authority except in accordance with –
   (a) a permit issued by the authority under section 68; or
   (b) an order made by the Charity Commissioners under section 72.

(2) Where a public charitable collection is conducted in contravention of subsection (1), any promoter of that collection shall be guilty of an offence and liable on summary conviction to a fine not exceeding the fourth level on the standard scale.

Permits

67. Applications for permits to conduct public charitable collections

(1) An application for a permit to conduct a public charitable collection in the area of a local authority shall be made to the authority by the person or persons proposing to promote that collection.

(2) Any such application –
   (a) shall specify the period for which it is desired that the permit, if issued, should have effect, being a period not exceeding 12 months; and
   (b) shall contain such information as may be prescribed by regulations under section 73.

(3) Any such application –
   (a) shall be made at least one month before the relevant day or before such later date as the local authority may in the case of that application allow,
   (b) . . .
and for this purpose 'the relevant day' means the day on which the collection is to be conducted or, where it is to be conducted on more than one day, the first of those days.

(4) Before determining any application duly made to them under this section, a local authority shall consult the chief officer of police for the police area which comprises or includes their area and may make such other inquiries as they think fit.

NOTE
Section shown as amended by the Deregulation and Contracting Out Act 1994.

---

68. Determination of applications and issue of permits

(1) Where an application for a permit is duly made to a local authority under section 67 in respect of a public charitable collection, the authority shall either –
   (a) issue a permit in respect of the collection, or
   (b) refuse the application on one or more of the grounds specified in section 69,
and, where they issue such a permit, it shall (subject to section 70) have effect for the period specified in the application in accordance with section 67(2)(a).

(2) A local authority may, at the time of issuing a permit under this section, attach to it such conditions as they think fit, having regard to the local circumstances of the collection; but the authority shall secure that the terms of any such conditions are consistent with the provisions of any regulations under section 73.

(3) Without prejudice to the generality of subsection (2), a local authority may attach conditions –

(a) specifying the day of the week, date, time or frequency of the collection;
(b) specifying the locality or localities within their area in which the collection may be
     conducted;
(c) regulating the manner in which the collection is to be conducted.

(4) Where a local authority –
   (a) refuse to issue a permit, or
   (b) attach any condition to a permit under subsection (2),
they shall serve on the applicant written notice of their decision to do so and of the reasons for
their decision; and that notice shall also state the right of appeal conferred by section 71(1) or (as
the case may be) section 71(2), and the time within which such an appeal must be brought.

69. Refusal of permits

(1) A local authority may refuse to issue a permit to conduct a public charitable collection on any
of the following grounds, namely –
   (a) that it appears to them that the collection would cause undue inconvenience to members
        of the public by reason of –
        (i)   the day of the week or date on which,
        (ii) the time at which,
        (iii) the frequency with which, or
        (iv) the locality or localities in which,
        it is proposed to be conducted;
   (b) that the collection is proposed to be conducted on a day on which another public
        charitable collection is already authorised (whether under section 68 or otherwise) to be
        conducted in the authority's area, or on the day falling immediately before, or immediately
        after, any such day;
   (c) that it appears to them that the amount likely to be applied for charitable, benevolent or
        philanthropic purposes in consequence of the collection would be inadequate, having
        regard to the likely amount of the proceeds of the collection;
   (d) that it appears to them that the applicant or any other person would be likely to receive an
        excessive amount by way of remuneration in connection with the collection;
   (e) that the applicant has been convicted –
        (i)   of an offence under section 5 of the 1916 Act, under the 1939 Act, under section 119
              of the 1982 Act or regulations made under it, or under this Part or regulations made
              under section 73 below, or
        (ii) of any offence involving dishonesty or of a kind the commission of which would in
              their opinion be likely to be facilitated by the issuing to him of a permit under section
              68 above;
   (f) where the applicant is a person other than a charitable, benevolent or philanthropic
        institution for whose benefit the collection is proposed to be conducted, that they are not
        satisfied that the applicant is authorised (whether by any such institution or by any person
        acting on behalf of any such institution) to promote the collection; or
   (g) that it appears to them that the applicant, in promoting any other collection authorised
        under this Part or under section 119 of the 1982 Act, failed to exercise due diligence –
        (i)   to secure that persons authorised by him to act as collectors for the purposes of the
              collection were fit and proper persons;
        (ii) to secure that such persons complied with the provisions of regulations under section
              73 below or (as the case may be) section 119 of the 1982 Act; or
        (iii) to prevent badges or certificates of authority being obtained by persons other than
              those he had so authorised.

(2) A local authority shall not, however, refuse to issue such a permit on the ground mentioned in subsection (1)(b) if it appears to them –

    (a) that the collection would be conducted only in one location, which is on land to which members of the public would have access only by virtue of the express or implied permission of the occupier of the land; and

    (b) that the occupier of the land consents to the collection being conducted there;

and for this purpose 'the occupier', in relation to unoccupied land, means the person entitled to occupy it.

(3) In subsection (1) –

    (a) in the case of a collection in relation to which there is more than one applicant, any reference to the applicant shall be construed as a reference to any of the applicants; and

    (b) (subject to subsection (4)) the reference in paragraph (g)(iii) to badges or certificates of authority is a reference to badges or certificates of authority in a form prescribed by regulations under section 73 below or (as the case may be) under section 119 of the 1982 Act.

(4) Subsection (1)(g) applies to the conduct of the applicant (or any of the applicants) in relation to any public charitable collection authorised under regulations made under section 5 of the 1916 Act (collection of money or sale of articles in a street or other public place), or authorised under the 1939 Act (collection of money or other property by means of visits from house to house), as it applies to his conduct in relation to a collection authorised under this Part, subject to the following modifications, namely –

    (a) in the case of a collection authorised under regulations made under the 1916 Act –

        (i) the reference in sub-paragraph (ii) to regulations under section 73 below shall be construed as a reference to the regulations under which the collection in question was authorised, and

        (ii) the reference in sub-paragraph (iii) to badges or certificates of authority shall be construed as a reference to any written authority provided to a collector pursuant to those regulations; and

    (b) in the case of a collection authorised under the 1939 Act –

        (i) the reference in sub-paragraph (ii) to regulations under section 73 below shall be construed as a reference to regulations under section 4 of that Act, and

        (ii) the reference in sub-paragraph (iii) to badges or certificates of authority shall be construed as a reference to badges or certificates of authority in a form prescribed by such regulations.

(5) In this section –

'the 1916 Act' means the Police, Factories, etc (Miscellaneous Provisions) Act 1916;

'the 1939 Act' means the House to House Collections Act 1939; and

'the 1982 Act' means the Civic Government (Scotland) Act 1982.

70. Withdrawal etc of permits

(1) Where a local authority who have issued a permit under section 68 –

    (a) have reason to believe that there has been a change in the circumstances which prevailed at the time when they issued the permit, and are of the opinion that, if the application for the permit had been made in the new circumstances of the case, the permit would not have been issued by them, or

    (b) have reason to believe that any information furnished to them by the promoter (or, in the case of a collection in relation to which there is more than one promoter, by any of them) for the purposes of the application for the permit was false in a material particular,

then (subject to subsection (2)) they may –

    (i)   withdraw the permit;

   (ii)   attach any condition to the permit; or

  (iii)   vary any existing condition of the permit.

(2) Any condition imposed by the local authority under subsection (1) (whether by attaching a new condition to the permit or by varying an existing condition) must be one that could have been attached to the permit under section 68(2) at the time when it was issued, assuming for this purpose –

  (a) that the new circumstances of the case had prevailed at that time, or

  (b) (in a case falling within paragraph (b) of subsection (1) above) that the authority had been aware of the true circumstances of the case at that time.

(3) Where a local authority who have issued a permit under section 68 have reason to believe that there has been or is likely to be a breach of any condition of it, or that a breach of such a condition is continuing, they may withdraw the permit.

(4) Where under this section a local authority withdraw, attach any condition to, or vary an existing condition of, a permit, they shall serve on the promoter written notice of their decision to do so and of the reasons for their decision; and that notice shall also state the right of appeal conferred by section 71(2) and the time within which such an appeal must be brought.

(5) Where a local authority so withdraw, attach any condition to, or vary an existing condition of, a permit, the permit shall nevertheless continue to have effect as if it had not been withdrawn or (as the case may be) as if the condition had not been attached or the variation had not been made –

  (a) until the time for bringing an appeal under section 71(2) has expired, or

  (b) if such an appeal is duly brought, until the determination or abandonment of the appeal.

71. Appeals

(1) A person who has duly applied to a local authority under section 67 for a permit to conduct a public charitable collection in the authority's area may appeal to a magistrates' court against a decision of the authority to refuse to issue a permit to him.

(2) A person to whom a permit has been issued under section 68 may appeal to a magistrates' court against –

  (a) a decision of the local authority under that section or section 70 to attach any condition to the permit; or

  (b) a decision of the local authority under section 70 to vary any condition so attached or to withdraw the permit.

(3) An appeal under subsection (1) or (2) shall be by way of complaint for an order, and the Magistrates' Courts Act 1980 shall apply to the proceedings; and references in this section to a magistrates' court are to a magistrates' court acting for the petty sessions area in which is situated the office or principal office of the local authority against whose decision the appeal is brought.

(4) Any such appeal shall be brought within 14 days of the date of service on the person in question of the relevant notice under section 68(4) or (as the case may be) section 70(4); and for the purposes of this subsection an appeal shall be taken to be brought when the complaint is made.

(5) An appeal against the decision of a magistrates' court on an appeal under subsection (1) or (2) may be brought to the Crown Court.

(6) On an appeal to a magistrates' court or the Crown Court under this section, the court may confirm, vary or reverse the local authority's decision and generally give such directions as it thinks fit, having regard to the provisions of this Part and of regulations under section 73.

(7) It shall be the duty of the local authority to comply with any directions given by the court under subsection (6); but the authority need not comply with any directions given by a magistrates' court –

(a) until the time for bringing an appeal under subsection (5) has expired, or

(b) if such an appeal is duly brought, until the determination or abandonment of the appeal.

Orders made by Charity Commissioners

72. Orders made by Charity Commissioners

(1) Where the Charity Commissioners are satisfied, on the application of any charity, that that charity proposes –

(a) to promote public charitable collections –

(i) throughout England and Wales, or

(ii) throughout a substantial part of England and Wales,

in connection with any charitable purposes pursued by the charity, or

(b) to authorise other persons to promote public charitable collections as mentioned in paragraph (a),

the Commissioners may make an order under this subsection in respect of the charity.

(2) Such an order shall have the effect of authorising public charitable collections which –

(a) are promoted by the charity in respect of which the order is made, or by persons authorised by the charity, and

(b) are so promoted in connection with the charitable purposes mentioned in subsection (1),

to be conducted in such area or areas as may be specified in the order.

(3) An order under subsection (1) may –

(a) include such conditions as the Commissioners think fit;

(b) be expressed (without prejudice to paragraph (c)) to have effect without limit of time, or for a specified period only;

(c) be revoked or varied by a further order of the Commissioners.

(4) Where the Commissioners, having made an order under subsection (1) in respect of a charity, make any further order revoking or varying that order, they shall serve on the charity written notice of their reasons for making the further order, unless it appears to them that the interests of the charity would not be prejudiced by the further order.

(5) In this section 'charity' and 'charitable purposes' have the same meaning as in the Charities Act 1960.

Supplementary

73. Regulations

(1) The Secretary of State may make regulations –

(a) prescribing the information which is to be contained in applications made under section 67;

(b) for the purpose of regulating the conduct of public charitable collections authorised under –

(i) permits issued under section 68; or

(ii) orders made by the Charity Commissioners under section 72.

(2) Regulations under subsection (1)(b) may, without prejudice to the generality of that provision, make provision –

(a) about the keeping and publication of accounts;

   (b) for the prevention of annoyance to members of the public;

   (c) with respect to the use by collectors of badges and certificates of authority, or badges incorporating such certificates, and to other matters relating to such badges and certificates, including, in particular, provision –

      (i) prescribing the form of such badges and certificates;

      (ii) requiring a collector, on request, to permit his badge, or any certificate of authority held by him for the purposes of the collection, to be inspected by a constable or a duly authorised officer of a local authority, or by an occupier of any premises visited by him in the course of the collection;

   (d) for prohibiting persons under a prescribed age from acting as collectors, and prohibiting others from causing them so to act.

(3) Regulations under this section may provide that any failure to comply with a specified provision of the regulations shall be an offence punishable on summary conviction by a fine not exceeding the second level on the standard scale.

74. Offences

(1) A person shall be guilty of an offence if, in connection with any charitable appeal, he displays or uses –

   (a) a prescribed badge or a prescribed certificate of authority which is not for the time being held by him for the purposes of the appeal pursuant to regulations under section 73, or

   (b) any badge or article, or any certificate or other document, so nearly resembling a prescribed badge or (as the case may be) a prescribed certificate of authority as to be likely to deceive a member of the public.

(2) A person guilty of an offence under subsection (1) shall be liable on summary conviction to a fine not exceeding the fourth level on the standard scale.

(3) Any person who, for the purposes of an application made under section 67, knowingly or recklessly furnishes any information which is false in a material particular shall be guilty of an offence and liable on summary conviction to a fine not exceeding the fourth level on the standard scale.

(4) In subsection (1) 'prescribed badge' and 'prescribed certificate of authority' mean respectively a badge and a certificate of authority in such form as may be prescribed by regulations under section 73.

SCHEDULE 5

Section 49

AMENDMENTS OF REDUNDANT CHURCHES AND OTHER RELIGIOUS
BUILDINGS ACT 1969

1. For section 4 of the Redundant Churches and Other Religious Buildings Act 1969 ('the 1969 Act') substitute –

'4. Transfer of certain redundant places of public worship

   (1) Subject to subsections (9) and (10) below, this section applies to any premises if –

      (a) the premises are held by or in trust for a charity ('the relevant charity'), and

      (b) the whole or part of the premises has been used as a place of public worship; but

      (c) the premises are not a church subject to the provisions of the Pastoral Measure 1983.

(2) If the court is satisfied, with respect to any premises to which this section applies ('the relevant premises') –

    (a) that those premises are no longer required (whether wholly or in part) for use as a place of public worship, and

    (b) that one of the following, namely –

        (i) the Secretary of State,

        (ii) the Commission, or

        (iii) a prescribed charity,

        is or are willing to enter into an agreement to acquire those premises by way of gift or for a consideration other than full consideration, but

    (c) that it is not within the powers of the persons in whom those premises are vested to carry out such an agreement except by virtue of this section,

the court may, under its jurisdiction with respect to charities, establish a scheme for the making and carrying out of such an agreement.

(3) A scheme established under subsection (2) above may, if it appears to the court proper to do so, provide for the acquirer of the relevant premises also to acquire (whether by gift or for a consideration other than full consideration or otherwise) –

    (a) any land held by or in trust for the relevant charity which is contiguous or adjacent to those premises; and

    (b) any objects which are or have been ordinarily kept on those premises.

(4) In subsections (2) and (3) above, in relation to the acquisition of the relevant premises or the acquisition of any land or object –

    (a) references to acquisition by the Secretary of State are references to acquisition by him under section 5 of the Historic Buildings and Ancient Monuments Act 1953 (acquisition by him of buildings of historic or architectural interest); and

    (b) references to acquisition by the Commission are references to acquisition by them under section 5A of that Act (acquisition by them of buildings of historic or architectural interest).

(5) A scheme established under subsection (2) above may also provide for conferring on the acquirer of the relevant premises –

    (a) such rights of way over any land held by or in trust for the relevant charity as appear to the court to be necessary –

        (i) for the purpose of the discharge of the acquirer's functions in relation to those premises or to any land acquired under the scheme, or

        (ii) for giving to the public reasonable access to those premises or to any such land, and

    (b) so far as is necessary for the purpose of the discharge of such functions or the giving of such access, any rights of way enjoyed by persons attending services at those premises.

(6) The Charity Commissioners may, on the application of the acquirer of the relevant premises, by order establish a scheme under section 18 of the Charities Act 1960 (Commissioners' concurrent jurisdiction with the High Court for certain purposes) making provision for the restoration of the relevant premises, or part of them, to use as a place of public worship.

(7) The Charity Commissioners may so establish any such scheme notwithstanding –

    (a) anything in subsection (4) of section 18 of that Act, or

    (b) that the relevant charity has ceased to exist;

and if the relevant charity has ceased to exist, any such scheme may provide for the constitution of a charity by or in trust for which the relevant premises are to be held on the restoration of those premises, or part of them, to use as a place of public worship.

(8) The Charity Commissioners shall have the same jurisdiction and powers in relation to the establishment of a scheme under subsection (2) above as they have under the provisions of section 18 of the Charities Act 1960 (except subsection (6)) in relation to the establishment of a scheme for the administration of a charity; and section 21 of that Act (publicity for proceedings under section 18, etc) shall accordingly have effect in relation to the establishment of a scheme under subsection (2) above as it has effect in relation to the establishment of a scheme for the administration of a charity.

(9) In relation to the Commission –
    (a) this section only applies to any premises falling within subsection (1) above if they are situated in England, and
    (b) references in this section to land are references only to land situated in England.

(10) In relation to a prescribed charity, this section only applies to any premises falling within subsection (1) above if they constitute either –
    (a) a listed building within the meaning of the Planning (Listed Buildings and Conservation Areas) Act 1990, or
    (b) a scheduled monument within the meaning of the Ancient Monuments and Archaeological Areas Act 1979.

(11) The Secretary of State may direct that any charity specified in the direction shall be a prescribed charity for the purposes of this section; and any direction under this subsection may be varied or revoked by a further direction given by the Secretary of State.

(12) References in this section to the acquirer of the relevant premises are references to the person or body acquiring those premises by virtue of a scheme established under subsection (2) above.

(13) In this section and section 5 below –
'the Commission' means the Historic Buildings and Monuments Commission for England;
'premises' includes a part of a building;
'prescribed charity' shall be construed by reference to subsection (11) above;
and sections 45 and 46 of the Charities Act 1960 (interpretation) shall have effect for the purposes of this section and section 5 below as they have effect for the purposes of that Act.'

2. For section 5 of the 1969 Act substitute –

'5. Trusts for repair etc of premises to continue after transfer under section 4

(1) Where any premises to which section 4 of this Act applies are acquired by the Secretary of State, the Commission or a prescribed charity in pursuance of that section, any property of a charity whose purposes include –
    (a) the repair and maintenance of those premises, or
    (b) the provision of objects for keeping on those premises, or
    (c) the maintenance of objects ordinarily kept there,
shall (subject to subsection (2) below) continue to be applicable for that purpose so long as the premises remain vested in the Secretary of State, the Commission or the prescribed charity, as the case may be.

(2) If so provided by the scheme under which the agreement for the acquisition of any such premises is made, subsection (1) above shall have effect in relation to the premises subject to and in accordance with any specified provisions of the scheme.

(3) Subsection (13) of section 4 of this Act has effect for the purposes of this section.'

CHARITIES ACT 1993

(1993 c 10)

ARRANGEMENT OF SECTIONS

PART I

THE CHARITY COMMISSIONERS AND THE OFFICIAL CUSTODIAN FOR CHARITIES

PART II

REGISTRATION AND NAMES OF CHARITIES

Registration of charities

Charity names

PART III

COMMISSIONERS' INFORMATION POWERS

PART IV

APPLICATION OF PROPERTY CY-PRES AND ASSISTANCE AND SUPERVISION OF CHARITIES BY COURT AND COMMISSIONERS

Extended powers of court and variation of charters

PART V

CHARITY LAND

PART VI

CHARITY ACCOUNTS, REPORTS AND RETURNS

PART VII

INCORPORATION OF CHARITY TRUSTEES

PART VIII

CHARITABLE COMPANIES

PART IX

MISCELLANEOUS

Powers of investment

Disqualification for acting as charity trustee

PART X

SUPPLEMENTARY

An Act to consolidate the Charitable Trustees Incorporation Act 1872 and, except for certain spent or transitional provisions, the Charities Act 1960 and Part I of the Charities Act 1992
[27 May 1993]

PART I

THE CHARITY COMMISSIONERS AND THE OFFICIAL CUSTODIAN FOR CHARITIES

1. The Charity Commissioners

(1) There shall continue to be a body of Charity Commissioners for England and Wales, and they shall have such functions as are conferred on them by this Act in addition to any functions under any other enactment for the time being in force.

(2) The provisions of Schedule 1 to this Act shall have effect with respect to the constitution and proceedings of the Commissioners and other matters relating to the Commissioners and their officers and employees.

(3) The Commissioners shall (without prejudice to their specific powers and duties under other enactments) have the general function of promoting the effective use of charitable resources by encouraging the development of better methods of administration, by giving charity trustees information or advice on any matter affecting the charity and by investigating and checking abuses.

(4) It shall be the general object of the Commissioners so to act in the case of any charity (unless it is a matter of altering its purposes) as best to promote and make effective the work of the charity in meeting the needs designated by its trusts; but the Commissioners shall not themselves have power to act in the administration of a charity.

(5) The Commissioners shall, as soon as possible after the end of every year, make to the Secretary of State a report on their operations during that year, and he shall lay a copy of the report before each House of Parliament.

2. The official custodian for charities

(1) There shall continue to be an officer known as the official custodian for charities (in this Act referred to as 'the official custodian') whose function it shall be to act as trustee for charities in the cases provided for by this Act; and the official custodian shall be by that name a corporation sole having perpetual succession and using an official seal which shall be officially and judicially noticed.

(2) Such officer of the Commissioners as they may from time to time designate shall be the official custodian.

(3) The official custodian shall perform his duties in accordance with such general or special directions as may be given him by the Commissioners, and his expenses (except those

re-imbursed to him or recovered by him as trustee for any charity) shall be defrayed by the Commissioners.

(4) Anything which is required to or may be done by, to or before the official custodian may be done by, to or before any officer of the Commissioners generally or specially authorised by them to act for him during a vacancy in his office or otherwise.

(5) The official custodian shall not be liable as trustee for any charity in respect of any loss or of the mis-application of any property unless it is occasioned by or through the wilful neglect or default of the custodian or of any person acting for him; but the Consolidated Fund shall be liable to make good to a charity any sums for which the custodian may be liable by reason of any such neglect or default.

(6) The official custodian shall keep such books of account and such records in relation thereto as may be directed by the Treasury and shall prepare accounts in such form, in such manner and at such times as may be so directed.

(7) The accounts so prepared shall be examined and certified by the Comptroller and Auditor General, and the report to be made by the Commissioners to the Secretary of State for any year shall include a copy of the accounts so prepared for any period ending in or with the year and of the certificate and report of the Comptroller and Auditor General with respect to those accounts.

PART II

REGISTRATION AND NAMES OF CHARITIES

Registration of charities

3. The register of charities

(1) The Commissioners shall continue to keep a register of charities, which shall be kept by them in such manner as they think fit.

(2) There shall be entered in the register every charity not excepted by subsection (5) below; and a charity so excepted (other than one excepted by paragraph (a) of that subsection) may be entered in the register at the request of the charity, but (whether or not it was excepted at the time of registration) may at any time, and shall at the request of the charity, be removed from the register.

(3) The register shall contain –
  (a) the name of every registered charity; and
  (b) such other particulars of, and such other information relating to, every such charity as the Commissioners think fit.

(4) Any institution which no longer appears to the Commissioners to be a charity shall be removed from the register, with effect, where the removal is due to any change in its purpose or trusts, from the date of that change; and there shall also be removed from the register any charity which ceases to exist or does not operate.

(5) The following charities are not required to be registered –
  (a) any charity comprised in Schedule 2 to this Act (in this Act referred to as an 'exempt charity');
  (b) any charity which is excepted by order or regulations;
  (c) any charity which has neither –

(i) any permanent endowment, nor

(ii) the use or occupation of any land,

and whose income from all sources does not in aggregate amount to more than £1,000 a year;

and no charity is required to be registered in respect of any registered place of worship.

(6) With any application for a charity to be registered there shall be supplied to the Commissioners copies of its trusts (or, if they are not set out in any extant document, particulars of them), and such other documents or information as may be prescribed by regulations made by the Secretary of State or as the Commissioners may require for the purpose of the application.

(7) It shall be the duty –

(a) of the charity trustees of any charity which is not registered nor excepted from registration to apply for it to be registered, and to supply the documents and information required by subsection (6) above; and

(b) of the charity trustees (or last charity trustees) of any institution which is for the time being registered to notify the Commissioners if it ceases to exist, or if there is any change in its trusts or in the particulars of it entered in the register, and to supply to the Commissioners particulars of any such change and copies of any new trusts or alterations of the trusts.

(8) The register (including the entries cancelled when institutions are removed from the register) shall be open to public inspection at all reasonable times; and copies (or particulars) of the trusts of any registered charity as supplied to the Commissioners under this section shall, so long as it remains on the register, be kept by them and be open to public inspection at all reasonable times, except in so far as regulations made by the Secretary of State otherwise provide.

(9) Where any information contained in the register is not in documentary form, subsection (8) above shall be construed as requiring the information to be available for public inspection in legible form at all reasonable times.

(10) If the Commissioners so determine, subsection (8) above shall not apply to any particular information contained in the register and specified in their determination.

(11) Nothing in the foregoing subsections shall require any person to supply the Commissioners with copies of schemes for the administration of a charity made otherwise than by the court, or to notify the Commissioners of any change made with respect to a registered charity by such a scheme, or require a person, if he refers the Commissioners to a document or copy already in the possession of the Commissioners, to supply a further copy of the document; but where by virtue of this subsection a copy of any document need not be supplied to the Commissioners, a copy of it, if it relates to a registered charity, shall be open to inspection under subsection (8) above as if supplied to the Commissioners under this section.

(12) If the Secretary of State thinks it expedient to do so –

(a) in consequence of changes in the value of money, or

(b) with a view to extending the scope of the exception provided for by subsection (5)(c) above,

he may by order amend subsection (5)(c) by substituting a different sum for the sum for the time being specified there.

(13) The reference in subsection (5)(b) above to a charity which is excepted by order or regulations is to a charity which –

(a) is for the time being permanently or temporarily excepted by order of the Commissioners; or

(b) is of a description permanently or temporarily excepted by regulations made by the Secretary of State, and which complies with any conditions of the exception.

(14) In this section 'registered place of worship' means any land or building falling within section 9 of the Places of Worship Registration Act 1855 (that is to say, the land and buildings which if the Charities Act 1960 had not been passed, would by virtue of that section as amended by subsequent enactments be partially exempted from the operation of the Charitable Trusts Act 1853), and for the purposes of this subsection 'building' includes part of a building.

4. Effect of, and claims and objections to, registration

(1) An institution shall for all purposes other than rectification of the register be conclusively presumed to be or to have been a charity at any time when it is or was on the register of charities.

(2) Any person who is or may be affected by the registration of an institution as a charity may, on the ground that it is not a charity, object to its being entered by the Commissioners in the register, or apply to them for it to be removed from the register; and provision may be made by regulations made by the Secretary of State as to the manner in which any such objection or application is to be made, prosecuted or dealt with.

(3) An appeal against any decision of the Commissioners to enter or not to enter an institution in the register of charities, or to remove or not to remove an institution from the register, may be brought in the High Court by the Attorney General, or by the persons who are or claim to be the charity trustees of the institution, or by any person whose objection or application under subsection (2) above is disallowed by the decision.

(4) If there is an appeal to the High Court against any decision of the Commissioners to enter an institution in the register, or not to remove an institution from the register, then until the Commissioners are satisfied whether the decision of the Commissioners is or is not to stand, the entry in the register shall be maintained, but shall be in suspense and marked to indicate that it is in suspense; and for the purposes of subsection (1) above an institution shall be deemed not to be on the register during any period when the entry relating to it is in suspense under this subsection.

(5) Any question affecting the registration or removal from the register of an institution may, notwithstanding that it has been determined by a decision on appeal under subsection (3) above, be considered afresh by the Commissioners and shall not be concluded by that decision, if it appears to the Commissioners that there has been a change of circumstances or that the decision is inconsistent with a later judicial decision, whether given on such an appeal or not.

5. Status of registered charity (other than small charity) to appear on official publications etc

(1) This section applies to a registered charity if its gross income in its last financial year exceeded £10,000.

(2) Where this section applies to a registered charity, the fact that it is a registered charity shall be stated in legible characters –
  (a) in all notices, advertisements and other documents issued by or on behalf of the charity and soliciting money or other property for the benefit of the charity;
  (b) in all bills of exchange, promissory notes, endorsements, cheques and orders for money or goods purporting to be signed on behalf of the charity; and
  (c) in all bills rendered by it and in all its invoices, receipts and letters of credit.

(2A) The statement required by subsection (2) above shall be in English, except that, in the case of a document which is otherwise wholly in Welsh, the statement may be in Welsh if it consists of or includes the words 'elusen cofrestredig' (the Welsh equivalent of 'registered charity').

(3) Subsection (2)(a) above has effect whether the solicitation is express or implied, and whether the money or other property is to be given for any consideration or not.

(4) If, in the case of a registered charity to which this section applies, any person issues or authorises the issue of any document falling within paragraph (a) or (c) of subsection (2) above which does not contain the statement required by that subsection, he shall be guilty of an offence and liable on summary conviction to a fine not exceeding level 3 on the standard scale.

(5) If, in the case of any such registered charity, any person signs any document falling within paragraph (b) of subsection (2) above which does not contain the statement required by that subsection, he shall be guilty of an offence and liable on summary conviction to a fine not exceeding level 3 on the standard scale.

(6) The Secretary of State may by order amend subsection (1) above by substituting a different sum for the sum for the time being specified there.

NOTE

Section shown as amended by the Welsh Language Act 1993 and the Charities Act 1993 (Substitution of Sums) Order 1995 (SI 1995/2696).

Charity names

6. Power of Commissioners to require charity's name to be changed

(1) Where this subsection applies to a charity, the Commissioners may give a direction requiring the name of the charity to be changed, within such period as is specified in the direction, to such other name as the charity trustees may determine with the approval of the Commissioners.

(2) Subsection (1) above applies to a charity if –
    (a) it is a registered charity and its name ('the registered name') –
        (i) is the same as, or
        (ii) is in the opinion of the Commissioners too like,
        the name, at the time when the registered name was entered in the register in respect of the charity, of any other charity (whether registered or not);
    (b) the name of the charity is in the opinion of the Commissioners likely to mislead the public as to the true nature –
        (i) of the purposes of the charity as set out in its trusts, or
        (ii) of the activities which the charity carries on under its trusts in pursuit of those purposes;
    (c) the name of the charity includes any word or expression for the time being specified in regulations made by the Secretary of State and the inclusion in its name of that word or expression is in the opinion of the Commissioners likely to mislead the public in any respect as to the status of the charity;
    (d) the name of the charity is in the opinion of the Commissioners likely to give the impression that the charity is connected in some way with Her Majesty's Government or any local authority, or with any other body of persons or any individual, when it is not so connected; or
    (e) the name of the charity is in the opinion of the Commissioners offensive;
and in this subsection any reference to the name of a charity is, in relation to a registered charity, a reference to the name by which it is registered.

(3) Any direction given by virtue of subsection (2)(a) above must be given within twelve months of the time when the registered name was entered in the register in respect of the charity.

(4) Any direction given under this section with respect to a charity shall be given to the charity trustees; and on receiving any such direction the charity trustees shall give effect to it notwithstanding anything in the trusts of the charity.

(5) Where the name of any charity is changed under this section, then (without prejudice to section 3(7)(b) above) it shall be the duty of the charity trustees forthwith to notify the Commissioners of the charity's new name and of the date on which the change occurred.

(6) A change of name by a charity under this section does not affect any rights or obligations of the charity; and any legal proceedings that might have been continued or commenced by or against it in its former name may be continued or commenced by or against it in its new name.

(7) Section 26(3) of the Companies Act 1985 (minor variations in names to be disregarded) shall apply for the purposes of this section as if the reference to section 26(1)(c) of that Act were a reference to subsection (2)(a) above.

(8) Any reference in this section to the charity trustees of a charity shall, in relation to a charity which is a company, be read as a reference to the directors of the company.

(9) Nothing in this section applies to an exempt charity.

7. Effect of direction under s 6 where charity is a company

(1) Where any direction is given under section 6 above with respect to a charity which is a company, the direction shall be taken to require the name of the charity to be changed by resolution of the directors of the company.

(2) Section 380 of the Companies Act 1985 (registration etc of resolutions and agreements) shall apply to any resolution passed by the directors in compliance with any such direction.

(3) Where the name of such a charity is changed in compliance with any such direction, the registrar of companies –
    (a) shall, subject to section 26 of the Companies Act 1985 (prohibition on registration of certain names), enter the new name on the register of companies in place of the former name, and
    (b) shall issue a certificate of incorporation altered to meet the circumstances of the case;
and the change of name has effect from the date on which the altered certificate is issued.

PART III

COMMISSIONERS' INFORMATION POWERS

8. General power to institute inquiries

(1) The Commissioners may from time to time institute inquiries with regard to charities or a particular charity or class of charities, either generally or for particular purposes, but no such inquiry shall extend to any exempt charity.

(2) The Commissioners may either conduct such an inquiry themselves or appoint a person to conduct it and make a report to them.

(3) For the purposes of any such inquiry the Commissioners, or a person appointed by them to conduct it, may direct any person (subject to the provisions of this section) –
    (a) to furnish accounts and statements in writing with respect to any matter in question at the inquiry, being a matter on which he has or can reasonably obtain information, or to return answers in writing to any questions or inquiries addressed to him on any such matter, and to verify any such accounts, statements or answers by statutory declaration;

(b) to furnish copies of documents in his custody or under his control which relate to any matter in question at the inquiry, and to verify any such copies by statutory declaration;

(c) to attend at a specified time and place and give evidence or produce any such documents.

(4) For the purposes of any such inquiry evidence may be taken on oath, and the person conducting the inquiry may for that purpose administer oaths, or may instead of administering an oath require the person examined to make and subscribe a declaration of the truth of the matters about which he is examined.

(5) The Commissioners may pay to any person the necessary expenses of his attendance to give evidence or produce documents for the purpose of an inquiry under this section, and a person shall not be required in obedience to a direction under paragraph (c) of subsection (3) above to go more than ten miles from his place of residence unless those expenses are paid or tendered to him.

(6) Where an inquiry has been held under this section, the Commissioners may either –

(a) cause the report of the person conducting the inquiry, or such other statement of the results of the inquiry as they think fit, to be printed and published, or

(b) publish any such report or statement in some other way which is calculated in their opinion to bring it to the attention of persons who may wish to make representations to them about the action to be taken.

(7) The council of a county or district, the Common Council of the City of London and the council of a London borough may contribute to the expenses of the Commissioners in connection with inquiries under this section into local charities in the council's area.

9. Power to call for documents and search records

(1) The Commissioners may by order –

(a) require any person to furnish them with any information in his possession which relates to any charity and is relevant to the discharge of their functions or of the functions of the official custodian;

(b) require any person who has in his custody or under his control any document which relates to any charity and is relevant to the discharge of their functions or of the functions of the official custodian –

(i) to furnish them with a copy of or extract from the document, or

(ii) (unless the document forms part of the records or other documents of a court or of a public or local authority) to transmit the document itself to them for their inspection.

(2) Any officer of the Commissioners, if so authorised by them, shall be entitled without payment to inspect and take copies of or extracts from the records or other documents of any court, or of any public registry or office of records, for any purpose connected with the discharge of the functions of the Commissioners or of the official custodian.

(3) The Commissioners shall be entitled without payment to keep any copy or extract furnished to them under subsection (1) above; and where a document transmitted to them under that subsection for their inspection relates only to one or more charities and is not held by any person entitled as trustee or otherwise to the custody of it, the Commissioners may keep it or may deliver it to the charity trustees or to any other person who may be so entitled.

(4) No person properly having the custody of documents relating only to an exempt charity shall be required under subsection (1) above to transmit to the Commissioners any of those documents, or to furnish any copy of or extract from any of them.

(5) The rights conferred by subsection (2) above shall, in relation to information recorded otherwise than in legible form, include the right to require the information to be made available in legible form for inspection or for a copy or extract to be made of or from it.

10. Disclosure of information to and by Commissioners

(1) Subject to subsection (2) below and to any express restriction imposed by or under any other enactment, a body or person to whom this section applies may disclose to the Charity Commissioners any information received by that body or person under or for the purposes of any enactment, where the disclosure is made by the body or person for the purpose of enabling or assisting the Commissioners to discharge any of their functions.

(2) Subsection (1) above shall not have effect in relation to the Commissioners of Customs and Excise or the Commissioners of Inland Revenue; but either of those bodies of Commissioners ('the relevant body') may disclose to the Charity Commissioners the following information –
- (a) the name and address of any institution which has for any purpose been treated by the relevant body as established for charitable purposes;
- (b) information as to the purposes of an institution and the trusts under which it is established or regulated, where the disclosure is made by the relevant body in order to give or obtain assistance in determining whether the institution ought for any purpose to be treated as established for charitable purposes; and
- (c) information with respect to an institution which has for any purpose been treated as so established but which appears to the relevant body –
  - (i) to be, or to have been, carrying on activities which are not charitable, or
  - (ii) to be, or to have been, applying any of its funds for purposes which are not charitable.

(3) In subsection (2) above, any reference to an institution shall, in relation to the Commissioners of Inland Revenue, be construed as a reference to an institution in England and Wales.

(4) Subject to subsection (5) below, the Charity Commissioners may disclose to a body or person to whom this section applies any information received by them under or for the purposes of any enactment, where the disclosure is made by the Commissioners –
- (a) for any purpose connected with the discharge of their functions, and
- (b) for the purpose of enabling or assisting that body or person to discharge any of its or his functions.

(5) Where any information disclosed to the Charity Commissioners under subsection (1) or (2) above is so disclosed subject to any express restriction on the disclosure of the information by the Commissioners, the Commissioners' power of disclosure under subsection (4) above shall, in relation to the information, be exercisable by them subject to any such restriction.

(6) This section applies to the following bodies and persons –
- (a) any government department (including a Northern Ireland department);
- (b) any local authority;
- (c) any constable; and
- (d) any other body or person discharging functions of a public nature (including a body or person discharging regulatory functions in relation to any description of activities).

(7) In subsection (6)(d) above the reference to any such body or person as is there mentioned shall, in relation to a disclosure by the Charity Commissioners under subsection (4) above, be construed as including a reference to any such body or person in a country or territory outside the United Kingdom.

(8) Nothing in this section shall be construed as affecting any power of disclosure exercisable apart from this section.

(9) In this section 'enactment' includes an enactment comprised in subordinate legislation (within the meaning of the Interpretation Act 1978).

11. Supply of false or misleading information to Commissioners, etc

(1) Any person who knowingly or recklessly provides the Commissioners with information which is false or misleading in a material particular shall be guilty of an offence if the information –
- (a) is provided in purported compliance with a requirement imposed by or under this Act; or
- (b) is provided otherwise than as mentioned in paragraph (a) above but in circumstances in which the person providing the information intends, or could reasonably be expected to know, that it would be used by the Commissioners for the purpose of discharging their functions under this Act.

(2) Any person who wilfully alters, suppresses, conceals or destroys any document which he is or is liable to be required, by or under this Act, to produce to the Commissioners shall be guilty of an offence.

(3) Any person guilty of an offence under this section shall be liable –
- (a) on summary conviction, to a fine not exceeding the statutory maximum;
- (b) on conviction on indictment, to imprisonment for a term not exceeding two years or to a fine, or both.

(4) In this section references to the Commissioners include references to any person conducting an inquiry under section 8 above.

12. Data protection

An order under section 30 of the Data Protection Act 1984 (exemption from subject access provisions of data held for the purpose of discharging designated functions in connection with the regulation of financial services etc) may designate for the purposes of that section, as if they were functions conferred by or under such an enactment as is there mentioned, any functions of the Commissioners appearing to the Secretary of State to be –
- (a) connected with the protection of charities against misconduct or mismanagement (whether by trustees or other persons) in their administration; or
- (b) connected with the protection of the property of charities from loss or misapplication or with the recovery of such property.

PART IV

APPLICATION OF PROPERTY CY-PRES AND ASSISTANCE AND SUPERVISION OF CHARITIES BY COURT AND COMMISSIONERS

Extended powers of court and variation of charters

13. Occasions for applying property cy-près

(1) Subject to subsection (2) below, the circumstances in which the original purposes of a charitable gift can be altered to allow the property given or part of it to be applied cy-près shall be as follows –
- (a) where the original purposes, in whole or in part –
  - (i) have been as far as may be fulfilled; or
  - (ii) cannot be carried out, or not according to the directions given and to the spirit of the gift; or
- (b) where the original purposes provide a use for part only of the property available by virtue of the gift; or

(c) where the property available by virtue of the gift and other property applicable for similar purposes can be more effectively used in conjunction, and to that end can suitably, regard being had to the spirit of the gift, be made applicable to common purposes; or

(d) where the original purposes were laid down by reference to an area which then was but has since ceased to be a unit for some other purpose, or by reference to a class of persons or to an area which has for any reason since ceased to be suitable, regard being had to the spirit of the gift, or to be practical in administering the gift; or

(e) where the original purposes, in whole or in part, have, since they were laid down, –

  (i) been adequately provided for by other means; or

  (ii) ceased, as being useless or harmful to the community or for other reasons, to be in law charitable; or

  (iii) ceased in any other way to provide a suitable and effective method of using the property available by virtue of the gift, regard being had to the spirit of the gift.

(2) Subsection (1) above shall not affect the conditions which must be satisfied in order that property given for charitable purposes may be applied cy-près except in so far as those conditions require a failure of the original purposes.

(3) References in the foregoing subsections to the original purposes of a gift shall be construed, where the application of the property given has been altered or regulated by a scheme or otherwise, as referring to the purposes for which the property is for the time being applicable.

(4) Without prejudice to the power to make schemes in circumstances falling within subsection (1) above, the court may by scheme made under the court's jurisdiction with respect to charities, in any case where the purposes for which the property is held are laid down by reference to any such area as is mentioned in the first column in Schedule 3 to this Act, provide for enlarging the area to any such area as is mentioned in the second column in the same entry in that Schedule.

(5) It is hereby declared that a trust for charitable purposes places a trustee under a duty, where the case permits and requires the property or some part of it to be applied cy-près, to secure its effective use for charity by taking steps to enable it to be so applied.

14. Application cy-près of gifts of donors unknown or disclaiming

(1) Property given for specific charitable purposes which fail shall be applicable cy-près as if given for charitable purposes generally, where it belongs –

(a) to a donor who after –

  (i) the prescribed advertisements and inquiries have been published and made, and

  (ii) the prescribed period beginning with the publication of those advertisements has expired,

  cannot be identified or cannot be found; or

(b) to a donor who has executed a disclaimer in the prescribed form of his right to have the property returned.

(2) Where the prescribed advertisements and inquiries have been published and made by or on behalf of trustees with respect to any such property, the trustees shall not be liable to any person in respect of the property if no claim by him to be interested in it is received by them before the expiry of the period mentioned in subsection (1)(a)(ii) above.

(3) For the purposes of this section property shall be conclusively presumed (without any advertisement or inquiry) to belong to donors who cannot be identified, in so far as it consists –

(a) of the proceeds of cash collections made by means of collecting boxes or by other means not adapted for distinguishing one gift from another; or

(b) of the proceeds of any lottery, competition, entertainment, sale or similar money-raising activity, after allowing for property given to provide prizes or articles for sale or otherwise to enable the activity to be undertaken.

(4) The court may by order direct that property not falling within subsection (3) above shall for the purposes of this section be treated (without any advertisement or inquiry) as belonging to donors who cannot be identified where it appears to the court either –

(a) that it would be unreasonable, having regard to the amounts likely to be returned to the donors, to incur expense with a view to returning the property; or

(b) that it would be unreasonable, having regard to the nature, circumstances and amounts of the gifts, and to the lapse of time since the gifts were made, for the donors to expect the property to be returned.

(5) Where property is applied cy-près by virtue of this section, the donor shall be deemed to have parted with all his interest at the time when the gift was made; but where property is so applied as belonging to donors who cannot be identified or cannot be found, and is not so applied by virtue of subsection (3) or (4) above –

(a) the scheme shall specify the total amount of that property; and

(b) the donor of any part of that amount shall be entitled, if he makes a claim not later than six months after the date on which the scheme is made, to recover from the charity for which the property is applied a sum equal to that part, less any expenses properly incurred by the charity trustees after that date in connection with claims relating to his gift; and

(c) the scheme may include directions as to the provision to be made for meeting any such claim.

(6) Where –

(a) any sum is, in accordance with any such directions, set aside for meeting any such claims, but

(b) the aggregate amount of any such claims actually made exceeds the relevant amount,

then, if the Commissioners so direct, each of the donors in question shall be entitled only to such proportion of the relevant amount as the amount of his claim bears to the aggregate amount referred to in paragraph (b) above; and for this purpose 'the relevant amount' means the amount of the sum so set aside for deduction of any expenses properly incurred by the charity trustees in connection with claims relating to the donors' gifts.

(7) For the purposes of this section, charitable purposes shall be deemed to 'fail' where any difficulty in applying property to those purposes makes that property or the part not applicable cy-près available to be returned to the donors.

(8) In this section 'prescribed' means prescribed by regulations made by the Commissioners; and such regulation may, as respects the advertisements which are to be published for the purposes of subsection (1)(a) above, make provision as to the form and content of such advertisements as well as the manner in which they are to be published.

(9) Any regulations made by the Commissioners under this section shall be published by the Commissioners in such manner as they think fit.

(10) In this section, except in so far as the context otherwise requires, references to a donor include persons claiming through or under the original donor, and references to property given include the property for the time being representing the property originally given or properly derived from it.

(11) This section shall apply to property given for charitable purposes, notwithstanding that it was so given before the commencement of this Act.

15. Charities governed by charter, or by or under statute

(1) Where a Royal charter establishing or regulating a body corporate is amendable by the grant and acceptance of a further charter, a scheme relating to the body corporate or to the administration of property held by the body (including a scheme for the cy-près application of any such property) may be made by the court under the court's jurisdiction with respect to charities notwithstanding that the scheme cannot take effect without the alteration of the charter, but shall be so framed that the scheme, or such part of it as cannot take effect without the alteration of the charter, does not purport to come into operation unless or until Her Majesty thinks fit to amend the charter in such manner as will permit the scheme or that part of it to have effect.

(2) Where under the court's jurisdiction with respect to charities or the corresponding jurisdiction of a court in Northern Ireland, or under powers conferred by this Act or by any Northern Ireland legislation relating to charities, a scheme is made with respect to a body corporate, and it appears to Her Majesty expedient, having regard to the scheme, to amend any Royal charter relating to that body, Her Majesty may, on the application of that body, amend the charter accordingly by Order in Council in any way in which the charter could be amended by the grant and acceptance of a further charter; and any such Order in Council may be revoked or varied in like manner as the charter it amends.

(3) The jurisdiction of the court with respect to charities shall not be excluded or restricted in the case of a charity of any description mentioned in Schedule 4 to this Act by the operation of the enactments or instruments there mentioned in relation to that description, and a scheme established for any such charity may modify or supersede in relation to it the provision made by any such enactment or instrument as if made by a scheme of the court, and may also make any such provision as is authorised by that Schedule.

Powers of Commissioners to make schemes and act for protection of charities etc

16. Concurrent jurisdiction with High Court for certain purposes

(1) Subject to the provisions of this Act, the Commissioners may by order exercise the same jurisdiction and powers as are exercisable by the High Court in charity proceedings for the following purposes –
   (a) establishing a scheme for the administration of a charity;
   (b) appointing, discharging or removing a charity trustee or trustee for a charity, or removing an officer or employee;
   (c) vesting or transferring property, or requiring or entitling any person to call for or make any transfer of property or any payment.

(2) Where the court directs a scheme for the administration of a charity to be established, the court may by order refer the matter to the Commissioners for them to prepare or settle a scheme in accordance with such directions (if any) as the court sees fit to give, and any such order may provide for the scheme to be put into effect by order of the Commissioners as if prepared under subsection (1) above and without any further order of the court.

(3) The Commissioners shall not have jurisdiction under this section to try or determine the title at law or in equity to any property as between a charity or trustee for a charity and a person holding or claiming the property or an interest in it adversely to the charity, or to try or determine any question as to the existence or extent of any charge or trust.

(4) Subject to the following subsections, the Commissioners shall not exercise their jurisdiction under this section as respects any charity, except –

(a) on the application of the charity; or

(b) on an order of the court under subsection (2) above; or

(c) in the case of a charity other than an exempt charity, on the application of the Attorney General.

(5) In the case of a charity which is not an exempt charity and whose income from all sources does not in aggregate exceed £500 a year, the Commissioners may exercise their jurisdiction under this section on the application –

(a) of any one or more of the charity trustees; or

(b) of any person interested in the charity; or

(c) of any two or more inhabitants of the area of the charity if it is a local charity.

(6) Where in the case of a charity, other than an exempt charity, the Commissioners are satisfied that the charity trustees ought in the interests of the charity to apply for a scheme, but have unreasonably refused or neglected to do so and the Commissioners have given the charity trustees an opportunity to make representations to them, the Commissioners may proceed as if an application for a scheme had been made by the charity but the Commissioners shall not have power in a case where they act by virtue of this subsection to alter the purposes of a charity, unless forty years have elapsed from the date of its foundation.

(7) Where –

(a) a charity cannot apply to the Commissioners for a scheme by reason of any vacancy among the charity trustees or the absence or incapacity of any of them, but

(b) such an application is made by such number of the charity trustees as the Commissioners consider appropriate in the circumstances of the case,

the Commissioners may nevertheless proceed as if the application were an application made by the charity.

(8) The Commissioners may on the application of any charity trustee or trustee for a charity exercise their jurisdiction under this section for the purpose of discharging him from his trusteeship.

(9) Before exercising any jurisdiction under this section otherwise than on an order of the court, the Commissioners shall give notice of their intention to do so to each of the charity trustees, except any that cannot be found or has no known address in the United Kingdom or who is party or privy to an application for the exercise of the jurisdiction; and any such notice may be given by post, and, if given by post, may be addressed to the recipient's last known address in the United Kingdom.

(10) The Commissioners shall not exercise their jurisdiction under this section in any case (not referred to them by order of the court) which, by reason of its contentious character, or of any special question of law or of fact which it may involve, or for other reasons, the Commissioners may consider more fit to be adjudicated on by the court.

(11) An appeal against any order of the Commissioners under this section may be brought in the High Court by the Attorney General.

(12) An appeal against any order of the Commissioners under this section may also, at any time within the three months beginning with the day following that on which the order is published, be brought in the High Court by the charity or any of the charity trustees, or by any person removed from any office or employment by the order (unless he is removed with the concurrence of the charity trustees or with the approval of the special visitor, if any, of the charity).

(13) No appeal shall be brought under subsection (12) above except with a certificate of the Commissioners that it is a proper case for an appeal or with the leave of one of the judges of the High Court attached to the Chancery Division.

(14) Where an order of the Commissioners under this section establishes a scheme for the administration of a charity, any person interested in the charity shall have the like right of appeal under subsection (12) above as a charity trustee, and so also, in the case of a charity which is a local charity in any area, shall any two or more inhabitants of the area and the council of any parish or (in Wales) any community comprising the area or any part of it.

(15) If the Secretary of State thinks it expedient to do so –
    (a) in consequence of changes in the value of money, or
    (b) with a view to increasing the number of charities in respect of which the Commissioners
        may exercise their jurisdiction under this section in accordance with subsection (5) above,
he may by order amend that subsection by substituting a different sum for the sum for the time being specified there.

17. Further powers to make schemes or alter application of charitable property

(1) Where it appears to the Commissioners that a scheme should be established for the administration of a charity, but also that it is necessary or desirable for the scheme to alter the provision made by an Act of Parliament establishing or regulating the charity or to make any other provision which goes or might go beyond the powers exercisable by them apart from this section, or that it is for any reason proper for the scheme to be subject to parliamentary review, then (subject to subsection (6) below) the Commissioners may settle a scheme accordingly with a view to its being given effect under this section.

(2) A scheme settled by the Commissioners under this section may be given effect by order of the Secretary of State, and a draft of the order shall be laid before Parliament.

(3) Without prejudice to the operation of section 6 of the Statutory Instruments Act 1946 in other cases, in the case of a scheme which goes beyond the powers exercisable apart from this section in altering a statutory provision contained in or having effect under any public general Act of Parliament, the order shall not be made unless the draft has been approved by resolution of each House of Parliament.

(4) Subject to subsection (5) below, any provision of a scheme brought into effect under this section may be modified or superseded by the court or the Commissioners as if it were a scheme brought into effect by order of the Commissioners under section 16 above.

(5) Where subsection (3) above applies to a scheme, the order giving effect to it may direct that the scheme shall not be modified or superseded by a scheme brought into effect otherwise than under this section, and may also direct that that subsection shall apply to any scheme modifying or superseding the scheme to which the order gives effect.

(6) The Commissioners shall not proceed under this section without the like application and the like notice of the charity trustees, as would be required if they were proceeding (without an order of the court) under section 16 above; but on any application for a scheme, or in a case where they act by virtue of subsection (6) or (7) of that section, the Commissioners may proceed under this section or that section as appears to them appropriate.

(7) Notwithstanding anything in the trusts of a charity, no expenditure incurred in preparing or promoting a Bill in Parliament shall without the consent of the court or the Commissioners be defrayed out of any moneys applicable for the purposes of a charity but this subsection shall not apply in the case of an exempt charity.

(8) Where the Commissioners are satisfied –
    (a) that the whole of the income of a charity cannot in existing circumstances be effectively
        applied for the purposes of the charity; and

(b) that, if those circumstances continue, a scheme might be made for applying the surplus cy-près; and

(c) that it is for any reason not yet desirable to make such a scheme;

then the Commissioners may by order authorise the charity trustees at their discretion (but subject to any conditions imposed by the order) to apply any accrued or accruing income for any purposes for which it might be made applicable by such a scheme, and any application authorised by the order shall be deemed to be within the purposes of the charity.

(9) An order under subsection (8) above shall not exceed to more than £300 out of income accrued before the date of the order, nor to income accruing more than three years after that date, nor to more than £100 out of the income accruing in any of those three years.

18. Power to act for protection of charities

(1) Where, at any time after they have instituted an inquiry under section 8 above with respect to any charity, the Commissioners are satisfied –

(a) that there is or has been any misconduct or mismanagement in the administration of the charity; or

(b) that it is necessary or desirable to act for the purpose of protecting the property of the charity or securing a proper application for the purposes of the charity of that property or of property coming to the charity,

the Commissioners may of their own motion do one or more of the following things –

(i) by order suspend any trustee, charity trustee, officer, agent or employee of the charity from the exercise of his office or employment pending consideration being given to his removal (whether under this section or otherwise);

(ii) by order appoint such number of additional charity trustees as they consider necessary for the proper administration of the charity;

(iii) by order vest any property held by or in trust for the charity in the official custodian, or require the persons in whom any such property is vested to transfer it to him, or appoint any person to transfer any such property to him;

(iv) order any person who holds any property on behalf of the charity, or of any trustee for it, not to part with the property without the approval of the Commissioners;

(v) order any debtor of the charity not to make any payment in or towards the discharge of his liability to the charity without the approval of the Commissioners;

(vi) by order restrict (notwithstanding anything in the trusts of the charity) the transactions which may be entered into, or the nature or amount of the payments which may be made, in the administration of the charity without the approval of the Commissioners;

(vii) by order appoint (in accordance with section 19 below) a receiver and manager in respect of the property and affairs of the charity.

(2) Where, at any time after they have instituted an inquiry under section 8 above with respect to any charity, the Commissioners are satisfied –

(a) that there is or has been any misconduct or mismanagement in the administration of the charity; and

(b) that it is necessary or desirable to act for the purpose of protecting the property of the charity or securing a proper application for the purposes of the charity of that property or of property coming to the charity,

the Commissioners may of their own motion do either or both of the following things –

(i) by order remove any trustee, charity trustee, officer, agent or employee of the charity who has been responsible for or privy to the misconduct or mismanagement or has by his conduct contributed to it or facilitated it;

    (ii) by order establish a scheme for the administration of the charity.

(3) The references in subsection (1) or (2) above to misconduct or mismanagement shall (notwithstanding anything in the trusts of the charity) extend to the employment for the remuneration or reward of persons acting in the affairs of the charity, or for other administrative purposes, of sums which are excessive in relation to the property which is or is likely to be applied or applicable for the purposes of the charity.

(4) The Commissioners may also remove a charity trustee by order made of their own motion –
  (a) where, within the last five years, the trustee –
    (i) having previously been adjudged bankrupt or had his estate sequestrated, has been discharged, or
    (ii) having previously made a composition or arrangement with, or granted a trust deed for, his creditors, has been discharged in respect of it;
  (b) where the trustee is a corporation in liquidation;
  (c) where the trustee is incapable of acting by reason of mental disorder within the meaning of the Mental Health Act 1983;
  (d) where the trustee has not acted, and will not declare his willingness or unwillingness to act;
  (e) where the trustee is outside England and Wales or cannot be found or does not act, and his absence or failure to act impedes the proper administration of the charity.

(5) The Commissioners may by order made of their own motion appoint a person to be a charity trustee –
  (a) in place of a charity trustee removed by them under this section or otherwise;
  (b) where there are no charity trustees, or where by reason of vacancies in their number or the absence or incapacity of any of their number the charity cannot apply for the appointment;
  (c) where there is a single charity trustee, not being a corporation aggregate, and the Commissioners are of opinion that it is necessary to increase the number for the proper administration of the charity;
  (d) where the Commissioners are of opinion that it is necessary for the proper administration of the charity to have an additional charity trustee because one of the existing charity trustees who ought nevertheless to remain a charity trustee either cannot be found or does not act or is outside England and Wales.

(6) The powers of the Commissioners under this section to remove or appoint charity trustees of their own motion shall include power to make any such order with respect to the vesting in or transfer to the charity trustees of any property as the Commissioners could make on the removal or appointment of a charity trustee by them under section 16 above.

(7) Any order under this section for the removal or appointment of a charity trustee or trustee for a charity, or for the vesting or transfer of any property, shall be of the like effects as an order made under section 16 above.

(8) Subject to subsection (9) below, subsections (11) to (13) of section 16 above shall apply to orders under this section as they apply to orders under that section.

(9) The requirement to obtain any such certificate or leave as is mentioned in section 16(13) above shall not apply to –
  (a) an appeal by a charity or any of the charity trustees of a charity against an order under subsection (1)(vii) above appointing a receiver and manager in respect of the charity's property and affairs, or
  (b) an appeal by a person against an order under subsection (2)(i) or (4)(a) above removing him from his office or employment.

(10) Subsection (14) of section 16 above shall apply to an order under this section which establishes a scheme for the administration of a charity as it applies to such an order under that section.

(11) The power of the Commissioners to make an order under subsection (1)(i) above shall not be exercisable so as to suspend any person from the exercise of his office or employment for a period of more than twelve months; but (without prejudice to the generality of section 89(1) below), any such order made in the case of any person may make provision as respects the period of his suspension for matters arising out of it, and in particular for enabling any person to execute any instrument in his name or otherwise act for him and, in the case of a charity trustee, for adjusting any rules governing the proceedings of the charity trustees to take account of the reduction in the number capable of acting.

(12) Before exercising any jurisdiction under this section otherwise than by virtue of subsection (1) above, the Commissioners shall give notice of their intention to do so to each of the charity trustees, except any that cannot be found or has no known address in the United Kingdom; and any such notice may be given by post and, if given by post, may be addressed to the recipient's last known address in the United Kingdom.

(13) The Commissioners shall, at such intervals as they think fit, review any order made by them under paragraph (i), or any of paragraphs (iii) to (vii), of subsection (1) above; and, if on any such review it appears to them that it would be appropriate to discharge the order in whole or in part, they shall so discharge it (whether subject to any savings or other transitional provisions or not).

(14) If any person contravenes an order under subsection (1)(iv), (v) or (vi) above, he shall be guilty of an offence and liable on summary conviction to a fine not exceeding level 5 on the standard scale.

(15) Subsection (14) above shall not be taken to preclude the bringing of proceedings for breach of trust against any charity trustee or trustee for a charity in respect of a contravention of an order under subsection (1)(iv) or (vi) above (whether proceedings in respect of the contravention are brought against him under subsection (14) above or not).

(16) This section shall not apply to an exempt charity.

19. Supplementary provisions relating to receiver and manager appointed for a charity

(1) The Commissioners may under section 18(1)(vii) above appoint to be receiver and manager in respect of the property and affairs of a charity such person (other than an officer or employee of theirs) as they think fit.

(2) Without prejudice to the generality of section 89(1) below, any order made by the Commissioners under section 18(1)(vii) above may make provision with respect to the functions to be discharged by the receiver and manager appointed by the order; and those functions shall be discharged by him under the supervision of the Commissioners.

(3) In connection with the discharge of those functions any such order may provide –
  (a) for the receiver and manager appointed by the order to have such powers and duties of the charity trustees of the charity concerned (whether arising under this Act or otherwise) as are specified in the order;
  (b) for any powers or duties exercisable or falling to be performed by the receiver and manager by virtue of paragraph (a) above to be exercisable or performed by him to the exclusion of those trustees.

(4) Where a person has been appointed receiver and manager by any such order –

(a) section 29 below shall apply to him and to his functions as a person so appointed as it applies to a charity trustee of the charity concerned and to his duties as such; and

(b) the Commissioners may apply to the High Court for directions in relation to any particular matter arising in connection with the discharge of those functions.

(5) The High Court may on an application under subsection (4)(b) above –
   (a) give such directions, or
   (b) make such orders declaring the rights of any persons (whether before the court or not),
as it thinks just; and the costs of any such application shall be paid by the charity concerned.

(6) Regulations made by the Secretary of State may make provision with respect to –
   (a) the appointment and removal of persons appointed in accordance with this section;
   (b) the remuneration of such persons out of the income of the charities concerned;
   (c) the making of reports to the Commissioners by such persons.

(7) Regulations under subsection (6) above may, in particular, authorise the Commissioners –
   (a) to require security for the due discharge of his functions to be given by a person so appointed;
   (b) to determine the amount of such a person's remuneration;
   (c) to disallow any amount of remuneration in such circumstances as are prescribed by the regulations.

20. Publicity for proceedings under ss 16 to 18

(1) The Commissioners shall not make any order under this Act to establish a scheme for the administration of a charity, or submit such a scheme to the court or the Secretary of State for an order giving it effect, unless not less than one month previously there has been given public notice of their proposals, inviting representations to be made to them within a time specified in the notice, being not less than one month from the date of such notice, and, in the case of a scheme relating to a local charity, other than on ecclesiastical charity, in a parish or (in Wales) a community, a draft of the scheme has been communicated to the parish or community council or, in the case of a parish not having a council, to the chairman of the parish meeting.

(2) The Commissioners shall not make any order under this Act to appoint, discharge or remove a charity trustee or trustee for a charity (other than the official custodian), unless not less than one month previously there has been given the like public notice as is required by subsection (1) above for an order establishing a scheme but this subsection shall not apply in the case of –
   (a) an order under section 18(1)(ii) above; or
   (b) an order discharging or removing a trustee if the Commissioners are of opinion that it is unnecessary and not in his interest to give publicity to the proposal to discharge to remove him.

(3) Before the Commissioners make an order under this Act to remove without his consent a charity trustee or trustee for a charity, or an officer, agent or employee of a charity, the Commissioners shall, unless he cannot be found or has no known address in the United Kingdom, give him not less than one month's notice of their proposal, inviting representations to be made to them within a time specified in the notice.

(4) Where notice is given of any proposals as required by subsections (1) to (3) above, the Commissioners shall take into consideration any representations made to them about the proposals within the time specified in the notice, and may (without further notice) proceed with the proposals either without modification or with such modifications as appear to them to be desirable.

(5) Where the Commissioners make an order which is subject to appeal under subsection (12) of section 16 above the order shall be published either by giving public notice of it or by giving notice of it to all persons entitled to appeal against it under that subsection, as the Commissioners think fit.

(6) Where the Commissioners make an order under this Act to establish a scheme for the administration of a charity, a copy of the order shall, for not less than one month after the order is published, be available for public inspection at all reasonable times at the Commissioners' office and also at some convenient place in the area of the charity, if it is a local charity.

(7) Any notice to be given under this section of any proposals or order shall give such particulars of the proposals or order, or such directions for obtaining information about them, as the Commissioners think sufficient and appropriate, and any public notice shall be given in such manner as they think sufficient and appropriate.

(8) Any notice to be given under this section, other than a public notice, may be given by post and, if given by post, may be addressed to the recipient's last known address in the United Kingdom.

Property vested in official custodian

21. Entrusting charity property to official custodian, and termination of trust

(1) The court may by order –
   (a) vest in the official custodian any land held by or in trust for a charity;
   (b) authorise or require the persons in whom any such land is vested to transfer it to him; or
   (c) appoint any person to transfer any such land to him;
but this subsection does not apply to any interest in land by way of mortgage or other security.

(2) Where property is vested in the official custodian in trust for a charity, the court may make an order discharging him from the trusteeship as respects all or any of that property.

(3) Where the official custodian is discharged from his trusteeship of any property, or the trusts on which he holds any property come to an end, the court may make such vesting orders and give such directions as may seem to the court to be necessary or expedient in consequence.

(4) No person shall be liable for any loss occasioned by his acting in conformity with an order under this section or by his giving effect to anything done in pursuance of such an order, or be excused from so doing by reason of the order having been in any respect improperly obtained.

22. Supplementary provisions as to property vested in official custodian

(1) Subject to the provisions of this Act, where property is vested in the official custodian in trust for a charity, he shall not exercise any powers of management, but he shall as trustee of any property have all the same powers, duties and liabilities, and be entitled to the same rights and immunities, and be subject to the control and orders of the court, as a corporation appointed custodian trustee under section 4 of the Public Trustee Act 1906 except that he shall have no power to charge fees.

(2) Subject to subsection (3) below, where any land is vested in the official custodian in trust for a charity, the charity trustees shall have power in his name and on his behalf to execute and do all assurances and things which they could properly execute or do in their own name and on their own behalf if the land were vested in them.

(3) If any land is so vested in the official custodian by virtue of an order under section 18 above, the power conferred on the charity trustees by subsection (2) above shall not be exercisable by

them in relation to any transaction affecting the land, unless the transaction is authorised by order of the court or of the Commissioners.

(4) Where any land is vested in the official custodian in trust for a charity, the charity trustees shall have the like power to make obligations entered into by them binding on the land as if it were vested in them; and any covenant, agreement or condition which is enforceable by or against the custodian by reason of the land being vested in him shall be enforceable by or against the charity trustees as if the land were vested in them.

(5) In relation to a corporate charity, subsections (2), (3) and (4) above shall apply with the substitution of references to the charity for references to the charity trustees.

(6) Subsections (2), (3) and (4) above shall not authorise any charity trustees or charity to impose any personal liability on the official custodian.

(7) Where the official custodian is entitled as trustee for a charity to the custody of securities or documents of title relating to the trust property, he may permit them to be in the possession or under the control of the charity trustees without thereby incurring any liability.

23. Divestment in the case of land subject to Reverter of Sites Act 1987

(1) Where –
    (a) any land is vested in the official custodian in trust for a charity, and
    (b) it appears to the Commissioners that section 1 of the Reverter of Sites Act 1987 (right of reverter replaced by trust for sale) will, or is likely to, operate in relation to the land at a particular time or in particular circumstances,
the jurisdiction which, under section 16 above, is exercisable by the Commissioners for the purpose of discharging a trustee for a charity may, at any time before section 1 of that Act ('the 1987 Act') operates in relation to the land, be exercised by them of their own motion for the purpose of –
    (i) making an order discharging the official custodian from his trusteeship of the land, and
    (ii) making such vesting orders and giving such directions as appear to them to be necessary or expedient in consequence.

(2) Where –
    (a) section 1 of the 1987 Act has operated in relation to any land which, immediately before the time when that section so operated, was vested in the official custodian in trust for a charity, and
    (b) the land remains vested in him but on the trust arising under that section,
the court or the Commissioners (of their own motion) may –
    (i) make an order discharging the official custodian from his trusteeship of the land, and
    (ii) (subject to the following provisions of this section) make such vesting orders and give such directions as appear to it or them to be necessary or expedient in consequence.

(3) Where any order discharging the official custodian from his trusteeship of any land –
    (a) is made by the court under section 21(2) above, or by the Commissioners under section 16 above, on the grounds that section 1 of the 1987 Act will, or is likely to, operate in relation to the land, or
    (b) is made by the court or the Commissioners under subsection (2) above,
the persons in whom the land is to be vested on the discharge of the official custodian shall be the relevant charity trustees (as defined in subsection (4) below), unless the court or (as the case may be) the Commissioners is or are satisfied that it would be appropriate for it to be vested in some other persons.

(4) In subsection (3) above 'the relevant charity trustees' means –
- (a) in relation to an order made as mentioned in paragraph (a) of that subsection, the charity trustees of the charity in trust for which the land is vested in the official custodian immediately before the time when the order takes effect, or
- (b) in relation to an order made under subsection (2) above, the charity trustees of the charity in trust for which the land was vested in the official custodian immediately before the time when section 1 of the 1987 Act operated in relation to the land.

(5) Where –
- (a) section 1 of the 1987 Act has operated in relation to any such land as is mentioned in subsection (2)(a) above, and
- (b) the land remains vested in the official custodian as mentioned in subsection (2)(b) above,

then (subject to subsection (6) below), all the powers, duties and liabilities that would, apart from this section, be those of the official custodian as trustee for sale of the land shall instead be those of the charity trustees of the charity concerned; and those trustees shall have power in his name and on his behalf to execute and do all assurances and things which they could properly execute or do in their own name and on their own behalf if the land were vested in them.

(6) Subsection (5) above shall not be taken to require or authorise those trustees to sell the land at a time when it remains vested in the official custodian.

(7) Where –
- (a) the official custodian has been discharged from his trusteeship of any land by an order under subsection (2) above, and
- (b) the land has, in accordance with subsection (3) above, been vested in the charity trustees concerned or (as the case may be) in any persons other than those trustees,

the land shall be held by those trustees, or (as the case may be) by those persons, as trustees for sale on the terms of the trust arising under section 1 of the 1987 Act.

(8) The official custodian shall not be liable to any person in respect of any loss or misapplication of any land vested in him in accordance with that section unless it is occasioned by or through any wilful neglect or default of his or of any person acting for him; but the Consolidated Fund shall be liable to make good to any person any sums for which the official custodian may be liable by reason of any such neglect or default.

(9) In this section any reference to section 1 of the 1987 Act operating in relation to any land is a reference to a trust for sale arising in relation to the land under that section.

Establishment of common investment or deposit funds

24. Schemes to establish common investment funds

(1) The court or the Commissioners may by order make and bring into effect schemes (in this section referred to as 'common investment schemes') for the establishment of common investment funds under trusts which provide –
- (a) for property transferred to the fund by or on behalf of a charity participating in the scheme to be invested under the control of trustees appointed to manage the fund; and
- (b) for the participating charities to be entitled (subject to the provisions of the scheme) to the capital and income of the fund in shares determined by reference to the amount or value of the property transferred to it by or on behalf of each of them and to the value of the fund at the time of the transfers.

(2) The court or the Commissioners may make a common investment scheme on the application of any two or more charities.

(3) A common investment scheme may be made in terms admitting any charity to participate, or the scheme may restrict the right to participate in any manner.

(4) A common investment scheme may make provision for, and for all matters connected with, the establishment, investment, management and winding up of the common investment fund, and may in particular include provision –

    (a) for remunerating persons appointed trustees to hold or manage the fund or any part of it, with or without provision authorising a person to receive the remuneration notwithstanding that he is also a charity trustee of or trustee for a participating charity;

    (b) for restricting the size of the fund, and for regulating as to time, amount or otherwise the right to transfer property to or withdraw it from the fund, and for enabling sums to be advanced out of the fund by way of loan to a participating charity pending the withdrawal of property from the fund by the charity;

    (c) for enabling income to be withheld from distribution with a view to avoiding fluctuations in the amounts distributed, and generally for regulating distributions of income;

    (d) for enabling money to be borrowed temporarily for the purpose of meeting payments to be made out of the funds;

    (e) for enabling questions arising under the scheme as to the right of a charity to participate, or as to the rights of participating charities, or as to any other matter, to be conclusively determined by the decision of the trustees managing the fund or in any other manner;

    (f) for regulating the accounts and information to be supplied to participating charities.

(5) A common investment scheme, in addition to the provision for property to be transferred to the fund on the basis that the charity shall be entitled to a share in the capital and income of the fund, may include provision for enabling sums to be deposited by or on behalf of a charity on the basis that (subject to the provisions of the scheme) the charity shall be entitled to repayment of the sums deposited and to interest thereon at a rate determined by or under the scheme; and where a scheme makes any such provision it shall also provide for excluding from the amount of capital and income to be shared between charities participating otherwise than by way of deposit such amounts (not exceeding the amounts properly attributable to the making of deposits) as are from time to time reasonably required in respect of the liabilities of the fund for the repayment of deposits and for the interest on deposits, including amounts required by way of reserve.

(6) Except in so far as a common investment scheme provides to the contrary, the rights under it of a participating charity shall not be capable of being assigned or charged, nor shall any trustee or other person concerned in the management of the common investment fund be required or entitled to take account of any trust or other equity affecting a participating charity or its property or rights.

(7) The powers of investment of every charity shall include power to participate in common investment schemes unless the power is excluded by a provision specifically referring to common investment schemes in the trusts of the charity.

(8) A common investment fund shall be deemed for all purposes to be a charity; and if the scheme admits only exempt charities, the fund shall be an exempt charity for the purposes of this Act.

(9) Subsection (8) above shall apply not only to common investment funds established under the powers of this section, but also to any similar fund established for the exclusive benefits of charities by or under any enactment relating to any particular charities or class of charity.

25. Schemes to establish common deposit funds

(1) The court or the Commissioners may by order make and bring into effect schemes (in this section referred to as 'common deposit schemes') for the establishment of common deposit funds under trusts which provide –

(a) for sums to be deposited by or on behalf of a charity participating in the scheme and invested under the control of trustees appointed to manage the fund; and

(b) for any such charity to be entitled (subject to the provisions of the scheme) to repayment of any sums so deposited and to interest thereon at a rate determined under the scheme.

(2) Subject to subsection (3) below, the following provisions of section 24 above, namely –

(a) subsections (2) to (4), and

(b) subsections (6) to (9),

shall have effect in relation to common deposit schemes and common deposit funds as they have effect in relation to common investment schemes and common investment funds.

(3) In its application in accordance with subsection (2) above, subsection (4) of that section shall have effect with the substitution for paragraphs (b) and (c) of the following paragraphs –

'(b) for regulating as to time, amount or otherwise the right to repayment of sums deposited in the fund;

(c) for authorising a part of the income for any year to be credited to a reserve account maintained for the purpose of counteracting any losses accruing to the fund, and generally for regulating the manner in which the rate of interest on deposits is to be determined from time to time;'.

Additional powers of Commissioners

26. Power to authorise dealings with charity property etc

(1) Subject to the provisions of this section, where it appears to the Commissioners that any action proposed or contemplated in the administration of a charity is expedient in the interests of the charity, they may by order sanction that action, whether or not it would otherwise be within the powers exercisable by the charity trustees in the administration of the charity; and anything done under the authority of such an order shall be deemed to be properly done in the exercise of those powers.

(2) An order under this section may be made so as to authorise a particular transaction, compromise or the like, or a particular application of property, or so as to give a more general authority, and (without prejudice to the generality of subsection (1) above) may authorise a charity to use common premises, or employ a common staff, or otherwise combine for any purpose of administration, with any other charity.

(3) An order under this section may give directions as to the manner in which any expenditure is to be borne and as to other matters connected with or arising out of the action thereby authorised; and where anything is done in pursuance of an authority given by any such order, any directions given in connection therewith shall be binding on the charity trustees for the time being as if contained in the trusts of the charity; but any such directions may on the application of the charity be modified or superseded by a further order.

(4) Without prejudice to the generality of subsection (3) above, the directions which may be given by an order under this section shall in particular include directions for meeting any expenditure out of a specified fund, for charging any expenditure to capital or to income, for requiring expenditure charged to capital to be recouped out of income within a specified period, for restricting the costs to be incurred at the expense of the charity, or for the investment of moneys arising from any transaction.

(5) An order under this section may authorise any act notwithstanding that it is prohibited by any of the disabling Acts mentioned in subsection (6) below or that the trusts of the charity provide for

the act to be done by or under the authority of the court; but no such order shall authorise the doing of any act expressly prohibited by Act of Parliament other than the disabling Acts or by the trusts of the charity or shall extend or alter the purposes of the charity.

(6) The Acts referred to in subsection (5) above as the disabling Acts are the Ecclesiastical Leases Act 1571, the Ecclesiastical Leases Act 1572, the Ecclesiastical Leases Act 1575 and the Ecclesiastical Leases Act 1836.

(7) An order under this section shall not confer any authority in relation to a building which has been consecrated and of which the use or disposal is regulated, and can be further regulated, by a scheme having effect under the Union of Benefices Measures 1923 to 1952, the Reorganisation Areas Measures 1944 and 1954, the Pastoral Measure 1968 or the Pastoral Measure 1983, the reference to a building being taken to include part of a building and any land which under such a scheme is to be used or disposed of with a building to which the scheme applies.

27. Power to authorise ex gratia payments etc

(1) Subject to subsection (3) below, the Commissioners may by order exercise the same power as is exercisable by the Attorney General to authorise the charity trustees of a charity –
    (a) to make any application of property of the charity, or
    (b) to waive to any extent, on behalf of the charity, its entitlement to receive any property,
in a case where the charity trustees –
        (i) (apart from this section) have no power to do so, but
        (ii) in all the circumstances regard themselves as being under a moral obligation to do so.

(2) The power conferred on the Commissioners by subsection (1) above shall be exercisable by them under the supervision of, and in accordance with such directions as may be given by, the Attorney General; and any such directions may in particular require the Commissioners, in such circumstances as are specified in the directions –
    (a) to refrain from exercising that power; or
    (b) to consult the Attorney General before exercising it.

(3) Where –
    (a) an application is made to the Commissioners for them to exercise that power in a case where they are not precluded from doing so by any such directions, but
    (b) they consider that it would nevertheless be desirable for the application to be entertained by the Attorney General rather than by them,
they shall refer the application to the Attorney General.

(4) It is hereby declared that where, in the case of any application made to them as mentioned in subsection (3)(a) above, the Commissioners determine the application by refusing to authorise charity trustees to take any action falling within subsection (1)(a) or (b) above, that refusal shall not preclude the Attorney General, on an application subsequently made to him by the trustees, from authorising the trustees to take that action.

28. Power to give directions about dormant bank accounts of charities

(1) Where the Commissioners –
    (a) are informed by a relevant institution –
        (i) that it holds one or more accounts in the name of or on behalf of a particular charity ('the relevant charity'), and
        (ii) that the account, or (if it so holds two or more accounts) each of the accounts, is dormant, and
    (b) are unable, after making reasonable inquiries, to locate that charity or any of its trustees,
they may give a direction under subsection (2) below.

(2) A direction under this subsection is a direction which –

(a) requires the institution concerned to transfer the amount, or (as the case may be) the aggregate amount, standing to the credit of the relevant charity in the account or accounts in question to such other charity as is specified in the direction in accordance with subsection (3) below; or

(b) requires the institution concerned to transfer to each of two or more other charities so specified in the direction such part of that amount or aggregate amount as is there specified in relation to that charity.

(3) The Commissioners may specify in a direction under subsection (2) above such other charity or charities as they consider appropriate, having regard, in a case where the purposes of the relevant charity are known to them, to those purposes and to the purposes of the other charity or charities; but the Commissioners shall not so specify any charity unless they have received from the charity trustees written confirmation that those trustees are willing to accept the amount proposed to be transferred to the charity.

(4) Any amount received by a charity by virtue of this section shall be received by the charity on terms that –

(a) it shall be held and applied by the charity for the purposes of the charity, but

(b) it shall, as property of the charity, nevertheless be subject to any restrictions on expenditure to which it was subject as property of the relevant charity

(5) Where –

(a) the Commissioners have been informed as mentioned in subsection (1)(a) above by any relevant institution, and

(b) before any transfer is made by the institution in pursuance of a direction under subsection (2) above, the institution has, by reason of any circumstances, cause to believe that the account, or (as the case may be) any of the accounts, held by it in the name of or on behalf of the relevant charity is no longer dormant,

the institution shall forthwith notify those circumstances in writing to the Commissioners; and, if it appears to the Commissioners that the account or accounts in question is or are no longer dormant, they shall revoke any direction under subsection (2) above which has previously been given by them to the institution with respect to the relevant charity.

(6) The receipt of any charity trustees or trustee for a charity in respect of any amount received from a relevant institution by virtue of this section shall be a complete discharge of the institution in respect of that amount.

(7) No obligation as to secrecy or other restriction on disclosure (however imposed) shall preclude a relevant institution from disclosing any information to the Commissioners for the purpose of enabling them to discharge their functions under this section.

(8) For the purposes of this section –

(a) an account is dormant if no transaction, other than –

(i) a transaction consisting in a payment into the account, or

(ii) a transaction which the institution holding the account has itself caused to be effected, has been effected in relation to the account within the period of five years immediately preceding the date when the Commisioners are informed as mentioned in paragraph (a) of subsection (1) above;

(b) a 'relevant institution' means –

(i) the Bank of England;

(ii) an institution which is authorised by the Bank of England to operate a deposit-taking business under Part I of the Banking Act 1987;

(iii) a European deposit-taker as defined in regulation 8(2) of the Banking Coordination (Second Council Directive) Regulations 1992;

(iv) a building society which is authorised by the Building Societies Commission under section 9 of the Building Societies Act 1986 to raise money from its members; or

(v) such other institution mentioned in Schedule 2 to the Banking Act 1987 as the Secretary of State may prescribe by regulations; and

(c) references to the transfer of any amount to a charity are references to its transfer –

(i) to the charity trustees, or

(ii) to any trustee for the charity,

as the charity trustees may determine (and any reference to any amount received by a charity shall be construed accordingly).

(9) For the purpose of determining the matters in respect of which any of the powers conferred by section 8 or 9 above may be exercised it shall be assumed that the Commissioners have no functions under this section in relation to accounts to which this subsection applies (with the result that, for example, a relevant institution shall not, in connection with the functions of the Commissioners under this section, be required under section 8(3)(a) above to furnish any statements, or answer any questions or inquiries, with respect to any such accounts held by the institution).

This subsection applies to accounts which are dormant accounts by virtue of subsection (8)(a) above but would not be such accounts if sub-paragraph (i) of that provision were omitted.

(10) Subsection (1) above shall not apply to any account held in the name of or on behalf of an exempt charity.

29. Power to advise charity trustees

(1) The Commissioners may on the written application of any charity trustee give him their opinion or advice on any matter affecting the performance of his duties as such.

(2) A charity trustee or trustee for a charity acting in accordance with the opinion or advice of the Commissioners given under this section with respect to the charity shall be deemed, as regards his responsibility for so acting, to have acted in accordance with his trust, unless, when he does so, either –

(a) he knows or has reasonable cause to suspect that the opinion or advice was given in ignorance of material facts; or

(b) the decision of the court has been obtained on the matter or proceedings are pending to obtain one.

30. Powers for preservation of charity documents

(1) The Commissioners may provide books in which any deed, will or other document relating to a charity may be enrolled.

(2) The Commissioners may accept for safe keeping any document of or relating to a charity, and the charity trustees or other persons having the custody of documents of or relating to a charity (including a charity which has ceased to exist) may with the consent of the Commissioners deposit them with the Commissioners for safe keeping, except in the case of documents required by some other enactment to be kept elsewhere.

(3) Where a document is enrolled by the Commissioners or is for the time being deposited with them under this section, evidence of its contents may be given by means of a copy certified by any

officer of the Commissioners generally or specially authorised by them to act for this purpose; and a document purporting to be such a copy shall be received in evidence without proof of the official position, authority or handwriting of the person certifying it or of the original document being enrolled or deposited as aforesaid.

(4) Regulations made by the Secretary of State may make provision for such documents deposited with the Commissioners under this section as may be prescribed by the regulations to be destroyed or otherwise disposed of after such period or in such circumstances as may be so prescribed.

(5) Subsections (3) and (4) above shall apply to any document transmitted to the Commissioners under section 9 above and kept by them under subsection (3) of that section, as if the document had been deposited with them for safe keeping under this section.

31. Power to order taxation of solicitor's bill

(1) The Commissioners may order that a solicitor's bill of costs for business done for a charity, or for charity trustees or trustees for a charity, shall be taxed, together with the costs of the taxation, by a taxing officer in such division of the High Court as may be specified in the order, or by the taxing officer of any other court having jurisdiction to order the taxation of the bill.

(2) On any order under this section for the taxation of a solicitor's bill the taxation shall proceed, and the taxing officer shall have the same powers and duties, and the costs of the taxation shall be borne, as if the order had been made, on the application of the person chargeable with the bill, by the court in which the costs are taxed.

(3) No order under this section for the taxation of a solicitor's bill shall be made after payment of the bill unless the Commissioners are of opinion that it contains exorbitant charges; and no such order shall in any case be made where the solicitor's costs are not subject to taxation on an order of the High Court by reason either of an agreement as to his remuneration or the lapse of time since payment of the bill.

Legal proceedings relating to charities

32. Proceedings by Commissioners

(1) Subject to subsection (2) below, the Commissioners may exercise the same powers with respect to –
  (a) the taking of legal proceedings with reference to charities or the property or affairs of charities, or
  (b) the compromise of claims with a view to avoiding or ending such proceedings,
as are exercisable by the Attorney General acting ex officio.

(2) Subsection (1) above does not apply to the power of the Attorney General under section 63(1) below to present a petition for the winding up of a charity.

(3) The practice and procedure to be followed in relation to any proceedings taken by the Commissioners under subsection (1) above shall be the same in all respects (and in particular as regards costs) as if they were proceedings taken by the Attorney General acting ex officio.

(4) No rule of law or practice shall be taken to require the Attorney General to be a party to any such proceedings.

(5) The powers exercisable by the Commissioners by virtue of this section shall be exercisable by them of their own motion, but shall be exercisable only with the agreement of the Attorney General on each occasion.

33. Proceedings by other persons

(1) Charity proceedings may be taken with reference to a charity either by the charity, or by any of the charity trustees, or by any person interested in the charity, or by any two or more inhabitants of the area of the charity if it is a local charity, but not by any other person.

(2) Subject to the following provisions of this section, no charity proceedings relating to a charity (other than an exempt charity) shall be entertained or proceeded with in any court unless the taking of the proceedings is authorised by order of the Commissioners.

(3) The Commissioners shall not, without special reasons, authorise the taking of charity proceedings where in their opinion the case can be dealt with by them under the powers of this Act other than those conferred by section 32 above.

(4) This section shall not require any order for the taking of proceedings in a pending cause or matter or for the bringing of any appeal.

(5) Where the foregoing provisions of this section require the taking of charity proceedings to be authorised by an order of the Commissioners, the proceedings may nevertheless be entertained or proceeded with if, after the order had been applied for and refused, leave to take the proceedings was obtained from one of the judges of the High Court attached to the Chancery Division.

(6) Nothing in the foregoing subsections shall apply to the taking of proceedings by the Attorney General, with or without a relator, or to the taking of proceedings by the Commissioners in accordance with section 32 above.

(7) Where it appears to the Commissioners, on an application for an order under this section or otherwise, that it is desirable for legal proceedings to be taken with reference to any charity (other than an exempt charity) or its property or affairs, and for the proceedings to be taken by the Attorney General, the Commissioners shall so inform the Attorney General, and send him such statements and particulars as they think necessary to explain the matter.

(8) In this section 'charity proceedings' means proceedings in any court in England or Wales brought under the court's jurisdiction with respect to charities, or brought under the court's jurisdiction with respect to trusts in relation to the administration of a trust for charitable purposes.

34. Report of s 8 inquiry to be evidence in certain proceedings

(1) A copy of the report of the person conducting an inquiry under section 8 above shall, if certified by the Commissioners to be a true copy, be admissible in any proceedings to which this section applies –
    (a) as evidence of any fact stated in the report; and
    (b) as evidence of the opinion of that person as to any matter referred to in it.

(2) This section applies to –
    (a) any legal proceedings instituted by the Commissioners under this Part of this Act; and
    (b) any legal proceedings instituted by the Attorney General in respect of a charity.

(3) A document purporting to be a certificate issued for the purposes of subsection (1) above shall be received in evidence and be deemed to be such a certificate, unless the contrary is proved.

Meaning of 'trust corporation'

35. Application of provisions to trust corporations appointed under s 16 or 18

(1) In the definition of 'trust corporation' contained in the following provisions –
    (a) section 117(xxx) of the Settled Land Act 1925,

(b) section 68(18) of the Trustee Act 1925,

(c) section 205 (xxviii) of the Law of Property Act 1925,

(d) section 55 (xxvi) of the Administration of Estates Act 1925, and

(e) section 128 of the Supreme Court Act 1981,

the reference to a corporation appointed by the court in any particular case to be a trustee includes a reference to a corporation appointed by the Commissioners under this Act to be a trustee.

(2) This section shall be deemed always to have had effect; but the reference to section 128 of the Supreme Court Act 1981 shall, in relation to any time before 1 January 1982, be construed as a reference to section 175(1) of the Supreme Court of Judicature (Consolidation) Act 1925.

PART V

CHARITY LAND

36. Restrictions on dispositions

(1) Subject to the following provisions of this section and section 40 below, no land held by or in trust for a charity shall be sold, leased or otherwise disposed of without an order of the court or of the Commissioners.

(2) Subsection (1) above shall not apply to a disposition of such land if –

(a) the disposition is made to a person who is not –

(i) a connected person (as defined in Schedule 5 to this Act), or

(ii) a trustee for, or nominee of, a connected person; and

(b) the requirements of subsection (3) or (5) below have been complied with in relation to it.

(3) Except where the proposed disposition is the granting of such a lease as is mentioned in subsection (5) below, the charity trustees must, before entering into an agreement for the sale, or (as the case may be) for a lease or other disposition, of the land –

(a) obtain and consider a written report on the proposed disposition from a qualified surveyor instructed by the trustees and acting exclusively for the charity;

(b) advertise the proposed disposition for such period and in such manner as the surveyor has advised in his report (unless he has there advised that it would not be in the best interests of the charity to advertise the proposed disposition); and

(c) decide that they are satisfied, having considered the surveyor's report, that the terms on which the disposition is proposed to be made are the best that can reasonably be obtained for the charity.

(4) For the purposes of subsection (3) above a person is a qualified surveyor if –

(a) he is a fellow or professional associate of the Royal Institution of Chartered Surveyors or of the Incorporated Society of Valuers and Auctioneers or satisfies such other requirement or requirements as may be prescribed by regulations made by the Secretary of State; and

(b) he is reasonably believed by the charity trustees to have ability in, and experience of, the valuation of land of the particular kind, and in the particular area, in question;

and any report prepared for the purposes of that subsection shall contain such information, and deal with such matters, as may be prescribed by regulations so made.

(5) Where the proposed disposition is the granting of a lease for a term ending not more than seven years after it is granted (other than one granted wholly or partly in consideration of a fine), the charity trustees must, before entering into an agreement for the lease –

(a) obtain and consider the advice on the proposed disposition of a person who is reasonably believed by the trustees to have the requisite ability and practical experience to provide them with competent advice on the proposed disposition; and

(b) decide that they are satisfied, having considered that person's advice, that the terms on which the disposition is proposed to be made are the best that can reasonably be obtained for the charity.

(6) Where –

(a) any land is held by or in trust for a charity, and

(b) the trusts on which it is so held stipulate that it is to be used for the purposes, or any particular purposes, of the charity,

then (subject to subsections (7) and (8) below and without prejudice to the operation of the preceding provisions of this section) the land shall not be sold, leased or otherwise disposed of unless the charity trustees have previously –

(i) given public notice of the proposed disposition, inviting representations to be made to them within a time specified in the notice, being not less than one month from the date of the notice; and

(ii) taken into consideration any representations made to them within that time about the proposed disposition.

(7) Subsection (6) above shall not apply to any such disposition of land as is there mentioned if –

(a) the disposition is to be effected with a view to acquiring by way of replacement other property which is to be held on the trusts referred to in paragraph (b) of that subsection; or

(b) the disposition is the granting of a lease for a term ending not more than two years after it is granted (other than one granted wholly or partly in consideration of a fine).

(8) The Commissioners may direct –

(a) that subsection (6) above shall not apply to dispositions of land held by or in trust for a charity or class of charities (whether generally or only in the case of a specified class of dispositions or land, or otherwise as may be provided in the direction), or

(b) that that subsection shall not apply to a particular disposition of land held by or in trust for a charity,

if, on an application made to them in writing by or on behalf of the charity or charities in question, the Commissioners are satisfied that it would be in the interests of the charity or charities for them to give the direction.

(9) The restrictions on disposition imposed by this section apply notwithstanding anything in the trusts of a charity; but nothing in this section applies –

(a) to any disposition for which general or special authority is expressly given (without the authority being made subject to the sanction of an order of the court) by any statutory provision contained in or having effect under an Act of Parliament or by any scheme legally established; or

(b) to any disposition of land held by or in trust for a charity which –

(i) is made to another charity otherwise than for the best price that can reasonably be obtained, and

(ii) is authorised to be so made by the trusts of the first-mentioned charity; or

(c) to the granting, by or on behalf of a charity and in accordance with its trusts, or a lease to any beneficiary under those trusts where the lease –

(i) is granted otherwise than for the best rent that can reasonably be obtained; and

(ii) is intended to enable the demised premises to be occupied for the purposes, or any particular purposes, of the charity.

(10) Nothing in this section applies –

(a) to any disposition of land held by or in trust for an exempt charity;

    (b) to any disposition of land by way of mortgage or other security; or

    (c) to any disposition of an advowson.

(11) In this section 'land' means land in England or Wales.

37. Supplementary provisions relating to dispositions

(1) Any of the following instruments, namely –

    (a) any contract for the sale, or for a lease or other disposition, of land which is held by or in trust for a charity, and

    (b) any conveyance, transfer, lease or other instrument effecting a disposition of such land,

and state –

       (i) that the land is held by or in trust for a charity,

     (ii) whether the charity is an exempt charity and whether the disposition is one falling within paragraph (a), (b) or (c) of subsection (9) of section 36 above, and

    (iii) if it is not an exempt charity and the disposition is not one falling within any of those paragraphs, that the land is land to which the restrictions on disposition imposed by that section apply.

(2) Where any land held by or in trust for a charity is sold, leased or otherwise disposed of by a disposition to which subsection (1) or (2) of section 36 above applies, the charity trustees shall certify in the instrument by which the disposition is effected –

    (a) (where subsection (1) of that section applies) that the disposition has been sanctioned by an order of the court or of the Commissioners (as the case may be), or

    (b) (where subsection (2) of that section applies) that the charity trustees have power under the trusts of the charity to effect the disposition, and that they have complied with the provisions of that section so far as applicable to it.

(3) Where subsection (2) above has been complied with in relation to any disposition of land, then in favour of a person who (whether under the disposition or afterwards) acquires an interest in the land for money or money's worth, it shall be conclusively presumed that the facts were as stated in the certificate.

(4) Where –

    (a) any land held by or in trust for a charity is sold, leased or otherwise disposed of by a disposition to which subsection (1) or (2) of section 36 above applies, but

    (b) subsection (2) above has not been complied with in relation to the disposition,

then in favour of a person who (whether under the disposition or afterwards) in good faith acquires an interest in the land for money or money's worth, the disposition shall be valid whether or not –

       (i) the disposition has been sanctioned by an order of the court or of the Commissioners, or

     (ii) the charity trustees have power under the trusts of the charity to effect the disposition and have complied with the provisions of that section so far as applicable to it.

(5) Any of the following instruments, namely –

    (a) any contract for the sale, or for a lease or other disposition, of land which will, as a result of the disposition, be held by or in trust for a charity, and

    (b) any conveyance, transfer, lease or other instrument effecting a disposition of such land,

shall state –

       (i) that the land will, as a result of the disposition, be held by or in trust for a charity,

     (ii) whether the charity is an exempt charity, and

    (iii) if it is not an exempt charity, that the restrictions on disposition imposed by section 36 above will apply to the land (subject to subsection (9) of that section).

(6) In section 29(1) of the Settled Land Act 1925 (charitable and public trusts) –

  (a) the requirements for a conveyance of land held on charitable, ecclesiastical or public trusts to state that it is held on such trusts shall not apply to any instrument to which subsection (1) above applies; and

  (b) the requirement imposed on a purchaser, in the circumstances mentioned in section 29(1) of that Act, to see that any consents or orders requisite for authorising a transaction have been obtained shall not apply in relation to any disposition in relation to which subsection (2) above has been complied with;

and expressions used in this subsection which are also used in that Act have the same meaning as in that Act.

(7) Where –

  (a) the disposition to be effected by any such instrument as is mentioned in subsection (1)(b) or (5)(b) above will be a registered disposition, or

  (b) any such instrument will on taking effect on an instrument to which section 123(1) of the Land Registration Act 1925 (compulsory registration of title) applies,

the statement which, by virtue of subsection (1) or (5) above, is to be contained in the instrument shall be in such form as may be prescribed.

(8) Where –

  (a) an application is duly made –

    (i) for registration of a disposition of registered land, or

    (ii) for registration of a person's title under a disposition of unregistered land, and

  (b) the instrument by which the disposition is effected contains a statement complying with subsections (5) and (7) above, and

  (c) the charity by or in trust for which the land is held as a result of the disposition is not an exempt charity,

the registrar shall enter in the register, in respect of the land, a restriction in such form as may be prescribed.

(9) Where –

  (a) any such restriction is entered in the register in respect of any land, and

  (b) the charity by or in trust for which the land is held becomes an exempt charity,

the charity trustees shall apply to the registrar for the restriction to be withdrawn; and on receiving any application duly made under this subsection the registrar shall withdraw the restriction.

(10) Where –

  (a) any registered land is held by or in trust for an exempt charity and the charity ceases to be an exempt charity, or

  (b) any registered land becomes, as a result of a declaration of trust by the registered proprietor, land held in trust for a charity (other than an exempt charity),

the charity trustees shall apply to the registrar for such a restriction as is mentioned in subsection (8) above to be entered in the register in respect of the land; and on receiving any application duly made under this subsection the registrar shall enter such a restriction in the register in respect of the land.

(11) In this section –

  (a) references to a disposition of land do not include references to –

    (i) a disposition of land by way of mortgage or other security,

    (ii) any disposition of an advowson, or

    (iii) any release of a rentcharge falling within section 40(1) below; and

  (b) 'land' means land in England or Wales;

and subsections (7) to (10) above shall be construed as one with the Land Registration Act 1925.

38. Restrictions on mortgaging

(1) Subject to subsection (2) below, no mortgage of land held by or in trust for a charity shall be granted without an order of the court or of the Commissioners.

(2) Subsection (1) above shall not apply to a mortgage of any such land by way of security for the repayment of a loan where the charity trustees have, before executing the mortgage, obtained and considered proper advice, given to them in writing, on the matters mentioned in subsection (3) below.

(3) Those matters are –
   (a) whether the proposed loan is necessary in order for the charity trustees to be able to pursue the particular course of action in connection with which the loan is sought by them;
   (b) whether the terms of the proposed loan are reasonable having regard to the status of the charity as a prospective borrower; and
   (c) the ability of the charity to repay on those terms the sum proposed to be borrowed.

(4) For the purposes of subsection (2) above proper advice is the advice of a person –
   (a) who is reasonably believed by the charity trustees to be qualified by his ability in and practical experience of financial matters; and
   (b) who has no financial interest in the making of the loan in question;
and such advice may constitute proper advice for those purposes notwithstanding that the person giving it does so in the course of his employment as an officer or employee of the charity or of the charity trustees.

(5) This section applies notwithstanding anything in the trusts of a charity; but nothing in this section applies to any mortgage for which general or special authority is given as mentioned in section 36(9)(a) above.

(6) In this section –
'land' means land in England or Wales;
'mortgage' includes a charge.

(7) Nothing in this section applies to an exempt charity.

39. Supplementary provisions relating to mortgaging

(1) Any mortgage of land held by or in trust for a charity shall state –
   (a) that the land is held by or in trust for a charity,
   (b) whether the charity is an exempt charity and whether the mortgage is one falling within subsection (5) of section 38 above, and
   (c) if it is not an exempt charity and the mortgage is not one falling within that subsection, that the mortgage is one to which the restrictions imposed by that section apply;
and where the mortgage will be a registered disposition any such statement shall be in such form as may be prescribed.

(2) Where subsection (1) or (2) of section 38 above applies to any mortgage of land held by or in trust for a charity, the charity trustees shall certify in the mortgage –
   (a) (where subsection (1) of that section applies) that the mortgage has been sanctioned by an order of the court or of the Commissioners (as the case may be), or
   (b) (where subsection (2) of that section applies) that the charity trustees have power under the trusts of the charity to grant the mortgage, and that they have obtained and considered such advice as is mentioned in that subsection.

(3) Where subsection (2) above has been complied with in relation to any mortgage, then in favour of a person who (whether under the mortgage or afterwards) acquires an interest in the

land in question for money or money's worth, it shall be conclusively presumed that the facts were as stated in the certificate.

(4) Where –

    (a) subsection (1) or (2) of section 38 above applies to any mortgage of land held by or in trust for a charity, but

    (b) subsection (2) above has not been complied with in relation to the mortgage,

then in favour of a person who (whether under the mortgage or afterwards) in good faith acquires an interest in the land for money or money's worth, the mortgage shall be valid whether or not –

        (i) the mortgage has been sanctioned by an order of the court or of the Commissioners, or

        (ii) the charity trustees have power under the trusts of the charity to grant the mortgage and have obtained and considered such advice as is mentioned in subsection (2) of that section.

(5) In section 29(1) of the Settled Land Act 1925 (charitable and public trusts) –

    (a) the requirement for a mortgage of land held on charitable, ecclesiastical or public trusts (as a 'conveyance' of such land for the purposes of that Act) to state that it is held on such trusts shall not apply to any mortgage to which subsection (1) above applies; and

    (b) the requirement imposed on a mortgagee (as a 'purchaser' for those purposes), in the circumstances mentioned in section 29(1) of that Act, to see that any consents or orders requisite for authorising a transaction have been obtained shall not apply in relation to any mortgage in relation to which subsection (2) above has been complied with;

and expressions used in this subsection which are also used in that Act have the same meaning as in that Act.

(6) In this section –

'mortgage' includes a charge, and 'mortgagee' shall be construed accordingly;

'land' means land in England or Wales;

'prescribed' and 'registered disposition' have the same meaning as in the Land Registration Act 1925.

40. Release of charity rentcharges

(1) Section 36(1) above shall not apply to the release by a charity of a rentcharge which it is entitled to receive if the release is given in consideration of the payment of an amount which is not less than ten times the annual amount of the rentcharge.

(2) Where a charity which is entitled to receive a rentcharge releases it in consideration of the payment of an amount not exceeding £500, any costs incurred by the charity in connection with proving its title to the rentcharge shall be recoverable by the charity from the person or persons in whose favour the rentcharge is being released.

(3) Neither section 36(1) nor subsection (2) above applies where a rentcharge which a charity is entitled to receive is redeemed under sections 8 to 10 of the Rentcharges Act 1977.

(4) The Secretary of State may by order amend subsection (2) above by substituting a different sum for the sum for the time being specified there.

PART VI

CHARITY ACCOUNTS, REPORTS AND RETURNS

41. Duty to keep accounting records

(1) The charity trustees of a charity shall ensure that accounting records are kept in respect of the charity which are sufficient to show and explain all the charity's transactions, and which are such as to –

    (a) disclose at any time, with reasonable accuracy, the financial position of the charity at that time, and

    (b) enable the trustees to ensure that, where any statements of accounts are prepared by them under section 42(1) below, those statements of accounts comply with the requirements of regulations under that provision.

(2) The accounting records shall in particular contain –

    (a) entries showing from day to day all sums of money received and expended by the charity, and the matters in respect of which the receipt and expenditure takes place; and

    (b) a record of the assets and liabilities of the charity.

(3) The charity trustees of a charity shall preserve any accounting records made for the purposes of this section in respect of which the charity for at least six years from the end of the financial year of the charity in which they are made.

(4) Where a charity ceases to exist within the period of six years mentioned in subsection (3) above as it applies to any accounting records, the obligation to preserve those records in accordance with that subsection shall continue to be discharged by the last charity trustees of the charity, unless the Commissioners consent in writing to the records being destroyed or otherwise disposed of.

(5) Nothing in this section applies to a charity which is a company.

42. Annual statements of accounts

(1) The charity trustees of a charity shall (subject to subsection (3) below) prepare in respect of each financial year of the charity a statement of accounts complying with such requirements as to its form and contents as may be prescribed by regulations made by the Secretary of State.

(2) Without prejudice to the generality of subsection (1) above, regulations under that subsection may make provision –

    (a) for any such statement to be prepared in accordance with such methods and principles as are specified or referred to in the regulations;

    (b) as to any information to be provided by way of notes to the accounts;

and regulations under that subsection may also make provision for determining the financial years of a charity for the purposes of this Act and any regulations made under it.

(3) Where a charity's gross income in any financial year does not exceed £100,000, the charity trustees may, in respect of that year, elect to prepare the following, namely –

    (a) a receipts and payments account, and

    (b) a statement of assets and liabilities,

instead of a statement of accounts under subsection (1) above.

(4) The charity trustees of a charity shall preserve –

(a) any statement of accounts prepared by them under subsection (1) above, or

(b) any account and statement prepared by them under subsection (3) above,

for at least six years from the end of the financial year to which any such statement relates or (as the case may be) to which any such account and statement relate.

(5) Subsection (4) of section 41 above shall apply in relation to the preservation of any such statement or account and statement as it applies in relation to the preservation of any accounting records (the references to subsection (3) of that section being read as references to subsection (4) above).

(6) The Secretary of State may by order amend subsection (3) above by substituting a different sum for the sum for the time being specified there.

(7) Nothing in this section applies to a charity which is a company.

NOTE

Section shown as amended by the Charities Act 1993 (Substitution of Sums) Order 1995 (SI 1995/2696).

---

43. Annual audit or examination of charity accounts

(1) Subsection (2) below applies to a financial year of a charity ('the relevant year') if the charity's gross income or total expenditure in any of the following, namely –

(a) the relevant year,

(b) the financial year of the charity immediately preceding the relevant year (if any), and

(c) the financial year of the charity immediately preceding the year specified in paragraph (b) above (if any),

exceeds £250,000.

(2) If this subsection applies to a financial year of a charity, the accounts of the charity for that year shall be audited by a person who –

(a) is, in accordance with section 25 of the Companies Act 1989 (eligibility for appointment), eligible for appointment as a company auditor, or

(b) is a member of a body for the time being specified in regulations under section 44 below and is under the rules of that body eligible for appointment as auditor of the charity.

(3) If subsection (2) above does not apply to a financial year of a charity and its gross income or total expenditure in that year exceeds £10,000, then (subject to subsection (4) below) the accounts of the charity for that year shall, at the election of the charity trustees, either –

(a) be examined by an independent examiner, that is to say an independent person who is reasonably believed by the trustees to have the requisite ability and practical experience to carry out a competent examination of the accounts, or

(b) be audited by such a person as is mentioned in subsection (2) above.

(4) Where it appears to the Commissioners –

(a) that subsection (2), or (as the case may be) subsection (3) above, has not been complied with in relation to a financial year of a charity within ten months from the end of that year, or

(b) that, although subsection (2) above does not apply to a financial year of a charity, it would nevertheless be desirable for the accounts of the charity for that year to be audited by such a person as is mentioned in that subsection, the Commissioners may by order require the accounts of the charity for that year to be audited by such a person as is mentioned in that subsection.

(5) If the Commissioners make an order under subsection (4) above with respect to a charity, then unless –
  (a) the order is made by virtue of paragraph (b) of that subsection, and
  (b) the charity trustees themselves appoint an auditor in accordance with the order,
the auditor shall be a person appointed by the Commissioners.

(6) The expenses of any audit carried out by an auditor appointed by the Commissioners under subsection (5) above, including the auditor's remuneration, shall be recoverable by the Commissioners –
  (a) from the charity trustees of the charity concerned, who shall be personally liable, jointly and severally, for those expenses; or
  (b) to the extent that it appears to the Commissioners not to be practical to seek recovery of those expenses in accordance with paragraph (a) above, from the funds of the charity.

(7) The Commissioners may –
  (a) give guidance to charity trustees in connection with the selection of a person for appointment as an independent examiner;
  (b) give such directions as they think appropriate with respect to the carrying out of an examination in pursuance of subsection (3)(a) above;
and any such guidance or directions may either be of general application or apply to a particular charity only.

(8) The Secretary of State may by order amend subsection (1) or (3) above by substituting a different sum for the sum for the time being specified there.

(9) Nothing in this section applies to a charity which is a company.

NOTE
Section shown as amended by the Deregulation and Contracting Out Act 1994 and the Charities Act 1993 (Substitution of Sums) Order 1995 (SI 1995/2696).

---

44. Supplementary provisions relating to audits etc

(1) The Secretary of State may by regulations make provision –
  (a) specifying one or more bodies for the purposes of section 43(2)(b) above;
  (b) with respect to the duties of an auditor carrying out an audit under section 43 above, including provision with respect to the making by him of a report on –
      (i)   the statement of accounts prepared for the financial year in question under section 42(1) above, or
      (ii) the account and statement so prepared under section 42(3) above,
      as the case may be;
  (c) with respect to the making by an independent examiner of a report in respect of an examination carried out by him under section 43 above;
  (d) conferring on such an auditor or on an independent examiner a right of access with respect to books, documents and other records (however kept) which relate to the charity concerned;
  (e) entitling such an auditor or an independent examiner to require, in the case of a charity, information and explanations from past or present charity trustees or trustees for the charity, or from past or present officers or employees of the charity;

(f) enabling the Commissioners, in circumstances specified in the regulations, to dispense with the requirements of section 43(2) or (3) above in the case of a particular charity or in the case of any particular financial year of a charity.

(2) If any person fails to afford an auditor or an independent examiner any facility to which he is entitled by virtue of subsection (1)(d) or (e) above, the Commissioners may by order give –
    (a) to that person, or
    (b) to the charity trustees for the time being of the charity concerned,
such directions as the Commissioners think appropriate for securing that the default is made good.

(3) Section 727 of the Companies Act 1985 (power of court to grant relief in certain cases) shall have effect in relation to an auditor or independent examiner appointed by a charity in pursuance of section 43 above as it has effect in relation to a person employed as auditor by a company within the meaning of that Act.

45. Annual reports

(1) The charity trustees of a charity shall prepare in respect of each financial year of the charity an annual report containing –
    (a) such a report by the trustees on the activities of the charity during that year, and
    (b) such other information relating to the charity or to its trustees or officers,
as may be prescribed by regulations made by the Secretary of State.

(2) Without prejudice to the generality of subsection (1) above, regulations under that subsection may make provision –
    (a) for any such report as is mentioned in paragraph (a) of that subsection to be prepared in accordance with such principles as are specified or referred to in the regulations;
    (b) enabling the Commissioners to dispense with any requirement prescribed by virtue of subsection (1)(b) above in the case of a particular charity or a particular class of charities, or in the case of a particular financial year of a charity or of any class of charities.

(3) Where in any financial year of a charity its gross income or total expenditure exceeds £10,000, the annual report required to be prepared under this section in respect of that year shall be transmitted to the Commissioners by the charity trustees –
    (a) within ten months from the end of that year, or
    (b) within such longer period as the Commissioners may for any special reason allow in the case of that report.

(3A) Where in any financial year of a charity neither its gross income nor its total expenditure exceeds £10,000, the annual report required to be prepared under this section in respect of that year shall, if the Commissioners so request, be transmitted to them by the charity trustees –
    (a) in the case of a request made before the end of seven months from the end of the financial year to which the report relates, within ten months from the end of that year, and
    (b) in the case of a request not so made, within three months from the date of the request,
or, in either case, within such longer period as the Commissioners may for any special reason allow in the case of that report.

(4) Subject to subsection (5) below, any annual report transmitted to the Commissioners under this section shall have attached to it the statement of accounts prepared for the financial year in question under section 42(1) above or (as the case may be) the account and statement so prepared under section 42(3) above, together with –
    (a) where the accounts of the charity for that year have been audited under section 43 above, a copy of the report made by the auditor on that statement of accounts or (as the case may be) on that account and statement;

(b) where the accounts of the charity for that year have been examined under section 43 above, a copy of the report made by the independent examiner in respect of the examination carried out by him under that section.

(5) Subsection (4) above does not apply to a charity which is a company, and any annual report transmitted by the charity trustees of such a charity under this section shall instead have attached to it a copy of the charity's annual accounts prepared for the financial year in question under Part VII of the Companies Act 1985, together with a copy of any auditors' report or report made for the purposes of section 249A(2) of that Act on those accounts.

(6) Any annual report transmitted to the Commissioners under this section, together with the documents attached to it, shall be kept by the Commissioners for such period as they think fit.

(7) The charity trustees of a charity shall preserve, for at least six years from the end of the financial year to which it relates, any annual report prepared by them under subsection (1) above which they have not been required to transmit to the Commissioners.

(8) Subsection (4) of section 41 above shall apply in relation to the preservation of any such annual report as it applies in relation to the preservation of any accounting records (the references in subsection (3) of that section being read as references to subsection (7) above).

(9) The Secretary of State may by order amend subsection (3) or (3A) above by substituting a different sum for the time being specified there.

NOTE

Section shown as amended by the Deregulation and Contracting Out Act 1994 and the Companies Act 1985 (Audit Exemption) Regulations 1994 (SI 1994/1935).

---

46. Special provision as respects accounts and annual reports of exempt and other excepted charities

(1) Nothing in sections 41 to 45 above applies to any exempt charity; but the charity trustees of an exempt charity shall keep proper books of account with respect to the affairs of the charity, and if not required by or under the authority of any other Act to prepare periodical statements of account shall prepare consecutive statements of account consisting on each occasion of an income and expenditure account relating to a period of not more than fifteen months and a balance sheet relating to the end of that period.

(2) The books of accounts and statements of account relating to an exempt charity shall be preserved for a period of six years at least unless the charity ceases to exist and the Commissioners consent in writing to their being destroyed or otherwise disposed of.

(3) Nothing in sections 43 to 45 above applies to any charity which –
   (a) falls within section 3(5)(c) above, and
   (b) is not registered.

(4) Except in accordance with subsection (7) below, nothing in section 45 above applies to any charity (other than an exempt charity or a charity which falls within section 3(5)(c) above) which –
   (a) is excepted by section 3(5) above, and
   (b) is not registered.

(5) If requested to do so by the Commissioners, the charity trustees of any such charity as is mentioned in subsection (4) above shall prepare an annual report in respect of such financial year of the charity as is specified in the Commissioners' request.

(6) Any report prepared under subsection (5) above shall contain –
   (a) such a report by the charity trustees on the activities of the charity during the year in question, and
   (b) such other information relating to the charity or to its trustees or officers,
as may be prescribed by regulations made under section 45(1) above in relation to annual reports prepared under that provision.

(7) Subsections (3) to (6) of section 45 (as originally enacted) above shall apply to any report required to be prepared under subsection (5) above as if it were an annual report required to be prepared under subsection (1) of that section.

(8) Any reference in this section to a charity which falls within section 3(5)(c) above includes a reference to a charity which falls within that provision but is also excepted from registration by section 3(5)(b) above.

NOTE
Section shown as amended by the Deregulation and Contracting Out Act 1994.

---

47. Public inspection of annual reports etc

(1) Any annual report or other document kept by the Commissioners in pursuance of section 45(6) above shall be open to public inspection at all reasonable times –
   (a) during the period for which it is so kept; or
   (b) if the Commissioners so determine, during such lesser period as they may specify.

(2) Where any person –
   (a) requests the charity trustees of a charity in writing to provide him with a copy of the charity's most recent accounts, and
   (b) pays them such reasonable fee (if any) as they may require in respect of the costs of complying with the request,
those trustees shall comply with the request within the period of two months beginning with the date on which it is made.

(3) In subsection (2) above the reference to a charity's most recent accounts is –
   (a) . . .
   (b) in the case of a charity other than one falling within paragraph (c) or (d) below, a reference to the statement of accounts or account and statement prepared in pursuance of section 42(1) or (3) above in respect of the last financial year of the charity in respect of which a statement of accounts or account and statement has or have been so prepared;
   (c) in the case of a charity which is a company, a reference to the most recent annual accounts of the company prepared under Part VII of the Companies Act 1985 in relation to which any of the following conditions is satisfied –
      (i) they have been audited;
      (ii) a report required for the purposes of section 249A(2) of that Act has been made in respect of them; or
      (iii) they relate to a year in respect of which the company is exempt from audit by virtue of section 249A(1) of that Act; and
   (d) in the case of an exempt charity, a reference to the accounts of the charity most recently audited in pursuance of any statutory or other requirement or, if its accounts are not required to be audited, the accounts most recently prepared in respect of the charity.

NOTE
Section shown as amended by the Deregulation and Contracting Out Act 1994 and the Companies Act 1985 (Audit Exemption) Regulations 1994 (SI 1994/1935).

48. Annual returns by registered charities

(1) Subject to subsection (1A) below, every registered charity shall prepare in respect of each of its financial years an annual return in such form, and containing such information, as may be prescribed by regulations made by the Commissioners.

(1A) Subsection (1) above shall not apply in relation to any financial year of a charity in which neither the gross income nor the total expenditure of the charity exceeds £10,000.

(2) Any such return shall be transmitted to the Commissioners by the date by which the charity trustees are, by virtue of section 45(3) above, required to transmit to them the annual report required to be prepared in respect of the financial year in question.

(3) The Commissioners may dispense with the requirements of subsection (1) above in the case of a particular charity or a particular class of charities, or in the case of a particular financial year of a charity or of any class of charities.

(4) The Secretary of State may by order amend subsection (1A) above by substituting a different sum for the sum for the time being specified there.

NOTE
Section shown as amended by the Deregulation and Contracting Out Act 1994.

49. Offences

Any person who, without reasonable excuse, is persistently in default in relation to any requirement imposed –
    (a) by section 45(3) or (3A) above (taken with section 45(4) or (5), as the case may require), or
    (b) by section 47(2) or 48(2) above,
shall be guilty of an offence and liable on summary conviction to a fine not exceeding level 4 on the standard scale.

NOTE
Section shown as amended by the Deregulation and Contracting Out Act 1994.

PART VII

INCORPORATION OF CHARITY TRUSTEES

50. Incorporation of trustees of a charity

(1) Where –
    (a) the trustees of a charity, in accordance with section 52 below, apply to the Commissioners for a certificate of incorporation of the trustees as a body corporate, and

(b) the Commissioners consider that the incorporation of the trustees would be in the interests
     of the charity,

the Commissioners may grant such a certificate, subject to such conditions or directions as they
think fit to insert in it.

(2) The Commissioners shall not, however, grant such a certificate in a case where the charity
appears to them to be required to be registered under section 3 above but is not so registered.

(3) On the grant of such a certificate –
   (a) the trustees of the charity shall become a body corporate by such name as is specified in the
        certificate; and
   (b) (without prejudice to the operation of section 54 below) any relevant rights or liabilities of
        those trustees shall become rights or liabilities of that body.

(4) After their incorporation the trustees –
   (a) may sue and be sued in their corporate name; and
   (b) shall have the same powers, and be subject to the same restrictions and limitations, as
        respects the holding, acquisition and disposal of property for or in connection with the
        purposes of the charity as they had or were subject to while unincorporated;

and any relevant legal proceedings that might have been continued or commenced by or against
the trustees may be continued or commenced by or against them in their corporate name.

(5) A body incorporated under this section need not have a common seal.

(6) In this section –
'relevant rights or liabilities' means rights or liabilities in connection with any property vesting in
   the body in question under section 51 below; and
'relevant legal proceedings' means legal proceedings in connection with any such property.

51. Estate to vest in body corporate

The certificate of incorporation shall vest in the body corporate all real and personal estate, of
whatever nature or tenure, belonging to or held by any person or persons in trust for the charity,
and thereupon any person or persons in whose name or names any stocks, funds or securities are
standing in trust for the charity, shall transfer them into the name of the body corporate, except
that the foregoing provisions shall not apply to property vested in the official custodian.

52. Applications for incorporation

(1) Every application to the Commissioners for a certificate of incorporation under this Part of
this Act shall –
   (a) be in writing and signed by the trustees of the charity concerned; and
   (b) be accompanied by such documents or information as the Commissioners may require for
        the purpose of the application.

(2) The Commissioners may require –
   (a) any statement contained in any such application, or
   (b) any document or information supplied under subsection (1)(b) above,
to be verified in such manner as they may specify.

53. Nomination of trustees, and filling up vacancies

(1) Before a certificate of incorporation is granted under this Part of this Act, trustees of the charity
must have been effectually appointed to the satisfaction of the Commissioners.

(2) Where a certificate of incorporation is granted vacancies in the number of the trustees of the charity shall from time to time be filled up so far as required by the constitution or settlement of the charity, or by any conditions or directions in the certificate, by such legal means as would have been available for the appointment of new trustees of the charity if no certificate of incorporation had been granted, or otherwise as required by such conditions or directions.

54. Liability of trustees and others, notwithstanding incorporation

After a certificate of incorporation has been granted under this Part of this Act all trustees of the charity, notwithstanding their incorporation, shall be chargeable for such property as shall come into their hands, and shall be answerable and accountable for their own acts, receipts, neglects, and defaults, and for the due administration of the charity and its property, in the same manner and to the same extent as if no such incorporation had been effected.

55. Certificate to be evidence of compliance with requirements for incorporation

A certificate of incorporation granted under this Part of this Act shall be conclusive evidence that all the preliminary requirements for incorporation under this Part of this Act have been complied with, and the date of incorporation mentioned in the certificate shall be deemed to be the date at which incorporation has taken place.

56. Power of Commissioners to amend certificate of incorporation

(1) The Commissioners may amend a certificate of incorporation either on the application of the incorporated body to which it relates or of their own motion.

(2) Before making any such amendment of their own motion, the Commissioners shall by notice in writing –
(a) inform the trustees of the relevant charity of their proposals, and
(b) invite those trustees to make representations to them within a time specified in the notice, being not less than one month from the date of the notice.

(3) The Commissioners shall take into consideration any representations made by those trustees within the time so specified, and may then (without further notice) proceed with their proposals either without modification or with such modifications as appear to them to be desirable.

(4) The Commissioners may amend a certificate of incorporation either –
(a) by making an order specifying the amendment; or
(b) by issuing a new certificate of incorporation taking account of the amendment.

57. Records of applications and certificates

(1) The Commissioners shall keep a record of all applications for, and certificates of, incorporation under this Part of this Act and shall preserve all documents sent to them under this Part of this Act.

(2) Any person may inspect such documents, under the direction of the Commissioners, and any person may require a copy or extract of any such document to be certified by a certificate signed by the secretary of the Commissioners.

58. Enforcement of orders and directions

All conditions and directions inserted in any certificate of incorporation shall be binding upon and performed or observed by the trustees as trusts of the charity, and section 88 below shall apply to any trustee who fails to perform or observe any such condition or direction as it applies to a person guilty of disobedience to any such order of the Commissioners as is mentioned in that section.

59. Gifts to charity before incorporation to have same effect afterwards

After the incorporation of the trustees of any charity under this Part of this Act every donation, gift and disposition of property, real or personal, lawfully made before the incorporation but not having actually taken effect, or thereafter lawfully made, by deed, will or otherwise to or in favour of the charity, or the trustees of the charity, or otherwise for the purposes of the charity, shall take effect as if made to or in favour of the incorporated body or otherwise for the like purposes.

60. Execution of documents by incorporated body

(1) This section has effect as respects the execution of documents by an incorporated body.

(2) If an incorporated body has a common seal, a document may be executed by the body by the affixing of its common seal.

(3) Whether or not it has a common seal, a document may be executed by an incorporated body either –
  (a) by being signed by a majority of the trustees of the relevant charity and expressed (in whatever form of words) to be executed by the body; or
  (b) by being executed in pursuance of an authority given under subsection (4) below.

(4) For the purposes of subsection (3)(b) above the trustees of the relevant charity in the case of an incorporated body may, subject to the trusts of the charity, confer on any two or more of their number –
  (a) a general authority, or
  (b) an authority limited in such manner as the trustees think fit,
to execute in the name and on behalf of the body documents for giving effect to transactions to which the body is a party.

(5) An authority under subsection (4) above –
  (a) shall suffice for any document if it is given in writing or by resolution of a meeting of the trustees of the relevant charity, notwithstanding the want of any formality that would be required in giving an authority apart from that subsection;
  (b) may be given so as to make the powers conferred exercisable by any of the trustees, or may be restricted to named persons or in any other way;
  (c) subject to any such restriction, and until it is revoked, shall, notwithstanding any change in the trustees of the relevant charity, have effect as a continuing authority given by the trustees from time to time of the charity and exercisable by such trustees.

(6) In any authority under subsection (4) above to execute a document in the name and on behalf of an incorporated body there shall, unless the contrary intention appears, be implied authority also to execute it for the body in the name and on behalf of the official custodian or of any other person, in any case in which the trustees could do so.

(7) A document duly executed by an incorporated body which makes it clear on its face that it is intended by the person or persons making it to be a deed has effect, upon delivery, as a deed; and it shall be presumed, unless a contrary intention is proved, to be delivered upon its being so executed.

(8) In favour of a purchaser a document shall be deemed to have been duly executed by such a body if it purports to be signed –
  (a) by a majority of the trustees of the relevant charity, or
  (b) by such of the trustees of the relevant charity as are authorised by the trustees of that charity to execute it in the name and on behalf of the body,
and, where the document makes it clear on its face that it is intended by the person or persons making it to be a deed, it shall be deemed to have been delivered upon its being executed.

For this purpose 'purchaser' means a purchaser in good faith for valuable consideration and includes a lessee, mortgagee or other person who for valuable consideration acquires an interest in property.

61. Power of Commissioners to dissolve incorporated body

(1) Where the Commissioners are satisfied –
- (a) that an incorporated body has no assets or does not operate, or
- (b) that the relevant charity in the case of an incorporated body has ceased to exist, or
- (c) that the institution previously constituting, or treated by them as constituting, any such charity has ceased to be, or (as the case may be) was not at the time of the body's incorporation, a charity, or
- (d) that the purposes of the relevant charity in the case of an incorporated body have been achieved so far as is possible or are in practice incapable of being achieved,

they may of their own motion make an order dissolving the body as from such date as is specified in the order.

(2) Where the Commissioners are satisfied, on the application of the trustees of the relevant charity in the case of an incorporated body, that it would be in the interests of the charity for that body to be dissolved, the Commissioners may make an order dissolving the body as from such date as is specified in the order.

(3) Subject to subsection (4) below, an order made under this section with respect to an incorporated body shall have the effect of vesting in the trustees of the relevant charity, in trust for that charity, all property for the time being vested –
- (a) in the body, or
- (b) in any other person (apart from the official custodian),

in trust for that charity.

(4) If the Commissioners so direct in the order –
- (a) all or any specified part of that property shall, instead of vesting in the trustees of the relevant charity, vest –
  - (i) in a specified person as trustee for, or nominee of, that charity, or
  - (ii) in such persons (other than the trustees of the relevant charity) as may be specified;
- (b) any specified investments, or any specified class or description of investments, held by any person in trust for the relevant charity shall be transferred –
  - (i) to the trustees of that charity, or
  - (ii) to any such person or persons as is or are mentioned in paragraph (a)(i) or (ii) above;

and for this purpose 'specified' means specified by the Commissioners in the order.

(5) Where an order to which this subsection applies is made with respect to an incorporated body –
- (a) any rights or liabilities of the body shall become rights or liabilities of the trustees of the relevant charity; and
- (b) any legal proceedings that might have been continued or commenced by or against the body may be continued or commenced by or against those trustees.

(6) Subsection (5) above applies to any order under this section by virtue of which –
- (a) any property vested as mentioned in subsection (3) above is vested –
  - (i) in the trustees of the relevant charity, or
  - (ii) in any persons as trustee for, or nominee of, that charity; or
- (b) any investments held by any person in trust for the relevant charity are required to be transferred –
  - (i) to the trustees of that charity, or

(ii) to any person as trustee for, or nominee of, that charity.

(7) Any order made by the Commissioners under this section may be varied or revoked by a further order so made.

62. Interpretation of Part VII

In this Part of this Act –

'incorporated body' means a body incorporated under section 50 above;

'the relevant charity', in relation to an incorporated body, means the charity the trustees of which have been incorporated as that body;

'the trustees', in relation to a charity, means the charity trustees.

PART VIII

CHARITABLE COMPANIES

63. Winding up

(1) Where a charity may be wound up by the High Court under the Insolvency Act 1986, a petition for it to be wound up under that Act by any court in England or Wales having jurisdiction may be presented by the Attorney General, as well as by any person authorised by that Act.

(2) Where a charity may be so wound up by the High Court, such a petition may also be presented by the Commissioners if, at any time after they have instituted an inquiry under section 8 above with respect to the charity, they are satisfied as mentioned in section 18(1)(a) or (b) above.

(3) Where a charitable company is dissolved, the Commissioners may make an application under section 651 of the Companies Act 1985 (power of court to declare dissolution of company void) for an order to be made under that section with respect to the company; and for this purpose subsection (1) of that section shall have effect in relation to a charitable company as if the reference to the liquidator of the company included a reference to the Commissioners.

(4) Where a charitable company's name has been struck off the register of companies under section 652 of the Companies Act 1985 (power of registrar to strike defunct company off register), the Commissioners may make an application under section 653(2) of that Act (objection to striking off by person aggrieved) for an order restoring the company's name to that register; and for this purpose section 653(2) shall have effect in relation to a charitable company as if the reference to any such person aggrieved as is there mentioned included a reference to the Commissioners.

(5) The powers exercisable by the Commissioners by virtue of this section shall be exercisable by them of their own motion, but shall be exercisable only with the agreement of the Attorney General on each occasion.

(6) In this section 'charitable company' means a company which is a charity.

64. Alteration of objects clause

(1) Where a charity is a company or other body corporate having power to alter the instruments establishing or regulating it as a body corporate, no exercise of that power which has the effect of the body ceasing to be a charity shall be valid so as to affect the application of –

(a) any property acquired under any disposition or agreement previously made otherwise than for full consideration in money or money's worth, or any property representing property so acquired,

(b) any property representing income which has accrued before the alteration is made, or

(c) the income from any such property as aforesaid.

(2) Where a charity is a company, any alteration by it –

(a) of the objects clause in its memorandum of association, or

(b) of any other provision in its memorandum of association, or any provision in its articles of association, which is a provision directing or restricting the manner in which property of the company may be used or applied,

is ineffective without the prior written consent of the Commissioners.

(3) Where a company has made any such alteration in accordance with subsection (2) above and –

(a) in connection with the alteration is required by virtue of –

(i) section 6(1) of the Companies Act 1985 (delivery of documents following alteration of objects), or

(ii) that provision as applied by section 17(3) of that Act (alteration of condition in memorandum which could have been contained in articles),

to deliver to the registrar of companies a printed copy of its memorandum, as altered, or

(b) is required by virtue of section 380(1) of that Act (registration etc of resolutions and agreements) to forward to the registrar a printed or other copy of the special resolution effecting the alteration,

the copy so delivered or forwarded by the company shall be accompanied by a copy of the Commissioner's consent.

(4) Section 6(3) of that Act (offences) shall apply to any default by a company in complying with subsection (3) above as it applies to any such default as is mentioned in that provision.

65. Invalidity of certain transactions

(1) Sections 35 and 35A of the Companies Act 1985 (capacity of company not limited by its memorandum; power of directors to bind company) do not apply to the acts of a company which is a charity except in favour of a person who –

(a) gives full consideration in money or money's worth in relation to the act in question, and

(b) does not know that the act is not permitted by the company's memorandum or, as the case may be, is beyond the powers of the directors,

or who does not know at the time the act is done that the company is a charity.

(2) However, where such a company purports to transfer or grant an interest in property, the fact that the act was not permitted by the company's memorandum or, as the case may be, that the directors in connection with the act exceeded any limitation on their powers under the company's constitution, does not affect the title of a person who subsequently acquires the property or any interest in it for full consideration without actual notice of any such circumstances affecting the validity of the company's act.

(3) In any proceedings arising out of subsection (1) above the burden of proving –

(a) that a person knew that an act was not permitted by the company's memorandum or was beyond the powers of the directors, or

(b) that a person knew that the company was a charity,

lies on the person making that allegation.

(4) Where a company is a charity, the ratification of an act under section 35(3) of the Companies Act 1985, or the ratification of a transaction to which section 322A of that Act applies (invalidity

of certain transactions to which directors or their associates are parties), is ineffective without the prior written consent of the Commissioners.

66. Requirement of consent of Commissioners to certain acts

(1) Where a company is a charity –
  (a) any approval given by the company for the purposes of any of the provisions of the Companies Act 1985 specified in subsection (2) below, and
  (b) any affirmation by it for the purposes of section 322(2)(c) of that Act (affirmation of voidable arrangements under which assets are acquired by or from a director or person connected with him),

is ineffective without the prior written consent of the Commissioners.

(2) The provisions of the Companies Act 1985 referred to in subsection (1)(a) above are –
  (a) section 312 (payment to director in respect of loss of office or retirement);
  (b) section 313(1) (payment to director in respect of loss of office or retirement made in connection with transfer of undertaking or property of company);
  (c) section 319(3) (incorporation in director's service contract of term whereby his employment will or may continue for a period of more than five years);
  (d) section 320(1) (arrangement whereby assets are acquired by or from director or person connected with him);
  (e) section 337(3)(a) (provision of funds to meet certain expenses incurred by director).

67. Name to appear on correspondence etc

Section 30(7) of the Companies Act 1985 (exemption from requirements relating to publication of name etc) shall not, in its application to any company which is a charity, have the effect of exempting the company from the requirements of section 349(1) of that Act (company's name to appear in its correspondence etc).

68. Status to appear on correspondence etc

(1) Where a company is a charity and its name does not include the word 'charity' or the word 'charitable' then, subject to subsection (1A), the fact that the company is a charity shall be stated in legible characters –
  (a) in all business letters of the company,
  (b) in all its notices and other official publications,
  (c) in all bills of exchange, promissory notes, endorsements, cheques and orders for money or goods purporting to be signed on behalf of the company,
  (d) in all conveyances purporting to be executed by the company, and
  (e) in all bills rendered by it and in all its invoices, receipts, and letters of credit.

(1A) Where a company's name includes the word 'elusen' or the word 'elusennol' (the Welsh equivalents of the words 'charity' and 'charitable'), subsection (1) above shall not apply in relation to any document which is wholly in Welsh.

(1B) The statement required by subsection (1) above shall be in English, except that, in the case of a document which is otherwise wholly in Welsh, the statement may be in Welsh if it consists of or includes the word 'elusen' or the word 'elusennol'.

(2) In subsection (1)(d) above 'conveyance' means any instrument creating, transferring, varying or extinguishing an interest in land.

(3) Subsections (2) to (4) of section 349 of the Companies Act 1985 (offences in connection with failure to include required particulars in business letters etc) shall apply in relation to a

contravention of subsection (1) above, taking the reference in subsection (3)(b) of that section to a bill of parcels as a reference to any such bill as is mentioned in subsection (1)(e) above.

NOTE

Section shown as amended by the Welsh Language Act 1993.

---

69. Investigation of accounts

(1) In the case of a charity which is a company the Commissioners may by order require that the condition and accounts of the charity for such period as they think fit shall be investigated and audited by an auditor appointed by them, being a person eligible for appointment as a company auditor under section 25 of the Companies Act 1989.

(2) An auditor acting under subsection (1) above –
    (a) shall have a right of access to all books, accounts and documents relating to the charity which are in the possession or control of the charity trustees or to which the charity trustees have access;
    (b) shall be entitled to require from any charity trustee, past or present, and from any past or present officer or employee of the charity such information and explanation as he thinks necessary for the performance of his duties;
    (c) shall at the conclusion or during the progress of the audit make such reports to the Commissioners about the audit or about the accounts or affairs of the charity as he thinks the case requires, and shall send a copy of any such report to the charity trustees.

(3) The expenses of any audit under subsection (1) above, including the remuneration of the auditor, shall be paid by the Commissioners.

(4) If any person fails to afford an auditor any facility to which he is entitled under subsection (2) above the Commissioners may by order give to that person or to the charity trustees for the time being such directions as the Commissioners think appropriate for securing that the default is made good.

PART IX

MISCELLANEOUS

Powers of investment

70. Relaxation of restrictions on wider-range investments

(1) The Secretary of State may by order made with the consent of the Treasury –
    (a) direct that, in the case of a trust fund consisting of property held by or in trust for a charity, any division of the fund in pursuance of section 2(1) of the Trustee Investments Act 1961 (trust funds to be divided so that wider-range and narrower-range investments are equal in value) shall be made so that the value of the wider-range part at the time of the division bears to the then value of the narrower-range part such proportion as is specified in the order;
    (b) provide that, in its application in relation to such a trust fund, that Act shall have effect subject to such modifications so specified as the Secretary of State considers appropriate in consequence of, or in connection with, any such direction.

(2) Where, before the coming into force of an order under this section, a trust fund consisting of property held by or in trust for a charity has already been divided in pursuance of section 2(1) of that Act, the fund may, notwithstanding anything in that provision, be again divided (once only) in pursuance of that provision during the continuance in force of the order.

(3) No order shall be made under this section unless a draft of the order has been laid before and approved by a resolution of each House of Parliament.

(4) Expressions used in this section which are also used in the Trustee Investments Act 1961 have the same meaning as in that Act.

(5) *(Applies to Scotland only.)*

71. Extension of powers of investment

(1) The Secretary of State may by regulations made with the consent of the Treasury make, with respect to property held by or in trust for a charity, provision authorising a trustee to invest such property in any manner specified in the regulations, being a manner of investment not for the time being included in any Part of Schedule 1 to the Trustee Investments Act 1961.

(2) Regulations under this section may make such provision –
    (a) regulating the investment of property in any manner authorised by virtue of subsection (1) above, and
    (b) with respect to the variation and retention of investments so made,
as the Secretary of State considers appropriate.

(3) Such regulations may, in particular, make provision –
    (a) imposing restrictions with respect to the proportion of the property held by or in trust for a charity which may be invested in any manner authorised by virtue of subsection (1) above, being either restrictions applying to investment in any such manner generally or restrictions applying to investment in any particular such manner;
    (b) imposing the like requirements with respect to the obtaining and consideration of advice as are imposed by any of the provisions of section 6 of the Trustee Investments Act 1961 (duty of trustees in choosing investments).

(4) Any power of investment conferred by any regulations under this section –
    (a) shall be in addition to, and not in derogation from, any power conferred otherwise than by such regulations; and
    (b) shall not be limited by the trusts of a charity (in so far as they are not contained in any Act or instrument made under an enactment) unless it is excluded by those trusts in express terms;
but any such power shall only be exercisable by a trustee in so far as a contrary intention is not expressed in any Act or in any instrument made under an enactment and relating to the powers of the trustee.

(5) No regulations shall be made under this section unless a draft of the regulations has been laid before and approved by a resolution of each House of Parliament.

(6) In this section 'property' –
    (a) in England and Wales, means real or personal property of any description, including money and things in action, but does not include an interest in expectancy; and
    (b) *(applies to Scotland only)*;
and any reference to property held by or in trust for a charity is a reference to property so held, whether it is for the time being in a state of investment or not.

(7) *(Applies to Scotland only.)*

Disqualification for acting as charity trustee

72. Persons disqualified for being trustees of a charity

(1) Subject to the following provisions of this section, a person shall be disqualified for being a charity trustee or trustee for a charity if –
   (a) he has been convicted of any offence involving dishonesty or deception;
   (b) he has been adjudged bankrupt or sequestration of his estate has been awarded and (in either case) he has not been discharged;
   (c) he has made a composition or arrangement with, or granted a trust deed for, his creditors and has not been discharged in respect of it;
   (d) he has been removed from the office of charity trustee or trustee for a charity by an order made –
      (i) by the Commissioners under section 18(2)(i) above, or
      (ii) by the Commissioners under section 20(1A)(i) of the Charities Act 1960 (power to act for protection of charities) or under section 20(1)(i) of that Act (as in force before the commencement of section 8 of the Charities Act 1992), or
      (iii) by the High Court,
      on the grounds of any misconduct or mismanagement in the administration of the charity for which he was responsible or to which he was privy, or which he by his conduct contributed to or facilitated;
   (e) he has been removed, under section 7 of the Law Reform (Miscellaneous Provisions) (Scotland) Act 1990 (powers of Court of Session to deal with management of charities), from being concerned in the management or control of any body;
   (f) he is subject to a disqualification order under the Company Directors Disqualification Act 1986 or to an order made under section 429(2)(b) of the Insolvency Act 1986 (failure to pay under county court administration order).

(2) In subsection (1) above –
   (a) paragraph (a) applies whether the conviction occurred before or after the commencement of that subsection, but does not apply in relation to any conviction which is a spent conviction for the purposes of the Rehabilitation of Offenders Act 1974;
   (b) paragraph (b) applies whether the adjudication of bankruptcy or the sequestration occurred before or after the commencement of that subsection;
   (c) paragraph (c) applies whether the composition or arrangement was made, or the trust deed was granted, before or after the commencement of that subsection; and
   (d) paragraphs (d) to (f) apply in relation to orders made and removals effected before or after the commencement of that subsection.

(3) Where (apart from this subsection) a person is disqualified under subsection (1)(b) above for being a charity trustee or trustee for any charity which is a company, he shall not be so disqualified if leave has been granted under section 11 of the Company Directors Disqualification Act 1986 (undischarged bankrupts) for him to act as director of the charity; and similarly a person shall not be disqualified under subsection (1)(f) above for being a charity trustee or trustee for such a charity if –
   (a) in the case of a person subject to a disqualification order, leave under the order has been granted for him to act as director of the charity, or
   (b) in the case of a person subject to an order under section 429(2)(b) of the Insolvency Act 1986, leave has been granted by the court which made the order for him to so act.

(4) The Commissioners may, on the application of any person disqualified under subsection (1) above, waive his disqualification either generally or in relation to a particular charity or a particular class of charities; but no such waiver may be granted in relation to any charity which is a company if –

  (a) the person concerned is for the time being prohibited, by virtue of –
     (i) a disqualification order under the Company Directors Disqualification Act 1986, or
     (ii) section 11(1) or 12(2) of that Act (undischarged bankrupts; failure to pay under county court administration order),
     from acting as director of the charity; and
  (b) leave has not been granted for him to act as director of any other company.

(5) Any waiver under subsection (4) above shall be notified in writing to the person concerned.

(6) For the purposes of this section the Commissioners shall keep, in such manner as they think fit, a register of all persons who have been removed from office as mentioned in subsection (1)(d) above either –

  (a) by an order of the Commissioners made before or after the commencement of subsection (1) above, or
  (b) by an order of the High Court made after the commencement of section 45(1) of the Charities Act 1992;

and, where any person is so removed from office by an order of the High Court, the court shall notify the Commissioners of his removal.

(7) The entries in the register kept under subsection (6) above shall be available for public inspection in legible form at all reasonable times.

73. Persons acting as charity trustee while disqualified

(1) Subject to subsection (2) below, any person who acts as a charity trustee or trustee for a charity while he is disqualified for being such a trustee by virtue of section 72 above shall be guilty of an offence and liable –

  (a) on summary conviction, to imprisonment for a term not exceeding six months or to a fine not exceeding the statutory maximum, or both;
  (b) on conviction on indictment, to imprisonment for a term not exceeding two years or to a fine, or both.

(2) Subsection (1) above shall not apply where –
  (a) the charity concerned is a company; and
  (b) the disqualified person is disqualified by virtue only of paragraph (b) or (f) of section 72(1) above.

(3) Any acts done as charity trustee or trustee for a charity by a person disqualified for being such a trustee by virtue of section 72 above shall not be invalid by reason only of that disqualification.

(4) Where the Commissioners are satisfied –
  (a) that any person has acted as charity trustee or trustee for a charity (other than an exempt charity) while disqualified for being such a trustee by virtue of section 72 above, and
  (b) that, while so acting, he has received from the charity any sums by way of remuneration or expenses, or any benefit in kind, in connection with his acting as charity trustee or trustee for the charity,

they may by order direct him to repay to the charity the whole or part of any such sums, or (as the case may be) to pay to the charity the whole or part of the monetary value (as determined by them) of any such benefit.

(5) Subsection (4) above does not apply to any sums received by way of remuneration or expenses in respect of any time when the person concerned was not disqualified for being a charity trustee or trustee for the charity.

74. Power to transfer all property, modify objects etc

(1) This section applies to a charity if –
    (a) its gross income in its last financial year did not exceed £5,000, and
    (b) it does not hold any land on trusts which stipulate that the land is to be used for the purposes, or any particular purposes, of the charity,
and it is neither an exempt charity nor a charitable company.

(2) Subject to the following provisions of this section, the charity trustees of a charity to which this section applies may resolve for the purposes of this section –
    (a) that all the property of the charity should be transferred to such other charity as is specified in the resolution, being either a registered charity or a charity which is not required to be registered;
    (b) that all the property of the charity should be divided, in such manner as is specified in the resolution, between such two or more other charities as are so specified, being in each case either a registered charity or a charity which is not required to be registered;
    (c) that the trusts of the charity should be modified by replacing all or any of the purposes of the charity with such other purposes, being in law charitable, as are specified in the resolution;
    (d) that any provision of the trusts of the charity –
        (i) relating to any of the powers exercisable by the charity trustees in the administration of the charity, or
        (ii) regulating the procedure to be followed in any respect in connection with its administration,
should be modified in such manner as is specified in the resolution.

(3) Any resolution passed under subsection (2) above must be passed by a majority of not less than two-thirds of such charity trustees as vote on the resolution.

(4) The charity trustees of a charity to which this section applies ('the transferor charity') shall not have power to pass a resolution under subsection (2)(a) or (b) above unless they are satisfied –
    (a) that the existing purposes of the transferor charity have ceased to be conducive to a suitable and effective application of the charity's resources; and
    (b) that the purposes of the charity or charities specified in the resolution are as similar in character to the purposes of the transferor charity as is reasonably practicable;
and before passing the resolution they must have received from the charity trustees of the charity, or (as the case may be) of each of the charities, specified in the resolution written confirmation that those trustees are willing to accept a transfer of property under this section.

(5) The charity trustees of any such charity shall not have power to pass a resolution under subsection (2)(c) above unless they are satisfied –
    (a) that the existing purposes of the charity (or, as the case may be, such of them as it is proposed to replace) have ceased to be conducive to a suitable and effective application of the charity's resources; and
    (b) that the purposes specified in the resolution are as similar in character to those existing purposes as is practical in the circumstances.

(6) Where charity trustees have passed a resolution under subsection (2) above, they shall –

(a) give public notice of the resolution in such manner as they think reasonable in the circumstances; and

(b) send a copy of the resolution to the Commissioners, together with a statement of their reasons for passing it.

(7) The Commissioners may, when considering the resolution, require the charity trustees to provide additional information or explanation –

(a) as to the circumstances in and by reference to which they have determined to act under this section, or

(b) relating to their compliance with this section in connection with the resolution;

and the Commissioners shall take into account any representations made to them by persons appearing to them to be interested in the charity where those representations are made within the period of six weeks beginning with the date when the Commissioners receive a copy of the resolution by virtue of subsection (6)(b) above.

(8) Where the Commissioners have so received a copy of a resolution from any charity trustees and it appears to them that the trustees have complied with this section in connection with the resolution, the Commissioners shall, within the period of three months beginning with the date when they receive the copy of the resolution, notify the trustees in writing either –

(a) that the Commissioners concur with the resolution; or

(b) that they do not concur with it.

(9) Where the Commissioners so notify their concurrence with the resolution, then –

(a) if the resolution was passed under subsection (2)(a) or (b) above, the charity trustees shall arrange for all the property of the transferor charity to be transferred in accordance with the resolution and on terms that any property so transferred –

(i) shall be held and applied by the charity to which it is transferred ('the transferee charity') for the purposes of that charity, but

(ii) shall, as property of the transferee charity, nevertheless be subject to any restrictions on expenditure to which it is subject as property of the transferor charity,

and those trustees shall arrange for it to be so transferred by such date as may be specified in the notification; and

(b) if the resolution was passed under subsection (2)(c) or (d) above, the trusts of the charity shall be deemed, as from such date as may be specified in the notification, to have been modified in accordance with the terms of the resolution.

(10) For the purpose of enabling any property to be transferred to a charity under this section, the Commissioners shall have power, at the request of the charity trustees of that charity, to make orders vesting any property of the transferor charity –

(a) in the charity trustees of the first-mentioned charity or in any trustee for that charity, or

(b) in any other person nominated by those charity trustees to hold the property in trust for that charity.

(11) The Secretary of State may by order amend subsection (1) above by substituting a different sum for the sum for the time being specified there.

(12) In this section –

(a) 'charitable company' means a charity which is a company or other body corporate; and

(b) references to the transfer of property to a charity are references to its transfer –

(i) to the charity trustees, or

(ii) to any trustee for the charity, or

(iii) to a person nominated by the charity trustees to hold it in trust for the charity,

as the charity trustees may determine.

75. Power to spend capital

(1) This section applies to a charity if –
   (a) it has a permanent endowment which does not consist of or comprise any land, and
   (b) its gross income in its last financial year did not exceed £1,000,
and it is neither an exempt charity nor a charitable company.

(2) Where the charity trustees of a charity to which this section applies are of the opinion that the property of the charity is too small, in relation to its purposes, for any useful purpose to be achieved by the expenditure of income alone, they may resolve for the purposes of this section that the charity ought to be freed from the restrictions with respect to expenditure of capital to which its permanent endowment is subject.

(3) Any resolution passed under subsection (2) above must be passed by a majority of not less than two-thirds of such charity trustees as vote on the resolution.

(4) Before passing such a resolution the charity trustees must consider whether any reasonable possibility exists of effecting a transfer or division of all the charity's property under section 74 above (disregarding any such transfer or division as would, in their opinion, impose on the charity an unacceptable burden of costs).

(5) Where charity trustees have passed a resolution under subsection (2) above, they shall –
   (a) give public notice of the resolution in such manner as they think reasonable in the circumstances; and
   (b) send a copy of the resolution to the Commissioners, together with a statement of their reasons for passing it.

(6) The Commissioners may, when considering the resolution, require the charity trustees to provide additional information or explanation –
   (a) as to the circumstances in and by reference to which they have determined to act under this section, or
   (b) relating to their compliance with this section in connection with the resolution;
and the Commissioners shall take into account any representations made to them by persons appearing to them to be interested in the charity where those representations are made within the period of six weeks beginning with the date when the Commissioners receive a copy of the resolution by virtue of subsection (5)(b) above.

(7) Where the Commissioners have so received a copy of a resolution from any charity trustees and it appears to them that the trustees have complied with this section in connection with the resolution, the Commissioners shall, within the period of three months beginning with the date when they receive the copy of the resolution, notify the trustees in writing either –
   (a) that the Commissioners concur with the resolution; or
   (b) that they do not concur with it.

(8) Where the Commissioners so notify their concurrence with the resolution, the charity trustees shall have, as from such date as may be specified in the notification, power by virtue of this section to expend any property of the charity without regard to any such restrictions as are mentioned in subsection (2) above.

(9) The Secretary of State may by order amend subsection (1) above by substituting a different sum for the sum for the time being specified there.

(10) In this section 'charitable company' means a charity which is a company or other body corporate.

76. Local authority's index of local charities

(1) The council of a county or of a district or London borough and the Common Council of the City of London may maintain an index of local charities or of any class of local charities in the council's area, and may publish information contained in the index, or summaries or extracts taken from it.

(2) A council proposing to establish or maintaining under this section an index of local charities or of any class of local charities shall, on request, be supplied by the Commissioners free of charge with copies of such entries in the register of charities as are relevant to the index or with particulars of any changes in the entries of which copies have been supplied before; and the Commissioners may arrange that they will without further request supply a council with particulars of any such changes.

(3) An index maintained under this section shall be open to public inspection at all reasonable times.

(4) A council may employ any voluntary organisation as their agent for the purposes of this section, on such terms and within such limits (if any) or in such cases as they may agree; and for this purpose 'voluntary organisation' means any body of which the activities are carried on otherwise than for profit, not being a public or local authority.

(5) A joint board discharging any of a council's functions shall have the same powers under this section as the council as respects local charities in the council's area which are established for purposes similar or complementary to any services provided by the board.

77. Reviews of local charities by local authority

(1) The council of a county or of a district or London borough and the Common Council of the City of London may, subject to the following provisions of this section, initiate, and carry out in co-operation with the charity trustees, a review of the working of any group of local charities with the same or similar purposes in the council's area, and may make to the Commissioners such report on the review and such recommendations arising from it as the council after consultation with the trustees think fit.

(2) A council having power to initiate reviews under this section may co-operate with other persons in any review by them of the working of local charities in the council's area (with or without other charities), or may join with other persons in initiating and carrying out such a review.

(3) No review initiated by a council under this section shall extend to any charity without the consent of the charity trustees, nor to any ecclesiastical charity.

(4) No review initiated under this section by the council of a district shall extend to the working in any county of a local charity established for purposes similar or complementary to any services provided by county councils unless the review so extends with the consent of the council of that county.

(5) Subsections (4) and (5) of section 76 above shall apply for the purposes of this section as they apply for the purposes of that section.

78. Co-operation between charities, and between charities and local authorities

(1) Any local council and any joint board discharging any functions of such a council –

(a) may make, with any charity established for purposes similar or complementary to services provided by the council or board, arrangements for co-ordinating the activities of the council or board and those of the charity in the interests of persons who may benefit from those services or from the charity; and

(b) shall be at liberty to disclose to any such charity in the interests of those persons any information obtained in connection with the services provided by the council or board, whether or not arrangements have been made with the charity under this subsection.

In this subsection 'local council' means the council of a county, or of a district, London borough, parish or (in Wales) community, and includes also the Common Council of the City of London and the Council of the Isles of Scilly.

(2) Charity trustees shall, notwithstanding anything in the trusts of the charity, have power by virtue of this subsection to do all or any of the following things, where it appears to them likely to promote or make more effective the work of the charity, and may defray the expense of so doing out of any income or money applicable as income of the charity, that is to say –

(a) they may co-operate in any review undertaken under section 77 above or otherwise of the working of charities or any class of charities;

(b) they may make arrangements with an authority acting under subsection (1) above or with another charity for co-ordinating their activities and those of the authority or of the other charity;

(c) they may publish information of other charities with a view to bringing them to the notice of those for whose benefit they are intended.

79. Parochial charities

(1) Where trustees hold any property for the purposes of a public recreation ground, or of allotments (whether under inclosure Acts or otherwise), for the benefit of inhabitants of a parish having a parish council, or for other charitable purposes connected with such a parish, except for an ecclesiastical charity, they may with the approval of the Commissioners and with the consent of the parish council transfer the property to the parish council or to persons appointed by the parish council; and the council or their appointees shall hold the property on the same trusts and subject to the same conditions as the trustees did.

This subsection shall apply to property held for any public purpose as it applies to property held for charitable purposes.

(2) Where the charity trustees of a parochial charity in a parish, not being an ecclesiastical charity nor a charity founded within the preceding forty years, do not include persons elected by the local government electors, ratepayers or inhabitants of the parish or appointed by the parish council or parish meeting, the parish council or parish meeting may appoint additional charity trustees, to such number as the Commissioners may allow; and if there is a sole charity trustee not elected or appointed as aforesaid of any such charity, the number of the charity trustees may, with the approval of the Commissioners, be increased to three of whom one may be nominated by the person holding the office of the sole trustee and one by the parish council or parish meeting.

(3) Where, under the trusts of a charity other than an ecclesiastical charity, the inhabitants of a rural parish (whether in vestry or not) or a select vestry were formerly (in 1894) entitled to appoint charity trustees for, or trustees or beneficiaries of, the charity, then –

(a) in a parish having a parish council, the appointment shall be made by the parish council or, in the case of beneficiaries, by persons appointed by the parish council; and

(b) in a parish not having a parish council, the appointment shall be made by the parish meeting.

(4) Where overseers as such or, except in the case of an ecclesiastical charity, churchwardens as such were formerly (in 1894) charity trustees of or trustees for a parochial charity in a rural parish, either alone or jointly with other persons, then instead of the former overseer or church warden trustees there shall be trustees (to a number not greater than that of the former overseer or churchwarden trustees) appointed by the parish council or, if there is no parish council, by the parish meeting.

(5) Where, outside Greater London (other than the outer London boroughs), overseers of a parish as such were formerly (in 1927) charity trustees of or trustees for any charity, either alone or jointly with other persons, then instead of the former overseer trustees there shall be trustees (to a number not greater than that of the former overseer trustees) appointed by the parish council or, if there is no parish council, by the parish meeting.

(6) In the case of an urban parish existing immediately before the passing of the Local Government Act 1972 which after 1 April 1974 is not comprised in a parish, the power of appointment under subsection (5) above shall be exercisable by the district council.

(7) In the application of the foregoing provisions of this section to Wales –
  (a) for references in subsections (1) and (2) to a parish or a parish council there shall be substituted respectively references to a community or a community council;
  (b) for references in subsections (3)(a) and (b) to a parish, a parish council or a parish meeting there shall be substituted respectively references to a community, a community council or the district council;
  (c) for references in subsections (4) and (5) to a parish council or a parish meeting there shall be substituted respectively references to a community council or the district council.

(8) Any appointment of a charity trustee or trustee for a charity which is made by virtue of this section shall be for a term of four years, and a retiring trustee shall be eligible for re-appointment but –
  (a) on an appointment under subsection (2) above, where no previous appointments have been made by virtue of that subsection or of the corresponding provision of the Local Government Act 1894 or the Charities Act 1960, and more than one trustee is appointed, half of those appointed (or as nearly as may be) shall be appointed for a term of two years; and
  (b) an appointment made to fill a casual vacancy shall be for the remainder of the term of the previous appointment.

(9) This section shall not affect the trusteeship, control or management of any voluntary school within the meaning of the Education Act 1944 or of any grant-maintained school.

(10) The provisions of this section shall not extend to the Isles of Scilly, and shall have effect subject to any order (including any future order) made under any enactment relating to local government areas or the powers of local authorities.

(11) In this section the expression 'formerly (in 1894)' relates to the period immediately before the passing of the Local Government Act 1894, and the expression 'formerly (in 1927)' to the period immediately before 1 April 1927; and the word 'former' shall be construed accordingly.

Scottish charities

80. Supervision by Commissioners of certain Scottish charities

(1) The following provisions of this Act, namely –
  (a) sections 8 and 9,
  (b) section 18 (except subsection (2)(ii)), and
  (c) section 19,

shall have effect in relation to any recognised body which is managed or controlled wholly or mainly in or from England or Wales as they have effect in relation to a charity.

(2) Where –
- (a) a recognised body is managed or controlled wholly or mainly in or from Scotland, but
- (b) any person in England and Wales holds any property on behalf of the body or of any person concerned in its management or control,

then, if the Commissioners are satisfied as to the matters mentioned in subsection (3) below, they may make an order requiring the person holding the property not to part with it without their approval.

(3) The matters referred to in subsection (2) above are –
- (a) that there has been any misconduct or mismanagement in the administration of the body; and
- (b) that it is necessary or desirable to make an order under that subsection for the purpose of protecting the property of the body or securing a proper application of such property for the purposes of the body;

and the reference in that subsection to the Commissioners being satisfied as to those matters is a reference to their being so satisfied on the basis of such information as may be supplied to them by the Lord Advocate.

(4) Where –
- (a) any person in England and Wales holds any property on behalf of a recognised body or of any person concerned in the management or control of such a body, and
- (b) the Commissioners are satisfied (whether on the basis of such information as may be supplied to them by the Lord Advocate or otherwise) –
  - (i) that there has been any misconduct or mismanagement in the administration of the body, and
  - (ii) that it is necessary or desirable to make an order under this subsection for the purpose of protecting the property of the body or securing a proper application of such property for the purposes of the body,

the Commissioners may by order vest the property in such recognised body or charity as is specified in the order in accordance with subsection (5) below, or require any persons in whom the property is vested to transfer it to any such body or charity, or appoint any person to transfer the property to any such body or charity.

(5) The Commissioners may specify in an order under subsection (4) above such other recognised body or such charity as they consider appropriate, being a body or charity whose purposes are, in the opinion of the Commissioners, as similar in character to those of the body referred to in paragraph (a) of that subsection as is reasonably practicable; but the Commissioners shall not so specify any body or charity unless they have received –
- (a) from the persons concerned in the management or control of the body, or
- (b) from the charity trustees of the charity,

as the case may be, written confirmation that they are willing to accept the property.

(6) In this section 'recognised body' has the same meaning as in Part I of the Law Reform (Miscellaneous Provisions) (Scotland) Act 1990 (Scottish charities).

Administrative provisions about charities

81. Manner of giving notice of charity meetings, etc

(1) All notices which are required or authorised by the trusts of a charity to be given to a charity trustee, member or subscriber may be sent by post, and, if sent by post, may be addressed to any

address given as his in the list of charity trustees, members or subscribers for the time being in use at the office or principle office of the charity.

(2) Where any such notice required to be given as aforesaid is given by post, it shall be deemed to have been given by the time at which the letter containing it would be delivered in the ordinary course of post.

(3) No notice required to be given as aforesaid of any meeting or election need be given to any charity trustee, member or subscriber, if in the list above mentioned he has no address in the United Kingdom.

82. Manner of executing instruments

(1) Charity trustees may, subject to the trusts of the charity, confer on any of their body (not being less than two in number) a general authority, or an authority limited in such manner as the trustees think fit, to execute in the names and on behalf of the trustees assurances or other deeds or instruments for giving effect to transactions to which the trustees are a party; and any deed or instrument executed in pursuance of an authority so given shall be of the same effect as if executed by the whole body.

(2) An authority under subsection (1) above –
  (a) shall suffice for any deed or instrument if it is given in writing or by resolution of a meeting of the trustees, notwithstanding the want of any formality that would be required in giving an authority apart from that subsection;
  (b) may be given so as to make the powers conferred exercisable by any of the trustees, or may be restricted to named persons or in any other way;
  (c) subject to any such restriction, and until it is revoked, shall, notwithstanding any change in the charity trustees, have effect as a continuing authority given by the charity trustees from time to time of the charity and exercisable by such trustees.

(3) In any authority under this section to execute a deed or instrument in the names and on behalf of charity trustees there shall, unless the contrary intention appears, be implied authority also to execute it for them in the name and on behalf of the official custodian or of any other person, in any case in which the charity trustees could do so.

(4) Where a deed or instrument purports to be executed in pursuance of this section, then in favour of a person who (then or afterwards) in good faith acquires for money or money's worth an interest in or charge on property or the benefit of any covenant or agreement expressed to be entered into by the charity trustees, it shall be conclusively presumed to have been duly executed by virtue of this section.

(5) The powers conferred by this section shall be in addition to and not in derogation of any other powers.

83. Transfer and evidence of title to property vested in trustees

(1) Where, under the trusts of a charity, trustees of property held for the purposes of the charity may be appointed or discharged by resolution of a meeting of the charity trustees, members or other persons, a memorandum declaring a trustee to have been so appointed or discharged shall be sufficient evidence of that fact if the memorandum is signed either at the meeting by the person presiding or in some other manner directed by the meeting and is attested by two persons present at the meeting.

(2) A memorandum evidencing the appointment or discharge of a trustee under subsection (1) above, if executed as a deed, shall have the like operation under section 40 of the Trustee Act 1925 (which relates to vesting declarations as respects trust property in deeds appointing or discharging trustees) as if the appointment or discharge were effected by the deed.

(3) For the purposes of this section, where a document purports to have been signed and attested as mentioned in subsection (1) above, then on proof (whether by evidence or as a matter of presumption) of the signature the document shall be presumed to have been so signed and attested, unless the contrary is shown.

(4) This section shall apply to a memorandum made at any time, except that subsection (2) shall apply only to those made after the commencement of the Charities Act 1960.

(5) This section shall apply in relation to any institution to which the Literary and Scientific Institutions Act 1854 applies as it applies in relation to a charity.

PART X

SUPPLEMENTARY

84. Supply by Commissioners of copies of documents open to public inspection

The Commissioners shall, at the request of any person, furnish him with copies of, or extracts from, any document in their possession which is for the time being open to inspection under Parts II to VI of this Act.

85. Fees and other amounts payable to Commissioners

(1) The Secretary of State may by regulations require the payment to the Commissioners of such fees as may be prescribed by the regulations in respect of –
  (a) the discharge by the Commissioners of such functions under the enactments relating to charities as may be so prescribed;
  (b) the inspection of the register of charities or of other material kept by them under those enactments, or the furnishing of copies of or extracts from documents so kept.

(2) Regulations under this section may –
  (a) confer, or provide for the conferring of, exemptions from liability to pay a prescribed fee;
  (b) provide for the remission or refunding of a prescribed fee (in whole or in part) in circumstances prescribed by the regulations.

(3) Any regulations under this section which require the payment of a fee in respect of any matter for which no fee was previously payable shall not be made unless a draft of the regulations has been laid before and approved by a resolution of each House of Parliament.

(4) The Commissioners may impose charges of such amounts as they consider reasonable in respect of the supply of any publications produced by them.

(5) Any fees and other payments received by the Commissioners by virtue of this section shall be paid into the Consolidated Fund.

86. Regulations and orders

(1) Any regulations or order of the Secretary of State under this Act –
  (a) shall be made by statutory instrument; and
  (b) (subject to subsection (2) below) shall be subject to annulment in pursuance of a resolution of either House of Parliament.

(2) Subsection (1)(b) above does not apply –
   (a) to an order under section 17(2), 70 or 99(2);
   (b) to any regulations under section 71; or
   (c) to any regulations to which section 85(3) applies.

(3) Any regulations of the Secretary of State or the Commissioners and any order of the Secretary of State under this Act may make –
   (a) different provision for different cases; and
   (b) such supplemental, incidental, consequential or transitional provision or savings as the Secretary of State or, as the case may be, the Commissioners consider appropriate.

(4) Before making any regulations under section 42, 44 or 45 above the Secretary of State shall consult such persons or bodies of persons as he considers appropriate.

87. Enforcement of requirements by order of Commissioners

(1) If a person fails to comply with any requirement imposed by or under this Act then (subject to subsection (2) below) the Commissioners may by order give him such directions as they consider appropriate for securing that the default is made good.

(2) Subsection (1) above does not apply to any such requirement if –
   (a) a person who fails to comply with, or is persistently in default in relation to, the requirement is liable to any criminal penalty; or
   (b) the requirement is imposed –
      (i) by an order of the Commissioners to which section 88 below applies, or
      (ii) by a direction of the Commissioners to which that section applies by virtue of section 90(2) below.

88. Enforcement of orders of Commissioners

A person guilty of disobedience –
   (a) to an order of the Commissioners under section 9(1), 44(2), 61, 73 or 80 above; or
   (b) to an order of the Commissioners under section 16 or 18 above requiring a transfer of property or payment to be called for or made; or
   (c) to an order of the Commissioners requiring a default under this Act to be made good;
may on the application of the Commissioners to the High Court be dealt with as for disobedience to an order of the High Court.

89. Other provisions as to orders of Commissioners

(1) Any order made by the Commissioners under this Act may include such incidental or supplementary provisions as the Commissioners think expedient for carrying into effect the objects of the order, and where the Commissioners exercise any jurisdiction to make such an order on an application or reference to them, they may insert any such provisions in the order notwithstanding that the application or reference does not propose their insertion.

(2) Where the Commissioners make an order under this Act, then (without prejudice to the requirements of this Act where the order is subject to appeal) they may themselves give such public notice as they think fit of the making or contents of the order, or may require it to be given by any person on whose application the order is made or by any charity affected by the order.

(3) The Commissioners at any time within twelve months after they have made an order under any provision of this Act other than section 61 if they are satisfied that the order was made by

mistake or on misrepresentation or otherwise than in conformity with this Act, may with or without any application or reference to them discharge the order in whole or in part, and subject or not to any savings or other transitional provisions.

(4) Except for the purposes of subsection (3) above or of an appeal under this Act, an order made by the Commissioners under this Act shall be deemed to have been duly and formally made and not be called in question on the ground only of irregularity or informality, but (subject to any further order) have effect according to its tenor.

90. Directions of the Commissioners

(1) Any direction given by the Commissioners under any provision contained in this Act –
    (a) may be varied or revoked by a further direction given under that provision; and
    (b) shall be given in writing.

(2) Sections 88 and 89(1), (2) and (4) above shall apply to any such directions as they apply to an order of the Commissioners.

(3) In subsection (1) above the reference to the Commissioners includes, in relation to a direction under subsection (3) of section 8 above, a reference to any person conducting an inquiry under that section.

(4) Nothing in this section shall be read as applying to any directions contained in an order made by the Commissioners under section 87(1) above.

91. Service of orders and directions

(1) This section applies to any order or direction made or given by the Commissioners under this Act.

(2) An order or direction to which this section applies may be served on a person (other than a body corporate) –
    (a) by delivering it to that person;
    (b) by leaving it at his last known address in the United Kingdom; or
    (c) by sending it by post to him at that address.

(3) An order or direction to which this section applies may be served on a body corporate by delivering it or sending it by post –
    (a) to the registered or principal office of the body in the United Kingdom, or
    (b) if it has no such office in the United Kingdom, to any place in the United Kingdom where it carries on business or conducts its activities (as the case may be).

(4) Any such order or direction may also be served on a person (including a body corporate) by sending it by post to that person at an address notified by that person to the Commissioners for the purposes of this subsection.

(5) In this section any reference to the Commissioners includes, in relation to a direction given under subsection (3) of section 8 above, a reference to any person conducting an inquiry under that section.

92. Appeals from Commissioners

(1) Provision shall be made by rules of court for regulating appeals to the High Court under this Act against orders or decisions of the Commissioners.

(2) On such an appeal the Attorney General shall be entitled to appear and be heard, and such other persons as the rules allow or as the court may direct.

93. Miscellaneous provisions as to evidence

(1) Where, in any proceedings to recover or compel payment of any rentcharge or other periodical payment claimed by or on behalf of a charity out of land or of the rents, profits or other income of land, otherwise than as rent incident to a reversion, it is shown that the rentcharge or other periodical payment has at any time been paid for twelve consecutive years to or for the benefit of the charity, that shall be prima facie evidence of the perpetual liability to it of the land or income, and no proof of its origin shall be necessary.

(2) In any proceedings, the following documents, that is to say, –
  (a) the printed copies of the reports of the Commissioners for enquiring concerning charities, 1818 to 1837, who were appointed under the Act 58 Geo 3 c 91 and subsequent Acts; and
  (b) the printed copies of the reports which were made for various counties and county boroughs to the Charity Commissioners by their assistant commissioners and presented to the House of Commons as returns to orders of various dates beginning with 8 December 1890, and ending with 9 September 1909,
shall be admissible as evidence of the documents and facts stated in them.

(3) Evidence of any order, certificate or other document issued by the Commissioners may be given by means of a copy retained by them, or taken from a copy so retained, and certified to be a true copy by any officer of the Commissioners generally or specially authorised by them to act for this purpose; and a document purporting to be such a copy shall be received in evidence without proof of the official position, authority or handwriting of the person certifying it.

94. Restriction on institution of proceedings for certain offences

(1) No proceedings for an offence under this Act to which this section applies shall be instituted except by or with the consent of the Director of Public Prosecutions.

(2) This section applies to any offence under –
  (a) section 5;
  (b) section 11;
  (c) section 18(14);
  (d) section 49; or
  (e) section 73(1).

95. Offences by bodies corporate

Where any offence under this Act is committed by a body corporate and is proved to have been committed with the consent or connivance of, or to be attributable to any neglect on the part of, any director, manager, secretary or other similar officer of the body corporate, or any person who was purporting to act in any such capacity, he as well as the body corporate shall be guilty of that offence and shall be liable to be proceeded against and punished accordingly.

  In relation to a body corporate whose affairs are managed by its members, 'director' means a member of the body corporate.

96. Construction of references to a 'charity' or to particular classes of charity

(1) In this Act, except in so far as the context otherwise requires –
'charity' means any institution, corporate or not, which is established for charitable purposes and is subject to the control of the High Court in the exercise of the court's jurisdiction with respect to charities;
'ecclesiastical charity' has the same meaning as in the Local Government Act 1894;
'exempt charity' means (subject to section 24(8) above) a charity comprised in Schedule 2 to this Act;

'local charity' means, in relation to any area, a charity established for purposes which are by their nature or by the trusts of the charity directed wholly or mainly to the benefit of that area or of part of it;

'parochial charity' means, in relation to any parish or (in Wales) community, a charity the benefits of which are, or the separate distribution of the benefits of which is, confined to inhabitants of the parish or community, or of a single ancient ecclesiastical parish which included that parish or community or part of it, or of an area consisting of that parish or community with not more than four neighbouring parishes or communities.

(2) The expression 'charity' is not in this Act applicable –

    (a) to any ecclesiastical corporation (that is to say, any corporation in the Church of England, whether sole or aggregate, which is established for spiritual purposes) in respect of the corporate property of the corporation, except to a corporation aggregate having some purposes which are not ecclesiastical in respect of its corporate property held for those purposes; or

    (b) to any Diocesan Board of Finance within the meaning of the Endowments and Glebe Measure 1976 for any diocese in respect of the diocesan glebe land of that diocese within the meaning of that Measure; or

    (c) to any trust of property for purposes for which the property has been consecrated.

(3) A charity shall be deemed for the purposes of this Act to have a permanent endowment unless all property held for the purposes of the charity may be expended for those purposes without distinction between capital and income, and in this Act 'permanent endowment' means, in relation to any charity, property held subject to a restriction on its being expended for the purposes of the charity.

(4) References in this Act to a charity whose income from all sources does not in aggregate amount to more than a specified amount shall be construed –

    (a) by reference to the gross revenues of the charity, or

    (b) if the Commissioners so determine, by reference to the amount which they estimate to be the likely amount of those revenues,

but without (in either case) bringing into account anything for the yearly value of land occupied by the charity apart from the pecuniary income (if any) received from that land; and any question as to the application of any such reference to a charity shall be determined by the Commissioners, whose decision shall be final.

(5) The Commissioners may direct that for all or any of the purposes of this Act an institution established for any special purposes of or in connection with a charity (being charitable purposes) shall be treated as forming part of that charity or as forming a distinct charity.

(6) The Commissioners may direct that for all or any of the purposes of this Act two or more charities having the same charity trustees shall be treated as a single charity.

NOTE

Section shown as amended by the Charities (Amendment) Act 1995.

---

97. General interpretation

(1) In this Act, except in so far as the context otherwise requires –

'charitable purposes' means purposes which are exclusively charitable according to the law of England and Wales;

'charity trustees' means the persons having the general control and management of the administration of a charity;

'the Commissioners' means the Charity Commissioners for England and Wales;

'company' means a company formed and registered under the Companies Act 1985 or to which the provisions of that Act apply as they apply to such a company;

'the court' means the High Court and, within the limits of its jurisdiction, any other court in England and Wales having a jurisdiction in respect of charities concurrent (within any limit of area or amount) with that of the High Court, and includes any judge or officer of the court exercising the jurisdiction of the court;

'financial year' –

(a) in relation to a charity which is a company, shall be construed in accordance with section 223 of the Companies Act 1985; and

(b) in relation to any other charity, shall be construed in accordance with regulations made by virtue of section 42(2) above;

but this definition is subject to the transitional provisions in section 99(4) below and Part II of Schedule 8 to this Act;

'gross income', in relation to charity, means its gross recorded income from all sources including special trusts;

'independent examiner', in relation to a charity, means such a person as is mentioned in section 43(3)(a) above;

'institution' includes any trust or undertaking;

'the official custodian' means the official custodian for charities;

'permanent endowment' shall be construed in accordance with section 96(3) above;

'the register' means the register of charities kept under section 3 above and 'registered' shall be construed accordingly;

'special trust' means property which is held and administered by or on behalf of a charity for any special purposes of the charity, and is so held and administered on separate trusts relating only to that property but a special trust shall not, by itself, constitute a charity for the purposes of Part VI of this Act;

'trusts' in relation to a charity, means the provisions establishing it as a charity and regulating its purposes and administration, whether those provisions take effect by way of trust or not, and in relation to other institutions has a corresponding meaning.

(2) In this Act, except in so far as the context otherwise requires, 'document' includes information recorded in any form, and, in relation to information recorded otherwise than in legible form –

(a) any reference to its production shall be construed as a reference to the furnishing of a copy of it in legible form; and

(b) any reference to the furnishing of a copy of, or extract from, it shall accordingly be construed as a reference to the furnishing of a copy of, or extract from, it in legible form.

(3) No vesting or transfer of any property in pursuance of any provision of Part IV or IX of this Act shall operate as a breach of a covenant or condition against alienation or give rise to a forfeiture.

98. Consequential amendments and repeals

(1) The enactments mentioned in Schedule 6 to this Act shall be amended as provided in that Schedule.

(2) The enactments mentioned in Schedule 7 to this Act are hereby repealed to the extent specified in the third column of the Schedule.

99. Commencement and transitional provisions

(1) Subject to subsection (2) below this Act shall come into force on 1st August 1993.

(2) Part VI, section 69 and paragraph 21(3) of Schedule 6 shall not come into force until such day

as the Secretary of State may by order appoint; and different days may be appointed for different provisions or different purposes.

(3) Until the coming into force of all the provisions mentioned in subsection (2) above the provisions mentioned in Part I of Schedule 8 to this Act shall continue in force notwithstanding their repeal.

(4) Part II of Schedule 8 to this Act shall have effect until the coming into force of the first regulations made by virtue of section 42(2) above for determining the financial year of a charity for the purposes of the provisions mentioned in that Part.

100. Short title and extent

(1) This Act may be cited as the Charities Act 1993.

(2) Subject to subsection (3) to (6) below, this Act extends only to England and Wales.

(3) Section 10 above and this section extend to the whole of the United Kingdom.

(4) Section 15(2) extends also to Northern Ireland.

(5) Sections 70 and 71 and so much of section 86 as relates to those sections extend also to Scotland.

(6) The amendments in Schedule 6 and the repeals in Schedule 7 have the same extent as the enactments to which they refer and section 98 above extends accordingly.

SCHEDULES

SCHEDULE 1

Section 1

CONSTITUTION ETC OF CHARITY COMMISSIONERS

1.   (1) There shall be a Chief Charity Commissioner and two other commissioners.

(2) Two at least of the commissioners shall be persons who have a seven year general qualification within the meaning of section 71 of the Courts and Legal Services Act 1990.

(3) The chief commissioner and the other commissioners shall be appointed by the Secretary of State, and shall be deemed for all purposes to be employed in the civil service of the Crown.

(4) There may be paid to each of the commissioners such salary and allowances as the Secretary of State may with the approval of the Treasury determine.

(5) If at any time it appears to the Secretary of State that there should be more than three commissioners, he may with the approval of the Treasury appoint not more than two additional commissioners.

2.   (1) The chief commissioner may, with the approval of the Treasury as to number and conditions of service, appoint such assistant commissioners and other officers and such employees as he thinks necessary for the proper discharge of the functions of the Commissioners and of the official custodian.

(2) There may be paid to officers and employees so appointed such salaries or remuneration as the Treasury may determine.

3.   (1) The Commissioners may use an official seal for the authentication of documents, and their seal shall be officially and judicially noticed.

(2) The Documentary Evidence Act 1868, as amended by the Documentary Evidence Act 1882, shall have effect as if in the Schedule to the Act of 1868 the Commissioners were included in the first column and any commissioner or assistant commissioner and any officer authorised to act on behalf of the Commissioners were mentioned in the second column.

(3) The Commissioners shall have power to regulate their own procedure and, subject to any such regulations and to any directions of the chief commissioner, any one commissioner or any assistant commissioner may act for and in the name of the Commissioners.

(4) Where the Commissioners act as a board, then –
- (a) if not more than four commissioners hold office for the time being, the quorum shall be two commissioners (of whom at least one must be a person having a qualification such as is mentioned in paragraph 1(2) above); and
- (b) if five commissioners so hold office, the quorum shall be three commissioners (of whom at least one must be a person having such a qualification);

and in the case of an equality of votes the chief commissioner or in his absence the commissioner presiding shall have a second or casting vote.

(5) The Commissioners shall have power to act notwithstanding any vacancy in their number.

(6) It is hereby declared that the power of a commissioner or assistant commissioner to act for and in the name of the Commissioners in accordance with sub-paragraph (3) above may, in particular, be exercised in relation to functions of the Commissioners under sections 8, 18, 19 and 63 of this Act, including functions under sections 8, 18 and 19 as applied by section 80(1).

4. Legal proceedings may be instituted by or against the Commissioners by the name of the Charity Commissioners for England and Wales, and shall not abate or be affected by any change in the persons who are the commissioners.

SCHEDULE 2

Sections 3 and 96

EXEMPT CHARITIES

The following institutions, so far as they are charities, are exempt charities within the meaning of this Act, that is to say –
- (a) any institution which, if the Charities Act 1960 had not been passed, would be exempted from the powers and jurisdiction, under the Charitable Trusts Acts 1853 to 1939, of the Commissioners or Minister of Education (apart from any power of the Commissioners or Minister to apply those Acts in whole or in part to charities otherwise exempt) by the terms of any enactment not contained in those Acts other than section 9 of the Places of Worship Registration Act 1855;
- (b) the universities of Oxford, Cambridge, London, Durham and Newcastle, the colleges and halls in the universities of Oxford, Cambridge, Durham and Newcastle, Queen Mary and Westfield College in the University of London and the colleges of Winchester and Eton;
- (c) any university, university college, or institution connected with a university or university college, which Her Majesty declares by Order in Council to be an exempt charity for the purposes of this Act;
- (d) a grant-maintained school;
- (da) the School Curriculum and Assessment Authority;
- (e) the National Curriculum Council;
- (f) the Curriculum and Assessment Authority for Wales;
- (g) the School Examinations and Assessment Council;

(h) a higher education corporation;

(i) a successor company to a higher education corporation (within the meaning of section 129(5) of the Education Reform Act 1988) at a time when an institution conducted by the company is for the time being designated under that section;

(j) a further education corporation;

(k) the Board of Trustees of the Victoria and Albert Museum;

(l) the Board of Trustees of the Science Museum;

(m) the Board of Trustees of the Armouries;

(n) the Board of Trustees of the Royal Botanic Gardens, Kew;

(o) the Board of Trustees of the National Museum and Galleries on Merseyside;

(p) the trustees of the British Museum and the trustees of the National History Museum;

(q) the Board of Trustees of the National Gallery;

(r) the Board of Trustees of the Tate Gallery;

(s) the Board of Trustees of the National Portrait Gallery;

(t) the Board of Trustees of the Wallace Collection;

(u) the Trustees of the Imperial War Museum;

(v) the Trustees of the National Maritime Museum;

(w) any institution which is administered by or on behalf of an institution included above and is established for the general purposes of, or for any special purpose of or in connection with, the last-mentioned institution;

(x) the Church Commissioners and any institution which is administered by them;

(y) any registered society within the meaning of the Industrial and Provident Societies Act 1965 and any registered society or branch within the meaning of the Friendly Societies Act 1974;

(z) the Board of Governors of the Museum of London;

(za) the British Library Board;

(zb) the National Lottery Charities Board.

NOTE

Schedule shown as amended by the Education Act 1993 and the National Lottery etc Act 1993.

SCHEDULE 3

Section 13

ENLARGEMENT OF AREAS OF LOCAL CHARITIES

Existing area	Permissible enlargement
1. Greater London	Any area comprising Greater London.
2. Any area in Greater London and not in, or partly in, the City of London.	(i) Any area in Greater London and not in, or partly in, the City of London; (ii) the area of Greater London exclusive of the City of London; (iii) any area comprising the area of Greater London, exclusive of the City of London; (iv) any area partly in Greater London and partly in any adjacent parish or parishes (civil or ecclesiastical), and not partly in the City of London.
3. A district	Any area comprising the district
4. Any area in a district	(i) Any area in the district; (ii) the district; (iii) any area comprising the district; (iv) any area partly in the district and partly in any adjacent district.
5. A parish (civil or ecclesiastical), or two or more parishes, or an area in a parish, or partly in each of two of more parishes.	Any area not extending beyond the parish or parishes comprising or adjacent to the area in column 1.
6. In Wales, a community, or two or more communities, or an area in a community, or partly in each of two or more communities.	Any area not extending beyond the community or communities comprising or adjacent to the area in column 1.

SCHEDULE 4

Section 15

COURT'S JURISDICTION OVER CERTAIN CHARITIES GOVERNED BY OR UNDER STATUTE

1. The court may by virtue of section 15(3) of this Act exercise its jurisdiction with respect to charities –

   (a) in relation to charities established or regulated by any provision of the Seamen's Fund Winding-up Act 1851 which is repealed by the Charities Act 1960;

   (b) in relation to charities established or regulated by schemes under the Endowed Schools Act 1869 to 1948, or section 75 of the Elementary Education Act 1870 or by schemes given effect under section 2 of the Education Act 1973;

   (c) ...

(d) in relation to fuel allotments, that is to say, land which, by any enactment relating to inclosure or any instrument having effect under such an enactment, is vested in trustees upon trust that the land or the rents and profits of the land shall be used for the purpose of providing poor persons with fuel;

(e) in relation to charities established or regulated by any provision of the Municipal Corporations Act 1883 which is repealed by the Charities Act 1960 or by any scheme having effect under any such provision;

(f) in relation to charities regulated by schemes under the London Government Act 1899;

(g) in relation to charities established or regulated by orders or regulations under section 2 of the Regimental Charitable Funds Act 1935;

(h) in relation to charities regulated by section 79 of this Act, or by any such order as is mentioned in that section.

2. Notwithstanding anything in section 19 of the Commons Act 1876 a scheme for the administration of a fuel allotment (within the meaning of the foregoing paragraph) may provide –

(a) for the sale or letting of the allotments or any part thereof, for the discharge of the land sold or let from any restrictions as to the use thereof imposed by or under any enactment relating to inclosure and for the application of the sums payable to the trustees of the allotment in respect of the sale or lease; or

(b) for the exchange of the allotment or any part thereof for other land, for the discharge as aforesaid of the land given in exchange by the said trustees, and for the application of any money payable to the said trustees for equality of exchange; or

(c) for the use of the allotment or any part thereof for any purposes specified in the scheme.

NOTE

Schedule shown as amended by the Statute Law (Repeals) Act 1993.

SCHEDULE 5

Section 36(2)

MEANING OF 'CONNECTED PERSON' FOR PURPOSES OF SECTION 36(2)

1. In section 36(2) of this Act 'connected person', in relation to a charity, means –

(a) a charity trustee or trustee for the charity;

(b) a person who is the donor of any land to the charity (whether the gift was made on or after the establishment of the charity);

(c) a child, parent, grandchild, grandparent, brother or sister of any such trustee or donor;

(d) an officer, agent or employee of the charity;

(e) the spouse of any person falling within any of sub-paragraphs (a) to (d) above;

(f) an institution which is controlled –
    (i) by any person falling within any of sub-paragraphs (a) to (e) above, or
    (ii) by two or more such persons taken together; or

(g) a body corporate in which –
    (i) any connected person falling within any of sub-paragraphs (a) to (f) above has a substantial interest, or
    (ii) two or more such persons, taken together, have a substantial interest.

2. (1) In paragraph 1(c) above 'child' includes a stepchild and an illegitimate child.

(2) For the purposes of paragraph 1(e) above a person living with another as that person's husband or wife shall be treated as that person's spouse.

3. For the purposes of paragraph 1(f) above a person controls an institution if he is able to secure that the affairs of the institution are conducted in accordance with his wishes.

4. (1) For the purposes of paragraph 1(g) above any such connected person as is there mentioned has a substantial interest in a body corporate if the person or institution in question –

(a) is interested in shares comprised in the equity share capital of that body of a nominal value of more than one-fifth of that share capital, or

(b) is entitled to exercise, or control the exercise of, more than one-fifth of the voting power at any general meeting of that body.

(2) The rules set out in Part I of Schedule 13 to the Companies Act 1985 (rules for interpretation of certain provisions of that Act) shall apply for the purposes of sub-paragraph (1) above as they apply for the purposes of section 346(4) of that Act ('connected persons' etc).

(3) In this paragraph 'equity share capital' and 'share' have the same meaning as in that Act.

SCHEDULE 6

Section 98(1)

CONSEQUENTIAL AMENDMENTS

The Places of Worship Registration Act 1855 (c 81)

1. (1) Section 9 of the Places of Worship Registration Act 1855 shall be amended as follows.

(2) For 'subsection (4) of section four of the Charities Act 1960' there shall be substituted 'subsection (5) of section 3 of the Charities Act 1993'.

(3) At the end there shall be added –

'(2) Section 89 of the said Act of 1993 (provisions as to orders under that Act) shall apply to any order under paragraph (b) above as it applies to orders under that Act.'

The Open Spaces Act 1906 (c 25)

2. At the end of section 4 of the Open Spaces Act 1906 there shall be added –

'(4) Section 89 of the Charities Act 1993 (provisions as to orders under that Act) shall apply to any order of the Charity Commissioners under this section as it applies to orders made by them under that Act.'

The New Parishes Measure 1943 (No 1)

3. (1) The New Parishes Measure 1943 shall be amended as follows.

(2) In subsection (1)(b) of section 14 for 'the Charities Act 1960' there shall be substituted 'the Charities Act 1993'.

(3) At the end of that section there shall be added –

'(4) Section 89 of the Charities Act 1993 (provisions as to orders under that Act) shall apply to any order under section (1)(b) above as it applies to orders under that Act.'

(4) In section 31 for 'the Charities Act 1960' there shall be substituted 'the Charities Act 1993'.

The Clergy Pensions Measure 1961 (No 3)

4. In section 33 of the Clergy Pensions Measure 1961 for 'section 32 of the Charities Act 1992' and 'the Charities Act 1960' there shall be substituted respectively 'section 36 of the Charities Act 1993' and 'that Act'.

The Finance Act 1963 (c 25)

5. In section 65(2) of the Finance Act 1963 at the end of paragraph (a) there shall be added 'or to any common investment scheme under section 24 or any common deposit scheme under section 25 of the Charities Act 1993;'.

The Cathedrals Measure 1963 (No 2)

6. (1) The Cathedrals Measure 1963 shall be amended as follows.

(2) In section 20(2)(iii) for 'section 32 of the Charities Act 1992' there shall be substituted 'section 36 of the Charities Act 1993'.

(3) In section 51 for 'the Charities Act 1960' there shall be substituted 'the Charities Act 1993'.

The Incumbents and Churchwardens (Trusts) Measure 1964 (No 2)

7. In section 1 of the Incumbents and Churchwardens (Trust) Measure 1964 for 'subsection (3) of section forty-five of the Charities Act 1960' there shall be substituted 'section 96(3) of the Charities Act 1993'.

The Leasehold Reform Act 1967 (c 88)

8. In section 23(4) of the Leasehold Reform Act 1967 for 'section 32 of the Charities Act 1992' there shall be substituted 'section 36 of the Charities Act 1993'.

The Greater London Council (General Powers) Act 1968 (c xxxix)

9. In section 43 of the Greater London Council (General Powers) Act 1968, in the definition of 'night café', for 'section 4 of the Charities Act 1960' and 'subsection (4) thereof' there shall be substituted respectively 'section 3 of the Charities Act 1993' and 'subsection (5) thereof'.

The Redundant Churches and other Religious Buildings Act 1969 (c 22)

10. (1) The Redundant Churches and other Religious Buildings Act 1969 shall be amended as follows.

(2) In subsection (6) of section 4 for 'section 18 of the Charities Act 1960' there shall be substituted 'section 16 of the Charities Act 1993'.

(3) In subsection (7) of that section for 'subsection (4) of section 18 of that Act' there shall be substituted 'subsection (4) of section 16 of that Act'.

(4) In subsection (8) of that section for 'section 18 of the Charities Act 1960' and (where next occurring) 'section 18' there shall be substituted respectively 'section 16 of the Charities Act 1993' and 'section 16' and for 'section 21' there shall be substituted 'section 20'.

(5) In subsection (13) of that section for 'sections 45 and 46 of the Charities Act 1960' there shall be substituted 'sections 96 and 97 of the Charities Act 1993'.

(6) In section 7(2) for 'the Charities Act 1960' and 'section 23' there shall be substituted respectively 'the Charities Act 1993' and 'section 26'.

The Sharing of Church Buildings Act 1969 (c 38)

11. (1) The Sharing of Church Buildings Act 1969 shall be amended as follows.

(2) In section 2(4) for 'the Charities Act 1960' there shall be substituted 'the Charities Act 1993'.

(3) In subsection (1) of section 8 for 'the Charities Act 1960' there shall be substituted 'the Charities Act 1993'.

(4) In subsection (2) of that section for 'section 45(2) of the Charities Act 1960' there shall be substituted 'section 96(2) of the Charities Act 1993'.

(5) In subsection (3) of that section for 'Section 32 of the Charities Act 1992' there shall be substituted 'Section 36 of the Charities Act 1993'.

The Local Government Act 1972 (c 70)

12.   (1) The Local Government Act 1972 shall be amended as follows.

(2) In sections 11(3)(c) and 29(3)(c) for 'section 37 of the Charities Act 1960' there shall be substituted 'section 79 of the Charities Act 1993'.

(3) In sections 123(6) and 127(4) for 'the Charities Act 1960' there shall be substituted 'the Charities Act 1993'.

(4) In section 131(3) for 'section 32 of the Charities Act 1992' and 'section 32(9)(a) of that Act' there shall be substituted respectively 'section 36 of the Charities Act 1993' and 'section 36(9)(a) of that Act'.

13. . . .

The Theatres Trust Act 1976 (c 27)

14. In section 2(2)(d) of the Theatres Trust Act 1976 for 'sections 32 and 34 of the Charities Act 1992' there shall be substituted 'sections 36 and 38 of the Charities Act 1993'.

The Interpretation Act 1978 (c 30)

15. In Schedule 1 to the Interpretation Act 1978, in the definition of 'Charity Commissioners' for 'section 1 of the Charities Act 1960' there shall be substituted 'section 1 of the Charities Act 1993'.

The Reserve Forces Act 1980 (c 9)

16.   (1) Section 147 of the Reserve Forces Act 1980 shall be amended as follows.

(2) In subsection (4) for 'section 28 of the Charities Act 1960' there shall be substituted 'section 33 of the Charities Act 1993'.

(3) In subsection (5) for 'section 28(5) of that Act of 1960' there shall be substituted 'section 33(5) of that Act of 1993'.

(4) In subsection (7) for 'section 18 of the Charities Act 1960' there shall be substituted 'section 16 of the Charities Act 1993'.

(5) In subsection (10)(b) for 'the Charities Act 1960' there shall be substituted 'the Charities Act 1993'.

17. . . .

The Pastoral Measure 1983 (No 1)

18.   (1) The Pastoral Measure 1983 shall be amended as follows.

(2) In section 55(1) for 'the Charities Act 1960' and 'section 45(2)(b)' there shall be substituted 'the Charities Act 1993' and 'section 96(2)(c)'.

(3) In section 63(3) for 'the Charities Act 1960' there shall be substituted 'the Charities Act 1993'.

(4) In section 87(1) for 'section 45 of the Charities Act 1960' there shall be substituted 'section 96 of the Charities Act 1993'.

(5) In paragraphs 11(6) and 16(1)(e) of Schedule 3 for 'section 18 of the Charities Act 1960' there shall be substituted 'section 16 of the Charities Act 1993'.

The Rates Act 1984 (c 33)

19. In section 3(9) of the Rates Act 1984 for 'section 4 of the Charities Act 1960' there shall be substituted 'section 3 of the Charities Act 1993'.

The Companies Act 1985 (c 6)

20. (1) The Companies Act 1985 shall be amended as follows.

(2) In sections 35(4) and 35A(6) for 'section 30B(1) of the Charities Act 1960' there shall be substituted 'section 56(1) of the Charities Act 1993'.

(3) In section 209(1)(c) and paragraph 11(b) of Schedule 13 after 'the Charities Act 1960' there shall be inserted 'or section 24 or 25 of the Charities Act 1993'.

The Housing Associations Act 1985 (c 69)

21. (1) The Housing Associations Act 1985 shall be amended as follows.

(2) In section 10(1) for 'sections 32 and 34 of the Charities Act 1992' there shall be substituted 'sections 36 and 38 of the Charities Act 1993'.

(3) In section 26(2) for the words from 'section 8' onwards there shall be substituted 'sections 41 to 45 of the Charities Act 1993 (charity accounts)'.

(4) In section 35(2)(c) for 'section 32 of the Charities Act 1992' there shall be substituted 'section 36 of the Charities Act 1993'.

(5) In section 38 –
  (a) in paragraph (a) for 'the Charities Act 1960' there shall be substituted 'the Charities Act 1993';
  (b) in paragraph (b) for 'section 4 of that Act' there shall be substituted 'section 3 of that Act'.

The Financial Services Act 1986 (c 60)

22. In section 45(1)(j) of the Financial Services Act 1986 after 'the Charities Act 1960' there shall be inserted ', section 24 or 25 of the Charities Act 1993'.

The Coal Industry Act 1987 (c 3)

23. (1) In section 5 of the Coal Industry Act 1987 for subsection (8) there shall be substituted –

'(8) Sections 16(3), (9), (11) to (14), 17(1) to (5) and (7) and 20 of the Charities Act 1993 shall apply in relation to the powers of the Charity Commissioners and the making of schemes under this section as they apply in relation to their powers and the making of schemes under that Act and sections 89, 91 and 92 of that Act shall apply to orders and decisions under this section as they apply to orders and decisions under that Act.'

(2) In subsection (8A) of that section for 'section 29' (in both places) there shall be substituted 'section 17'.

The Reverter of Sites Act 1987 (c 15)

24. In section 4(4) of the Reverter of Sites Act 1987 for 'sections 40, 40A and 42 of the Charities Act 1960' there shall be substituted 'sections 89, 91 and 92 of the Charities Act 1993'.

The Income and Corporation Taxes Act 1988 (c 1)

25. In Schedule 20 to the Income and Corporation Taxes Act 1988 –
   (a) in paragraph 3 after 'the Charities Act 1960' there shall be inserted ', section 24 of the Charities Act 1993';
   (b) in paragraph 3A after 'the Charities Act 1960' there shall be inserted 'or section 25 of the Charities Act 1993'.

The Courts and Legal Services Act 1990 (c 41)

26. In Schedule 11 to the Courts and Legal Services Act 1990, in the reference to a Charity Commissioner, for 'under the First Schedule to the Charities Act 1960' there shall be substituted 'as provided in Schedule 1 to the Charities Act 1993'.

The London Local Authorities Act 1990 (c vii)

27. In section 4 of the London Local Authorities Act 1990, in the definition of 'night café', for 'section 4 of the Charities Act 1960' and 'subsection (4) thereof' there shall be substituted respectively 'section 3 of the Charities Act 1993' and 'subsection (5) thereof'.

The London Local Authorities Act 1991 (c xiii)

28. In section 4 of the London Local Authorities Act 1991, in the definition of 'establishment for special treatment', for 'section 4 of the Charities Act 1960' and 'subsection (4) of that section' there shall be substituted respectively 'section 3 of the Charities Act 1993' and 'subsection (5) of that section'.

29. . . .

Other amendments

30. In the following provisions for 'the Charities Act 1960' there shall be substituted 'the Charities Act 1993' –

The National Health Service Reorganisation Act 1973 section 30(5).
The Consumer Credit Act 1974 section 189(1).
The Rent (Agriculture) Act 1976 section (5)(3)(f).
The Rent Act 1977 section 15(2)(b).
The National Health Service Act 1977 section 96(2).
The Dioceses Measure 1978 section 19(4).
The Ancient Monuments and Archaeological Areas Act 1979 section 49(3).
The Greater London Council (General Powers) Act 1984 section 10(2)(n).
The Local Government Act 1985 section 90(4).
The Housing Act 1985 sections 525 and 622.
The Landlord and Tenant Act 1987 section 60(1).
The Education Reform Act 1988 sections 128(5) and 192(11).
The Copyright Designs and Patents Act 1988 Schedule 6 paragraph 7.
The Housing Act 1988 Schedule 2 Part I Ground 6.
The University of Wales College of Cardiff Act 1988 section 9.
The Imperial College Act 1988 section 10.
The Local Government and Housing Act 1989 section 138(1).

SCHEDULE 7

REPEALS

Chapter	Short title	Extent of repeal
35 & 36 Vic c 24	The Charitable Trustees Incorporation Act 1872	The whole Act so far as unrepealed.
10 & 11 Geo 5 c 16	The Imperial War Museum Act 1920	Section 5.
24 & 25 Geo 5 c 43	The National Maritime Museum Act 1934	Section 7.
8 & 9 Eliz 2 c 58	The Charities Act 1960	The whole Act so far as unrepealed except – section 28(9) section 35(6) section 38(3) to (5) section 39(2) sections 48 and 49 Schedule 6.
1963 c 33	The London Government Act 1963	Section 81(9)(b) and (c).
1963 c xi	The Universities of Durham and Newcastle-upon-Tyne Act 1963	Section 10.
1965 c 17	The Museum of London Act 1965	Section 11.
1972 c 54	The British Library Act 1972	Section 4(2)
1972 c 70	The Local Government Act 1972	Section 210(9)
1973 c 16	The Education Act 1973	In section 2(7) the words from 'but' onwards. In Schedule 1, paragraph 1(1) and (3).
1976 No 4	The Endowments and Glebe Measure 1976	Section 44.
1983 c 47	The National Heritage Act 1983	In Schedule 5, paragraph 4.
1985 c 9	The Companies Consolidation (Consequential Provisions) Act 1985	In Schedule 2 the entry relating to the Charities Act 1960.
1985 c 20	The Charities Act 1985	Section 1.
1986 c 60	The Financial Services Act 1986	In Schedule 16, paragraph 1.
1988 c 40	The Education Reform Act 1988	In Schedule 12, paragraphs 9, 10, 63 and 64.
1989 c 40	The Companies Act 1989	Section 111.
1989 c xiii	The Queen Mary and Westfield College Act 1989	Section 10.

Chapter	Short title	Extent of repeal
1990 c 41	The Courts and Legal Services Act 1990	In Schedule 10, paragraph 14.
1992 c 13	The Further and Higher Education Act 1992	In Schedule 8, paragraph 69.
1992 c 41	The Charities Act 1992	The whole of Part I except – section 1(1) and (4) sections 29 and 30 section 36 sections 49 and 50 Section 75(b). Section 76(1)(a). In section 77, subsection (2)(a), (b) and (c) and in subsection (4) the figures 20, 22 and 23. Section 79(4) and (5). Schedules 1 to 4. In Schedule 6, paragraph 13(2). In Schedule 7, the entries relating to section 8 of the Charities Act 1960 and (so far as not in force at the date specified in section 99(1) of this Act) the Charities Act 1985.
1992 c 44	The Museums and Galleries Act 1992	In Schedule 8, paragraphs 4 and 10. In Schedule 9, the entry relating to the Charities Act 1960.

SCHEDULE 8

Section 99(3), (4)

TRANSITIONAL PROVISIONS

PART I

PROVISIONS APPLYING PENDING COMING INTO FORCE OF PART VI ETC

1. In the Charities Act 1960 –
   section 8
   section 32
   Part V so far as relevant to those sections.

2. In the Charities Act 1985
   section 1
   sections 6 and 7 so far as relevant to section 1.

PART II

PROVISIONS APPLYING PENDING COMING INTO FORCE OF 'FINANCIAL YEAR' REGULATIONS

Section 5

In section 5(1) of this Act 'financial year' –

(a) in relation to a charity which is a company, shall be construed in accordance with section 223 of the Companies Act 1985;

(b) in relation to any other charity, means any period in respect of which an income and expenditure account is required to be prepared whether under section 32 of the Charities Act 1960 or by or under the authority of any other Act, whether that period is a year or not.

Sections 74 and 75

In sections 74(1)(a) and 75(1)(b) of this Act 'financial year' means any period in respect of which an income and expenditure account is required to be prepared whether under section 32 of the Charities Act 1960 or by or under the authority of any other Act, whether that period is a year or not.

HOUSE TO HOUSE COLLECTIONS ACT 1939

(2 & 3 Geo 6 c 44)

ARRANGEMENT OF SECTIONS

*An Act to provide for the regulation of house to house collections for charitable purposes; and for matters
connected therewith*   [28 July 1939]

1.   Charitable collections from house to house to be licensed

(1) Subject to the provisions of this Act, no collection for a charitable purpose shall be made
unless the requirements of this Act as to a licence for the promotion thereof are satisfied.

(2) If a person promotes a collection for a charitable purpose, and a collection for that purpose is
made in any locality pursuant to his promotion, then, unless there is in force, throughout the
period during which the collection is made in that locality, a licence authorising him, or
authorising another under whose authority he acts, to promote a collection therein for that
purpose, he shall be guilty of an offence.

(3) If a person acts as a collector in any locality for the purposes of a collection for a charitable
purpose, then, unless there is in force, at all times when he so acts, a licence authorising a promoter
under whose authority he acts, or authorising the collector himself, to promote a collection
therein for that purpose, he shall be guilty of an offence.

(4) If the chief officer of police for the police area comprising a locality in which a collection for a
charitable purpose is being, or is proposed to be, made is satisfied that that purpose is local in
character and that the collection is likely to be completed within a short period of time, he may
grant to a person who appears to him to be principally concerned in the promotion of the
collection a certificate in the prescribed form, and, where a certificate is so granted, the provisions
of this Act, except the provisions of sections five and six thereof and the provisions of section eight
thereof in so far as they relate to those sections, shall not apply, in relation to a collection made for
that purpose within such locality and within such period as may be specified in the certificate, to
the person to whom the certificate is granted or to any person authorised by him to promote the
collection or to act as a collector for the purposes thereof.

2. Licences

(1) Where a person who is promoting, or proposes to promote, a collection in any locality for a
charitable purpose makes to the licensing authority for the ... area comprising that locality an

application in the prescribed manner specifying the purpose of the collection and the locality (whether being the whole of the area of the authority or a part thereof) within which the collection is to be made, and furnishes them with the prescribed information, the authority shall, subject to the following provisions of this section, grant to him a licence authorising him to promote a collection within that locality for that purpose.

(1A) In this section 'licensing authority' means –
   (a) in relation to the City of London, the Common Council;
   (b) in relation to the Metropolitan Police District, the Commissioner of Police for the Metropolis; and
   (c) in relation to a district exclusive of any part thereof within the Metropolitan Police District, the district council.

(2) A licence shall be granted for such period, not being longer than twelve months, as may be specified in the application, and shall, unless it is previously revoked, remain in force for the period so specified:

Provided that, if it appears to a licensing authority to be expedient to provide for the simultaneous expiration of licences to be granted by them in respect of collections which in their opinion are likely to be proposed to be made annually or continuously over a long period, they may, on the grant of such a licence, grant it for a period shorter or longer than that specified in the application therefor, or for a period longer than twelve months (but not exceeding eighteen months), as may be requisite for that purpose.

(3) A licensing authority may refuse to grant a licence, or, where a licence has been granted, may revoke it, if it appears to the authority –
   (a) that the total amount likely to be applied for charitable purposes as the result of the collection (including any amount already so applied) is inadequate in proportion to the value of the proceeds likely to be received (including any proceeds already received);
   (b) that remuneration which is excessive in relation to the total amount aforesaid is likely to be, or has been, retained or received out of the proceeds of the collection by any person;
   (c) that the grant of a licence would be likely to facilitate the commission of an offence under section three of the Vagrancy Act 1824, or that an offence under that section has been committed in connection with the collection;
   (d) that the application or the holder of the licence is not a fit and proper person to hold a licence by reason of the fact that he has been convicted in the United Kingdom of any of the offences specified in the Schedule to this Act, or has been convicted in any part of His Majesty's dominions of any offence conviction for which necessarily involved a finding that he acted fraudulently or dishonestly, or of an offence of a kind the commission of which would be likely to be facilitated by the grant of a licence;
   (e) that the applicant or the holder of the licence, in promoting a collection in respect of which a licence has been granted to him, has failed to exercise due diligence to secure that persons authorised by him to act as collectors for the purposes of the collection were fit and proper persons, to secure compliance on the part of persons so authorised with the provisions of regulations made under this Act, or to prevent prescribed badges or prescribed certificates of authority being obtained by persons other than persons so authorised; or
   (f) that the applicant or holder of the licence has refused or neglected to furnish to the authority such information as they may have reasonably required for the purpose of informing themselves as to any of the matters specified in the foregoing paragraphs.

(4) When a licensing authority refuse to grant a licence or revoke a licence which has been granted, they shall forthwith give written notice to the applicant or holder of the licence stating upon which one or more of the grounds set out in subsection (3) of this section the licence has

been refused or revoked and informing him of the right of appeal given by this section, and the applicant or holder of the licence may thereupon appeal to the Secretary of State against the refusal or revocation of the licence as the case may be and the decision of the Secretary of State shall be final.

(5) The time within which any such appeal may be brought shall be fourteen days from the date on which notice is given under subsection (4) of this section.

(6) If the Secretary of State decides that the appeal shall be allowed, the licensing authority shall forthwith issue a licence or cancel the revocation as the case may be in accordance with the decision of the Secretary of State.

NOTE

Section shown as amended by the Local Government Act 1972.

---

3. Exemptions in the case of collections over wide areas

(1) Where the Secretary of State is satisfied that a person pursues a charitable purpose throughout the whole of England or a substantial part thereof and is desirous of promoting collections for that purpose, the Secretary of State may by order direct that he shall be exempt from the provisions of subsection (2) of section one of this Act as respects all collections for that purpose in such localities as may be prescribed in the order, and whilst an order so made in the case of any person is in force as respects collections in any locality, the provisions of this Act shall have effect in relation to the person exempted, to a promoter of a collection in that locality for that purpose who acts under the authority of the person exempted, and to a person who so acts as a collector for the purposes of any such collection, as if a licence authorising the person exempted to promote a collection in that locality for that purpose had been in force.

(2) Any order made under this section may be revoked or varied by a subsequent order made by the Secretary of State.

4. Regulations

(1) The Secretary of State may make regulations for prescribing anything which by this Act is required to be prescribed, and for regulating the manner in which collections, in respect of which licences have been granted or orders have been made under the last foregoing section, may be carried out and the conduct of promoters and collectors in relation to such collections.

(2) Without prejudice to the generality of the powers conferred by the foregoing subsection, regulations made thereunder may make provision for all or any of the following matters, that is to say –
   (a) for requiring and regulating the use by collectors, of prescribed badges and prescribed certificates of authority, and the issue, custody, production and return thereof, and, in particular, for requiring collectors on demand by a police constable or by any occupant of a house visited to produce their certificates of authority.
   (b) in the case of collections in respect of which licences have been granted, for requiring that the prescribed certificates of authority of the collectors shall be authenticated in a manner approved by the chief officer of police for the area in respect of which the licence was granted, and that their prescribed badges shall have inserted therein or annexed thereto in a manner and form so approved a general indication of the purpose of the collection;
   (c) for prohibiting persons below a prescribed age from acting, and others from causing them to act, as collectors;

(d) for preventing annoyance to the occupants of houses visited by collectors;

(e) for requiring the prescribed information with respect to the expenses, proceeds and application of the proceeds of collections to be furnished, in the case of collections in respect of which licences have been granted, by the person to whom the licence was granted to the authority by whom it was granted, and, in the case of collections in respect of which an order has been made, by the person thereby exempted from the provisions of subsection (2) of section one of this Act to the Secretary of State, and for requiring the information furnished to be vouched and authenticated in such manner as may be prescribed.

(3) Any person who contravenes or fails to comply with the provisions of a regulation made under this Act shall be guilty of an offence.

(4) Any regulations made under this Act shall be laid before Parliament as soon as may be after they are made, and if either House of Parliament, within the period of forty days beginning with the date on which the regulations are laid before it, resolves that the regulations be annulled, the regulations shall thereupon become void, without prejudice, however, to anything previously done thereunder or to the making of new regulations.

In reckoning any such period of forty days as aforesaid, no account shall be taken of any time during which Parliament is dissolved or prorogued or during which both Houses are adjourned for more than four days.

NOTE

Section shown as amended by the Local Government Act 1972.

---

5. Unauthorised use of badges, etc

If any person, in connection with any appeal made by him to the public in association with a representation that the appeal is for a charitable purpose, displays or uses –

(a) a prescribed badge, or a prescribed certificate of authority, not being a badge or certificate for the time being held by him for the purposes of the appeal pursuant to regulations made under this Act, or

(b) any badge or device, or any certificate or other document, so nearly resembling a prescribed badge or, as the case may be, a prescribed certificate of authority as to be calculated to deceive,

he shall be guilty of an offence.

6. Collector to give name, etc, to police on demand

A police constable may require any person whom be believes to be acting as a collector for the purposes of a collection for a charitable purpose to declare to him immediately his name and address and to sign his name, and if any person fails to comply with a requirement duly made to him under this section, he shall be guilty of an offence.

7. Delegation of functions

(1) ...

(2) The functions conferred on a chief officer of police by this Act or regulations made thereunder may be delegated by him to any police officer not below the rank of inspector.

NOTE

Section shown as amended by the Local Government Act 1972.

---

8.   Penalties

(1) Any promoter guilty of an offence under subsection (2) of section one of this Act shall be liable, on summary conviction, to imprisonment for a term not exceeding six months or to a fine not exceeding level 3 on the standard scale or to both such imprisonment and such fine.

(2) Any collector guilty of an offence under subsection (3) of section one of this Act shall be liable, on summary conviction, to a fine not exceeding level 2 on the standard scale or imprisonment for a term not exceeding three months, or to both such imprisonment and such fine.

(3) Any person guilty of an offence under subsection (3) of section four of this Act shall be liable, on summary conviction, to a fine not exceeding level 1 on the standard scale.

(4) Any person guilty of an offence under section five of this Act shall be liable, on summary conviction, to imprisonment for a term not exceeding six months or to a fine not exceeding level 3 on the standard scale, or to both such imprisonment and such fine.

(5) Any person guilty of an offence under section six of this Act shall be liable, on summary conviction, to a fine not exceeding level 1 on the standard scale.

(6) If any person in furnishing any information for the purposes of this Act knowingly or recklessly makes a statement false in a material particular, he shall be guilty of an offence, and shall be liable, on summary conviction, to imprisonment for a term not exceeding six months or to a fine not exceeding level 3 on the standard scale, or to both such imprisonment and such fine.

(7) Where an offence under this Act committed by a corporation is proved to have been committed with the consent or connivance of, or to be attributable to any culpable neglect of duty on the part of, any director, manager, secretary, or other officer of the corporation, he, as well as the corporation, shall be deemed to be guilty of that offence and shall be liable to be proceeded against and punished accordingly.

NOTE
Section shown as amended by the Criminal Justice Act 1982.

------

9.   Application to metropolitan police district

(1) ...

(2) The functions which may be delegated by a chief officer of police by virtue of subsection (2) of section seven of this Act shall not include any functions conferred on the Commissioner of Police for the Metropolis by virtue of his being a licensing authority within the meaning of section 2 of this Act.

NOTE
Section shown as amended by the Local Government Act 1972.

★   ★   ★   ★

11.   Interpretation

(1) In this Act the following expressions have the meanings hereby respectively assigned to them, that is to say −

'charitable purposes' means any charitable, benevolent or philanthropic purpose, whether or not the purpose is charitable within the meaning of any rule of law;

'collection' means an appeal to the public, made by means of visits from house to house, to give, whether for consideration or not, money or other property; and 'collector' means, in relation to a collection, a person who makes the appeal in the course of such visits as aforesaid;

'house' includes a place of business;

'licence' means a licence under this Act;

.   .   .

'prescribed' means prescribed by regulations made under this Act;

'proceeds' means, in relation to a collection, all money and all other property given, whether for consideration or not, in response to the appeal made;

'promoter' means, in relation to a collection, a person who causes others to act, whether for remuneration or otherwise, as collectors for the purposes of the collection; and 'promote' and 'promotion' have corresponding meanings.

(2) For the purposes of this Act, a collection shall be deemed to be made for a particular purpose where the appeal is made in association with a representation that the money or other property appealed for, or part thereof, will be applied for that purpose.

NOTE
Section shown as amended by the Police Act 1964.

12. Short title, commencement, interpretation and extent

(1) This Act may be cited as the House to House Collections Act 1939.

(2) . . .

(3) References in this Act to any enactment shall be construed as references to that enactment as amended by any subsequent enactment.

(4) This Act shall not extend to Northern Ireland.

NOTE
Section shown as amended by the Statute Law Revision Act 1950.

SCHEDULE
Section 2

OFFENCES TO WHICH PARAGRAPH (D) OF SUBSECTION (3) OF SECTION TWO APPLIES

Offences under sections forty-seven to fifty-six of the Offences against the Person Act 1861. Robbery, burglary and blackmail

Offences in Scotland involving personal violence or lewd, indecent, or libidinous conduct, or dishonest appropriation of property.

Offences under the Street Collections Regulation (Scotland) Act 1915.

Offences under section five of the Police, Factories, etc (Miscellaneous Provisions) Act 1916.

NOTE
Section shown as amended by the Theft Act 1968.

POLICE, FACTORIES, ETC (MISCELLANEOUS PROVISIONS) ACT 1916

(6 & 7 Geo 5 c 31)

An Act to amend the Enactments relating to the Police and certain other Enactments with the administration of which the Secretary of State for the Home Department is concerned

[3 August 1916]

PART I

POLICE

*   *   *   *

5.   Regulation of street collections

(1) Each of the authorities specified in subsection (1A) below may make regulations with respect to the places where and the conditions under which persons may be permitted in any street or public place, within their area, to collect money or sell articles for the benefit of charitable or other purposes, and any person who acts in contravention of any such regulation shall be liable on summary conviction to a fine not exceeding level 1 on the standard scale:

Provided that –

(a) regulations made under this section shall not come into operation until they have been confirmed by the Secretary of State, and published for such time and in such manner as the Secretary of State may direct; and

(b) regulations made under this section shall not apply to the selling of articles in any street or public place when the articles are sold in the ordinary course of trade, and for the purpose of earning a livelihood, and no representation is made by or on behalf of the seller that any part of the proceeds of sale will be devoted to any charitable purpose.

(1A) The authorities referred to in subsection (1) above are –

(a) the Common Council of the City of London,

(b) the police authority for the Metropolitan Police District, and

(c) the council of each district;

but any regulations made by a district council under that subsection shall not have effect with respect to any street or public place which is within the Metropolitan Police District as well as within the district.

(2) This section, except subsection (3) thereof, shall apply to Ireland with the following modifications –

(a) references to the Secretary of State shall be construed as references to the Lord Lieutenant; and

(b) references to a police authority shall be construed as references to the Inspector General of the Royal Irish Constabulary.

(3) ...

(4) In this section –

the expression 'street' includes any highway and any public bridge, road, lane, footway, square, court, alley, or passage, whether a thoroughfare or not.

NOTE

Section shown as amended by the Local Government Act 1972, the Criminal Justice Act 1982, the Statute Law Revision Act 1927 and the Civic Government (Scotland) Act 1982.

---

6. Extent of Part I

This Part of this Act shall not apply, except where otherwise expressly provided, to Scotland or Ireland.

★   ★   ★   ★

13. Short title

This Act may be cited as the Police, Factories, etc (Miscellaneous Provisions) Act 1916.

APPENDIX 2

STATUTORY INSTRUMENTS

HOUSE TO HOUSE COLLECTIONS REGULATIONS 1947
(SR & O 1947/2662)

1. Title and extent

(1) These regulations may be cited as the House to House Collections Regulations, 1947, and shall come into operation on the twenty-ninth day of December, 1947.

(2) These regulations shall not extend to Scotland.

2. Interpretation

(1) In these regulations, unless the context otherwise requires, –

'The Act' means the House to House Collections Act, 1939;

'chief promoter', in relation to a collection, means a person to whom a licence has been granted authorising him to promote that collection or in respect of whom an order has been made directing that he shall be exempt from the provisions of subsection (2) of section 1 of the Act as respects that collection;

'collecting box' means a box or other receptacle for monetary contributions, securely closed and sealed in such a way that it cannot be opened without breaking the seal;

'licence' means a licence granted by a police authority under section 2 of the Act;

'order' means an order made by the Secretary of State under section 3 of the Act;

'prescribed badge' means a badge in the form set out in the Fourth Schedule to these regulations;

'prescribed certificate of authority' means a certificate in the form set out in the Third Schedule to these regulations;

'receipt book' means a book of detachable forms of receipt consecutively numbered with counterfoils or duplicates correspondingly numbered;

'street collection' means a collection or sale to which regulations made under section 5 of the Police, Factories, etc (Miscellaneous Provisions) Act, 1916, apply.

(2) A mark shall for the purposes of these regulations be deemed to have been made on a collecting box if it is made on a wrapper securely gummed to the collecting box.

(3) The Interpretation Act, 1889, applies to the interpretation of these regulations as it applies to the interpretation of an Act of Parliament.

3. Local collections of a transitory nature

(1) Every certificate granted under subsection (4) of section 1 of the Act shall be in the form set out in the First Schedule to these regulations, and section 5 and 6 and subsections (4) and (5) of section 8 of the Act shall be set forth on the back of every such certificate.

(2) Where such a certificate is granted as aforesaid, the provisions of these regulations shall not apply, in relation to a collection made for the purpose specified on the certificate, within the locality and within the period so specified, to the person to whom the certificate is granted or to any person authorised by him to act as a collector for the purposes of that collection.

4. Applications for licences and orders

(1) An application for a licence shall be in the form set out in the Second Schedule to these regulations, and shall give the particulars there specified.

1

(2) An application for a licence or for an order shall be made not later than the first day of the month preceding that in which it is proposed to commence the collection:

Provided that the police authority or, as the case may be, the Secretary of State may grant the application notwithstanding that it was not made within the time required by this paragraph if satisfied that there are special reasons for so doing.

5.   Responsibility of promoters as respects collectors

Every promoter of a collection shall exercise all due diligence –
- (a) to secure that persons authorised to act as collectors for the purposes of the collection are fit and proper persons; and
- (b) to secure compliance on the part of persons so authorised with the provisions of these regulations.

6.   Certificates of authority, badges, collecting boxes and receipt books

(1) No promoter of a collection shall permit any person to act as a collector, unless he has issued or caused to be issued to that person –
- (a) a prescribed certificate of authority duly completed (except as regards the signature of the collector) and signed by or on behalf of the chief promoter of the collection;
- (b) a prescribed badge, having inserted therein or annexed thereto a general indication of the purpose of the collection; and
- (c) if money is to be collected, a collecting box or receipt book marked with a clear indication of the purpose of the collection and a distinguishing number, which indication and number shall, in the case of a receipt book, also be marked on every receipt contained therein in addition to the consecutive number of the receipt.

(2) Every promoter of a collection shall exercise all due diligence to secure –
- (a) that no prescribed certificate of authority, prescribed badge, collecting box or receipt book is issued, unless the name and address of the collector to whom it is issued have been entered on a list showing in respect of any collecting box or receipt book the distinguishing number thereof; and
- (b) that every prescribed certificate of authority, prescribed badge, collecting box or receipt book issued by him or on his behalf is returned when the collection is completed or when for any other reason a collector ceases to act as such.

(3) In the case of a collection in respect of which a licence has been granted –
- (a) every prescribed certificate of authority shall be given on a form obtained from His Majesty's Stationery Office, and every prescribed badge shall be so obtained; and
- (b) every prescribed certificate of authority shall be authenticated, and the general indication on every prescribed badge of the purpose of the collection shall be inserted therein or annexed thereto, in a manner approved by the chief officer of police for the area in respect of which the licence was granted.

7.   Duties of collectors in relation to certificates and badges

Every collector shall –
- (a) sign his name on the prescribed certificate of authority issued to him and produce it on the demand of any police constable or of any occupant of a house visited by him for the purpose of collection;
- (b) sign his name on the prescribed badge issued to him and wear the badge prominently whenever he is engaged in collecting; and

(c) keep such certificate and badge in his possession and return them to a promoter of the collection on replacement thereof or when the collection is completed or at any other time on the demand of a promoter of the collection.

8.   Age limit

No person under the age of 16 years shall act or be authorised to act as a collector of money.

NOTE
Regulation shown as amended by SI 1963/684.

9.   Importuning

No collector shall importune any person to the annoyance of such person, or remain in, or at the door of, any house if requested to leave by any occupant thereof.

10.   Collection of money

(1) Where a collector is collecting money by means of a collecting box, he shall not receive any contribution save by permitting the person from whom it is received to place it in a collecting box issued to him by a promoter of the collection.

(2) Where a collector is collecting money by other means than a collecting box, he shall, upon receiving a contribution from any person, forthwith and in the presence of such person enter on a form of receipt in a receipt book issued to him by a promoter of the collection and on the corresponding counterfoil or duplicate the date, the name of the contributor and the amount contributed, and shall sign the form of receipt, the entries and signature being in ink or indelible pencil, and shall hand the form of receipt to the person from whom he received the contribution.

11.   Duty of collectors to return boxes and books

Every collector, to whom a collecting box or receipt book has been issued, shall –
   (a) when the collecting box is full or the receipt book is exhausted, or
   (b) upon the demand of a promoter of the collection, or
   (c) when he does not desire to act as a collector, or
   (d) upon the completion of the collection,
return to a promoter of the collection that collecting box with the seal unbroken or that receipt book with a sum equal to the total amount of the contributions (if any) entered therein.

12.   Examination of boxes and books

(1) Subject as provided in paragraph (2) of this regulation, a collecting box when returned shall be examined by, and, if it contains money, be opened in the presence of, a promoter of the collection and another responsible person.

(2) Where a collecting box is delivered unopened to a bank, it may be examined and opened by an official of the bank in the absence of a promoter of the collection.

(3) As soon as a collecting box has been opened, the contents shall be counted and the amount shall be entered with the distinguishing number of the collecting box on a list, which shall be certified by the persons making the examination.

(4) Every receipt book when returned and all sums received therewith shall be examined by a promoter of the collection and another responsible person, and the amount of the contributions entered in the receipt book shall be checked with the money and entered with the distinguishing

number of the receipt book on a list, which shall be certified by the persons making the examination.

13.   Provision for envelope collections

(1) Where the promoter of a collection to whom an order has been granted informs the Secretary of State that he desires to promote an envelope collection, and the Secretary of State is of opinion that the collection is for a charitable purpose of major importance and is suitably administered, the Secretary of State may, if he thinks fit, give permission for the promotion of an envelope collection.

(2) Where an envelope collection is made in accordance with this regulation –
    (a) every envelope used shall have a gummed flap by means of which it can be securely closed;
    (b) no collector shall receive a contribution except in an envelope which has been so closed; and
    (c) these regulations shall have effect subject to the following modifications:
        (i) sub-paragraph (c) of paragraph (1) of regulation 6 shall not apply;
        (ii) regulation 10 shall not apply;
        (iii) regulations 11 and 12 shall have effect as if each envelope in which a contribution is received were a collecting box;
        (iv) in regulation 11 for the words 'with the seal unbroken' there shall be substituted the word 'unopened';
        (v) in paragraph (3) of regulation 12 for the words 'As soon as a collecting box has been opened' there shall be substituted the words 'As soon as the envelope has been opened' and the words 'with the distinguishing number of the collecting box' shall be omitted.

(3) In this regulation 'envelope collection' means a collection made by persons going from house to house leaving envelopes in which money may be placed and which are subsequently called for.

14.   Promoters to furnish accounts

(1) The chief promoter of a collection in respect of which a licence has been granted shall furnish an account of the collection of the police authority by which the licence was granted within one month of the expiry of the licence:

Provided that if licences are granted to the same person for collections to be made for the same purpose in more than one police area, a combined account of the collections made in all or any of those police areas may, by agreement between the chief promoter and the respective police authorities, be made only to such of the respective police authorities as may be so agreed.

(2) The chief promoter of a collection in respect of which an order has been made shall furnish an account annually to the Secretary of State so long as the order remains in force, and if the order is revoked a final account shall be furnished within three months of the date of the revocation of the order.

(3) The police authority or the Secretary of State may extend the period within which an account is required to be furnished to the authority or to him, as the case may be, if satisfied that there are special reasons for so doing.

(4) The chief promoter of a collection which is made in connection in whole or in part with a street collection of which an account is required to be furnished to a police authority by regulations made under section 5 of the Police, Factories, etc. (Miscellaneous Provisions) Act,

1916, may, if the said police authority agrees, combine the accounts of the house to house collection, in so far as it is made in connection with the street collection, with the accounts of the street collection, and the amount so included in the combined account shall not be required to form part of the account required to be furnished under paragraph (1) or, as the case may be, paragraph (2) of this regulation, so, however, that in the case of an account furnished under the said paragraph (2) the account shall show, in addition to an account in respect of moneys received from house to house collections not made in connection with a street collection, a statement showing the total proceeds of all combined collections, the total expenses and the balance applied to charitable purposes.

15. Form and certification of accounts

The account required by the preceding regulation –

(a) where money has been collected, shall be furnished in the form set out in the Fifth Schedule to these regulations and, where property has been collected and sold, shall be furnished in the form set out in the Sixth Schedule to these regulations, and in either case shall be certified by the chief promoter of the collection and by an independent responsible person as auditor; and

(b) where property (other than money) has been collected and given away or used, shall be furnished in the form set out in the Seventh Schedule to these regulations and shall be certified by the chief promoter and by every person responsible for the disposal of the property collected.

16. Vouching of accounts

(1) Every account furnished under paragraph (a) of regulation 15 of these regulations shall be accompanied by vouchers for each item of the expenses and application of the proceeds and, in the case of a collection of money, by every receipt book used for the purposes of the collection and by the list referred to in paragraph (2) of regulation 6 of these regulations and the list referred to in regulation 12 of these regulations.

(2) Paragraph (1) of this regulation shall not apply to an account certified by an auditor who is a member of an association or society of accountants incorporated at the date of these regulations or is on other grounds accepted as competent by the authority to which the account is submitted, but where in such a case the vouchers, receipt books and lists mentioned in the said paragraph (1) are not submitted with an account, the chief promoter shall ensure that they are available for three months after the account is submitted and shall, if the authority to which the account was submitted so requires at any time within that period, submit them to that authority.

17. Disposal of disused certificates of authority, etc

The chief promoter of a collection shall exercise all due diligence to secure that all forms of prescribed certificates of authority and prescribed badges obtained by him for the purposes of the collection are destroyed when no longer required in connection with that collection or in connection with a further collection which he has been authorised to promote for the same purpose.

FIRST SCHEDULE   Regulation 3

FORM OF CERTIFICATE OF EXEMPTION OF A LOCAL COLLECTION OF A TRANSITORY NATURE

In pursuance of section 1(4) of the House to House Collections Act, 1939, I hereby certify that I am satisfied that the collection, of which particulars are given below, is for a charitable purpose which is local in character, and is likely to be completed within a short period of time.

Accordingly the provisions of that Act (other than those set forth over-leaf★) will not apply, in relation to a collection made for the purpose and within the locality and period indicated below, to the promoter(s) named below or to any person authorised by＿＿ him to act as a collector for the purposes of the collection.   them

(*Signed*) ....

PARTICULARS OF COLLECTION

Name(s) of promoter(s).
Purpose of collection.
Locality to which collection is to be confined.
Date of commencement of collection.
Date beyond which collection must not continue.

★ *Sections 5, 6, 8(4) and 8(5) of the Act are to be set forth on the back of the certificate.*

SECOND SCHEDULE   Regulation 4

FORM OF APPLICATION FOR LICENCE

To the Police Authority for (*here insert name of police area*).

In pursuance of section 2 of the House to House Collections Act, 1939, I hereby apply for a licence authorising me to promote the collection, of which particulars are given below.

Date..   (*Signed*)..

PARTICULARS OF COLLECTION

1. Surname of applicant (*in block letters*). Other names.

2. Address of applicant.

3. Particulars of charitable purposes to which proceeds of collection are to be applied. (Full particulars should be given and, where possible, the most recent account of any charity which is to benefit should be enclosed.)

4. Over what parts of the police area is it proposed that the collection should extend?

5. During what period of the year is it proposed that the collection should be made?

6. Is it proposed to collect money?

7. Is it proposed to collect other property? If so, of what nature? and is it proposed to sell such property or to give it away or to use it?

8. Approximately how many persons is it proposed to authorise to act as collectors in the area of the police authority to which the application is addressed?

9. Is it proposed that remuneration should be paid out of the proceeds of the collection—
   (*a*) to collectors?
   (*b*) to other persons?
   If so, at what rates and to what classes of persons?

10. Is application being made for licences for collections for the same purpose in other police areas?
    If so, to what police authorities?
    And, approximately, how many persons in all is it proposed to authorise to act as collectors?

11. Has the applicant, or to the knowledge of the applicant, anyone associated with the promotion of the collection, been refused a licence or order under the Act, or had a licence or order revoked?
    If so, give particulars.

12. Is it proposed to promote this collection in conjunction with a street collection? If so, is it desired that the accounts of this collection should be combined wholly or in part with the account of the street collection?

13. If the collection is for a War Charity, state if such charity has been registered or exempted from registration under the War Charities Act, 1940, and give name of registration authority and date of registration or exemption.

FORM OF PRESCRIBED CERTIFICATE OF AUTHORITY

HOUSE TO HOUSE COLLECTIONS ACT

COLLECTOR'S CERTIFICATE OF AUTHORITY

(*Here insert name of collector in block letters*)

of (*here insert address of collector*)

is hereby authorised to collect for

(*here insert the purpose of the collection*)

in (*here insert the area within which the collector is authorised to collect, being an area within which the collection has been authorised*)

*during the period (*here insert the period during which the collector is authorised to collect, being a period during which the collection has been authorised*)

Signature of collector—	*Signed—*

★ This entry may be omitted in the case of a collection in respect of which an order has been made.

Regulation 7 is to be set forth on the back of the certificate.

FOURTH SCHEDULE Regulations 2 and 6

FORM OF PRESCRIBED BADGE

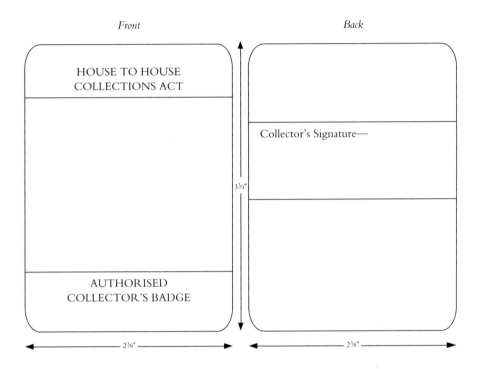

Front *Back*

HOUSE TO HOUSE
COLLECTIONS ACT

Collector's Signature—

3¾″

AUTHORISED
COLLECTOR'S BADGE

2⅛″ 2⅛″

FIFTH SCHEDULE Regulation 15

FORM OF ACCOUNT OF EXPENSES, PROCEEDS AND APPLICATION
OF PROCEEDS OF COLLECTION OF MONEY

(*a*) Surname of chief promoter (*in block letters*).
(*b*) Other names (*in block letters*).
Address of chief promoter.
Purpose of collection.
Area to which account relates.
Period to which account relates.

All amounts to be entered *gross*.

Proceeds of Collection	£ s. d.	Expenses and Application of Proceeds	£ s. d.
From collectors, as in lists of collectors and amounts attached hereto.		Printing and stationery ..	
		Postage	
Bank Interest		Advertising	
Other items (if any):–		Collecting boxes	
....		Other items (if any):–	
....		....	
....		....	
		Disposal of Balance (insert particulars):–	
		....	
		....	
		....	
Total		Total	

CERTIFICATE OF CHIEF PROMOTER

I certify that to the best of my knowledge and belief the above is a true account of the expenses, proceeds and application of the proceeds of the collection to which it relates.

Date ....   (*Signed*) ....

CERTIFICATE OF AUDITOR

I certify that I have obtained all the information and explanations required by me as auditor and that the above is in my opinion a true account of the expenses, proceeds and application of the proceeds of the collection to which it relates.

Date ....   (*Signed*) ....
                    Qualifications ....

SIXTH SCHEDULE   Regulation 15

FORM OF ACCOUNT OF EXPENSES, PROCEEDS AND APPLICATION OF PROCEEDS OF COLLECTION OF PROPERTY SOLD OR COLLECTED FOR SALE

(*a*) Surname of chief promoter (*in block letters*).
(*b*) Other names (*in block letters*).

Address of chief promoter.
Purpose of collection.
Area to which account relates.
Period to which account relates.

CASH ACCOUNT

All amounts to be entered gross.

MONETARY RECEIPTS	£ s. d.	EXPENSES AND APPLICATION OF MONETARY RECEIPTS	£ s. d.	£ s. d.
Amount obtained during period of account by sales of property collected. Bank Interest .. .. Other items (if any):–		Items of expense incurred during period of account, *other than* expenses incurred for the purpose of converting property collected into cash, viz.:–		£
		Items of expense incurred during period of account for the purpose of converting property collected into cash, viz.:–		£
		Disposal of Balance (insert particulars):–		£
Total		Total		

VALUATION OF PROPERTY COLLECTED

Estimated value of property collected during period of
    account   ..   ..
    If the estimated value is not equal to the difference between the "amount obtained by sales of property collected" and the total of the "items of expense incurred during period of account for the purpose of converting property collected into cash", as stated in the cash account, an explanation should be given.

CERTIFICATE OF CHIEF PROMOTER

I certify that to the best of my knowledge and belief the above is a true account of the expenses and the value and application of the proceeds of the collection to which it relates, and that none of the property to which it relates has been disposed of otherwise than by sale, unless found useless and destroyed or otherwise disposed of as rubbish.

Date .... (*Signed*) ....

CERTIFICATE OF AUDITOR

I certify that I have obtained all the information and explanations required by me as auditor and that the above is in my opinion a true account of the monetary receipts and expenses and application of the monetary receipts of the collection to which it relates.

Date .... (*Signed*) ....

SEVENTH SCHEDULE   Regulation 15

FORM OF ACCOUNT OF COLLECTION OF PROPERTY (OTHER THAN MONEY) GIVEN AWAY, USED OR COLLECTED FOR GIVING AWAY

(*a*) Surname of chief promoter (*in block letters*).
(*b*) Other names (*in block letters*).
Address of chief promoter.
Purpose of collection.
Area to which account relates.
Period to which account relates.

I certify that to the best of my knowledge and belief all property collected in the collection of which particulars are given above (unless found useless and destroyed or otherwise disposed of as rubbish) has been given away or used for charitable purposes as follows:–

(*Here insert particulars of disposal of property collected.*)

(*Signed*) ....Chief promoter.

....
....
....

Date ....

I further certify that the above certificate has been signed by every person responsible for the disposal of the property collected.

Date .... (*Signed*) ....

Chief promoter.

CHARITABLE COLLECTIONS (TRANSITIONAL PROVISIONS) ORDER 1974

(SI 1974/140)

NOTE

Prior to 1 April 1974, the functions of making regulations for the control of street collections under the Police, Factories, etc (Miscellaneous Provisions) Act 1916 were vested in various existing police and local authorities. On that date, these functions were transferred by the Local Government Act 1972 to district councils. This order, now largely spent, made transitional provision for the exercise of these functions. It terminated existing street collection regulations. Scheduled to the order are model street collection regulations as set out below.

1.　Model Street Collection Regulations

In these Regulations, unless the context otherwise requires –

'collection' means a collection of money or a sale of articles for the benefit of charitable or other purposes and the word 'collector' shall be construed accordingly;

'promoter' means a person who causes others to act as collectors;

'the licensing authority' means (†　　　　　　　　　　);

'permit' means a permit for a collection;

'contributor' means a person who contributes to a collection and includes a purchaser of articles for sale for the benefit of charitable or other purposes;

'collecting box' means a box or other receptacle for the reception of money from contributors.

2.　No collection, other than a collection taken at a meeting in the open air, shall be made in any street or public place within (★　　　　　　　　　) unless a promoter shall have obtained from the licensing authority a permit.

3.　Application for a permit shall be made in writing not later than one month before the date on which it is proposed to make the collection:

Provided that the licensing authority may reduce the period of one month if satisfied that there are special reasons for so doing.

4.　No collection shall be made except upon the day and between the hours stated in the permit.

5.　The licensing authority may, in granting a permit, limit the collection to such streets or public places or such parts thereof as it thinks fit.

6.　(1) No person may assist or take part in any collection without the written authority of a promoter.

(2) Any person authorised under paragraph (1) above shall produce such written authority forthwith for inspection on being requested to do so by a duly authorised officer of the licensing authority or any constable.

7.　No collection shall be made in any part of the carriage way of any street which has a footway:

Provided that the licensing authority may, if it thinks fit, allow a collection to take place on the said carriage way where such collection has been authorised to be held in connection with a procession.

8.　No collection shall be made in a manner likely to inconvenience or annoy any person.

---

†Insert the name of the licensing authority granting the permit.

★Insert the name of the new licensing area.

9.   No collector shall importune any person to the annoyance of such person.

10.   While collecting—
(a)   a collector shall remain stationary; and
(b)   a collector or two collectors together shall not be nearer to another collector than 25 metres:
    Provided that the licensing authority may, if it thinks fit, waive the requirements of this Regulation in respect of a collection which has been authorised to be held in connection with a procession.

11.   No promoter, collector or person who is otherwise connected with a collection shall permit a person under the age of sixteen years to act as a collector.

12.   (1) Every collector shall carry a collecting box.

(2) All collecting boxes shall be numbered consecutively and shall be securely closed and sealed in such a way as to prevent them being opened without the seal being broken.

(3) All money received by a collector from contributors shall immediately be placed in a collecting box.

(4) Every collector shall deliver, unopened, all collecting boxes in his possession to a promoter.

13.   A collector shall not carry or use any collecting box, receptacle or tray which does not bear displayed prominently thereon the name of the charity or fund which is to benefit nor any collecting box which is not duly numbered.

14.   (1) Subject to paragraph (2) below a collecting box shall be opened in the presence of a promoter and another responsible person.

(2) Where a collecting box is delivered, unopened, to a bank, it may be opened by an official of the bank.

(3) As soon as a collecting box has been opened, the person opening it shall count the contents and shall enter the amount with the number of the collecting box on a list which shall be certified by that person.

15.   (1) No payment shall be made to any collector.

(2) No payments shall be made out of the proceeds of a collection, either directly or indirectly, to any other person connected with the promotion or conduct of such collection for, or in respect of, services connected therewith, except such payments as may have been approved by the licensing authority.

16.   (1) Within one month after the date of any collection the person to whom a permit has been granted shall forward to the licensing authority –
(a)   a statement in the form set out in the Schedule to these Regulations, or in a form to the like effect, showing the amount received and the expenses and payments incurred in connection with such collection, and certified by that person and a qualified accountant;
(b)   a list of the collectors;
(c)   a list of the amounts contained in each collecting box;
and shall, if required by the licensing authority, satisfy it as to the proper application of the proceeds of the collection.

(2) The said person shall also, within the same period, at the expense of that person and after a qualified accountant has given his certificate under paragraph (1)(a) above, publish in such newspaper or newspapers as the licensing authority may direct a statement showing the name of the person to whom the permit has been granted, the area to which the permit relates, the name of

the charity or fund to benefit, the date of the collection, the amount collected, and the amount of the expenses and payments incurred in connection with such collection.

(3) The licensing authority may, if satisfied there are special reasons for so doing extend the period of one month referred to in paragraph (1) above.

(4) For the purposes of this Regulation 'a qualified accountant' means a member of one or more of the following bodies:
   the Institute of Chartered Accountants in England and Wales;
   the Institute of Chartered Accountants of Scotland;
   the Association of Certified Accountants;
   the Institute of Chartered Accountants in Ireland.

17.   These regulations shall not apply –
   (a) in respect of a collection taken at a meeting in the open air; or
   (b) to the selling of articles in any street or public place when the articles are sold in the ordinary course of trade.

18.   Any person who acts in contravention of any of the foregoing regulations shall be liable on summary conviction to a fine not exceeding two pounds or in the case of a second or subsequent offence not exceeding five pounds.

STREET COLLECTIONS (METROPOLITAN POLICE DISTRICT) REGULATIONS 1979

(SI 1979/1230)

1. (1) These Regulations may be cited as the Street Collections (Metropolitan Police District) Regulations 1979.

(2) These Regulations shall be published in the London Gazette on a day not later than 15 November 1979 and shall come into operation on 1 January 1980.

2. In these Regulations, unless the context otherwise requires –
'chief promoter' means a society, committee or body consisting of not less than three persons to which a permit for a street collection has been granted;
'collecting box' means a box or other receptacle for the reception of money from contributors;
'Commissioner' means the Commissioner of Police of the Metropolis;
'collection' means –
   (i) a collection of money; or
   (ii) a sale of articles
in any street or public place within the Metropolitan Police District for the benefit of charitable or other purposes, and 'collector' shall be construed accordingly;
'contributor' means a person who contributes to a collection, and includes a purchaser of articles for sale for the benefit of charitable or other purposes;
'permit' means a permit for a collection;
'promoter' means a person, authorised in that behalf by the chief promoter, who causes others to act as collectors.

3. These Regulations shall not apply –
   (a) in respect of a collection taken at a meeting in the open air; or
   (b) to the selling of articles in any street or public place when the articles are sold in the ordinary course of trade and for the purpose of earning a livelihood and no representation is made by or on behalf of the seller that any part of the proceeds of sale will be devoted to any charitable purpose.

4. No collection shall be made unless a permit therefor has been obtained from the Commissioner.

5. (1) Every application for a permit shall be made in writing to the Commissioner in the form set out in Schedule 1 to these Regulations not later than the first day of the month preceding the month in which it is proposed to hold the collection:
   Provided that the Commissioner may consider an application made later than that date if he is satisfied that there are special reasons for so doing.

(2) Every application shall be made by a society, committee or other body consisting of not less than three members acting through not less than three members thereof who shall be jointly responsible for the collection.

(3) Every application shall be referred by the Commissioner to an Advisory Committee appointed by him with the approval of the Secretary of State, and, in deciding whether to grant a permit, he may have regard to any recommendation of the Advisory Committee.

6. No collection shall be made except upon the day and between the hours stated in the permit.

7. The Commissioner may, in granting a permit, limit the collection to such districts, streets or public places or such parts thereof as he thinks fit.

8.   (1) No person may assist or take part in any collection unless he is in possession of a written authority signed on behalf of the chief promoter.

(2) Any person authorised under paragraph (1) above shall produce that authority forthwith for inspection on being requested to do so by any constable.

9.   No collection shall be made in any part of the carriage way of any street:

Provided that the Commissioner may, if he thinks fit, allow a collection to take place on such a carriage way where that collection has been authorised to be held in connection with a procession.

10.   No collection shall be made in such a manner as to cause, or be likely to cause, danger, obstruction, inconvenience or annoyance to any person.

11.   No collector shall importune any person to the annoyance of such person.

12.   While collecting –
   (a) a collector shall remain stationary; and
   (b) a collector or two collectors together shall not be nearer to another collector than 25 metres:

Provided that the Commissioner may, if he thinks fit, waive the requirements of this Regulation in respect of a collection which has been authorised to be held in connection with a procession.

13.   No promoter, collector or person who is otherwise connected with a collection shall permit a person under the age of sixteen years to act as a collector:

Provided that in the case of a collection which has been authorised to be held in connection with a procession, the Commissioner may, if he thinks fit, authorise the chief promoter to permit persons of less than sixteen but not less than fourteen years to act as collectors after receipt of a written assurance by such chief promoter that each of such persons will at all times be accompanied by a responsible able-bodied adult.

14.   No collector shall be accompanied by any animal.

15.   (1) Every collector shall carry a collecting box.

(2) All collecting boxes shall be numbered consecutively and shall be securely closed and sealed in such a way as to prevent them being opened without the seal being broken.

(3) All money received by a collector from contributors shall immediately be placed in a collecting box.

(4) Every collector shall deliver, unopened, all collecting boxes in his possession to a promoter.

16.   A collector shall not carry or use any collecting box, receptacle or tray which does not bear displayed prominently thereon the name of the charity or fund which is to benefit, or any collecting box which is not duly numbered.

17.   (1) Subject to paragraph (2) below a collecting box shall be opened in the presence of a promoter and another responsible person.

(2) Where a collecting box is delivered unopened to a bank it may be opened by an official of the bank.

(3) As soon as a collecting box has been opened the person opening it shall count the contents and shall enter the amount with the number of the collecting box on a list which shall be certified by that person.

18.   (1) No payment by way of reward shall be made to any collector.

(2) No payment shall be made out of the proceeds of a collection, either directly or indirectly, to any other person connected with the promotion or conduct of such collection for, or in respect of, services connected therewith, except such payments as may have been specified in the form of application for a permit and approved by the Commissioner.

19. (1) Within three months after the date of a collection, the chief promoter shall forward to the Commissioner –

(a) a statement in the form set out in Schedule 2 to these Regulations showing the amount received and the expenses and payments incurred in connection with the collection and certified by two of the persons responsible for the collection referred to in Regulation 5(2) above and by a qualified accountant:

Provided that if a collection results in a sum of £400 or less being collected, the Commissioner may, if he thinks fit, waive the requirement for certification by a qualified accountant and substitute therefor a requirement for certification by an independent responsible person, unless, after examination of the statement, he decides that it should be certified by a qualified accountant;

(b) a list showing the names of the collectors; and

(c) a list of the amounts contained in each collecting box,

and shall, if required by the Commissioner, satisfy him as to the proper application of the proceeds of the collection.

(2) The chief promoter shall also, within the same period, at the expense of the chief promoter and after any certification required under paragraph (1)(a) above, publish in such newspaper or newspapers as the Commissioner may direct a statement showing the name of the chief promoter, the area to which the permit relates, the name of the charity or fund to benefit, the date of the collection, the amount collected, the amount distributed to each charity or fund to benefit, and the amount of the expenses and payments incurred in connection with such collection.

Provided that the Commissioner may, if he thinks fit, waive the requirements of this paragraph in respect of a collection which results in a sum of £400 or less being collected.

(3) Not later than seven days after the publication of a newspaper containing the statement required by paragraph (2) above the chief promoter shall send a copy of that newspaper to the Commissioner.

(4) For the purposes of this Regulation 'a qualified accountant' means a member of one or more of the following bodies:

the Institute of Chartered Accountants in England and Wales;
the Institute of Chartered Accountants of Scotland;
the Association of Certified Accountants;
the Institute of Chartered Accountants in Ireland.

NOTE

Regulation shown as amended by SI 1986/1696.

---

20. (1) This Regulation applies to a collection in respect of which the Chief Superintendent in charge of the police division where it is to be held has issued a certificate for the purposes of this Regulation to the person who appears to him to be principally concerned in promoting the collection and which is made in accordance with the terms of that certificate.

(2) No certificate shall be issued under paragraph (1) above unless it appears to the Chief Superintendent that the collection is to be made in the period from 1 to 24 December in any year and in connection with the singing or playing (including the reproduction of recordings) of Christmas carols by two or more persons assembled together.

(3) In the case of a collection to which this Regulation applies –

    (a) Regulations 4, 5, 12(b), 17 and 19, and, in so far as they relate to the numbering of collecting boxes, Regulations 15(2) and 16, shall not have effect; and

    (b) Regulations 6, 7, 8(1), 9, 12 (except paragraph (b)) and 13 shall be construed as if any reference to a permit or the Commissioner were, respectively, a reference to the certificate under paragraph (1) and the Chief Superintendent, as if any reference to the chief promoter or a promoter were a reference to the person to whom the certificate is issued, and as if the reference in the proviso to regulation 13 to a collection which has been authorised to be held in connection with a procession were a reference to any collection.

NOTE

Regulation shown as amended by SI 1986/1696.

---

21.   (1) The Regulations made and confirmed by the Secretary of State under section 5 of the Police, Factories, etc (Miscellaneous Provisions) Act 1916 and dated 2 July 1926 and the Street Collections (Metropolitan Police District) Regulations 1963 are hereby revoked.

(2) Where a permit has been granted under the Regulations mentioned in paragraph (1) above in respect of a collection to be made after the coming into operation of these Regulations, these Regulations (including paragraph (1) above) shall not have effect in relation to that collection.

CHARITIES (MISLEADING NAMES) REGULATIONS 1992

(SI 1992/1901)

In exercise of the powers conferred upon me by section 4(2)(c) of the Charities Act 1992. I hereby make the following Regulations:

1. These regulations may be cited as the Charities (Misleading Names) Regulations 1992 and shall come into force on 1 September 1992.

2. The words and expressions set out in the Schedule to these Regulations, together (where appropriate) with the plural and possessive forms of those words and expressions and any abbreviation of them, are hereby specified for the purposes of section 4(2)(c) of the Charities Act 1992.

SCHEDULE   Regulation 2

SPECIFICATION OF WORDS AND EXPRESSIONS FOR THE PURPOSES OF SECTION 4(2)(c) OF THE CHARITIES ACT 1992

Assurance	King
Authority	National
Bank	Nationwide
Benevolent	Northern Ireland
British	Northern Irish
Building Society	Official
Church	Polytechnic
Co-operative	Prince
England	Princess
English	Queen
Europe	Registered
European	Royal
Friendly Society	Royale
Grant-Maintained	Royalty
Great Britain	School
Great British	Scotland
Her Majesty	Scottish
His Majesty	Trade Union
Industrial & Provident	United Kingdom
Society	University
International	Wales
Ireland	Welsh
Irish	Windsor

CHARITIES (RECEIVER AND MANAGER) REGULATIONS 1992

(SI 1992/2355)

1. Citation, commencement and interpretation

(1) These Regulations may be cited as the Charities (Receiver and Manager) Regulations 1992 and shall come into force on 1 November 1992.

(2) In these Regulations –
'the 1960 Act' means the Charities Act 1960;
'the appointed person' means a person appointed by order under section 20(1)(vii) of the 1960 Act to be receiver and manager in respect of the property and affairs of a charity;
'the relevant charity' means the charity in respect of which that person was appointed; and
'the relevant order' means the order by which that person was appointed.

2. Security by appointed person

The Commissioners are hereby authorised to require the appointed person to give security to them for the due discharge of his functions within such time and in such form as they may specify.

3. Remuneration of appointed person

(1) The Commissioners are hereby authorised to determine the amount of an appointed person's remuneration.

(2) The remuneration of an appointed person shall be payable out of the income of the relevant charity.

(3) The Commissioners are hereby authorised to disallow any amount of remuneration of an appointed person where, on the expiry of the time specified in the notice referred to in regulation 4(2) below and after consideration of such representations, if any, as are duly made in response to such a notice, they are satisfied that he has failed in such manner as is set out in paragraph (a) or (b) of regulation 4(1) below and specified in such a notice.

4. Notice of failure to, and removal of, appointed person

(1) Where it appears to the Commissioners that an appointed person has failed –
(a) to give security within such time or in such form as they have specified, or
(b) satisfactorily to discharge any function imposed on him by or by virtue of the relevant order or by regulation 5 below,
and they wish to consider exercising their powers under regulation 3(3) above or paragraph (3) below, they shall give him, whether in person or by post, a written notice complying with paragraph (2) below.

(2) A notice given to an appointed person under paragraph (1) above shall inform him of –
(a) any failure under paragraph (1)(a) or (b) above in respect of which the notice is issued;
(b) of the Commissioners' power under regulation 3(3) above to authorise the disallowance of any amount of remuneration if satisfied as to any such failure;
(c) of their power under paragraph (3) below to remove him if satisfied as to any such failure; and

(d) of his right to make representations to them in respect of any such alleged failure within such reasonable time as is specified in the notice.

(3) On the expiry of the time specified in the notice referred to in paragraph (2) above and after consideration of such representations, if any, as are duly made in response to such a notice, the Commissioners may remove an appointed person where they are satisfied that he has failed in such manner as is set out in paragraph (1)(a) or (b) above and specified in such notice (whether or not they also exercise the power conferred by regulation 3(3) above).

5. Reports by appointed person

(1) This regulation makes provision in respect of the reports which are to be made by an appointed person to the Commissioners (and which, in addition to the matters which are required to be included by virtue of paragraphs (2) to (4) below, may also include particulars of any matter which, in his opinion, should be brought to their attention).

(2) An appointed person shall make a report to the Commissioners not later than three months after the date of his appointment setting out –
- (a) an estimate by him of the total value of the property of the relevant charity on, or shortly after, the date of his appointment;
- (b) such information about the property and affairs of the relevant charity immediately prior to his appointment as he believes should be included in the report, notwithstanding that it may also be eventually included in a report under section 6 of the 1960 Act; and
- (c) his strategy for discharging the functions conferred on him by or by virtue of the relevant order.

(3) For as long as an appointed person holds office as such, he shall make a report to the Commissioners not later than one month after each anniversary of his appointment setting out –
- (a) an estimate by him of the total value of the property of the relevant charity on that anniversary of his appointment in respect of which the report is required to be made;
- (b) a summary of the discharge by him of the functions conferred on him by or by virtue of the relevant order during the twelve months ending with that anniversary; and
- (c) where there are changes to his strategy as last set out in a report in accordance with paragraph (2)(c) above or, as the case may be, this sub-paragraph, those changes.

(4) Subject to paragraph (5) below, an appointed person shall make a report to the Commissioners not later than three months after the date when he ceased to hold office as such setting out –
- (a) an estimate by him of the total value of the property of the relevant charity on that date; and
- (b) a summary of the discharge by him of the functions conferred on him by or by virtue of the relevant order during the period ending with that date and beginning with either –
    - (i)   the date of his appointment; or
    - (ii) if that date is more than twelve months before the date when he ceased to hold office as an appointed person, the day immediately after the last anniversary of his appointment.

(5) Paragraph (4) above does not apply where an appointed person ceased to hold office one month or less after an anniversary of his appointment and a report had been made to the Commissioners in accordance with paragraph (3) above in respect of that anniversary.

CHARITIES (QUALIFIED SURVEYORS' REPORTS) REGULATIONS 1992

(SI 1992/2980)

1. (1) These Regulations may be cited as the Charities (Qualified Surveyors' Reports) Regulations 1992 and shall come into force on 1 January 1993.

(2) In these Regulations –
'relevant land' means the land in respect of which a report is being obtained for the purposes of section 32(3) of the Charities Act 1992; and
'the surveyor' means the qualified surveyor from whom such a report is being obtained.

2. A report prepared for the purposes of section 32(3) of the Charities Act 1992 (requirements to be complied with in respect of the disposition of land held by or in trust for a charity otherwise than with an order of the court or of the Charity Commissioners or where section 32(5) of that Act applies) shall contain such information and deal with such matters as are prescribed by the Schedule to these Regulations (together with such other information and such other matters as the surveyor believes should be drawn to the attention of the charity trustees).

SCHEDULE

INFORMATION TO BE CONTAINED IN, AND MATTERS TO BE DEALT WITH BY, QUALIFIED SURVEYORS' REPORTS

1. (1) A description of the relevant land and its location, to include –
(a) the measurements of the relevant land;
(b) its current use;
(c) the number of buildings (if any) included in the relevant land;
(d) the measurements of any such buildings; and
(e) the number of rooms in any such buildings and the measurements of those rooms.

(2) Where any information required by sub-paragraph (1) above may be clearly given by means of a plan, it may be so given and any such plan need not be drawn to scale.

2. Whether the relevant land, or any part of it, is leased by or from the charity trustees and, if it is, details of –
(a) the length of the lease and the period of it which is outstanding;
(b) the rent payable under the lease;
(c) any service charge which is so payable;
(d) the provisions in the lease for any review of the rent payable under it or any service charge so payable;
(e) the liability under the lease for repairs and dilapidations; and
(f) any other provision in the lease which, in the opinion of the surveyor, affects the value of the relevant land.

3. Whether the relevant land is subject to the burden of, or enjoys the benefit of, any easement or restrictive covenant or is subject to any annual or other periodic sum charged on or issuing out of the land except rent reserved by a lease or tenancy.

4. Whether any buildings included in the relevant land are in good repair and, if not, the surveyor's advice –

- (a) as to whether or not it would be in the best interests of the charity for repairs to be carried out prior to the proposed disposition;
- (b) as to what those repairs, if any, should be; and
- (c) as to the estimated cost of any repairs he advises.

5. Where, in the opinion of the surveyor, it would be in the best interests of the charity to alter any buildings included in the relevant land prior to disposition (because, for example, adaptations to the buildings for their current use are not such as to command the best market price on the proposed disposition), that opinion and an estimate of the outlay required for any alterations which he suggests.

6. Advice as to the manner of disposing of the relevant land so that the terms on which it is disposed of are the best that can reasonably be obtained for the charity, including –

- (a) where appropriate, a recommendation that the land should be divided for the purposes of the disposition;
- (b) unless the surveyor's advice is that it would not be in the best interests of the charity to advertise the proposed disposition, the period for which and the manner in which the proposed disposition should be advertised;
- (c) where the surveyor's advice is that it would not be in the best interests of the charity to advertise the proposed disposition, his reasons for that advice (for example, that the proposed disposition is the renewal of a lease to someone who enjoys statutory protection or that he believes someone with a special interest in acquiring the relevant land will pay considerably more than the market price for it); and
- (d) any view the surveyor may have on the desirability or otherwise of delaying the proposed disposition and, if he believes such delay is desirable, what the period of that delay should be.

7. (1) Where the surveyor feels able to give such advice and where such advice is relevant, advice as to the chargeability or otherwise of value added tax on the proposed disposition and the effect of such advice on the valuations given under paragraph 8 below.

(2) Where either the surveyor does not feel able to give such advice or such advice is not in his opinion relevant, a statement to that effect.

8. The surveyor's opinion as to –

- (a) the current value of the relevant land having regard to its current state or repair and current circumstances (such as the presence of a tenant who enjoys statutory protection) or, where the proposed disposition is a lease, the rent which could be obtained under it having regard to such matters;
- (b) what the value of the relevant land or what the rent under the proposed disposition would be –
    - (i) where he has given advice under paragraph 4 above, if that advice is followed; or
    - (ii) where he has expressed an opinion under paragraph 5 above, if that opinion is acted upon; or
    - (iii) if both that advice is followed and that opinion is acted upon;
- (c) where he has made a recommendation under paragraph 6(a) above, the increase in the value of the relevant land or rent in respect of it if the recommendation were followed;
- (d) where his advice is that it would not be in the best interests of the charity to advertise the proposed disposition because he believes a higher price can be obtained by not doing so, the amount by which that price exceeds the price that could be obtained if the proposed disposition were advertised; and

(e) where he has advised a delay in the proposed disposition under paragraph 6(d) above, the amount by which he believes the price which could be obtained consequent on such a delay exceeds the price that could be obtained without it.

9.   Where the surveyor is of the opinion that the proposed disposition is not in the best interests of the charity because it is not a disposition that makes the best use of the relevant land, that opinion and the reasons for it, together with his advice as to the type of disposition which would constitute the best use of the land (including such advice as may be relevant as to the prospects of buying out any sitting tenant or of succeeding in an application for change of use of the land under the laws relating to town and country planning etc).

CHARITY COMMISSIONERS' FEES (COPIES AND EXTRACTS) REGULATIONS 1992

(SI 1992/2986)

1. (1) These Regulations may be cited as the Charity Commissioners' Fees (Copies and Extracts) Regulations 1992 and shall come into force on 1 January 1993.

(2) In these Regulations 'relevant document' means any document which is kept by the Commissioners under the enactments relating to charities and of or from which section 9 of the Charities Act 1960 or section 7 of the Charitable Trustees Incorporation Act 1872 requires the Commissioners to furnish copies or extracts at the request of any person.

2. Where a photocopier is used in response to a request to furnish a copy of, or extract from, a relevant document, there shall, subject to regulation 6 below, be payable to the Commissioners for such a copy or extract –
   (a) where there are not more than six sheets of photocopied material, a fee of £1.80; and
   (b) where there are more than six sheets of photocopied material, a fee of £1.80 and an additional 30p for each such sheet in excess of the first six.

3. (1) Where a request is made for a copy of, or extract from, a relevant document and the information contained in that document is recorded otherwise than in legible form, there shall, subject to paragraph (2) and regulation 6 below, be payable to the Commissioners for such a copy or extract (which, by virtue of section 46(2) of the Charities Act 1960, must be furnished in legible form) a fee of 60p for each sheet of paper on which such a copy or extract is printed.

(2) Paragraph (1) above shall not apply for the purposes of the calculation of the fee payable on the furnishing of extracts from a relevant document where –
   (a) the extracts requested are such that the request is capable of being dealt with as a request under regulation 4 below, and
   (b) the fee payable under that regulation for such extracts is lower than the fee which would otherwise be payable under paragraph (2) above.

4. (1) This regulation applies to a request for an extract (or extracts) from the register of charities (which is a relevant document because section 9 of the Charities Act 1960 applies to it by virtue of the requirement in section 4(7) of that Act that the register be kept open to public inspection) where –
   (a) the information contained in that register is recorded otherwise than in legible form, and
   (b) the request is in respect of any registered charity (or charities) identified by either its name (or their names) or the number under which it is registered (or the numbers under which they are registered).

(2) Subject to regulation 6 below, where a request of the kind described in paragraph (1) above is for a short extract (or extracts) from the register of charities, there shall be payable to the Commissioners in respect of furnishing it (or them) a fee of £2 with an additional 15p for each charity in respect of which a short extract is so furnished.

(3) Subject to regulation 6 below, where a request of the kind described in paragraph (1) above is for a standard extract (or extracts) from the register of charities, there shall be payable to the Commissioners in respect of furnishing it (or them) a fee of £2 with an additional 20p for each charity in respect of which a standard extract is so furnished.

(4) Subject to regulation 6 below, where a request of the kind described in paragraph (1) above is for a detailed extract (or extracts) from the register of charities, there shall be payable to the Commissioners in respect of furnishing it (or them) a fee of £2 with an additional 25p for each

charity in respect of which a detailed extract is so furnished or, where it is not possible to furnish such an extract (because the criterion which distinguishes a detailed extract from a standard extract and is referred to in paragraph (5) below is not satisfied) 20p for each charity in respect of which a standard extract is so furnished.

(5) In this regulation and regulation 5 below –

'a short extract' means an extract (not being a standard or detailed extract) which includes the name and registration number of the charity in question;

'a standard extract' means an extract (not being a detailed extract) which, in addition to the information about the charity in question included in a short extract, also includes the purposes of that charity and an address for correspondence with the charity trustees; and

'a detailed extract' means an extract which, in addition to the information about the charity in question included in a standard extract, also includes the names of any other (subsidiary) charity registered in the register of charities under the same number as that charity.

5. (1) This regulation applies to a request for an extract (or extracts) from the register of charities where –

(a) the information contained in that register is recorded otherwise than in legible form, and

(b) the request is framed by reference to criteria other than the name of any registered charity (or charities) or the number under which it is registered (or the numbers under which they are registered).

(2) Subject to regulation 6 below, there shall be payable to the Commissioners in respect of the furnishing of an extract (or extracts) from the register of charities in response to a request of the kind described in paragraph (1) above a fee of £2 with an additional £40 for each criterion by reference to which the extracts are to be identified, and an additional –

(a) 15p for each extract which is a short extract;

(b) 20p for each extract which is a standard extract; or

(c) 25p for each extract which is a detailed extract.

6. Where it appears to the Commissioners appropriate to do so, they may confer such exemption as they see fit from the liability to pay a fee prescribed by regulations 2 to 5 above.

CHARITIES (CY-PRÈS ADVERTISEMENTS, INQUIRIES AND DISCLAIMER) REGULATIONS 1993

1.　(1) These regulations may be cited as the Charity (Cy-Près Advertisements, Inquiries and Disclaimer) Regulations 1993 and shall come into force on the date on which they are made.

(2) In these Regulations –

'the Act' means the Charities Act 1960;

'advertisement' means an advertisement published in pursuance of section 14(1)(a)(i) of the Act;

'appeal' means an invitation to the public or a section of the public whether in writing, by means of television or radio or otherwise;

'property' means property given for specific charitable purposes which have failed.

2.　(1) Advertisements shall be in the form specified in Schedule 1 to these Regulations or in a form equivalent to that form in any other language required or permitted by paragraph (2) of this Regulation.

(2) Advertisements shall be published –

(a) in English in every case; and

(b) where the appeal was published in another language, in that language;

and may, in addition, be published in Welsh in any case where the appeal was not made in Welsh.

3.　Any advertisement published in pursuance of section 14(1)(a)(i) of the Act shall be published in the manner specified in Schedule 2 to these Regulations.

4.　Any inquiry made in pursuance of section 14(1)(a)(i) of the Act shall –

(a) be made in writing;

(b) be sent by post to the address of each donor recorded in the records of the trustees of the property; and

(c) contain at least the information specified in Schedule 3 to these Regulations.

5.　The period prescribed for the purposes of section 14(1)(a)(ii) of the Act shall be three months.

6.　Any disclaimer executed in pursuance of section 14(1)(b) of the Act shall either:

(a) be executed in English in the form specified in Schedule 4 to these Regulations; or

(b) be executed in Welsh in the form equivalent in that language to the form specified in Schedule 4 to these Regulations.

SCHEDULE 1　　　　　　　　　　　　　　　　　Regulation 2

FORM OF ADVERTISEMENT PRESCRIBED FOR THE PURPOSES OF SECTION 14(1)(a)(i) OF THE CHARITIES ACT 1960

<u>'ADVERTISEMENT</u>

Name of charity (if applicable):

Registered charity number (if applicable):

Purpose for which money or other property was given:

NOTICE is given that money and other property given for this purpose cannot be used for that purpose because [state reasons].

2.   If you gave money or other property for that purpose you are entitled to claim it back. If you wish to do so you must tell [insert name] of [insert address] within 3 months of [specify date: see note below]. If you wish the money or other property to go to a similar charitable purpose and to disclaim your right to the return of the money or other property, you must ask the person named above for a form of disclaimer.

3.   If you do not either make a claim within the 3 months or sign a disclaimer, the Charity Commissioners may make a Scheme applying the property to other charitable purposes. You will still be able to claim the return of your money or other property (less expenses), but *only if you do so within 6 months from the date of any Scheme made by the Commissioners.*

4.   Date of this notice: [*specify date: see note below*]'

[*Note: [This Note does not form part of the prescribed advertisement]* If this advertisement is to be published in a newspaper or other periodical, the words 'the date of this publication' should be inserted in paragraphs 2 and 4 above.

If this advertisement is to be published on a public notice board, the date inserted here should be the date on which the advertisement was fixed to the public notice board.]

SCHEDULE 2   Regulation 3

MANNER OF PUBLISHING ADVERTISEMENTS IN PURSUANCE OF SECTION 14(1)(a)(i) OF THE ACT

1.   Every advertisement shall be published in a newspaper or other periodical which is:
   (a) written in the same language as the advertisement; and
   (b) is sold or distributed throughout the area in which the appeal was made.

2.   Where the purposes of the appeal were directed towards the benefit of an area contained wholly or mainly within a local authority district or a London Borough or the City of London, a copy of every advertisement published under paragraph 1 shall also be published by fixing copies of it to two public notice boards in the relevant area.

SCHEDULE 3   Regulation 4

INFORMATION TO BE CONTAINED IN INQUIRIES TO BE MADE IN PURSUANCE OF SECTION 14(1)(a)(i) OF THE ACT

1.   The name and address of the charity to which the property was given by the donor;

2.   A description of the specific charitable purpose for which the property was given by the donor;

3.   The reasons why that purpose has failed;

4.   A description of the property (including the amount of any money) given for that purpose by the donor;

5.   A statement of the donor's right to have the property returned;

6.   A statement that the donor may disclaim the right to have the property described in paragraph 4 above returned by executing a disclaimer in the prescribed form;

7. A statement that, where the donor disclaims his right in respect of such property, the property may be applied for other charitable purposes similar to those for which it was given by a Scheme established by the Commissioners or by the court; and

8. A statement that, where the donor has not replied in writing to the inquiry within three months from the date of service of the inquiry, he will be treated for the purposes of section 14(1)(a) as a donor who cannot be identified or found, but that he will be able to claim the property, less expenses, within six months from the date of any Scheme made by the Commissioners or the court.

SCHEDULE 4   Regulation 6

FORM OF DISCLAIMER PRESCRIBED FOR THE PURPOSES OF
SECTION 14(1)(a)(ii) OF THE CHARITIES ACT 1960

'DISCLAIMER

I HEREBY DISCLAIM my right to the return of *the sum of £ . . . . . . / the property consisting of (insert description of property)*★ given by me for (insert name of charity to which, or description of purposes for which, the money or property was given).

Signed	....
Name in capitals	....
Address	....
Date	....
Signed†	....
Name in capitals	....
Address	....
Date	....',

★ Delete as appropriate.
†This paragraph may be repeated if further signatures are required.

The Seal of the Charity Commissioners for England and Wales was affixed hereto by order of the Commissioners.

24 June 1993

TRUSTEE INVESTMENTS (ADDITIONAL POWERS) ORDER 1994

(SI 1994/265)

Citation and commencement

1. This Order may be cited as the Trustee Investments (Additional Powers) Order 1994 and shall come into force on 11 March 1994.

Addition to Part I of the First Schedule to the Trustee Investments Act 1961

2. The powers of investment conferred by section 1 of the Trustee Investments Act 1961 shall be extended by adding National Savings Pensioners Guaranteed Income Bonds to paragraph 1 of Part I of the First Schedule thereto.

TRUSTEE INVESTMENTS (ADDITIONAL POWERS) (NO 2) ORDER 1994

(SI 1994/1908)

1. Citation and commencement

This Order may be cited as the Trustee Investments (Additional Powers) (No 2) Order 1994 and shall come into force on 22 August 1994.

2. New powers of investment of trustees

(1) For paragraph 10A of Part II of Schedule 1 to the Trustee Investments Act 1961 there shall be substituted –

'**10A.** In any units of a gilt unit trust scheme.

References in this Schedule to a gilt unit trust scheme are references to a collective investment scheme –

    (a) which is an authorised unit trust scheme within the meaning of the Financial Services Act 1986, a recognised scheme within the meaning of that Act or a UCITS; and

    (b) whose objective is to invest not less than 90% of the property of the scheme in loan stock, bonds and other instruments creating or acknowledging indebtedness which are transferable and which are issued or guaranteed by –

        (i) the government of the United Kingdom or elsewhere,

        (ii) by a local authority in the United Kingdom or in a relevant state, or

        (iii) by an international organisation the members of which include the United Kingdom or a relevant state;

and, in respect of the remainder of the property of the scheme, whose objective is to invest in any instrument falling within any of the paragraphs 1 to 3, 5 or 6 of Schedule 1 to the Financial Services Act 1986.'.

(2) After paragraph 15 of Part II of that Schedule, there shall be inserted –

'**16.** In fixed-interest or variable interest securities issued by the government of a relevant state.

17. In any securities the payment of interest on which is guaranteed by the government of a relevant state.

18. In fixed-interest securities issued in any relevant state by any public authority or nationalised industry or undertaking in that state.

19. In fixed-interest or variable interest securities issued in a relevant state by the government of any overseas territory within the Commonwealth or by any public or local authority within such a territory.

References in this paragraph to an overseas territory or to the government of such a territory shall be construed as if they occurred in the Overseas Development and Co-operation Act 1980.

20. In fixed-interest or variable interest securities issued in a relevant state by –

    (a) the African Development Bank;

    (b) the Asian Development Bank;

    (c) the Caribbean Development Bank;

    (d) the International Finance Corporation;

    (e) the International Monetary Fund;

    (f) the International Bank for Reconstruction and Development;

    (g) the Inter-American Development Bank;

(h) the European Atomic Energy Community;
(i) the European Bank for Reconstruction and Development;
(j) the European Economic Community;
(k) the European Investment Bank; or
(l) the European Coal and Steel Community.

21.   In debentures issued in any relevant state by a company incorporated in that state.

22.   In loans to any authority to which this paragraph applies secured on all or any of the revenues of the authority or on a fund into which all or any of those revenues are payable, in fixed-interest or variable interest securities issued in a relevant state by any such authority in that state for the purpose of borrowing money so secured, and in deposits with any authority to which this paragraph applies by way of temporary loan made on the giving of a receipt for the loan by the treasurer or other similar officer of the authority and on the giving of an undertaking by the authority that, if requested to charge the loan as aforesaid, it will either comply with the request or repay the loan.
   This paragraph applies to the following authorities, that is to say –
(a) any local authority in a relevant state; or
(b) any authority all the members of which are appointed or elected by one or more local authorities in any such state.

23.   In deposits with a mutual investment society whose head office is located in a relevant state.

24.   In loans secured on any interest in property in a relevant state which corresponds to an interest in property falling within paragraph 13 of this Part of this Schedule.'.

(3) After paragraph 3 of Part III of the Schedule there shall be inserted –
   '**4.** In any securities issued in any relevant state by a company incorporated in that state or by any unincorporated body constituted under the law of that state, not being (in either case) securities falling within Part II of this Schedule or paragraph 6 of this Part of this Schedule.

5.   In shares in a mutual investment society whose head office is located in a relevant state.

6.   In any units of a collective investment scheme which is –
(a) a recognised scheme within the meaning of the Financial Services Act 1986 which is constituted in a relevant state; or
(b) a UCITS;
and which does not fall within Part II of this Schedule.'.

3.   Minor and consequential amendments related to Article 2

(1) Part IV of Schedule 1 to the Trustee Investments Act 1961 shall be amended as follows.

(2) At the end of paragraph 1, there shall be inserted the words ', in the currency of a relevant state or in the european currency unit (as defined in article 1 of Council Regulation No 3180/78/EEC)'.

(3) In paragraph 2, after the words 'the Financial Services Act 1986' there shall be inserted the words 'or on an investment exchange which constitutes the principal or only market established in a relevant state on which securities admitted to official listing are dealt in or traded'.

(4) After paragraph 2, there shall be inserted –
   '**2A.**   The securities mentioned in paragraphs 16 to 21 of Part II of this Schedule, other than securities traded on a relevant money market or securities falling within paragraph 22 of Part II of this Schedule, and the securities mentioned in paragraph 4 of Part III of this Schedule do not include –

(a) securities the price for which is not quoted on a recognised investment exchange within the meaning of the Financial Services Act 1986 or on an investment exchange which constitutes the principal or only market established in a relevant state on which securities admitted to official listing are dealt in or traded;

(b) shares or debenture stock not fully paid up (except shares or debenture stock which by the terms of issue are required to be fully paid up within nine months of the date of issue or shares issued with no nominal value).'.

(5) In paragraph 3 –

(a) after the words 'securities mentioned in paragraph 6' there shall be inserted the words 'and 21';

(b) after the words 'and paragraph 1' there shall be inserted the words 'or 4';

(c) after sub-paragraph (a), there shall be inserted –

'(ab) shares or debentures of an incorporated company of which the total issued and paid up share capital at any time on the business day before the investment is made is less than the equivalent of one million pounds in the currency of a relevant state (at the exchange rate prevailing in the United Kingdom at the close of business on the day before the investment is made);'.

(6) In paragraph 4 –

(a) after the definition of 'local authority' there shall be inserted –

'"mutual investment society" means a credit institution which operates on mutual principles and which is authorised by the appropriate supervisory authority of a relevant state;

"relevant money market" means a money market which is supervised by the central bank, or a government agency, of a relevant state;

"relevant state" means Austria, Finland, Iceland, Norway, Sweden or a member state other than the United Kingdom;';

(b) in the definition of 'securities', after the words 'units within paragraph 3' there shall be inserted the words 'or 6'.

(7) In paragraph 6, at the beginning there shall be inserted the words 'In relation to the United Kingdom,'.

(8) After paragraph 6 there shall be inserted –

'**6A.** References in this Schedule to a UCITS are references to a collective investment scheme which is constituted in a relevant state and which complies with the conditions necessary for it to enjoy the rights conferred by Council Directive 85/611/EEC co-ordinating the laws, regulations and administrative provisions relating to undertakings for collective investment in transferable securities; and section 86(8) of the Financial Services Act 1986 (meaning of 'constituted in a member state') shall apply for the purposes of this paragraph as it applies for the purposes of that section but as if for references in that section to a member state there were substituted references to a relevant state.'.

CHARITABLE INSTITUTIONS (FUND-RAISING) REGULATIONS 1994

(SI 1994/3024)

1. Citation, commencement and interpretation

(1) These Regulations may be cited as the Charitable Institutions (Fund-Raising) Regulations 1994 and shall come into force on 1 March 1995.

(2) In these Regulations, the expression –
'bank' means –
  (a) the Bank of England; or
  (b) an institution which is authorised by the Bank of England to operate a deposit-taking business under Part I of the Banking Act 1987;
'building society' means a building society which is authorised by the Building Societies Commission under section 9 of the Building Societies Act 1986 to raise money from its members.

(3) In these Regulations, any reference, in relation to an agreement made for the purposes of section 59 of the Charities Act 1992, to a charitable institution, commercial participator or professional fund-raiser, shall, unless the contrary intention appears, be construed as a reference to any charitable institution, commercial participator or professional fund-raiser, respectively, which is or who is a party to the agreement.

2. Agreements between charitable institutions and professional fund-raisers

(1) The requirements as to form and content of an agreement made for the purposes of section 59(1) of the Charities Act 1992 are those set out in the following provisions of this regulation.

(2) Such an agreement (hereinafter in this regulation referred to as 'the agreement') shall be in writing and shall be signed by or on behalf of the charitable institution and the professional fund-raiser.

(3) The agreement shall specify –
  (a) the name and address of each of the parties to the agreement;
  (b) the date on which the agreement was signed by or on behalf of each of those parties;
  (c) the period for which the agreement is to subsist;
  (d) any terms relating to the termination of the agreement prior to the date on which that period expires; and
  (e) any terms relating to the variation of the agreement during that period.

(4) The agreement shall also contain –
  (a) a statement of its principal objectives and the methods to be used in pursuit of those objectives;
  (b) if there is more than one charitable institution party to the agreement, provision as to the manner in which the proportion in which the institutions which are so party are respectively to benefit under the agreement is to be determined; and
  (c) provision as to the amount by way of remuneration or expenses which the professional fund-raiser is to be entitled to receive in respect of things done by him in pursuance of the agreement and the manner in which that amount is to be determined.

3. Agreements between charitable institutions and commercial participators

(1) The requirements as to form and content of an agreement made for the purposes of section 59(2) of the Charities Act 1992 are those set out in the following provisions of this regulation.

(2) Such an agreement (hereafter in this regulation referred to as 'the agreement') shall be in writing and shall be signed by or on behalf of the charitable institution and the commercial participator.

(3) The agreement shall specify –
  (a) the name and address of each of the parties to the agreement;
  (b) the date on which the agreement was signed by or on behalf of each of those parties;
  (c) the period for which the agreement is to subsist;
  (d) any terms relating to the termination of the agreement prior to the date on which that period expires; and
  (e) any terms relating to the variation of the agreement during that period.

(4) The agreement shall also contain –
  (a) a statement of its principal objectives and the methods to be used in pursuit of those objectives;
  (b) provision as to the manner in which are to be determined –
      (i) if there is more than one charitable institution party to the agreement, the proportion in which the institutions which are so party are respectively to benefit under the agreement; and
      (ii) the proportion of the consideration given for goods or services sold or supplied by the commercial participator, or of any other proceeds of a promotional venture undertaken by him, which is to be given to or applied for the benefit of the charitable institution, or
      (iii) the sums by way of donations by the commercial participator in connection with the sale or supply of any goods or services sold or supplied by him which are to be so given or applied,
    as the case may require; and
  (c) provision as to any amount by way of remuneration or expenses which the commercial participator is to be entitled to receive in respect of things done by him in pursuance of the agreement and the manner in which any such amount is to be determined.

(5) The statement of methods referred to in paragraph (4)(a) above shall include, in relation to each method specified, a description of the type of charitable contributions which are to be given to or applied for the benefit of the charitable institution and of the circumstances in which they are to be so given or applied.

4. Notice prior to injunction to prevent unauthorised fund-raising

A notice served under subsection (3) of section 62 of the Charities Act 1992 shall, in addition to satisfying the requirements of that subsection, specify the circumstances which gave rise to the serving of the notice and the grounds on which an application under that section is to be made.

5. Availability of books, documents or other records

(1) A professional fund-raiser or commercial participator who is a party to an agreement made for the purposes of section 59 of the Charities Act 1992 shall, on request and at all reasonable times, make available to any charitable institution which is a party to that agreement any books, documents or other records (however kept) which relate to that institution and are kept for the purposes of the agreement.

(2) In the case of any record which is kept otherwise than in legible form, the reference in paragraph (1) above to making that record available shall be construed as a reference to making it available in legible form.

6. Transmission of money and other property to charitable institutions

(1) Any money or other property acquired by a professional fund-raiser or commercial participator for the benefit of, or otherwise falling to be given to or applied by such a person for the benefit of, a charitable institution (including such money or other property as is referred to in section 64(3) of the Charities Act 1992) shall, notwithstanding any inconsistent term in an agreement made for the purposes of section 59 of that Act, be transmitted to that institution in accordance with the following provisions of this regulation.

(2) A professional fund-raiser or commercial participator holding any such money or property as is referred to in paragraph (1) above shall, unless he has a reasonable excuse –

    (a) in the case of any money, and any negotiable instrument which is payable to or to the account of the charitable institution, as soon as is reasonably practicable after its receipt and in any event not later than the expiration of 28 days after that receipt or such other period as may be agreed with the institution –

        (i) pay it to the person or persons having the general control and management of the administration of the institution; or

        (ii) pay it into an account held by a bank or building society in the name of or on behalf of the institution which is under the control of the person, or any of the persons, specified in sub-paragraph (i) above; and

    (b) in the case of any other property, deal with it in accordance with any instructions given for that purpose, either generally or in a particular case, by the charitable institution:
    Provided that –

        (i) any property in the possession of the professional fund-raiser or commercial participator either pending the obtaining of such instructions as are referred to above or in accordance with such instructions shall be securely held by him;

        (ii) the proceeds of the sale or other disposal of any property shall, from the time of their receipt by the professional fund-raiser or commercial participator, be subject to the requirements of sub-paragraph (a) above.

7. Fund-raising for charitable etc purposes otherwise than by professional fund-raisers or commercial participators

(1) This regulation applies to any person who carries on for gain a business other than a fund-raising business but, in the course of that business, engages in any promotional venture in the course of which it is represented that charitable contributions are to be applied for charitable, benevolent or philanthropic purposes of any description (rather than for the benefit of one or more particular charitable institutions).

(2) Where any person to whom this regulation applies makes a representation to the effect that charitable contributions are to be applied for such charitable, benevolent or philanthropic purposes as are mentioned in paragraph (1) above he shall, unless he has a reasonable excuse, ensure that the representation is accompanied by a statement clearly indicating –

    (a) the fact that the charitable contributions referred to in the representation are to be applied for those purposes and not for the benefit of any particular charitable institution or institutions;

    (b) (in general terms) the method by which it is to be determined –

        (i) what proportion of the consideration given for goods or services sold or supplied by him, or of any other proceeds of a promotional venture undertaken by him, is to be applied for those purposes, or

        (ii) what sums by way of donations by him in connection with the sale or supply of any such goods or services are to be so applied,

    as the case may require; and

(c) the method by which it is to be determined how the charitable contributions referred to in the representation are to be distributed between different charitable institutions.

8.   Offences and penalties

(1) Failure to comply with any of the provisions of these Regulations specified in paragraph (2) below shall be an offence punishable on summary conviction by a fine not exceeding the second level on the standard scale.

(2) The provisions referred to in paragraph (1) above are –
    (a) regulation 5(1);
    (b) regulation 6(2); and
    (c) regulation 7(2).

CHARITIES (TRUSTEE INVESTMENTS ACT 1961) ORDER 1995

(SI 1995/1092)

1. This Order may be cited as the Charities (Trustee Investments Act 1961) Order 1995 and shall come into force on the fourteenth day after the day on which it is made.

2. It is hereby directed that, in the case of a trust fund consisting of property held by or in trust for a charity, any division of the fund in pursuance of section 2(1) of the Trustee Investments Act 1961 shall be made so that the value of the wider-range part at the time of the division bears to the then value of the narrower-range part the proportion of three to one.

3. (1) The Trustee Investments Act 1961 shall, in its application in relation to a trust fund consisting of property held by or in trust for a charity, have effect subject to the modifications specified in the following paragraphs of this article, being modifications which the Secretary of State consists appropriate in consequence of, or in connection with, the direction contained in article 2 of this Order.

(2) Paragraph (b) of section 2(3) and sub-paragraph (b) of paragraph 3 of the Second Schedule shall have effect as if for the words from 'each' to the end there were substituted the words 'the wider-range part of the fund is increased by an amount which bears the specified proportion to the amount by which the value of the narrower-range part of the fund is increased'.

(3) Section 4(3) shall have effect as if for the words 'so as either to be equal, or to bear to each other' there were substituted the words 'so as to bear to each other either the specified proportion or'.

(4) Section 17 shall have effect as if at the end there were added the following subsection –
'(6) In this Act, "the specified proportion" means the proportion specified in article 2 of the Charities (Trustee Investments Act 1961) Order 1995.'.

CHARITIES ACT 1993 (SUBSTITUTION OF SUMS) ORDER 1995

(SI 1995/2696)

1.   (1) This Order may be cited as the Charities Act 1993 (Substitution of Sums) Order 1995.

(2) This article and paragraphs (1) and (2) of article 2 of this Order shall come into force on 1 December 1995 and paragraphs (3) and (4) of article 2 of this Order shall come into force on 1 March 1996.

2.   (1) The Charities Act 1993 shall be amended in accordance with the following provisions of this article.

(2) In subsection (1) of section 5 (status of registered charity (other than small charity) to appear on official publications etc), for the sum of £5,000 there shall be substituted the sum of £10,000.

(3) In subsection (3) of section 42 (annual statements of accounts), for the sum of £25,000 there shall be substituted the sum of £100,000.

(4) In subsection (1) of section 43 (annual audit or examination of charity accounts), for the sum of £100,000 there shall be substituted the sum of £250,000.

CHARITIES (ACCOUNTS AND REPORTS) REGULATIONS 1995

(SI 1995/2724)

1. Citation and commencement

These Regulations may be cited as the Charities (Accounts and Reports) Regulations 1995 and shall come into force on 1 March 1996.

2. Interpretation

(1) In these Regulations, the expression –

'common deposit fund' means a common deposit fund established by a scheme under section 25 of the 1993 Act;

'common investment fund' means a common investment fund established by a scheme under section 24 of the 1993 Act, other than a fund the trusts of which provide for property to be transferred to the fund only by or on behalf of a participating charity of which the charity trustees are the trustees appointed to manage the fund;

'financial year' shall be construed in accordance with regulation 5 below;

'institution or body corporate connected with the charity', in relation to a charity, means an institution or body corporate which –

  (a) in the case of an institution, is controlled by,

  (b) in the case of a body corporate, in which a substantial interest is held by,

    the charity or any one or more of the charity trustees acting in his or their capacity as such;

'recognised stock exchange' has the meaning assigned to it by section 841 of the Income and Corporation Taxes Act 1988; and

'the 1993 Act' means the Charities Act 1993.

(2) For the purposes of these Regulations, a person is connected with a charity trustee if –

  (a) he is the child, parent, grandchild, grandparent, brother or sister of the charity trustee;

  (b) he is the spouse of the charity trustee or of any person connected with him by virtue of sub-paragraph (a) above;

  (c) he is a trustee of any trust, not being a charity, the beneficiaries or potential beneficiaries of which include the charity trustee or any person connected with him by virtue of sub-paragraph (a) or (b) above and is acting in his capacity as such;

  (d) he is a partner of the charity trustee or of any person connected with him by virtue of sub-paragraph (a), (b) or (c) above and is acting in his capacity as such; or

  (e) the person is a body corporate, not being a company which is connected with a charitable institution within the meaning of section 58(5) of the Charities Act 1992, in which the charity trustee has, or the charity trustee and any other charity trustee or trustees or person or persons connected with him by virtue of sub-paragraph (a), (b), (c) or (d) above, taken together, have, a substantial interest.

(3) Any expression in this regulation which also appears in Schedule 5 to the 1993 Act shall be construed in accordance with paragraphs 2 to 4 of that Schedule.

3. Form and content of statements of accounts

(1) Subject to regulation 4 below, the requirements as to form and contents of a statement of accounts prepared in accordance with section 42(1) of the 1993 Act are those set out in the following provisions of this regulation.

(2) The statement shall consist of the following, that is to say –

(a) a statement of financial activities which satisfies the requirements set out in Part I of Schedule 1 to these Regulations; and

(b) a balance sheet which satisfies the requirements set out in Part II of that Schedule.

(3) The statement shall be prepared in accordance with the methods and principles specified and referred to in Part III of Schedule 1 to these Regulations.

(4) There shall be provided by way of notes to the accounts the information specified in Part IV of Schedule 1 to these Regulations.

(5) Part V of Schedule 1 to these Regulations shall have effect for the purposes of defining expressions used in that Schedule.

(6) The balance sheet shall be signed by one or more of the charity trustees of the charity, each of whom has been authorised to do so, and shall specify the date on which the accounts to which the statement relates were approved by the charity trustees.

4.   Form and contents: special cases

(1) In the case of a common investment fund or a common deposit fund which is deemed to be a charity by virtue of section 24(8), including that subsection as applied by section 25(2), of the 1993 Act, the requirements as to form and contents of a statement of accounts prepared in accordance with section 42(1) of the 1993 Act are those set out in paragraphs (2) to (6) below.

(2) Subject to paragraph (8) below, the statement shall consist of the following, that is to say –

(a) a statement of total return which satisfies the requirements set out in Part I of Schedule 2 to these Regulations;

(b) a statement of movement in funds which satisfies the requirements set out in Part II of Schedule 2 to these Regulations; and

(c) a balance sheet which satisfies the requirements set out in Part III of Schedule 2 to these Regulations.

(3) The statement shall be prepared in accordance with the methods and principles specified and referred to in Part IV of Schedule 2 to these Regulations.

(4) There shall be provided by way of notes to the accounts the information specified in Part V of Schedule 2 to these Regulations.

(5) Part VI of Schedule 2 to these Regulations shall have effect for the purposes of defining expressions used in that Schedule.

(6) The balance sheet shall be signed by one or more of the trustees appointed to manage the fund, each of whom has been authorised to do so, and shall specify the date on which the accounts to which the statement relates were approved by the trustees appointed to manage the fund in accordance with the scheme by which the fund was established.

(7) In the case of a charity which –

(a) is a registered housing association within the meaning of the Housing Associations Act 1985 and whose registration has been recorded under section 5(3) of that Act; or

(b) has during the financial year in question –

(i) conducted an institution in relation to which a designation made, or having effect as if made, under section 129 of the Education Reform Act 1988 or section 28 of the Further and Higher Education Act 1992 has effect;

(ii) received financial support from funds administered by a higher education funding council or further education funding council within the meaning of that Act of 1992 in respect of expenditure incurred or to be incurred by the charity in connection with that institution; and

(iii) incurred no expenditure for charitable purposes other than the purposes of that institution or any other such institution,

the requirements as to form and contents of a statement of accounts prepared in pursuance of section 42(1) of the 1993 Act are that the statement shall consist of a balance sheet as at the end of the financial year in respect of which the statement of accounts is prepared and an income and expenditure account.

(8) In the case of any financial year of a common deposit fund in which there are no gains or losses on disposal or revaluation of assets, paragraph (2) above shall have effect as if sub-paragraph (b) were omitted.

5. Financial year

(1) The financial year of a charity shall, for the purposes of the 1993 Act and regulations made thereunder, be determined in accordance with the following provisions of this regulation.

(2) The first financial year of a charity shall be –
   (a) in the case of a charity which is established before the date on which these Regulations come into force, the period beginning with the day immediately following the end of the period in respect of which a statement of accounts was required to be prepared under any statutory provision contained in or having effect under an Act of Parliament applicable to that charity before the coming into force of section 42 of the 1993 Act and ending with the accounting reference date of the charity or such other date, not more than seven days before or after the accounting reference date, as the charity trustees may determine;
   (b) in the case of a charity which is established on or after the date on which these Regulations come into force, the period beginning with the day on which the charity is established and ending with the accounting reference date of the charity or such other date, not more than seven days before or after the accounting reference date, as the charity trustees may determine.

(3) Subsequent financial years of a charity begin with the day immediately following the end of the charity's previous financial year and end with its accounting reference date or such other date, not more than seven days before or after the accounting reference date, as the charity trustees may determine.

(4) The accounting reference date of a charity shall, for the purposes of this regulation, be –
   (a) in the first financial year of a charity which is established before the date on which these Regulations come into force, such date, not less than 6 months nor more than 18 months after the date on which that financial year began, as the charity trustees may determine;
   (b) in the first financial year of a charity which is established on or after the date on which these Regulations come into force, such date, not less than 6 months nor more than 18 months after the date on which the charity was established, as the charity trustees may determine;
   (c) in any subsequent financial year of a charity, the date 12 months after the previous accounting reference date of the charity or such other date, not less than 6 months nor more than 18 months after the previous accounting reference date of the charity as the trustees may determine:
Provided that –
   (i) the charity trustees shall not exercise their powers under sub-paragraph (c) of this paragraph so as to determine an accounting reference date in respect of any financial year which is consecutive, or follows immediately after a financial year which is consecutive, to a previous financial year in respect of which that power was exercised; and

(ii) the charity trustees shall exercise their powers under sub-paragraph (a) or (c) of this paragraph so as to determine a date earlier or later than 12 months from the beginning of the financial year only where satisfied that there are exceptional reasons to do so (which reasons shall, in the case of a charity subject to the requirements of regulation 3(4) or 4(4) above, be disclosed in a note to the accounts).

6.   Annual audit of charity accounts

(1) The duties of an auditor carrying out an audit of the accounts of a charity under section 43 of the 1993 Act shall be those specified in the following provisions of this regulation.

(2) Where a statement of accounts has been prepared under section 42(1) of the 1993 Act for the financial year in question the auditor shall make a report on that statement to the charity trustees which –
   (a) states the name and address of the auditor and the name of the charity concerned;
   (b) is signed by him or, where the office of auditor is held by a body corporate or partnership, in its name by a person authorised to sign on its behalf and states that the auditor is a person falling within paragraph (a) or, as the case may be, (b) of section 43(2) of the 1993 Act;
   (c) is dated and specifies the financial year in respect of which the accounts to which it relates have been prepared;
   (d) specifies that it is a report in respect of an audit carried out under section 43 of the 1993 Act and in accordance with regulations made under section 44 of that Act;
   (e) states whether in the auditor's opinion the statement of accounts complies with the requirements of regulation 3 or, as the case may be, 4, above and gives a true and fair view of the state of affairs of the charity at the end of the financial year in question and of the incoming resources and application of the resources of the charity in that year;
   (f) where the auditor has formed the opinion –
      (i) that accounting records have not been kept in respect of the charity in accordance with section 41 of the 1993 Act; or
      (ii) that the statement of accounts does not accord with those records; or
      (iii) that any information contained in the statement of accounts is inconsistent in any material respect with any report of the charity trustees prepared under section 45 of the 1993 Act in respect of the financial year in question; or
      (iv) that any information or explanation to which he is entitled under regulation 8 below has not been afforded to him,
      contains a statement of that opinion and of his grounds for forming it.

(3) Where a receipts and payments account and statement of assets and liabilities have been prepared under section 42(3) of the 1993 Act for the financial year in question the auditor shall make a report on that account and statement to the charity trustees which –
   (a) states the name and address of the auditor and the name of the charity concerned;
   (b) is signed by him or, where the office of auditor is held by a body corporate or partnership, in its name by a person authorised to sign on its behalf and states that the auditor is a person falling within paragraph (a) or, as the case may be, (b) of section 43(2) of the 1993 Act;
   (c) is dated and specifies the financial year in respect of which the accounts to which it relates have been prepared;
   (d) specifies that it is a report in respect of an audit carried out under section 43 of the 1993 Act and in accordance with regulations made under section 44 of that Act;
   (e) states whether in the auditor's opinion –
      (i) the account and statement properly present the receipts and payments of the charity for the financial year in question and its assets and liabilities as at the end of that year; and

(ii) the account and statement adequately distinguish any material special trust or other restricted fund of the charity;

(f) where the auditor has formed the opinion –

(i) that accounting records have not been kept in respect of the charity in accordance with section 41 of the 1993 Act; or

(ii) that the account and statement do not accord with those records; or

(iii) that any information or explanation to which he is entitled under regulation 8 below has not been afforded to him,

contains a statement of that opinion and of his grounds for forming it.

(4) The auditor shall, in preparing his report for the purposes of paragraph (2) or, as the case may be, (3) above, carry out such investigations as will enable him to form an opinion as to the matters specified in sub-paragraph (e) and (f) of that paragraph.

(5) The auditor shall communicate to the Commissioners, in writing, any matter of which the auditor becomes aware in his capacity as such which relates to the activities or affairs of the charity or of any institution or body corporate connected with the charity and which the auditor has reasonable cause to believe is, or is likely to be, of material significance for the exercise, in relation to the charity of the Commissioners' functions under section 8 (general power to institute inquiries) or 18 (power to act for protection of charities) of the 1993 Act.

(6) Where an auditor appointed by charity trustees ceases for any reason to hold office he shall send to the charity trustees a statement of any circumstances connected with his ceasing to hold office which he considers should be brought to their attention or, if he considers that there are no such circumstances, a statement that there are none; and the auditor shall send a copy of any statement sent to the charity trustees under this paragraph (except a statement that there are no such circumstances) to the Commissioners.

(7) In the case of an auditor appointed by the Commissioners, the report required by paragraph (2) or, as the case may be, (3) above shall be made to the Commissioners instead of to the charity trustees.

7.   Independent examination of charity accounts

An independent examiner who has carried out an examination of the accounts of a charity under section 43 of the 1993 Act shall make a report to the charity trustees which –

(a) states his name and address and the name of the charity concerned;

(b) is signed by him and specifies any relevant professional qualifications or professional body of which he is a member;

(c) is dated and specifies the financial year in respect of which the accounts to which it relates have been prepared;

(d) specifies that it is a report in respect of an examination carried out under section 43 of the 1993 Act and in accordance with any directions given by the Commissioners under subsection (7)(b) of that section which are applicable;

(e) states whether or not any matter has come to the examiner's attention in connection with the examination which gives him reasonable cause to believe that in any material respect –

(i) accounting records have not been kept in respect of the charity in accordance with section 41 of the 1993 Act; or

(ii) the accounts do not accord with those records; or

(iii) in the case of an examination of accounts a statement of which has been prepared under section 42(1) of the 1993 Act, the statement of accounts does not comply with any of the requirements of regulation 3 or, as the case may be, 4 above except the requirements specified in paragraph 1 of Part III of Schedule 1 to these Regulations;

(f) states whether or not any matter has come to the examiner's attention in connection with the examination to which, in his opinion, attention should be drawn in the report in order to enable a proper understanding of the accounts to be reached;

(g) where any of the following matters has become apparent to the examiner during the course of the examination, namely, that –

    (i) there has been any material expenditure or action which appears not to be in accordance with the trusts of the charity; or

    (ii) any information or explanation to which he is entitled under regulation 8 below has not been afforded to him; or

    (iii) in the case of an examination of accounts a statement of which has been prepared under section 42(1) of the 1993 Act, any information contained in the statement of accounts is inconsistent in any material respect with any report of the charity trustees prepared under section 45 of the 1993 Act in respect of the financial year in question,

contains a statement to that effect.

8.   Audit and independent examination: supplementary provisions

(1) An auditor or independent examiner carrying out an audit or examination of the accounts of a charity under section 43 of the 1993 Act shall have a right of access to any books, documents and other records (however kept) which relate to the charity concerned and which the auditor or examiner in question considers it necessary to inspect for the purposes of carrying out the audit or, as the case may be, examination.

(2) Such an auditor or independent examiner shall be entitled to require, in the case of the charity concerned, such information and explanations from past or present charity trustees or trustees for the charity, or from past or present officers or employees of the charity, as he considers it necessary to obtain for the purposes of carrying out the audit or, as the case may be, examination.

9.   Dispensations from audit or examination requirements

(1) The Commissioners may, in the circumstances specified in paragraph (2) below, dispense with the requirements of section 43(2) or (3) of the 1993 Act in the case of a particular charity or of a particular financial year of a charity.

(2) The circumstances referred to in paragraph (1) above are where the Commissioners:

(a) are satisfied that the accounts of the charity concerned are required to be audited in accordance with any statutory provision contained in or having effect under an Act of Parliament which, in the opinion of the Commissioners, imposes requirements which are sufficiently similar to the requirements of section 43(2) for those requirements to be dispensed with;

(b) are satisfied that the accounts of the charity concerned have been audited by the Comptroller and Auditor General;

(c) are satisfied that the accounts of the charity concerned for the financial year in question have been audited or, as the case may be, examined in accordance with requirements or arrangements which, in the opinion of the Commissioners, are sufficiently similar to the relevant requirements of section 43 of the 1993 Act applicable to that financial year of that charity for those requirements to be dispensed with;

(d) are satisfied that there has in the financial year in question been no transaction on the part of the charity concerned which would be required to be shown and explained in the accounting records kept in pursuance of section 41 of the 1993 Act;

(e) consider that, although the financial year in question of the charity concerned is one to which subsection (2) of section 43 of the 1993 Act applies, there are exceptional circumstances which justify the examination of the accounts by an independent examiner instead of their audit in accordance with that subsection, and the accounts have been so examined,

and where the charity trustees of the charity concerned have supplied to the Commissioners any report made to them with respect to the accounts of that charity for the financial year in question which the Commissioners have requested.

10.   Annual reports

(1) Subject to paragraph (4) below, the report on the activities of a charity during the year which is required to be contained in the annual report in respect of each financial year of the charity prepared under section 45 of the 1993 Act shall specify the financial year to which it relates and shall –

(a)   in the case of any financial year of a charity in which its gross income does not exceed £100,000, be a brief summary of the main activities and achievements of the charity during the year in relation to its objects;

(b)   in the case of any financial year of a charity in which its gross income exceeds £100,000, be a review of all activities, including material transactions, significant developments, and achievements, of the charity during the year in relation to its objects, any significant changes in those activities during the year, any important events affecting those activities which have occurred since the end of the year and any likely future developments in those activities; and

(c)   in either case, be dated and be signed by one or more of the charity trustees, each of whom has been authorised to do so.

(2) Subject to paragraphs (4), (5) and (6) below, the information relating to a charity and to its trustees and officers which is required to be contained in that annual report shall be –

(a)   the name of the charity as it appears in the register and any other name by which it makes itself known;

(b)   the number assigned to it in the register and, in the case of a charitable company, the number with which it is registered as a company;

(c)   the principal address of the charity and, in the case of a charitable company, the address of its registered office;

(d)   a description of the trusts of the charity;

(e)   the names of the charity trustees or, in the case of a charity having more than 50 charity trustees, the names of 50 of those trustees including any charity trustee who is also an officer of the charity and the name of any other person who has at any time during the financial year in question been a charity trustee and of any person or body entitled to appoint a charity trustee of the charity;

(f)   a description of the organisational structure of the charity; and

(g)   a description of any assets held by the charity, or on behalf of the charity by any trustee of the charity, for another charity, and particulars of any special arrangements made with respect to the safe custody of such assets and their segregation from assets of the charity not so held and of the objects of the charity on whose behalf the assets are held.

(3) The Commissioners may, where they are satisfied that, in the case of a particular charity or class of charities, or of a particular financial year of a charity or class of charities, –

(a)   the disclosure of the name of any person whose name is required by paragraph (2)(e) above to be contained in the annual report of a charity could lead to that person being placed in any personal danger; or

(b)   the disclosure of the principal address of the charity in accordance with paragraph (2)(c) above could lead to any such person being placed in any personal danger,

dispense with the requirement –

(i)   in sub-paragraph (e) of that paragraph so far as it applies to the name of any such person; or

(ii) in sub-paragraph (c) of that paragraph so far as it applies to the principal address of the charity,

as the case may require.

(4) In the case of a common investment fund or a common deposit fund which is deemed to be a charity by virtue of section 24(8), including that section as applied by section 25(2), of the 1993 Act, this regulation shall have effect as if –

(a) for sub-paragraphs (a) to (c) of paragraph (1) above there were substituted the following sub-paragraphs:

'(a)   be a review of the investment activities and policies of the trustees during that year;

(b)   contain particulars of any significant alteration in the terms of the scheme by which the fund was established or in the investment policies of the trustees during that year;

(c)   specify any material events affecting the fund which have occurred since the end of the year;

(d)   contain a statement as to whether the trustees have examined whether any person to whom they have delegated their functions in respect of the management of the fund has complied with the terms of the scheme by which the fund was established and with any agreement between the trustees and that person;

(e)   be dated and signed by one or more of the trustees appointed to manage the fund, each of whom has been authorised to do so.';

(b) for sub-paragraph (e) of paragraph (2) above there were substituted the following sub-paragraph:

'(e)   the names and any professional qualifications of the trustees appointed to manage the fund and any other person who has been a trustee of the fund during the financial year in question and of any person or body entitled to appoint such a trustee;';

(c) for sub-paragraph (g) of paragraph (2) above there were substituted the following sub-paragraphs:

'(g)   the name and address of any person to whom the trustees have delegated their functions in respect of the management of the fund or the holding of property transferred to, or sums deposited in, the fund or whom they have appointed to advise them on investment matters;

(h)   the name of any regulatory body of which any person referred to in sub-paragraph (g) above is a member; and

(i)   a description of any powers delegated by the trustees and of the procedures adopted to ensure that those powers are exercised consistently with the scheme by which the fund was established and the investment policies of the trustees.'; and

(d) paragraph (3) were omitted.

(5) In the case of a report prepared under section 46(5) of the 1993 Act (excepted charities which are not registered), paragraph (2) above shall have effect as if –

(a) in sub-paragraph (a) the words from 'as it appears in the register' to the end, and

(b) in sub-paragraph (b) the words 'the number assigned to it in the register and,',

were omitted.

(6) In the case of a report in respect of a financial year of a charity in which its gross income does not exceed £100,000, paragraph (2) above shall have effect as if sub-paragraphs (f) and (g) were omitted.

SCHEDULE 1   Regulation 3

FORM AND CONTENTS OF STATEMENTS OF ACCOUNTS

PART I

Statement of Financial Activities

1. The statement of financial activities shall show the total incoming resources and application of the resources, together with any other movements in the total resources, of the charity during the financial year in respect of which the statement of accounts is prepared.

2. The information required by paragraph 1 above shall be analysed by reference to –
   (a) the nature of the incoming resources or application of or movements in resources concerned, in accordance with paragraph 3 below; and
   (b) the type of fund to which it relates, in accordance with paragraph 4 below.

3. Subject to paragraph 5 below, the analysis required by paragraph 2(a) above is as follows:
   (a) all incoming resources other than those required to be entered by sub-paragraph (e) below, divided into –
      (i) incoming resources from donors;
      (ii) income from investment;
      (iii) income from trading activities –
         (A) which are in furtherance of the objects of the charity, and
         (B) which are for commercial or fund-raising purposes; and
      (iv) any other incoming resources;
   (b) all resources expended, divided into –
      (i) expenditure directly relating to the objects of the charity;
      (ii) expenditure on fund-raising and publicity; and
      (iii) expenditure on the cost of managing and administering the charity;
   (c) gross transfers between the funds of the charity;
   (d) net incoming or outgoing resources for the financial year before calculation of gains or losses on disposal of fixed assets intended for investment or on revaluation of fixed assets intended for use or investment (that is to say, the aggregate of all amounts entered in pursuance of sub-paragraphs (a), (b) and (c) above);
   (e) any gains or losses on disposal of fixed assets intended for investment or on revaluation of fixed assets intended for use or investment, divided into –
      (i) gains or losses on disposal of assets intended for investment;
      (ii) unrealised gains or losses on revaluation of assets intended for investment; and
      (iii) unrealised gains or losses on revaluation of assets intended for use;
   (f) net movement in funds in the financial year (that is to say, the total of all entries made in pursuance of sub-paragraphs (d) and (e) above);
   (g) the total of funds brought forward from the previous financial year; and
   (h) the total of funds carried forward to the next financial year (that is to say, the amount entered in pursuance of sub-paragraph (f) above plus the amount entered in pursuance of sub-paragraph (g) above).

4. The analysis required by paragraph 2(b) above is as follows:
   (a) unrestricted income funds;
   (b) income funds which are restricted as to their use;

(c) capital funds; and

(d) the total for all funds of the charity (that is to say, the total of the amounts entered in pursuance of sub-paragraphs (a), (b) and (c) above).

5.   In the case of any financial year of a charity in which the gross income of the charity does not exceed £100,000 but in respect of which the charity trustees have made no election in pursuance of section 42(3) of the 1993 Act, paragraph 3(b) above shall have effect as if for the words from 'divided into' to the end there were substituted the words 'divided into such categories as reasonably enable the user to gain an appreciation of the expenditure of the charity during the year'.

PART II

Balance Sheet

1.   The balance sheet shall show, by reference to the information specified in paragraph 2 below, the state of affairs of the charity as at the end of the financial year in respect of which the statement of accounts is prepared.

2.   The information referred to in paragraph 1 above is as follows:
   (a) fixed assets, divided into –
      (i)   intangible assets;
      (ii) tangible assets for use by the charity; and
      (iii) investments; and
   (b) current assets, divided into –
      (i)   stock and work in progress;
      (ii) debtors;
      (iii) investments; and
      (iv) cash at bank and in hand;
   (c) short-term creditors;
   (d) net current assets or liabilities (that is to say, the difference between the total amount entered in pursuance of sub-paragraph (b) above and the total amount entered in pursuance of sub-paragraph (c) above);
   (e) total assets after deduction of current liabilities (that is to say, the total amount entered in pursuance of sub-paragraph (a) above plus the amount entered in pursuance of sub-paragraph (d) above);
   (f) long term creditors;
   (g) provisions for liabilities or charges;
   (h) net assets (that is to say, the amount entered in pursuance of sub-paragraph (e) above less the total amounts entered in pursuance of sub-paragraphs (f) and (g) above); and
   (i) funds of the charity, divided into –
      (i)   unrestricted income funds;
      (ii) income funds which are restricted as to their use; and
      (iii) capital funds.

PART III

Methods and Principles

1.   (1) The statement of financial activities shall give a true and fair view of the incoming resources and application of the resources of the charity in, and the balance sheet shall give a true and fair view of the state of affairs of the charity at the end of, the financial year in respect of which the statement of accounts is prepared.

(2) Where compliance with Part I, or, as the case may be, Part II and Part IV of this Schedule would not be sufficient to give a true and fair view, the necessary additional information shall be given in the accounts or a note to them.

(3) If in special circumstances compliance with any of those provisions is inconsistent with the requirement to give a true and fair view, the charity trustees shall depart from that provision to the extent necessary to give a true and fair view; particulars of any such departure, the reasons for it and its effect shall be given in a note to the accounts.

2. (1) In respect of every amount required by paragraph 3 or 4(d) of Part I of this Schedule to be shown in the statement of financial activities or by Part II of this Schedule to be shown in the balance sheet, the corresponding amount for the financial year immediately preceding that to which the statement or balance sheet relates shall also be shown.

(2) Where that corresponding amount is not comparable with the amount to be shown for the item in question in respect of the financial year to which the statement of financial activities or balance sheet relates, the former amount shall be adjusted; particulars of any material adjustment under this sub-paragraph shall be disclosed in a note to the accounts.

(3) Where in the financial year to which the statement of accounts relates there is nothing required to be shown by one or more of the provisions specified in sub-paragraph (1) above but an amount was required to be shown by that provision in the immediately preceding financial year, this paragraph shall have effect as if such an amount were required to be shown in the financial year to which the statement of accounts relates and that amount were nil.

3. The values of assets and liabilities of the charity shall, for the purposes of entry in the accounts, be determined in accordance with the methods and principles for inclusion of assets and liabilities in the balance sheet set out in the Statement of Recommended Practice for Accounting by Charities issued in October 1995.

PART IV

Notes to the Accounts

1. Subject to paragraph 2 below, the information to be provided by way of notes to the accounts shall, insofar as not provided in the statement of accounts, be as follows:
   (a) a description of the accounting policies of, and assumptions made for the purposes of preparing the statement of accounts by, the charity trustees, including any material change in these, the reason for such change and its effect (if material) on the accounts;
   (b) a description of the nature and purpose of all significant funds of the charity;
   (c) a statement as to whether any remuneration or other benefits (together with the amount of such remuneration or, as the case may be, the monetary value of such benefits) has been paid or is payable to any charity trustee or person connected with such a trustee directly or indirectly from the funds of the charity or from the property of any institution or body corporate connected with the charity and the name of that person;
   (d) particulars of the cost to the charity of –
      (i) any policies of insurance against loss arising from the neglect or default of any of the charity trustees or trustees for the charity; of
      (ii) indemnifying the charity trustees, or any of the trustees, for the charity in respect of the consequences of any such loss;
   (e) particulars of any transaction undertaken in the name of or on behalf of the charity in which any charity trustee or person connected with such a trustee has a material interest;

(f) a description of any incoming resources which represent capital, according to whether or not that capital is permanent endowment;

(g) an itemised analysis of any material movement between any of the restricted funds of the charity, or between a restricted and an unrestricted fund of the charity, together with an explanation of the nature and purpose of each of those funds;

(h) the name of any institution or body corporate connected with the charity, together with a description of the nature of the charity's relationship with that institution or body corporate and of its activities, including, where material, its turnover and net profit or loss for the corresponding financial year of the institution or body corporate and any qualification expressed in an auditor's report on its accounts;

(i) particulars of any loan or guarantee secured against any of the assets of the charity;

(j) particulars of any remuneration paid to an auditor or independent examiner in respect of auditing or examining the accounts of the charity and particulars of any remuneration paid to him in respect of any other services rendered to the charity;

(k) such particulars of any grant made by the charity to another institution of which the Statement of Recommended Practice for Accounting by Charities issued in October 1995 requires disclosure as may be required by that Statement;

(l) an analysis of any entry in the balance sheet relating to fixed assets –

    (i) in the case of tangible assets for use by the charity, according to the following categories –

        (A) freehold interests in land and buildings;

        (B) any other interest in land or buildings;

        (C) plant and machinery;

        (D) fixtures, fittings and equipment; and

        (E) payments on account and assets in course of construction;

    (ii) in the case of investments, according to the following categories –

        (A) investment properties;

        (B) investments listed on a recognised stock exchange;

        (C) investments in a common deposit fund, a common investment fund or any other collective investment scheme within the meaning of section 75 of the Financial Services Act 1986;

        (D) investments in an institution or body corporate connected with the charity;

        (E) securities which are not listed on a recognised stock exchange;

        (F) cash; and

        (G) other investments;

    (iii) in the case of any such entry, which records –

        (A) the aggregate value of assets specified in each of paragraphs (i) to (iii) of paragraph 2(a) of Part II of this Schedule at the beginning of the financial year to which the balance sheet relates and at the date of the balance sheet, determined in accordance with the methods and principles specified in paragraph 3 of Part III of this Schedule but without making provision for depreciation or diminution in value;

        (B) the effect on the entry in the balance sheet made in pursuance of each of those paragraphs of any acquisitions, disposals or transfers of assets, or revisions in their recorded value, made during that financial year; and

        (C) the cumulative amount of provisions for depreciation or diminution in value of assets specified in each of those paragraphs as at each of the dates referred to in sub-paragraph (A) above, the amount of any such provisions made in respect of that financial year, the amount of any adjustments made in respect of any such provisions during that year in consequence of the disposal of any assets and the amount of any other adjustments made in respect of any such provisions during that year;

(m) an analysis of any entry in the balance sheet relating to debtors, according to the following categories –
  (i) trade debtors;
  (ii) amounts owed by any institution or body corporate connected with the charity;
  (iii) other debtors; and
  (iv) prepayments and accrued income;

(n) an analysis of any entry in the balance sheet relating to creditors (whether short-term or long-term creditors), according to the following categories –
  (i) loans and overdrafts;
  (ii) trade creditors;
  (iii) amounts owed to any institution or body corporate connected with the charity;
  (iv) other creditors; and
  (v) accruals and deferred income;

(o) the following particulars of any contingent liability, that is to say, its amount or estimated amount, its legal nature and whether any valuable security has been provided by the charity in connection with that liability and, if so, what;

(p) particulars of any other financial commitments which have not been provided for and are relevant to assessment of the state of affairs of the charity;

(q) in the case of any amount required by any of the preceding sub-paragraphs (other than sub-paragraph (g), (k) or (l)(iii)) to be disclosed, the corresponding amount for the financial year immediately preceding that to which the accounts relate;

(r) a statement as to whether or not the accounts have been prepared in accordance with any applicable accounting standards and statements of recommended practice and particulars of any material departure from those standards and practices and the reasons for such departure;

(s) where the charity trustees have exercised their powers under regulation 5(4)(a) or (c) above, a statement of their reasons for doing so; and

(t) any other information which is required by these Regulations to be disclosed in a note to the accounts or which may reasonably assist the user to understand the statement of accounts.

2. Sub-paragraphs (d) and (r) of paragraph 1 above shall not apply in the case of any financial year of a charity in which the gross income of the charity does not exceed £100,000 but in respect of which the charity trustees have made no election in pursuance of section 42(3) of the 1993 Act.

PART V

Interpretation

1. In this Schedule the following expressions have the meanings hereafter assigned to them –
'fixed assets' means the assets of a charity which are intended for use or investment on a continuing basis;
'long-term creditor' means an amount falling due after more than one year from the end of the financial year;
'provisions for liabilities or charges' means any amount retained as reasonably necessary for the purpose of providing for any liability or loss which is either likely to be incurred, or certain to be incurred but uncertain as to amount or as to the date on which it will arise;
'resources expended' means all charges relating to the financial year in respect of which the statement of accounts is prepared, including provision for depreciation and permanent diminution in value of fixed assets, calculated on the basis that the charity is carrying on its activities as a going concern; and

'short-term creditor' means an amount falling due within one year.

2.   For the purposes of paragraph 1 above, an amount shall be treated as falling due on the earliest date on which payment of any part of it may be required by the person entitled to payment, if he exercised all options and rights available to him.

SCHEDULE 2   Regulation 4

FORM AND CONTENTS OF STATEMENTS OF ACCOUNTS: COMMON INVESTMENT FUNDS AND COMMON DEPOSIT FUNDS

PART I

Statement of Total Return

1.   The statement of total return shall show the net gain or loss on investments, gross income, total expenditure and total return of the fund, and the total amount distributed or due, including interest paid or payable, to participating charities out of the fund, during the financial year in respect of which the statement of accounts is prepared.

2.   The information required by paragraph 1 above shall be analysed by reference to –
   (a) net gains or losses on investments, indicated by –
       (i)   gains or losses on investments sold during the financial year in question, based on the historical cost of the investment sold;
       (ii) any net appreciation or depreciation of such investments recognised in earlier accounting periods;
       (iii) the gains or losses on such investments based on their value as shown in the accounts (that is to say, the difference between or, as the case may be, the sum of the amounts entered in pursuance of paragraphs (i) and (ii) above); and
       (iv) net unrealised appreciation or depreciation of investments during the financial year in question;
   (b) gains or losses on other assets;
   (c) gross income, divided into –
       (i)   dividends in respect of shares;
       (ii) scrip dividends;
       (iii) interest on securities;
       (iv) interest on deposits at banks and building societies;
       (v)   underwriting commission; and
       (vi) other income;
   (d) expenditure incurred in the administration of the scheme under which the fund was established, divided into –
       (i)   amounts payable directly or indirectly by way of remuneration, reimbursement of expenses or otherwise to any trustee appointed to manage the fund or person connected with such a trustee;
       (ii) amounts payable directly or indirectly by way of remuneration, reimbursement of expenses or otherwise to any person to whom the trustees have delegated their functions in relation to management of the fund or to any person connected with that person;

      (iii) fees payable in respect of any audit carried out by an auditor under section 43 of the 1993 Act;

      (iv) any fees payable to the person carrying out such an audit in respect of other services for the fund provided by him;

      (v) any fees payable in respect of the safe custody of assets; and

      (vi) other expenditure divided into such categories as reasonably enable the user to gain an appreciation of the expenditure incurred;

  (e) tax borne by the fund in respect of income, profits or gains during the financial year in question, divided into –

      (i) income tax or capital gains tax to which the fund is liable in the United Kingdom; and

      (ii) overseas tax;

  (f) net income (that is to say, the total amount entered in pursuance of sub-paragraph (c) above less the total of the amounts entered in pursuance of sub-paragraphs (d) and (e) above);

  (g) total return (that is to say, the total of the amounts entered in pursuance of sub-paragraphs (a), (b) and (f) above);

  (h) the amount distributed or due in respect of income and accumulation shares, and interest paid or payable to charities who have deposited sums, during the financial year in question; and

  (i) net increase or decrease in the value of the fund resulting from its activities (that is to say, the difference between the amounts entered in pursuance of sub-paragraphs (g) and (h) above).

3.   In the case of a common investment fund established by a scheme which, in pursuance of section 24(5) of the 1993 Act, includes provision for enabling sums to be deposited by or on behalf of a charity on the basis that (subject to the provisions of the scheme) the charity shall be entitled to repayment of the sums deposited and to interest thereon at a rate determined by or under the scheme, the analysis required by paragraph 2 above shall distinguish between the amount of capital and income to be shared between charities participating otherwise than by way of deposit and the amounts excluded from such amount under provision made in pursuance of section 24(5) of the 1993 Act (that is, such amounts as are from time to time reasonably required in respect of the liabilities of the fund for the repayment of deposits and for the interest on deposits, including amounts required by way of reserve).

4.   In respect of any information required by a sub-paragraph of paragraph 2 above to be divided into separate categories denoted by paragraphs of that sub-paragraph, the division of that information into such separate categories may, if the trustees appointed to manage the fund so elect, be effected by means of a note to the accounts made in pursuance of Part V of this Schedule rather than by division in pursuance of that sub-paragraph.

PART II

Statement of Movement in Funds

1.   The statement of movement in funds shall provide a reconciliation between the net assets of the fund at the beginning of the financial year in respect of which the statement of accounts is prepared and the net assets of the fund at the end of that year.

2.   The reconciliation referred to in paragraph 1 above shall show –

  (a) the value of the net assets at the beginning of the financial year in question;

  (b) in the case of a common investment fund, the amount or value of any property transferred to or withdrawn from the fund during that year by participating charities;

(c) the net increase or decrease in the value of the fund resulting from its activities during that
year (that is to say, the amount entered in pursuance of sub-paragraph (i) of paragraph 2 of
Part I of this Schedule);

(d) in the case of a common investment fund, the amount of any distribution of income due in
respect of accumulation shares; and

(e) the value of the net assets at the end of the financial year in question.

3.   In the case of a common investment fund such as is described in paragraph 3 of Part I of this
Schedule, the analysis required by paragraph 2 above shall distinguish between the amount of
capital and income to be shared between charities participating otherwise than by way of deposit
and the amounts excluded from such amount under provision made in pursuance of section 24(5)
of the 1993 Act.

PART III

Balance Sheet

1.   The balance sheet shall show, by reference to the information specified in paragraph 2 or, as
the case may be, 3 below, the state of affairs of the fund as at the end of the financial year.

2.   Subject to paragraph 4 below, in the case of a common investment fund, the information
referred to in paragraph 1 above is as follows:

(a) tangible fixed assets for use by the fund;

(b) investments;

(c) current assets, divided into –
   (i)   debtors;
   (ii) deposits and loans;
   (iii) cash at bank and in hand; and
   (iv) others;

(d) liabilities, divided into –
   (i)   creditors;
   (ii) bank overdrafts;
   (iii) other loans; and
   (iv) distributions payable to participating charities;

(e) net current assets less liabilities (that is to say, the difference between the total amount
entered in pursuance of sub-paragraph (c) above and the total entered in pursuance of
sub-paragraph (d) above); and

(f) net assets (that is to say, the total of the amounts entered in pursuance of sub-paragraphs (a),
(b) and (e) above); and

(g) total funds of the common investment fund.

3.   In the case of a common deposit fund, the information referred to in paragraph 1 above is as
follows:

(a) cash at bank and in hand;

(b) debtors;

(c) deposits and investments, divided into –
   (i)   deposits at building societies within the meaning of the Building Societies Act 1986;
   (ii) deposits at the Bank of England or any institution which is authorised by the Bank of
England to operate a deposit-taking business under Part I of the Banking Act 1987;
   (iii) other bank deposits;
   (iv) other deposits; and
   (v)   other investments;

(d) current assets not included in any of paragraphs (a) to (c) above;

(e) tangible fixed assets for use by the fund;

(f) gross assets (that is to say, the total of the amounts entered in pursuance of sub-paragraphs (a) to (e) above);

(g) sums deposited by participating charities;

(h) other liabilities, divided into –

  (i) creditors;

  (ii) bank overdrafts;

  (iii) other loans; and

  (iv) interest accrued or payable to participating charities;

(i) total liabilities (that is to say, the total of the amounts entered in pursuance of sub-paragraphs (g) and (h) above); and

(j) total funds of the common deposit fund (that is to say, the amount entered in pursuance of sub-paragraph (f) above less the amount entered in pursuance of sub-paragraph (i) above).

4. In the case of a common investment fund such as is described in paragraph 3 of Part I of this Schedule, the information referred to in paragraph 1 above is –

(a) in relation to the amount of capital and income to be shared between charities participating otherwise than by way of deposit, the information specified in paragraph 2 above; and

(b) in relation to the amounts excluded from such amount under provision made in pursuance of section 24(5) of the 1993 Act, the information specified in paragraph 3 above.

5. In respect of any information required by sub-paragraph (c) of paragraph 3 above to be divided into separate categories denoted by paragraphs of that sub-paragraph, the division of that information into such separate categories may, if the trustees appointed to manage the fund so elect, be effected by means of a note to the accounts made in pursuance of Part V of this Schedule rather than by division in pursuance of that sub-paragraph.

PART IV

Methods and Principles

1. The methods and principles specified and referred to in Part III of Schedule 1 to these Regulations shall apply for the purposes of the preparation of the statement of accounts of a common investment fund or common deposit fund as they do for the purposes of the preparation of the statement of accounts of a charity to which that Schedule applies, subject to the following modifications.

2. (1) For any reference to 'the charity' or 'charity trustees' there is substituted a reference to the fund or, as the case may be, the trustees appointed to manage the fund.

(2) In paragraph 1(1), for 'statement of financial activities' there is substituted 'statement of total return'.

(3) After paragraph 1(1), there is inserted the following sub-paragraph:

'(1A) The statement of movement in funds shall give a true and fair view of the movements in the net assets of the fund between their position at the beginning of that year and their position at the end of that year.'.

(4) In paragraph 1(2), for 'Part I or, as the case may be, Part II and Part IV of this Schedule' there is substituted 'Part I, II or, as the case may be, III and Part V of Schedule 2 to these Regulations'.

(5) For paragraph 2(1), there is substituted the following sub-paragraph:

'(1) In respect of every amount required by paragraph 2 of Part I of Schedule 2 to these Regulations to be shown in the statement of total return, or by paragraph 2 of Part II of that

Schedule to be shown in the statement of movement in funds, or by paragraph 2 or, as the case may be, 3 of Part III of that Schedule to be shown in the balance sheet, the corresponding amount for the financial year immediately preceding that to which the statement or balance sheet relates shall also be shown.'.

(6) In paragraph 2(2), for 'statement of financial activities' there is substituted 'statement of total return, statement of movement in funds'.

(7) In paragraph 3, for 'Statement of Recommended Practice for Accounting by Charities issued in October 1995' there is substituted 'Statement of Recommended Practice for Authorised Unit Trust Schemes issued in April 1991'.

PART V

Notes to the Accounts

1. The information to be provided by way of notes to the accounts of a common investment fund or common deposit fund is the information specified in Part IV of Schedule 1 to these Regulations in relation to the accounts of charities to which that Schedule applies, modified in accordance with the following provisions of this Part.

2. (1) For any reference to 'the charity' there is substituted a reference to the fund and for any reference to 'the charity trustees' or 'trustees for the charity' or to any of them there is substituted a reference to the trustees appointed to manage the fund or to any of them, as the case may require.

(2) For paragraph 1(a) and (b) there are substituted the following sub-paragraphs:
'(a) a description of the accounting policies of the trustees, particularly regarding the basis of valuation of investments, the recognition of dividend income or intrest and the conversion of any amounts expressed in currency other than pounds sterling, and of the accounting assumptions made by them, including any material change in these, the reason for such change and its effect (if material) on the accounts;
(b) where the trustees appointed to manage the fund have during the financial year in question entered into any transaction, agreement or arrangement made for the purpose of minimising the risk of loss to the fund in consequence of fluctuations in interest rates or in the market value of securities or in the rates of foreign exchange, or entered into any other transaction in financial futures or options relating to shares, securities, foreign currency or other financial instrument which is a trading transaction in its own right, the nature of and reason for entering the transaction, agreement or arrangement and the total value of, and the maximum extent of financial exposure as at the date of the balance sheet resulting from, that transaction, agreement or arrangement;'.

(3) In paragraph 1(c), (d)(i) and (ii) and (e), after 'trustees appointed to manage the fund' there is inserted 'or any person to whom they have delegated their functions in relation to management of the fund'.

(4) For paragraph 1(f) and (g) there are substituted the following sub-paragraphs:
'(f) an analysis of the amount and date of any distribution in respect of income and accumulation shares or payment of interest to participating charities;
(g) a note of any adjustments made in the statement of total return to reflect the amount of income included in the creation or cancellation price of a unit or share in the fund;'.

(5) For paragraph 1(j) to (n) there are substituted the following sub-paragraphs –
'(j) an explanation of any amount entered in pursuance of paragraph 2(e)(i) of Part I of this Schedule (United Kingdom tax);
(k) an analysis of any entry in the balance sheet relating to:
(i) tangible fixed assets for use by the fund, according to the following categories –

       (A) freehold interests in land and buildings;

       (B) any other interest in land or buildings;

       (C) payments on account and assets in course of construction; and

       (D) plant, machinery, fixtures, fittings and equipment;

  (ii) debtors, according to the following categories –

       (A) in the case of a common investment fund, amounts receivable in respect of property transferred to the fund;

       (B) amounts receivable in respect of securities sold;

       (C) accrued income; and

       (D) other debtors;

  (iii) creditors, according to the following categories –

       (A) in the case of a common investment fund, amounts payable in respect of property withdrawn from the fund;

       (B) amounts payable in respect of securities purchased;

       (C) accrued expenses; and

       (D) other creditors;

(l) in the case of a common investment fund, the following statements, made up to the date of the balance sheet, that is to say –

  (i) a portfolio statement, specifying –

       (A) details of each investment held by or on behalf of the fund, including its market value at that date;

       (B) the category of each such investment according to its geographical area or industrial sector;

       (C) the percentage of net assets represented by each investment so held and by each category of investment specified under paragraph (B) above; and

       (D) whether or not the investment in question is listed on a recognised stock exchange;

  (ii) a statement of major changes in the portfolio, specifying –

       (A) whether the aggregate value of purchases or sales of a particular investment during the financial year in question exceeds 2 per cent of net assets at the beginning of that year, that value;

       (B) unless disclosed in pursuance of paragraph (A) above, the value of the 20 largest purchases and sales of a particular investment during the financial year in question; and

       (C) the total cost of purchase and net proceeds from sales of investments during the financial year in question;

  (iii) a statement of the number of shares issued as at the beginning of the year and as at the date of the balance sheet and the value of each income or accumulation shares as at each of those dates, calculated by reference to the net asset value of the fund; and

  (iv) a statement of the amount, if any, in the dividend equalisation reserve;

(m) in the case of a common deposit fund, details of sums deposited by participating charities as at the date of the balance sheet, divided into –

  (i) sums repayable on demand; and

  (ii) deposits with agreed maturity dates or periods of notice, divided into –

       (A) those repayable in not more than three months;

       (B) those repayable in more than three months but not more than one year;

       (C) those repayable in more than one year but not more than five years; and

       (D) those repayable in more than five years;

(n) in the case of a common deposit fund, details as at the date of the balance sheet of –

  (i) sums placed on deposit, divided into –

(A) sums repayable on demand; and

(B) other deposits, indicating whether they are repayable in not more than 3 months, more than 3 months but not more than 1 year, more than 1 year but not more than 5 years or more than 5 years; and

   (ii) investments other than deposits, analysed in accordance with sub-paragraph (m) above;'.

(6) For paragraph 1(q) there shall be substituted the following sub-paragraph:

'(q) in the case of any amount required by any of the preceding sub-paragraphs (other than sub-paragraph (l)(i) and (ii) to be disclosed, or the percentage of net assets represented by each category of investment required by sub-paragraph (l)(i)(C) above to be disclosed, the corresponding amount or percentage for the financial year immediately preceding that to which the accounts relate;'.

PART VI

Interpretation

1. In this Schedule, 'dividend equalisation reserve' means income withheld from distribution with a view to avoiding fluctuations in the amounts distributed.

2. For the purposes of this Schedule, a person is connected with a trustee appointed to manage the fund or a person to whom the trustees appointed to manage the fund have delegated their functions in relation to management of the fund (in this paragraph referred to as 'the manager') if—

(a) he is the child, parent, grandchild, grandparent, brother or sister of the manager;

(b) he is the spouse of the manager or of any person connected with him by virtue of sub-paragraph (a) above;

(c) he is the trustee of any trust, not being a charity, the beneficiaries or potential beneficiaries of which include the manager or any person connected with him by virtue of sub-paragraph (a) or (b) above and is acting in his capacity as such;

(d) he is a partner of the manager or of any person connected with him by virtue of sub-paragraph (a), (b) or (c) above and is acting in his capacity as such; or

(e) the person is a body corporate, not being a company which is connected with a charitable institution within the meaning of section 58(5) of the Charities Act 1992, in which the manager has, or the manager and any other manager or managers or person or persons connected with him by virtue of sub-paragraph (a), (b), (c) or (d) above, taken together, have, a substantial interest.

3. Any expression in paragraph 2 above which also appears in Schedule 5 to the 1993 Act shall be construed in accordance with paragraphs 2 to 4 of that Schedule.

INDEX

References are to paragraph numbers.